Philosophical Documents in Education

Second Edition

Edited by

Ronald F. Reed
Late of Texas Wesleyan University

Tony W. Johnson
West Chester University

 LONGMAN

An imprint of Addison Wesley Longman, Inc.

New York • Reading, Massachusetts • Menlo Park, California • Harlow, England
Don Mills, Ontario • Sydney • Mexico City • Madrid • Amsterdam

Editor-in-Chief: Priscilla McGeehon
Acquisitions Editor: Arthur Pomponio
Associate Editor: Arianne J. Weber
Full Service Production Manager: Valerie Zaborski
Project Coordination and Text Design: Elm Street Publishing Services, Inc.
Electronic Page Makeup: Elm Street Publishing Services, Inc.
Cover Design Manager: Nancy Danahy
Cover Designer: Keithley & Associates
Senior Print Buyer: Hugh Crawford
Printer and Binder: The Maple-Vail Book Manufacturing Group
Cover Printer: Phoenix Color Corps.

Library of Congress Cataloging-in-Publication Data

Philosophical documents in education/edited by Ronald F. Reed,
  Tony W. Johnson. —2nd ed.
      p.   cm.
  Includes bibliographical references and index.
  ISBN 0-8013-3316-4
  1. Education—Philosophy.   I. Reed, Ronald F. II. Johnson, Tony W.
  LB7.P5432   2000
  370'.1—dc21   99-12144
                                                                         CIP

Please visit our website at http://www.awlonline.com

ISBN 0-8013-3316-4

678910--MA--03

In Memoriam

Ronald F. Reed died suddenly and unexpectedly of a heart attack on August 23, 1998. Though he did not live to see it published, Ron was pleased with the changes we made in the second edition. We finished and submitted the manuscript for the second edition on Thursday prior to his death on Sunday.

Ron Reed was many things—a devoted husband and father, a down-to-earth friend and colleague, and an outstanding scholar and thinker, but, most of all, he was a teacher. He combined a "natural" ability to work with people of all ages and backgrounds with a willingness to reexamine his own teaching in a never-ending quest for better, more effective ways of helping others to think and learn. *Philosophical Documents,* by inviting and enabling potential and practicing teachers to participate in the conversation concerning the nature and purpose of education, contributes to and continues Ron's educational legacy.

Much like the great minds included in this volume, Ron truly impacted the lives of all who knew him. He will be missed, but, through such works as *Philosophical Documents,* his teaching voice will continue to be heard.

Tony W. Johnson

for Ann Reed and Fran Johnson

Contents

Preface

The response to the first edition of *Philosophical Documents in Education* has been gratifying. As we move into the second edition, we would like to mention how this edition is similar to and different from its predecessor.

In regard to similarity, we have picked selections, both new and old, with an eye toward answering a basic question: "What is an educated person?" Our assumption continues to be twofold—that this is the sort of question that leads to the posing and answering of other, if not all, important educational questions and that the way philosophers have answered the question is, at least, helpful for classroom teachers who must deal with the same question, on a daily basis, in the course of their practice.

We continue to think that education students and classroom teachers are capable of dealing directly with great philosophical literature in and about education. We recognize, of course, that the literature is not easy, and that it takes an enormous amount of work on the parts of students and instructors to create an environment in which, say, Plato's "Allegory of the Cave" becomes understandable to contemporary students and applicable to current educational problems. Still, when that environment is created the advantages may be incalculable. Imagine being able to ask Aristotle or John Locke or Maxine Greene for advice about classroom practice. *Philosophical Documents in Education* is the attempt to create an environment in which we can speak to them, and they to us.

Finally, as we say in the Introduction, we continue to think of *Documents* as a door through which students might walk to enter traditions that are as rich and wide as imagination will allow. The door continues to be Pragmatic, and Western, and so on—it continues to reflect our perspectives, if not biases—but it does open into a world that is "interestingly complex."

In regard to differences between this edition and the previous one, the reader will find a number, ranging from the mundane to the substantive. Time lines have been updated as necessary; questions at the end of selections have been modified; and the text, we hope, is cleaner and more free of typographical glitches.

In addition, the following are what we consider substantive changes:

1. There have been significant cuts and changes in the William James section. Those changes, in turn, may lead the reader to focus more on James' "What Pragmatism Means." That article may be crucial in underscoring the change of world view that runs through Dewey and may culminate (for now) in Richard Rorty's "Postmodernist Bourgeois Liberalism."

2. The section from *Democracy and Education* has been edited so that the emphasis is placed more on Dewey's understanding of community and less on the historical survey he presents regarding other educational philosophies. To understand community is to begin to see how important democracy is for Dewey and how novel is Dewey's definition of democracy.

3. Maxine Greene's "In Search of a Critical Pedagogy" has been replaced by what we think is a more representative and accessible article by that philosopher.

4. There was an overlap in the selections from Jane Roland Martin which was noticed by a number of readers. This has been addressed in the second edition.

5. In the Freire section, we have added a more recent work by the late Brazilian philosopher and educator. We think that Friere's "Letter" not only clarifies but contextualizes the theory contained in *Pedagogy of the Oppressed.*

6. The Lipman section has undergone rather important changes. We have deleted a number of pages from Lipman's *Thinking in Education* and replaced them with a little known article from a Finnish journal. The excerpt from *Thinking in Education* was meant to serve as an introduction to philosophy for children. We think the Finnish article does a better job of introducing philosophy for children to a general audience, *i.e.,* an audience with a limited acquaintance with that critical thinking movement as it has developed in the United States over the course of the past two decades.

7. We have added three new sections—one on Gareth Matthews whose works in philosophy and childhood seem to be growing in importance and scope; one on Nel Noddings who, among other things, has rediscovered the importance of the affective in the philosophy of education; and one on Kieran Egan whose works seems to extend, so well, the story-telling approach exemplified by Plato in his allegories and Rousseau in *Emile.*

8. We have made some changes to the introduction to the Rorty section. Our reviews have been split on Rorty's "Postmodernist Bourgeois Liberalism." Some have found it, and Professor Rorty, too technical for their students, while others have urged a less technical piece. While we are aware of the difficulty that Rorty's writing presents for beginning students in education, we continue to think, especially in light of his recent *Achieving Our Country: Leftist Thought in Twentieth Century America,* that his thought is so

important (whether one agrees with him or not) that it cannot be safely disregarded. Since we have not been able to find a better introduction to Rorty's thought than the article which graced our first edition, we have attempted to do a better job of introducing that article.

There is a final point we would like to make. We think that philosophy is very important in the education of those who are to be teachers, but just as importantly we think that philosophy—the sense of wondering, of looking for explanations, of trying to figure out what is worthy of belief and action—is a birthright of all students, both young and old. We hope that *Philosophical Documents in Education* will be used to help achieve that birthright.

Tony Johnson
Ron Reed

Acknowledgments

Anthologies, as we have learned, are the most collaborative of efforts. They exist only through the cooperation of a wide variety of sources. Although it is relatively easy to describe this book—an anthology of primary sources in philosophy that can be read with profit by students of education—turning the description into a book has occurred only because of the efforts of many people.

We acknowledge and deeply appreciate the permission of philosophers and publishers to reprint their work. Specific acknowledgments are presented at the beginning of each excerpt or section.

The Sid Richardson Foundation, through its support of the Creative and Critical Teaching Center, has provided invaluable financial support. Linda Nowell, assistant director of the center, has done a wonderful job compiling time lines, securing permissions, dealing with computer-related problems, and managing a host of other activities. Her scholarship and professionalism are always appreciated.

We are also grateful to the following individuals who reviewed the manuscript for the second edition and provided helpful comments:

Maike Philipsen, Virginia Commonwealth University

Anthony Rud, Purdue University

Linda Shadiow, Northern Arizona University

Marilyn Watt, Northeastern State University, Oklahoma

Finally, our special thanks to Ann Reed and Fran Johnson.

Introduction

Philosophical Documents in Education rests on a very basic assumption—that students of education, and potential and practicing teachers, can learn something of significance in terms of both theory and practice from reading, thinking about, and discussing the great philosophic tradition in education. Thus, this book is an attempt to bring that tradition to you in such a way that you may understand it and use it to formulate your own theory and practice.

We recognize, of course, that philosophical writing is not the easiest thing to read and understand. Frequently, it is rife with technical language, refers back to previous books and articles with which readers may not be familiar, and, in general, has a density and rigor of presentation and argumentation that is not typical of much of the other writing to which students of education are exposed.

As much as possible, we have tried to minimize the first two characteristics. The articles and excerpts presented here have a limited amount of technical language. You will not need to have an extensive philosophical vocabulary in order to read the articles. In addition, although the articles exist within a tradition and, as such, constitute a sort of conversation both among themselves and with articles and philosophers not presented here, explicit reference to other articles, and the corresponding assumption that readers will be familiar with those articles, has been avoided. The articles and excerpts, we believe, stand on their own.

The last characteristic, however, is a different story. A powerful philosophical position or argument cannot be reduced to a sentence or a paragraph without significant loss of force, evocativeness, and beauty. As readers of philosophy, we tend to distrust capsule summaries, and as editors, we have avoided them. Recognizing that students do not have unlimited time and energy, however, we have tried to limit the volume and number of the excerpts. The text is deliberately lean, and it is our hope that you will treat the excerpts as you would poetry: Read them slowly, carefully, and frequently.

The text is comprised of selections from 18 philosophers. Classical philosophers such as Plato, Augustine, John Locke, Jean-Jacques Rousseau, and John Dewey are represented here. At the same time, we have tried to provide a wide range of contemporary commentary on the philosophical ramifications of educational issues. Thus, we have included selections from Paulo Freire, Maxine Greene, Cornel West, and Richard Rorty, among others. A benefit of

1

the contemporary slant is that it exposes readers to the views of women and minorities, views that are typically underrepresented in foundation anthologies.

Each selection comes with a brief, informal introductory essay on the philosopher. These are meant to give you an impressionistic feel for the philosopher and what she or he was attempting to do. The thread that ties the introductory essays together is our attempt to frame the selections within the context of a basic question: What are the characteristics of an educated person?

We have also provided historical-biographical time lines on each, and a series of questions at the end of each chapter that are meant to open up the text for students.

Anthologies, of necessity, are selective and limited and reflect the interests, values, perspectives, and biases of the compilers. They are always open to legitimate criticism: Why this philosopher and not that? Why, in this anthology, Dewey and not Whitehead? Why this excerpt and not that? In this anthology, why the *Apology* but no reference to the *Meno* and the remembrance theory of knowledge?

Every anthology will have its idiosyncrasies. Every anthology will reflect the particular purposes—and biases—of those who compiled it, no matter how comprehensive it is intended to be. *This* anthology is not intended to be comprehensive. This anthology is meant to serve as an *invitation* to a tradition of scholarship. If you accept the invitation, if you use this anthology as a means for going deeper into that tradition, if you use it as a stepping-stone to further reading, we will consider our purpose achieved. It is our hope that you will realize the limits of this anthology and go beyond it to its sources.

View this anthology as a door through which you might enter a room in which an extended conversation about educational issues is taking place. The door has specific historical and geographic dimensions—it is pragmatic, it is Western, and so on—but once you have moved through it into the room, things become interestingly complex. Read any of the scholars in this anthology, take them seriously, go beyond the excerpts and articles you'll find here and read the original manuscripts, see the excerpts in their contexts, and almost inevitably you will begin a journey that corrects the inherent limitations of the anthology. Dewey will lead the inquiring student to Whitehead (and both might introduce you to such analytic thinkers as Israel Scheffler and R. S. Peters). The *Apology* will lead you to the *Meno*. The Western tradition itself will foster an examination of its roots in and connections to the Middle and Far East.

The door that this anthology provides opens into a room that is almost without limits—a room in which conversation about the nature and purpose of education takes place.

chapter 1

Socrates and Plato

TIME LINE FOR SOCRATES

470 BC	Is born in Athens, Greece, the son of Sophroniscus, a stonemason, and Phaenarete, a midwife.
470–400	Grows up during the "golden age" of Greece—his father, an intimate friend of the son of Aristides the Just, provides Socrates an acquaintanceship with the members of the Pericles circle.
	Serves with valor in the Peloponnesian War.
	Marries Xanthippe. They have seven or eight children.
	Is declared the wisest man by the Oracle at Delphi.
	Is put on trial for corrupting the minds of the youth of Athens.
399	Is found guilty and forced to drink hemlock.

Socrates wrote nothing. All that we know of him is from the writings of Aristophenes (The Clouds), *Plato, and Xenophon.*

TIME LINE FOR PLATO

427 BC	Is born in Athens, Greece, to a prominent family. Following his father's death his mother marries Pyrilampes, a close friend of Pericles.
405–400	Studies with Socrates.
399	Attends the trial and execution of Socrates.
387	Establishes the Academy. Later, Eudoxius, respected mathematician, unites his school, located at Cyzicus, with the Academy.

| **367** | Accepts Aristotle into the Academy. |
| **347** | Dies in Athens. |

Although scholars continue to debate the time frame of Plato's writings, the following are generally attributed to each period:

Early Period	Works, usually referred to as Socratic dialogues, focus on ethics. Included in this period are *Apology, Crito, Charmides, Laches, Euthyphro, Euthydemus, Cratylus, Protagoras,* and *Gorgias.*
Middle Period	Works focus on theory of ideas and metaphysical doctrines. Included in this period are *Meno, Symposium, Phaedo, The Republic,* and *Phaedrus.*
Late Period	Works focus on a reconsideration of the middle period, most notably the theory of ideas. Included in this period are *Theaetetus, Parmenides, Sophist, Statesman, Philebus, Timaeus,* and *The Laws.*

Introduction

Philosophy begins in the West with a group of philosophers variously known as the natural philosophers or the pre-Socratics. Men—and the history of Western philosophy has been dominated by males—such as Thales, Anaximander, Anaximenes, Parmenides, Empedocles, and Heraclitus were all engaged in an attempt to discover the secrets of the natural world, to reduce the mass of phenomena to a few manageable principles, and to understand their natural environments. What held them together was a belief that one could reason one's way to the truth, that by looking at natural effects one could deduce their causes. What distinguished one from the other was that they each reasoned their way to different causes. For some the natural world was reducible to one immovable substance. For others, there were four basic elements (earth, air, fire, and water). Others saw five or six or even more basic causes.

This led a group of philosophers, the Sophists, to react against the program of the natural philosophers. Where the natural philosophers assumed that an educated person, a wise person, was one knew the *truth* about things *natural,* the Sophists claimed that since "reason" generated so many different conclusions, there was something unreliable about reason itself. If, the Sophists suggested, reason were a reliable tool, it should always yield the same results. It did not; hence, the Sophists shifted inquiry away from an attempt to discover the truth about the natural world to an attempt to teach a useful skill.

The Sophists were the first professional teachers. They went around to the families of young boys—again, notice this orientation toward males—and offered to teach those boys how to argue persuasively. The Sophists said, in effect: We don't care what your position is. We don't care whether you are telling the truth or not.

We will teach you how to make your case and how to win arguments. This was an especially valuable skill because eventually those boys would, as heads of households, have to speak in the public forums that constituted Greek democracy. If they could not speak well, their family's fortune would suffer.

Into this mix—a mix that included a switch from the educated person as she or he who knew the truth about the natural world to the educated person as she or he who could argue persuasively regardless of the truth or falsity of the position—came the character Socrates.

If one reads the dialogue *Apology* carefully, one will see that two of the accusations against Socrates suggest that Socrates was both a natural philosopher and a Sophist at the same time. Certainly, since one was a reaction against the other, Socrates cannot be both. But what was Socrates? What was his doctrine? Why was he so important? We will try to answer those questions in the second part of this introduction.

Most of what we know about Socrates comes from three sources. Socrates did not write; indeed, he distrusted the written word, and so we must rely on the plays of Aristophenes and the dialogues of Xenophon and Plato.[1] For our purposes, we will concentrate on those writings that are clearly the most important, both philosophically and historically, that is, the writing of Socrates' student, Plato.

Most commentators divide Plato's writing into three major periods. In the early dialogues, *Apology, Charmides,* and *Phaedo,* for example, Plato gives a fairly accurate portrayal of Socrates. Plato was almost like a "fly on the wall" or a tape recorder, and one "hears" dialogues that may actually have taken place. This is the place to go to find out what Socrates was about and what he was teaching. In the middle period, *The Republic* is a good example of Plato's using Socrates to espouse his (Plato's) own doctrine. That doctrine is called the Theory of the Forms, and the middle period is the place to go if one wants to see what the mature Plato thought. Toward the end of his career, Plato had some doubts about his theory; in later dialogues like *Parmenides, Theaetetus,* and *Sophist,* one sees Plato rethinking and, perhaps, rejecting the theory. At the same time, because Socrates was Plato's mouthpiece in the middle period, the character of Socrates now becomes a minor figure, becomes a figure of ridicule and scorn, or drops out altogether. The later dialogues are not the place to go to get an accurate picture of Socrates.

So who was Socrates and what did he espouse? The dialogue *Apology* is probably the best place to start. As mentioned previously, Socrates was on trial for his life. After rejecting a number of the more far-fetched accusations (accusations that suggested he was a natural philosopher and a Sophist), Socrates wonders what the real charge against him is. He settles on the charge that he is guilty of corrupting the morals of the youth of Athens.

As one will see, "Socratic irony" is an apt description. Socrates, in the company of his students, engaged those with a reputation for wisdom in a dialogue. Over the course of those dialogues, Socrates discovered, and so did his students and the people who were questioned, that those with a reputation for wisdom did not always deserve it. Socrates was wiser than the "wisest" people because he knew his own limits: he knew that he did not know, while they mistakenly thought they did. For Socrates, the educated person is precisely the person who knows her or his limitations, who knows that she or he does not know.

There are two points that are worthy of consideration. The first is that this person, whom many consider to be one of the two great teachers in the Western tradition (Jesus is the other), professed to have virtually no doctrine and said that what he knew was unimportant. Over and over again, in the *Apology,* the *Phaedrus,* and the *Charmides,* Socrates suggests that true wisdom is the property of the gods, and that what he has—this human wisdom, this knowledge of his own limitations— is worth hardly anything at all.

The second point is that Socrates puts an enormous amount of weight, some might call it faith, on the power of the dialogue, that back-and-forth linguistic motion between speakers, to uncover the truth. When Socrates discusses ideas with those with a reputation for wisdom, a truth always emerges from the dialogue. The dialogue allows the truth to emerge—in the excerpt from *The Republic,* the truth is about some mistaken claims to knowledge. Socrates is different from the Sophists because he thinks there is a "truth" to be discovered. He is different from the natural philosophers because the method that he uses—discourse, dialogue, conversation—is public and communal; it is open to scrutiny in a way that reasoning, as a purely mental activity, is not.

Plato, as one would expect from a student, took much from his teacher Socrates. For Plato, education is a matter of leading a person from mere belief to true knowledge. In his classic "Allegory of the Cave," Plato suggests that we, as uneducated persons, are chained in a cave, seeing shadows on the wall and mistakenly believing that the shadows (and the cave itself) are the real things. Education involves breaking those chains and leading a person from the cave into the bright sunshine. The good teacher does this through the dialectical process, leading the student as far as she or he is capable. The best students, those most philosophical, those best educated, will use the dialectical process to discover true beauty, goodness, and justice. Plato is different from his teacher, Socrates, precisely because the wisdom that Plato's students would discover is worth a good deal; that is, it involves knowledge of objective standards (the Forms) that will enable people to lead good, productive lives.

The following selections include one from the *Apology* and two from *The Republic.* The first section from *The Republic* presents an introduction to the Theory of the Forms. In the second, Plato presents a story, "The Allegory of the Cave," which is meant to shed light on the theory.

Note

1. A dialogue is perhaps best understood as a focused attempt by a group of speakers to solve a limited number of problems or to answer a few questions.

From Plato's *Apology* (ca. 399 BC) wisdom

I dare say that some one will ask the question, "Why is this, Socrates, and what is the origin of these accusations of you: for there must have been something strange which you have been doing? All this great fame and talk about you would never have arisen if you had been like other men: tell us, then, why this is, as we should be sorry to judge hastily of you." Now I regard this as a fair challenge, and I will endeavor to explain to you the origin of this name of "wise," and of this evil fame. Please to attend then. And although some of you may think that I am joking, I declare that I will tell you the entire truth. Men of Athens, this reputation of mine has come of a certain sort of wisdom which I possess. If you ask me what kind of wisdom, I reply, such wisdom as is attainable by man, for to that extent I am inclined to believe that I am wise; whereas the persons of whom I was speaking have a superhuman wisdom, which I may fail to describe, because I have it not myself; and he who says that I have, speaks falsely, and is taking away my character. And here, O men of Athens, I must beg you not to interrupt me, even if I seem to say something extravagant. For the word which I will speak is not mine. I will refer you to a witness who is worthy of credit, and will tell you about my wisdom—whether I have any, and of what sort—and that witness shall be the God of Delphi. You must have known Chaerephon; he was early a friend of mine, and also a friend of yours, for he shared in the exile of the people, and returned with you. Well, Chaerephon, as you know, was very impetuous in all his doings, and he went to Delphi and boldly asked the oracle to tell him whether—as I was saying, I must beg you not to interrupt—he asked the oracle to tell him whether there was any one wiser than I was, and the Pythian prophetess answered, that there was no man wiser. Chaerephon is dead himself; but his brother, who is in court, will confirm the truth of this story.

Why do I mention this? Because I am going to explain to you why I have such an evil name. When I heard the answer, I said to myself, What can the god mean? and what is the interpretation of this riddle? for I know that I have no wisdom, small or great. What then can he mean when he says that I am the wisest of men? And yet he is a god, and can not lie; that would be against his nature. After long consideration, I at last thought of a method of trying the question. I reflected that if I could only find a man wiser than myself, then I might go to the god with a refutation in my hand. I should to say to him, "Here is a man who is wiser than I am; but you said that I was the wisest." Accordingly, I went to one who had the reputation of wisdom, and observed him—his name I need not mention; he was a politician whom I selected for examination—and the result was as follows: When I began to talk with him, I could not help thinking that he was not really wise, although he was thought wise by many, and wiser still by himself; and I went and tried to explain to him that he thought himself wise, but was not really wise, and the consequence was that he hated me, and his enmity was shared by several who were present and heard me. So I left him, saying to myself, as I went away: Well, although I do not suppose that either of us knows anything really beautiful and good, I am better off than he is,—for he knows nothing, and thinks that he knows. I neither know nor think that I know. In this latter particular, then, I seem to have slightly the advantage of him. Then I went to another who had still higher philosophical pretensions, and my conclusion was exactly the same. I made another enemy of him, and of many others besides him.

After this I went to one man after another, being not unconscious of the enmity which I provoked, and I lamented and feared this: but necessity was laid upon me—the word of God, I thought, ought to be considered first. And I said to myself, Go I must to all who appear to know, and find out the meaning of the oracle. And I swear to you, Athenians, by the dog I swear!—for I must tell you the truth—the result of my mission was just this: I found that the men most in repute were all but the most foolish; and that some inferior men were really wiser and better. I will tell you the tale of my wanderings and of the "Herculean" labors, as I may call them, which I endured only to find at last the oracle irrefutable. When I left the politicians, I went to the poets; tragic, dithyrambic, and all sorts. And there, I said to myself, you will be detected; now you will find out that you are more ignorant than they are. Accordingly, I took them some of the most elaborate passages in their own writings, and asked what was the meaning of them—thinking that they would teach me something. Will you believe me? I am almost ashamed to speak of this, but still I must say that there is hardly a person present who would not have talked better about their poetry than they did themselves. That showed me in an instant that not by wisdom do poets write poetry, but by a sort of genius and inspiration; they are like diviners or soothsayers who also say many fine things, but do not understand the meaning of them. And the poets appeared to me to be much in the same case; and I further observed that upon the strength of their poetry they believed themselves to be the wisest of men in other things in which they were not wise. So I departed, conceiving myself to be superior to them for the same reason that I was superior to the politicians.

At last I went to the artisans, for I was conscious that I knew nothing at all, as I may say, and I was sure that they knew many fine things; and in this I was not mistaken, for they did know many things of which I was ignorant, and in this they certainly were wiser than I was. But I observed that even the good artisans fell into the same error as the poets;—because they were good workmen they thought that they also knew all sorts of high matters, and this defect in them overshadowed their wisdom—therefore I asked myself on behalf of the oracle, whether I would like to be as I was, neither having their knowledge nor their ignorance, or like them in both; and I made answer to myself and the oracle that I was better off as I was.

This investigation has led to my having many enemies of the worst and most dangerous kind, and has given occasion also to many calumnies. And I am called wise, for my hearers always imagine that I myself possess the wisdom which I find wanting in others: but the truth is, O men of Athens, that God only is wise; and in this oracle he means to say that the wisdom of men is little or nothing; he is not speaking of Socrates, he is only using my name as an illustration, as if he said, He, O men, is the wisest who, like Socrates, knows that his wisdom is in truth worth nothing. And so I go my way, obedient to the god, and make inquisition into the wisdom of any one, whether citizen or stranger, who appears to be wise; and if he is not wise, then in vindication of the oracle I show him that he is not wise; and this occupation quite absorbs me, and I have no time to give either to any public matter of interest or to any concern of my own, but I am in utter poverty by reason of my devotion to the god. . . .

From Plato's *The Republic* (ca. 366 BC)

Book VI

Conceive then, said I, as we were saying, that there are these two entities, and that one of them is sovereign over the intelligible order and region and the other over the world of the eyeball, not to say the sky-ball, but let that pass. You surely apprehend the two types, the visible and the intelligible.

I do.

Represent them then, as it were, by a line divided into two unequal sections and cut each section again in the same ratio—the section, that is, of the visible and that of the intelligible order—and then as an expression of the ratio of their comparative clearness and obscurity you will have, as one of the sections of the visible world, images. By images I mean, first, shadows, and then reflections in water and on surfaces of dense, smooth, and bright texture, and everything of that kind, if you apprehend.

I do.

As the second section assume that of which this is a likeness or an image, that is, the animals about us and all plants and the whole class of objects made by man.

I so assume it, he said.

Would you be willing to say, said I, that the division in respect of reality and truth or the opposite is expressed by the proportion—as is the opinable to the knowable so is the likeness to that of which it is a likeness?

I certainly would.

Consider then again the way in which we are to make the division of the intelligible section.

In what way?

By the distinction that there is one section of it which the soul is compelled to investigate by treating as images the things imitated in the former division, and by means of assumptions from which it proceeds not up to a first principle but down to a conclusion, while there is another section in which it advances from its assumption to a beginning or principle that transcends assumption, and in which it makes no use of the images employed by the other section, relying on ideas only and progressing systematically through ideas.

I don't fully understand what you mean by this, he said.

Well, I will try again, said I, for you will better understand after this preamble. For I think you are aware that students of geometry and reckoning and such subjects first postulate the odd and the even and the various figures and three kinds of angles and other things akin to these in each branch of science, regard them as known, and, treating them as absolute assumptions, do not deign to render any further account of them to themselves or others, taking if for granted that they are obvious to everybody. They take their start from these, and pursuing the inquiry from this point on consistently, conclude with that for the investigation of which they set out.

Certainly, he said, I know that.

And do you not also know that they further make use of the visible forms and talk about them, though they are not thinking of them but of those things of which they are a likeness, pursuing their inquiry for the sake of the square as such and the diagonal as such, and not for the sake of the image of it which they draw? And so in all cases. The very things which they mold and draw, which have shadows and images of themselves in water, these things they treat in their turn as only images, but what they really seek is to get sight of those realities which can be seen only by the mind.

True, he said.

This then is the class that I described as intelligible, it is true, but with the reservation first that the soul is compelled to employ assumptions in the investigation of it, not proceeding to a first principle because of its inability to extricate itself from the rise above its assumptions, and second, that it uses as images or likenesses the very objects that are themselves copied and adumbrated by the class below them, and that in comparison with these latter are esteemed as clear and held in honor.

I understand, said he, that you are speaking of what falls under geometry and the kindred arts.

Understand then, said I, that by the other section of the intelligible I mean that which the reason itself lays hold of by the power of dialectic, treating its assumptions not as absolute beginnings but literally as hypotheses, underpinnings, footings, and springboards so to speak, to enable it to rise to that which requires no assumption and is the starting point of all, and after attaining to that again taking hold of the first dependencies from it, so to proceed downward to the conclusion, making no use whatever of any object of sense but only of pure ideas moving on through ideas to ideas and ending with ideas.

I understand, he said, not fully, for it is no slight task that you appear to have in mind, but I do understand that you mean to distinguish the aspect of reality and the intelligible, which is contemplated by the power of dialectic, as something truer and more exact than the object of the so-called arts and that those who contemplate them are compelled to use their understanding and not their senses, yet because they do not go back to the beginning in the study of them but start from assumptions you do not think they possess true intelli-

gence about them although the things themselves are intelligibles when appre-
hended in conjunction with a first principle. And I think you call the mental
habit of geometers and their like mind or understanding and not reason because
you regard understanding as something intermediate between opinion and
reason.

Your interpretation is quite sufficient, I said. And now, answering to these
four sections, assume these four affections occurring in the soul—intellection or
reason for the highest, understanding for the second, belief for the third, and for
the last, picture thinking or conjecture—and arrange them in a proportion, as
their objects partake of truth and reality.

I understand, he said. I concur and arrange them as you bid.

Book VII

Next, said I, compare our nature in respect of education and its lack to such an
experience as this. Picture men dwelling in a sort of subterranean cavern with a
long entrance open to the light on its entire width. Conceive them as having
their legs and necks fettered from childhood, so that they remain in the same
spot, able to look forward only, and prevented by the fetters from turning their
heads. Picture further the light from a fire burning higher up and at a distance
behind them, and between the fire and the prisoners and above them a road
along which a low wall has been built, as the exhibitors of puppet shows have
partitions before the men themselves, above which they show the puppets.

All that I see, he said.

See also, then, men carrying past the wall implements of all kinds that rise
above the wall, and human images and shapes of animals as well, wrought in
stone and wood and every material, some of these bearers presumably speaking
and others silent.

A strange image you speak of, he said, and strange prisoners.

Like to us, I said. For, to begin with, tell me do you think that these men
would have seen anything of themselves or of one another except the shadows
cast from the fire on the wall of the cave that fronted them?

How could they, he said, if they were compelled to hold their heads
unmoved through life?

And again, would not the same be true of the objects carried past them?

Surely.

If then they were able to talk to one another, do you not think that they
would suppose that in naming the things that they saw they were naming the
passing objects?

Necessarily.

And if their prison had an echo from the wall opposite them, when one of
the passers-by uttered a sound, do you think that they would suppose anything else than the passing shadow to be the speaker?

By Zeus, I do not, said he.

Then in every way such prisoners would deem reality to be nothing else
than the shadows of the artificial objects.

Quite inevitably, he said.

Consider, then, what would be the manner of the release and healing from these bonds and this folly if in the course of nature something of this sort should happen to them. When one was freed from his fetters and compelled to stand up suddenly and turn his head around and walk and to lift up his eyes to the light, and in doing all this felt pain and, because of the dazzle and glitter of the light, was unable to discern the objects whose shadows he formerly saw, what do you suppose would be his answer if someone told him that what he had seen before was all a cheat and an illusion, but that now, being nearer to reality and turned toward more real things, he saw more truly? And if also one should point out to him each of the passing objects and constrain him by questions to say what it is, do you not think that he would be at a loss and that he would regard what he formerly saw as more real than the things now pointed out to him?

Far more real, he said.

And if he were compelled to look at the light itself, would not that pain his eyes, and would he not turn away and flee to those things which he is able to discern and regard them as in very deed more clear and exact than the objects pointed out?

It is so, he said.

And if, said I, someone should drag him thence by force up the ascent which is rough and steep, and not let him go before he had drawn him out into the light of the sun, do you not think that he would find it painful to be so haled along, and would chafe at it, and when he came out into the light, that his eyes would be filled with its beams so that he would not be able to see even one of the things that we call real?

Why, no, not immediately, he said.

Then there would be need of habituation, I take it, to enable him to see the things higher up. And at first he would most easily discern the shadows and, after that, the likenesses or reflections in water of men and other things, and later, the things themselves, and from these he would go on to contemplate the appearances in the heavens and heaven itself, more easily by night, looking at the light of the stars and the moon, than by day the sun and the sun's light.

Of course.

And so, finally, I suppose, he would be able to look upon the sun itself and see its true nature, not by reflections in water or phantasms of it in an alien setting, but in and by itself in its own place.

Necessarily, he said.

And at this point he would infer and conclude that this it is that provides the seasons and the courses of the year and presides over all things in the visible region, and is in some sort the cause of all these things that they had seen.

Obviously, he said, that would be the next step.

Well then, if he recalled to mind his first habitation and what passed for wisdom there, and his fellow bondsmen, do you not think that he would count himself happy in the change and pity them?

He would indeed.

And if there had been honors and commendations among them which they bestowed on one another and prizes for the man who is quickest to make out the shadows as they pass and best able to remember their customary precedences, sequences, and coexistences, and so most successful in guessing at what was to come, do you think he would be very keen about such rewards, and that he would envy and emulate those who were honored by these prisoners and lorded it among them, or that he would feel with Homer and greatly prefer while living on earth to be serf of another, a landless man, and endure anything rather than opine with them and live that life?

Yes, he said, I think that he would choose to endure anything rather than such a life.

And consider this also, said I. If such a one should go down again and take his old place would he not get his eyes full of darkness, thus suddenly coming out of the sunlight?

He would indeed.

Now if he should be required to contend with these perpetual prisoners in 'evaluating' these shadows while his vision was still dim and before his eyes were accustomed to the dark—and this time required for habituation would not be very short—would he not provoke laughter, and would it not be said of him that he had returned from his journey aloft with his eyes ruined and that it was not worth while even to attempt the ascent? And if it were possible to lay hands on and to kill the man who tried to release them and lead them up, would they not kill him?

They certainly would, he said. . . .

Questions

1. What is Socrates' definition of wisdom in the *Apology?*
2. Do you think Socrates was treated fairly? Explain.
3. Was Socrates really surprised by the charges brought against him? Explain.
4. Should he have been surprised? Explain.
5. What do you think of Socrates' teaching style?
6. Have you had teachers like Socrates?
7. If so, did you learn much from them? Explain.
8. Draw a picture representing the story of the cave, and then explain the picture to your neighbor.
9. Would those persons chained in the cave have reason to believe the person who returned to the cave? Explain.
10. Assume you were the person who had escaped. How would you explain the world outside the cave to the prisoners?
11. Restate the Theory of the Forms in your own words.

12. How is the definition of wisdom offered in *The Republic* different from that offered in the *Apology?*

13. In what ways is the educational system implicit in *The Republic* similar to (or different from) the American system?

14. In what ways is it better (or worse)?

15. Formulate your own definition of an educated person.

chapter 2

Aristotle

TIME LINE FOR ARISTOTLE

384 BC	Is born in Stagira, Chalcidice, to Nicomachus, the court physician to Amyntas II, king of Macedonia. Is brought up by Proxenus, a guardian, following the death of his father.
367	Enters Plato's Academy.
347	Leaves Academy following Plato's death. Accepts invitation of Hermeias, ruler of Assos (which is near Troy), to join his court. Studies, writes, and teaches during the time at court. Marries Hermeias's niece and adopted daughter, Pythias. Fathers a daughter.
345	Moves to Mytilene on the island of Lesbos. During this time, he conducts zoological research.
342–339	Serves as tutor for son of Philip II of Macedon—Alexander the Great—at Pella.
335	Returns to Athens and opens the Lyceum. Shortly after arriving in Athens his wife dies and he takes a mistress, Herpyllis. The union produces one son, Nicomachus.
323	Is charged with impiety (the death of Alexander the Great gave rise to anti-Macedonian sentiment). Flees Athens to Chalcis.
322	Dies in Chalcis, Euboea.

TIME LINE OF HIS WRITINGS

367–347   Reflect empathetic and enthusiastic support of Platonism. Included in this period are *Eudemus* and *On the Good*.

347–335   Are critical of Platonic thought, in particular, the Theory of the Forms. Included in this period is *On Philosophy*.

335–322   Reject essential features of Platonic thought. His thinking becomes based on empirical science; included in this period are *Metaphysics, Politics,* and *Nicomachean Ethics*.

Introduction

Characterized by Dante as "the master of those who know," for centuries, Aristotle was called "The Philosopher." He is generally recognized as the best educated individual of his or any time, and his mastery of all the world's knowledge places him on "the shortest of lists of the giants of Western thought." As Renford Bambrough explains:

> All studies in formal logic until very recent times were footnotes to his work. In the study of ethics, politics, and literary criticism he set standards of sanity, urbanity, and penetration by which his successors two thousand years later may still be severely judged....There is no problem in any of the branches of what is still called philosophy—ontology, epistemology, metaphysics, ethics—on which his remarks do not continue to deserve the most careful attention from the modern inquirer.[1]

Born in the Macedonian town of Stagira in 384 BC, Aristotle acquired his taste for biology and the other sciences from his father, the physician to the court of the Macedonian king. Known today as the philosophical grandson of Socrates, Aristotle never gained full acceptance as a true Greek. Though honored and revered by subsequent generations, his contemporaries often referred to him, somewhat pejoratively, as "the son of the physician from Stagira" or as the "Stagirite philosopher."

Despite losing both parents at an early age, Aristotle received an outstanding education. At age 18, his guardian, Proxenus, sent him to Athens to study at Plato's Academy. For 20 years he studied with Plato, who described him as "the mind of the Academy." Upon Plato's death in 347 BC, Aristotle left Athens and spent the next few years traveling in the Aegean Islands. A crucial turning point occurred in 343 BC with his appointment as tutor to Prince Alexander, the heir to the Macedonian throne. While the relationship between Aristotle and his soon-to-be-famous student was often strained, their association proved mutually beneficial. Alexander, the eventual conqueror of the Hellenic world, shipped back to his former teacher an enormous amount of information from those parts of the world about which the Greeks knew little or nothing. Included in this bounty were constitutions and descriptions of the culture and customs of the people encountered during these exploits. Biological and botanical specimens were also sent back, affording Aristotle and his students the opportunity to systematize and categorize the whole spectrum of human knowledge.

By this time, Aristotle had established in Athens the Lyceum, a school located near a favorite meeting place of Socrates. Here, for more than a decade, Aristotle lectured to students on philosophic and scientific topics in the morning and on more general topics to a more popular audience in the afternoon. A creature of habit, Aristotle often walked while he talked, with his students following close behind. Here, too, Aristotle composed his most significant works, summing up in an encyclopedic fashion the results of a life of all-embracing study and thought.

These very productive years ended all too soon as word reached Athens of Alexander's death. Longing for their cherished freedom, Athenians moved quickly to cast off the yoke of the hated Macedonians. Due, in part, to his association with the Macedonians, the Athenians charged Aristotle with crimes similar to those brought against Socrates several generations earlier. Refusing, as he put it, to allow the Athenians to sin a second time against philosophy, Aristotle withdrew to the Macedonian community of Chalcis, dying there of natural causes in 322 BC.

The body of data available to him enabled Aristotle to develop a "number of amazingly wide-ranging and precisely argued treatises, which have had an enormous influence upon the Western world."[2] In his early works, Aristotle mimicked the style of his mentor, Plato, but in these later, more mature works, Aristotle refuses to allow the human mind to impose its intuitive patterns on the natural world. For Aristotle, as for Plato, there are absolutes or universals, but the method Aristotle employed to attain those absolutes differs significantly from Plato's. Believing that as much data as possible should be collected and analyzed before drawing a conclusion, Aristotle placed his trust in the careful observation and analysis of nature as our best hope of arriving at the truth.

Spending his mature years observing and analyzing a body of knowledge "never before available to one man,"[3] Aristotle concluded that all things possess an essence or nature. Inherent in this essence or nature is the potential to be actualized in accordance with that nature. For example, every acorn has the potential to be actualized as a giant oak tree. Whether and to what extent the potential is actualized depend upon the conditions enhancing or impeding the acorn's natural inclination to become an oak tree.

After a lifetime of study, Aristotle concluded that every substance, whether found in the natural world or created by human agency, is unique in that each is striving toward an *end* consistent with its nature or essence. To understand any substance, one must understand the end that particular substance seeks. Each substance has certain characteristics or performs certain functions that no other substance has or can perform. For example, just as animals are a special kind of organism because they perform certain functions that plants do not, human beings are unique animals in that they perform certain functions no other animal is capable of. The defining characteristic of human beings is their ability to ask general questions and to seek answers to them through observation and analysis. In short, human beings are rational animals, that is, questioning and thinking animals, capable of philosophical thought.

For a variety of reasons, not all acorns fulfill their potential of becoming oak trees, and, obviously, too few humans attain the ideal of becoming rational, contemplative beings. Just as a forester or a farmer, by nurturing the acorn at the right time in the right way, can enhance the acorn's chances of fulfilling its inherent potential, an educator—by appropriately exposing human beings to the great minds struggling with the perennial problems of humankind—can enhance the human being's natural desire to know.

A human being who, through education, has cultivated this natural desire to know comes as close as it is possible in this world to actualizing the human potential. When engaged in contemplation—not as a means to some other end but as an end in itself—humans become godlike, no longer moving from potentiality toward actuality. While the union of potentiality and actuality is not possible in this world, it remains the ideal or aspiration of humankind to "soar after the wings of God, [our] maker, the cause of all things."[4]

Aristotle implies that human beings, at their most sublime, are the most complex substances known in this world. Given this exalted status, it is appropriate for human beings to seek the highest good. As discussed in the selection from the *Nicomachean Ethics,* Aristotle suggests that the highest good "is to be found in human happiness." Since human beings are essentially rational creatures, Aristotle argues that they attain true happiness to the extent that they act in accordance with reason. In continuing the largely Greek idea that to know the good is to do the good, Aristotle suggests that, ideally, an educated person unites morality and reason in virtuous action. While the potential for such virtuous being is present at birth, that potential must be nurtured if it is to be actualized. For human beings to develop as they should demands that they be properly educated. Since, according to Aristotle, human beings achieve moral excellence by performing good acts, the development of good habits is a crucial part of their education. The ultimate goal of education is to assist human beings in developing their unique capacity to contemplate the world and their role in it. In addition to achieving human happiness, such individuals become ideal citizens ready and able to perform their duties as rational members of a community.

Notes

1. Renford Bambrough, *The Philosophy of Aristotle* (New York: New American Library, 1963), p. 11.
2. Paul Nash, *Models of Man: Explorations in the Western Educational Traditions* (New York: John Wiley & Sons, Inc., 1968), p. 33.
3. Ibid.
4. Robert Ulich, ed., *Three Thousand Years of Educational Wisdom: Selections from Great Documents* (Cambridge, MA: Harvard University Press, 1979), p. 88.

From *Nicomachean Ethics* (ca. 330 BC)

Book I

Our discussion will be adequate if it has as much clearness as the subject-matter admits of, for precision is not to be sought for alike in all discussions, any more than in all the products of the crafts. Now fine and just actions, which political science investigates, admit of much variety and fluctuation of opinion, so that they may be thought to exist only by convention, and not by nature. And goods also give rise to a similar fluctuation because they bring harm to many people; for before now men have been undone by reason of their wealth, and others by reason of their courage. We must be content, then, in speaking of such subjects and with such premises to indicate the truth roughly and in outline, and in speaking about things which are only for the most part true and with premises of the same kind to reach conclusions that are no better. In the same spirit, therefore, should each type of statement be *received*; for it is the mark of an educated man to look for precision in each class of things just so far as the nature of the subject admits; it is evidently equally foolish to accept probable reasoning from a mathematician and to demand from a rhetorician scientific proofs.

Now each man judges well the things he knows, and of these he is a good judge. And so the man who has been educated in a subject is a good judge of that subject, and the man who has received an all-round education is a good judge in general. Hence a young man is not a proper hearer of lectures on political science; for he is inexperienced in the actions that occur in life, but its discussions start from these and are about these; and, further, since he tends to follow his passions, his study will be vain and unprofitable, because the end aimed at is not knowledge but action. And it makes no difference whether he is young in years or youthful in character; the defect does not depend on time, but on his living, and pursuing each successive object, as passion directs. For to such persons, as to the incontinent, knowledge brings no profit; but to those who desire and act in accordance with a rational principle knowledge about such matters will be of great benefit. . . .

Let us again return to the good we are seeking, and ask what it can be. It seems different in different actions and arts; it is different in medicine, in strategy, and in the other arts likewise. What then is the good of each? Surely that for whose sake everything else is done. In medicine this is health, in strategy victory, in architecture a house, in any other sphere something else, and in every action and pursuit the end; for it is for the sake of this that all men do whatever else they do. Therefore, if there is an end for all that we do, this will be the good achievable by action, and if there are more than one, these will be the goods achievable by action.

So the argument has by a different course reached the same point; but we must try to state this even more clearly. Since there are evidently more than

Reprinted from Aristotle's *Nicomachean Ethics* translated by W. D. Ross (1925) by permission of Oxford University Press.

one end, and we choose some of these (e.g. wealth, flutes, and in general instruments) for the sake of something else, clearly not all ends are final ends; but the chief good is evidently something final. Therefore, if there is only one final end, this will be what we are seeking, and if there are more than one, the most final of these will be what we are seeking. Now we call that which is in itself worthy of pursuit more final than that which is worthy of pursuit for the sake of something else, and that which is never desirable for the sake of something else more final than the things that are desirable both in themselves and for the sake of that other thing, and therefore we call final without qualification that which is always desirable in itself and never for the sake of something else.

Now such a thing happiness, above all else, is held to be; for this we choose always for itself and never for the sake of something else, but honour, pleasure, reason, and every virtue we choose indeed for themselves (for if nothing resulted from them we should still choose each of them), but we choose them also for the sake of happiness, judging that by means of them we shall be happy. Happiness, on the other hand, no one chooses for the sake of these, nor, in general, for anything other than itself.

From the point of view of self-sufficiency the same result seems to follow; for the final good is thought to be self-sufficient. Now by self-sufficient we do not mean that which is sufficient for a man by himself, for one who lives a solitary life, but also for parents, children, wife, and in general for his friends and fellow citizens, since man is born for citizenship. But some limit must be set to this; for if we extend our requirement to ancestors and descendants and friends' friends, we are in for an infinite series. Let us examine this question, however, on another occasion; the self-sufficient we now define as that which when isolated makes life desirable and lacking in nothing; and such we think happiness to be; and further we think it most desirable of all things, without being counted as one good thing among others—if it were so counted it would clearly be made more desirable by the addition of even the least of goods; for that which is added becomes an excess of goods, and of goods the greater is always more desirable. Happiness, then, is something final and self-sufficient, and is the end of action.

Presumably, however, to say that happiness is the chief good seems a platitude, and a clearer account of what it is still desired. This might perhaps be given, if we could first ascertain the function of man. For just as for a flute-player, a sculptor, or any artist, and, in general, for all things that have a function or activity, the good and the "well" is thought to reside in the function, so would it seem to be for man, if he has a function. Have the carpenter, then, and the tanner certain functions or activities, and has man none? Is he born without a function? Or as eye, hand, foot, and in general each of the parts evidently has a function, may one lay it down that man similarly has a function apart from all these? What then can this be? Life seems to be common even to plants, but we are seeking what is peculiar to man. Let us exclude, therefore, the life of nutrition and growth. Next there would be a life of perception, but *it* also seems to be common even to the horse, the ox, and every animal. There remains, then, an active life of the element that has a rational principle; of this, one part has such a principle in the sense of being obedient to one, the other in the sense of possessing one and exercising thought. And, as "life of the rational element" also has two meanings, we must state that life in the sense of activity is what we mean; for this seems to be the more proper sense of the term. Now if the function of man is an activity of soul which follows or implies a rational principle, and if we say "a so-and-so" and "a good so-and-so" have a function which is the same kind, e. g. a lyre-player and a good lyre-player, and so without qualification in all cases, eminence in respect of goodness being added to the name of the function (for the function of a lyre-player is to play the lyre, and that of a good lyre-player is to do so well): if this is the case, [and we state the function of man to be a certain kind of life, and this to be an activity or actions of the soul implying a rational principle, and the function of a good man to be the good and noble performance of these, and if any action is well performed when it is performed in accordance with the appropriate excellence: if this is the case,] human good turns out to be activity of soul in accordance with virtue, and if there are more than one virtue, in accordance with the best and most complete. . . .

With those who identify happiness with virtue or some one virtue our account is harmony; for to virtue belongs virtuous activity. But it makes, perhaps, no small difference whether we place the chief good in possession or in use, in state of mind or inactivity. For the state of mind may exist without producing any good result, as in a man who is asleep or in some other way quite inactive, but activity cannot; for one who has the activity will of necessity be acting, and acting well. And as in the Olympic Games it is not the most beautiful and the strongest that are crowned but those who compete (for it is some of these that are victorious), so those who act win, and rightly win, the noble and good things in life. . . .

Book II

Virtue, then being of two kinds, intellectual and moral, intellectual virtue in the main owes both its birth and its growth to teaching (for which reason it requires experience and time), while moral virtue comes about as a result of habit, whence also its name ($\eta\theta\iota\kappa\eta$) is one that is formed by a slight variation from the word $\epsilon\theta\circ\zeta$ (habit). From this it is also plain that none of the moral virtues arises in us by nature; for nothing that exists by nature can form a habit contrary to its nature. For instance the stone which by nature moves downwards cannot be habituated to move upwards, not even if one tries to train it by throwing it up ten thousand times; nor can fire be habituated to move downward, nor can anything else that by nature behaves in one way be trained to behave in another. Neither by nature, then, nor contrary to nature do the virtues arise in us; rather we are adapted by nature to receive them, and are made perfect by habit.

Again, of all the things that come to us by nature we first acquire the potentiality and later exhibit the activity (this is plain in the case of the senses; for it was not by often seeing or often hearing that we got these senses, but on the contrary we had them before we used them, and did not come to have them by using them); but the virtues we get by first exercising them, as also happens in the case of the arts as well. For the things we have to learn before we can do them, we learn by doing them, e.g. men become builders by building and lyre-players by playing the lyre; so too we become just by doing just acts, temperate by doing temperate acts, brave by doing brave acts.

This is confirmed by what happens in states: for legislators make the citizens good by forming habits in them, and this is the wish of every legislator, and those who do not effect it miss their mark, and it is in this that a good constitution differs from a bad one.

Again, it is from the same causes and by the same means that every virtue is both produced and destroyed, and similarly every art; for it is from playing the lyre that both good and bad lyre-players are produced. And the corresponding statement is true of builders and of all the rest; men will be good or bad builders as a result of building well or badly. For if this were not so, there would have been no need of a teacher, but all men would have been born good or bad at their craft. This, then, is the case with the virtues also; by doing the acts that we do in our transactions with other men we become just or unjust, and by doing the acts that we do in the presence of danger, and being habituated to feel fear or confidence, we become brave or cowardly. The same is true of appetites and feelings of anger; some men become temperate and good-tempered, others self-indulgent and irascible, by behaving in one way or the other in the appropriate circumstances. Thus, in one word, states of character arise out of like activities. This is why the activities we exhibit must be of a certain kind; it is because the states of character correspond to the differences between these. It makes no small difference, then, whether we form habits of one kind or of another from our very youth; it makes a very great difference, or rather *all* the difference. . . .

It is the nature of such things to be destroyed by defect and excess, as we see in the case of strength and of health (for to gain light on things imperceptible we must use the evidence of sensible things); both excessive and defective exercise destroys the strength, and similarly drink or food which is above or below a certain amount destroys the health, while that which is proportionate both produces and increases and preserves it. So too is it, then, in the case of temperance and courage and the other virtues. For the man who flies from and fears everything and does not stand his ground against anything becomes a coward, and the man who fears nothing at all but goes to meet every danger becomes rash; and similarly the man who indulges in every pleasure and abstains from none becomes self-indulgent, while the man who shuns every pleasure, as boors do, becomes in a way insensible; temperance and courage, then, are destroyed by excess and defect, and preserved by the mean.

But not only are the sources and causes of their origination and growth the same as those of their destruction, but also the sphere of their actualization will be the same; for this is also true of the things which are more evident to sense, e.g., of strength; it is produced by taking much food and undergoing much exertion, and it is the strong man that will be most able to do these things. So too is it with the virtues; by abstaining from pleasures we become temperate, and it is when we have become so that we are most able to abstain from them; and similarly too in the case of courage; for by being habituated to despise things that are terrible and to stand our ground against them we become brave, and it is when we have become so that we shall be most able to stand our ground against them. . . .

Virtue, then, is a state of character concerned with choice, lying in a mean, i.e. the mean relative to us, this being determined by a rational principle, and by that principle by which the man of practical wisdom would determine it. Now it is a mean between two vices, that which depends on excess and that which depends on defect; and again it is a mean because the vices respectively fall short of or exceed what is right in both passions and actions, while virtue both finds and chooses that which is intermediate. Hence in respect of its substance and the definition which states its essence virtue is a mean, with regard to what is best and right an extreme.

But not every, action nor every passion admits of a mean; for some have names that already imply badness, e.g. spite, shamelessness, envy, and in the case of actions adultery, theft, murder; for all of these and suchlike things imply by their names that they are themselves bad, and not the excesses or deficiencies of them. It is not possible, then, ever to be right with regard to them; one must always be wrong. Nor does goodness or badness with regard to such things depend on committing adultery with the right woman, at the right time, and in the right way, but simply to do any of them is to go wrong. It would be equally absurd, then, to expect that in unjust, cowardly, and voluptuous action there should be a mean, an excess, and a deficiency; for at that rate there would be a mean of excess and of deficiency, an excess of excess, and a deficiency of deficiency. But as there is no excess and deficiency of temperance and courage because what is intermediate is in a sense an extreme, so too of the actions we have mentioned there is no mean nor any excess and deficiency, but however they are done they are wrong; for in general there is neither a mean of excess and deficiency, nor excess and deficiency of a mean. . . .

Book X

If happiness is activity in accordance with virtue, it is reasonable that it should be in accordance with the highest virtue; and this will be that of the best thing in us. Whether it be reason or something else that is this element which is thought to be our natural ruler and guide and to take thought of things noble and divine, whether it be itself also divine or only the most divine element in us, the activity of this in accordance with its proper virtue will be perfect happiness. That this activity is contemplative we have already said.

Now this would seem to be in agreement both with what we said before and with the truth. For, firstly, this activity is the best (since not only is reason the best thing in us, but the objects of reason are the best of knowable objects); and, secondly, it is the most continuous, since we can contemplate truth more continuously than we can *do* anything. And we think happiness has pleasure mingled with it, but the activity of philosophic wisdom is admittedly the pleasantest of virtuous activities; at all events the pursuit of it is thought to offer pleasures marvellous for their purity and their enduringness, and it is to be expected that those who know will pass their time more pleasantly than those who inquire. And the self-sufficiency that is spoken of must belong to the contemplative activity. For while a philosopher, as well as a just man or one possessing any other virtue, needs the necessaries of life, when they are sufficiently equipped with things of that sort the just man needs people towards whom and with whom he shall act justly, and the temperate man, the brave man, and each of the others is in the same case, but the philosopher, even when by himself, can contemplate truth, and the better the wiser he is; he can perhaps do so better if he has fellow-workers, but still he is the most self-sufficient. And this activity alone would seem to be loved for its own sake; for nothing arises from it apart from the contemplating, while from practical activities we gain more or less apart from the action. And happiness is thought to depend on leisure; for we are busy that we may have leisure, and make war that we may live in peace. Now the activity of the practical virtues is exhibited in political or military affairs, but the actions concerned with these seem to be unleisurely. Warlike actions are completely so (for no one chooses to be at war, or provokes war, for the sake of being at war; any one would seem absolutely murderous if he were to make enemies of his friends in order to bring about battle and slaughter); but the action of the statesman is also unleisurely, and—apart from the political action itself—aims at despotic power and honours, or at all events happiness, for him and his fellow citizens—a happiness different from political action, and evidently sought as being different. So if among virtuous actions political and military actions are distinguished by nobility and greatness, and these are unleisurely and aim at an end and are not desirable for their own sake, but the activity of reason, which is contemplative, seems both to be superior in serious worth and to aim at no end beyond itself, and to have its pleasure proper to itself (and this augments the activity), and the self-sufficiency, leisureliness, unweariedness (so far as this is possible for man), and all the other attributes ascribed to the supremely happy man are evidently those connected with this activity, it follows that this will be the complete happiness of man, if it be allowed a complete term of life (for none of the attributes of happiness is *in*complete).

But such a life would be too high for man; for it is not in so far as he is man that he will live so, but in so far as something divine is present in him; and by so much as this is superior to our composite nature is its activity superior to that which is the exercise of the other kind of virtue. If reason is divine, then, in comparison with man, the life according to it is divine in comparison with human life. But we must not follow those who advise us, being men, to think of human things, and, being mortal, of mortal things, but must, so far as we can, make ourselves immortal, and strain every nerve to live in accordance with the best thing in us; for even if it be small in bulk, much more does it in power and worth surpass everything. This would seem, too, to be each man himself, since it is the authoritative and better part of him. It would be strange, then, if he were to choose not the life of his self but that of something else. And what we said before will apply now; that which is proper to each thing is by nature best and most pleasant for each thing; for man, therefore, the life according to reason is best and pleasantest, since reason more than anything else *is* man. This life therefore is also the happiest. . . .

But that perfect happiness is a contemplative activity will appear from the following consideration as well. We assume the gods to be above all other beings blessed and happy; but what sort of actions must we assign to them? Acts of justice? Will not the gods seem absurd if they make contracts and return deposits, and so on? Acts of brave man, then, confronting dangers and running risks because it is noble to do so? Or liberal acts? To whom will they give? It will be strange if they are really to have money or anything of the kind. And what would their temperate acts be? Is not such praise tasteless, since they have no bad appetites? If we were to run through them all, the circumstances of action would be found trivial and unworthy of gods. Still, every one supposes that they *live* and therefore that they are active; we cannot suppose them to sleep like Endymion. Now if you take away from a living being action, and still more production, what is left but contemplation? Therefore the activity of God, which surpasses all others in blessedness, must be contemplative; and of human activities, therefore, that which is most akin to this must be most of the nature of happiness.

This is indicated, too, by the fact that the other animals have no share in happiness, being completely deprived of such activity. For while the whole life of gods is blessed, and that of men too in so far as some likeness of such activity belongs to them, none of the other animals is happy, since they in no way share in contemplation. Happiness extends, then, just so far as contemplation does, and those to whom contemplation more fully belongs are more truly happy, not as a mere concomitant but in virtue of the contemplation; for this is in itself precious. Happiness, therefore, must be some form of contemplation. . . .

Now he who exercises his reason and cultivates it seems to be both in the best state of mind and most dear to the gods. For if the gods have any care for human affairs, as they are thought to have, it would be reasonable both that they should delight in that which was best and most akin to them (i.e. reason) and that they should reward those who love and honour this most, as caring for the things that are dear to them and acting both rightly and nobly. And that all these attributes belong most of all to the philosopher is manifest. He, therefore, is the dearest to the gods. And he who is that will presumably be also the happiest; so that in this way too the philosopher will more than any other be happy. . . .

Now some think that we are made good by nature, others by habituation, others by teaching Nature's part evidently does not depend on us, but as a result of some divine causes is present in those who are truly fortunate; while argument and teaching, we may suspect, are not powerful with all men, but the soul of the student must first have been cultivated by means of habits for noble joy and noble hatred, like earth which is to nourish the seed. For he who lives as passion directs will not hear argument that dissuades him, nor understand it if he does; and how can we persuade one in such a state to change his ways. And in general passion seems to yield not to argument but to force. The character, then, must somehow be there already with a kinship to virtue, loving what is noble and hating what is base.

But it is difficult to get from youth up a right training for virtue if one has not been brought up under right laws; for to live temperately and hardily is not pleasant to most people, especially when they are young. For this reason their nurture and occupations should be fixed by law; for they will not be painful when they have become customary. But it is surely not enough that when they are young they should get the right nurture and attention; since they must, even when they are grown up, practise and be habituated to them, we shall need laws for this as well, and generally speaking to cover the whole life; for most people obey necessity rather than argument, and punishments rather than the sense of what is noble.

This is why some think that legislators ought to stimulate men to virtue and urge them forward by the motive of the noble, on the assumption that those who have been well advanced by the formation of habits will attend to such influences; and that punishments and penalties should be imposed on those who disobey and are of inferior nature, while the incurably bad should be completely banished. . . .

Now it is best that there should be a public and proper care for such matters; but if they are neglected by the community it would seem right for each man to help his children and friends towards virtue, and that they should have the power, or at least the will, to do this.

It would seem from what has been said that he can do this better if he makes himself capable of legislating. For public control is plainly effected by laws, and good control by good laws; whether written or unwritten would seem to make no difference, nor whether they are providing for the education of individuals or of groups—any more than it does in the case of music or gymnastics and other such pursuits. For as in cities laws and prevailing types of character have force, so in households do the injunctions and the habits of the father, and these have even more because of the tie of blood and the benefits he confers; for the children start with a natural affection and disposition to obey. Further, private education has an advantage over public, as private medical treatment has; for while in general rest and abstinence from food are good for a man in a fever, for a particular man they may not be; and a boxer presumably does not prescribe the same style of fighting to all his pupils. It would seem, then, that the detail is worked out with more precision if the control is private; for each person is more likely to get what suits his case.

But the details can be best looked after, one by one, by a doctor or gymnastic instructor or any one else who has the general knowledge of what is good for every one or for people of a certain kind (for the sciences both are said to be, and are, concerned with what is universal); not but what some particular detail may perhaps be well looked after by an unscientific person, if he has studied accurately in the light of experience what happens in each case, just as some people seem to be their own best doctors, though they could give no help to any one else. None the less, it will perhaps be agreed that if a man does wish to become master of an art or science he must go to the universal, and come to know it as well as possible; for, as we have said, it is with this that the sciences are concerned.

And surely he who wants to make men, whether many or few, better by his care must try to become capable of legislating, if it is through laws that we can become good. For to get any one whatever—any one who is put before us—into the right condition is not for the first chance comer; if any one can do it, it is the man who knows, just as in medicine and all other matters which give scope for care and prudence.

Questions

1. What does Aristotle mean by happiness?
2. Is happiness intrinsically or instrumentally valuable? Explain.
3. What is the difference between intellectual and moral virtue?
4. What role, if any, does habit play in developing virtue?
5. What role, if any, does nature play in humankind's development of virtue?
6. Explain why habit plays such a significant role in Aristotle's educational scheme.
7. Why did Aristotle refuse to allow the Athenians to sin a second time against philosophy?
8. What is the relationship between virtue, happiness, and leisure?
9. In what ways is the philosopher like the just human being, the temperate human being, and the brave human being?
10. How does the philosopher differ from those human beings?
11. Do you think Aristotle would be pleased with the way contemporary human beings use their leisure time? Explain.
12. What argument does Aristotle offer in support of the statement that the most blessed and happy activity of the gods is contemplation?
13. According to Aristotle, what is it about human beings that make them unique?
14. How did Aristotle arrive at his beliefs about human nature or essence?
15. In what ways is Aristotle like his mentor, Plato, and in what ways does he differ from Plato?
16. In your own words, describe Aristotle's vision of the ideally educated human being.

chapter 3

St. Augustine

TIME LINE FOR ST. AUGUSTINE

354 AD	Is born in Thagaste, North Africa (now Algeria). His father is a pagan; his mother is a devout Christian.
370	Begins the study of rhetoric in Carthage.
370–384	Takes a mistress with whom he has a son. Embraces Manichaean doctrine.
384	Leaves Africa (without his mistress and son) and moves to Milan, where he is municipal professor of rhetoric. Takes another mistress.
386	Converts to Christianity.
389	Writes *Concerning the Teacher.*
395	Is appointed bishop of Hippo.
400	Writes *Confessions.*
413–427	Writes *City of God* and *City of Man*
430	Dies in Hippo.

Introduction

St. Augustine is best known for his *Confessions,* a classic description of sin and redemption that has inspired religious believers and church leaders for centuries, and his twin volumes, *City of Man* and *City of God,* detailing the relationship of the human and the political to the religious. What is frequently overlooked about Augustine is his pivotal position in educational thought. He stands at the beginning of the medieval period and sets the themes that will define that era. At the same time, given his pagan studies, described throughout the *Confessions*, there is a very real Platonic (or Neoplatonic) feel to Augustine's thought. Finally, as the selection from *Concerning the Teacher* shows, with its stress on experience, Augustine is a harbinger of the pragmatic-progressive tradition that finds its clearest exposition in the writings of John Dewey.

Augustine was born in Thagaste, a North African town situated close to what is now the border between Algeria and Tunisia, in AD 354. His youth and young manhood were spent being drawn between the worldly materialism of his Roman father's tradition and the religious piety of his mother's Christian faith. Eventually, somewhere around 386, Augustine chose the latter and was baptized. By 391, he was ordained a priest, and in 395 he replaced Valerius as bishop of Hippo. He remained bishop until his death in 430.

To understand Augustine, to begin to understand his conception of an educated person, it is helpful to contrast medieval thought with modern thought.

The modern period is generally said to begin with the French philosopher René Descartes and to have had its clearest flowering in the French Enlightenment. Descartes's program, which he labeled "systematic doubt," is a fairly simple one. Descartes realized that it is commonplace for people to be deceived, for them to make mistakes. If those mistakes come at the beginning of inquiry, if they are "foundational," everything built upon them will crumble as the foundation is shown to be faulty. His program, then, was to examine all beliefs until he arrived at a belief that could not be doubted and that could serve as a foundation on which to build a secure system. Again, one rejects all beliefs that can be doubted until one gets to some indubitable core, which for Descartes was the Classic *"Je pense, donc je suis"* ("I think, therefore I am"), and then one goes about building a secure system. In the French Enlightenment, and throughout the modern era, that method for building a secure system was called the "scientific method."

For Augustine, as both heir to the classical Greek tradition and harbinger of medievalism, there is, simply, something very strange about the modern search for foundations. Socrates, given the option of fleeing the city after he has been found guilty of "corrupting the morals of the youth of Athens," reaffirms his decision to stay and, in effect, acquiesces to his own execution. It is not only that Socrates owes a debt to the city and its laws—the city has given "birth" to him, it has nurtured and supported him, it has given him many benefits. It would be unseemly to accept all the benefits and then flee when the "bill" was being presented. Even more importantly, it is that the city and its laws are part of Socrates: They define him, and to run away from the city is, in effect, to run away from himself. Socrates does not have to search for a foundation, for a firm and secure starting place. It is given in the polis, in the shared living that constitutes the city. Furthermore, it is membership in the polis that makes possible the discovery of those universal truths that Plato in *The Republic* will call the Forms.

In a similar way, Augustine does not have to search for a foundation. As a true medievalist, he sees inquiry as beginning with an existing community of religious believers. Those believers (in Augustine's case, the believers are Christians, but in other cases they can be Jews or Mohammedans) have a set of preexisting beliefs, dogmas, traditions, institutions, practices, and so on, which define them as a community. One starts, using John Dewey's telling phrase, from the "likemindedness" of the community, and one uses that likemindedness as an instrument for getting closer and closer to the truth. For Augustine the truth is found in Christ.

The distinction between the Greek/medieval notions of inquiry and the educated person and the modern notions of the same is worth stressing. For both the Greeks and the medieval person, it is precisely membership in a particular cultural and historical group that makes possible the discovery of a truth that is transcultural and ahistorical. Membership in *this* church, at *this* time, observations of its rituals and practices, make possible the discovery of a truth that is said to be timeless and universal. The modern thinker, exemplified by Descartes, tries to *begin* with a foundation that is transcultural and ahistorical, that is true for all times and for all places.

Having pointed out differences between Augustine and modern thinkers such as Descartes, one should also point out similarities between Augustine and the American philosopher and educator John Dewey. This twentieth-century thinker is the one person who puts experience at the heart of education. For Dewey, education was basically about giving children new and varied experiences and creating environments in which children were encouraged to wrest as much meaning as possible from those experiences, to reconstruct them, and to make sense of them. Dewey was reacting against a system in which one person, the teacher-expert, simply told the child-student what was important and in which the student's task was to record the information and give it back to the teacher on examination day. Dewey viewed that as dry, lifeless, and most importantly a-educational or anti-educational.

Nearly one thousand years before Dewey's stirring "My Pedagogic Creed," St. Augustine was saying similar things. He recast the role of the teacher from one of mere conveyor of information to one who is most concerned with creating an environment in which children are encouraged either to have new experiences or to recall old ones. The teacher-expert might believe that words have a kind of magical quality, that is, that words have meaning "attached" to them and that by simply uttering a word or series of words, teachers can be assured that their students will understand them and use them appropriately. The Augustinian teacher believes that words become meaningful only to the extent that they can be connected with a set of experiences. Thus, she or he busies herself or himself with speaking and acting so that the classroom becomes a place in which students have experiences and are encouraged to evaluate those experiences using the criteria provided by religion.

To repeat, the educated person, for Augustine, is the individual whose membership in a religious community allows her or him to discover standards and criteria (the Truth as found in the person of Christ) that enable the person to deal meaningfully with her or his experience. The following excerpts show some of the classical Greek, medieval Christian, and pragmatic strands that constitute the philosophy of St. Augustine.

From *Confessions* (ca. 400)

Book I

Chapter XIX.—How He Was More Careful to Avoid Barbarisms of Speech, Than Corruption of Manners

In the threshold of these customs lay I, wretched boy, and upon that stage I played my prizes; where I more feared to commit a barbarism in speaking, than I took care when I committed any, not to envy those that committed none. All this I declare and confess to thee, my God; but in these things I was by them applauded, to please whom, I then accounted equal to living honestly. For then I discerned not that whirlpool of filthiness whereinto I was cast from thine eyes. For in thine eyes, what was more filthy than I? Where also I displeased such as myself; with innumerable lies deceiving both my tutor, and masters, and parents: all for love of play, out of a desire to see toys, and a restless desire to imitate the stage.

Thievery also I committed out of my father's buttery and table; either gluttony oft commanding me, or that I might have something to give my playfellows, selling me their baubles, although they were as much delighted with them as myself. In these playgames I being often over-matched, did with a vain desire to be counted excellent, aspire to win though by foul play. And what was I so unwilling to endure, and what if I found out the deceit would I so fiercely wrangle at, as even those very tricks which I would put upon others? And being myself taken with the manner, I would fall flat out, than yield to it.

Is this that childish innocency? It is not, Lord, it is not. I cry thee mercy, O my God: for these are the same things, the very same, which as our years go on, leaving tutors and masters, leaving nuts, and balls, and birds, are done with regard to kings and governors, to the getting of gold, and manor houses, and slaves. But this boy's play passes over as more years come on, just as greater punishments follow after the ferule. Thou therefore, O our King, hast approved of the character of humility in the stature of childhood, when thou sayest: To such belongeth the Kingdom of God. . . .

Book III

Chapter IV.—How Tully's Hortensius Provoked Him to Study Philosophy

Amongst these mad companions in that tender age of mine learned I the books of eloquence, wherein my ambition was to be eminent, all out of a damnable and vainglorious end, puffed up with a delight of human glory. By the ordinary course of study I fell upon a certain book of one Cicero, whose tongue almost every man admires, though not so his heart. This book of his contains an exhortation to Philosophy, and 'tis called Hortensius. Now this book quite altered my

Reprinted by permission of the publishers and the Loeb Classical Library from *St. AUGUSTINE: CONFESSIONS*, Cambridge, Mass.: Harvard University Press, 1912, 1930.

affection, turned my prayers to thyself, O Lord, and made me have clean other purposes and desires. All my vain hopes I thenceforth slighted; and with an incredible heat of spirit I thirsted after the immortality of wisdom, and began now to rouse up myself, that I might turn again to theeward. For I made not use of that book to file my tongue with, which I seemed to buy with that exhibition which my mother allowed me, in that nineteenth year of my age, my father being dead two years before. I made not use of that book, I say, to sharpen my tongue withal, nor had it persuaded me to affect the fine language in it, but the matter of it.

How did I burn then, my God, how did I burn to fly from earthly delights towards thee, and yet I knew not what thou meanedst to do with me! For with thee is wisdom. That love of wisdom is in Greek called Philosophy, with which that book inflamed me. Some there be that seduce others through Philosophy, under a great, a fair promising, and an honest name, colouring over and palliating their own errors: and almost all those who in the same and former ages had been of that stamp, are in that book censured and set forth: there also is that most wholesome advice of thy Spirit, given by thy good and devout servant, made plain: Beware lest any man spoil you through Philosophy and vain deceit after the tradition of men, after the rudiments of the world, and not after Christ. For in him dwelleth all the Fulness of the Godhead bodily. For my part, thou Light of my heart knowest, that the Apostolical Scriptures were scarce known to me at that time: but this was it that so delighted me in that exhortation, that it did not engage me to this or that sect, but left me free to love, and seek, and obtain, and hold, and embrace Wisdom itself, whatever it was. Perchance it was that book I was stirred up, and enkindled, and inflamed by: This thing only in such a heat of zeal took me off, that the name of Christ was not in it. For this Name, according to thy mercy, O Lord, this Name of my Savior thy Son, had my tender heart even together with my mother's milk devoutly drunken in, and charily treasured up: so that what book soever was without that Name, though never so learned, politely and truly penned, did not altogether take my approbation.

Chapter V.—He Sets Lightly by the Holy Scriptures Because of the Simplicity of the Style

I resolved thereupon to bend my studies towards the Holy Scriptures, that I might see what they were. But behold, I espy something in them not revealed to the proud, not discovered unto children, humble in style, sublime in operation, and wholly veiled over in mysteries; and I was not so fitted at that time, as to pierce into the sense, or stoop my neck to its coming. For when I attentively read these Scriptures, I thought not then so of them, as I now speak; but they seemed to me far unworthy to be compared to the stateliness of the Ciceronian eloquence. For my swelling pride soared above the temper of their style, nor was my sharp wit able to pierce into their sense. And yet such are thy Scriptures as grew up together with thy little ones. But I much disdained to be held a little one; and big swollen with pride, I took myself to be some great man. . . .

From *Concerning the Teacher* (ca. 389)

Internal Light, Internal Truth

Now, if regarding colors we consult light; and regarding the other sensible objects we consult the elements of this world constituting the bodies of which we have sense experience, and the senses themselves which the mind uses as interpreters to know such things; and if, moreover, regarding those things which are objects of intelligence we consult the truth within us through reasoning—then what can be advanced as proof that words teach us anything beyond the mere sound which strikes the ears? For everything we perceive, we perceive either through a sense of the body or by the mind. The former we call sensible, the latter, intelligible; or, to speak in the manner of our own authors, we call the former carnal, and the latter spiritual. When we are asked concerning the former, we answer, if the things of which we have sense knowledge are present; as when we are looking at a new moon we are asked what sort of a thing it is or where it is. In this case if the one who puts the question does not see the object, he believes words; and often he does not believe them. But learn he does not all, unless he himself sees what is spoken about; and in that case he learns not by means of spoken words, but by means of the realities themselves and his senses. For the words have the same sound for the one who sees the object as for the one who does not see it. But when a question is asked not regarding things which we perceive while they are present, but regarding things of which we had sense knowledge in the past, then we express in speech, not the realities themselves, but the images impressed by them on the mind and committed to memory. How we can speak at all of these as true when we see they are false, I do not know—unless it be because we report on them not as things we actually see and perceive, but as things we have seen and perceived. Thus we bear these images in the depths of memory as so many attestations, so to say, of things previously perceived by the senses. Contemplating these in the mind, we have the good conscience that we are not lying when we speak. But even so, these attestations are such for us only. If one who hears me has personally perceived these things and become aware of them, he does not learn them from my words, but recognizes them from the images that are stored away within himself. If, however, he has had no sense knowledge of them, he clearly believes rather than learns by means of the words.

Now, when there is question of those things which we perceive by the mind—that is, by means of the intellect and by reason—we obviously express in speech the things which we behold immediately in that interior light of truth which effects enlightenment and happiness in the so-called inner man. And at the same time if the one who hears me likewise sees those things with

From *ST. AUGUSTINE* translated by Joseph M. Colleran, C.SS.R., PhD. c 1950 by Rev. Johannes Quasten and Rev. Joseph C. Plumpe c 1978 by Rev. Johannes Quasten and Rose Mary L. Plumple.

an inner and undivided eye, he knows the matter of which I speak by his own contemplation, not by means of my words. Hence, I do not teach even such a one, although I speak what is true and he sees what is true. For he is taught not by my words, but by the realities themselves made manifest to him by God revealing them to his inner self. Thus, if he were asked, he could also give answers regarding these things. What could be more absurd than to think that he is taught by my speech, when even before I spoke he could explain those same things, if he were asked about them?

As for the fact that, as often happens, one denies something when he is asked about it, but is brought around by further questions to affirm it, this happens by reason of the weakness of his vision, not permitting him to consult that light regarding the matter as a whole. He is prompted to consider the problem part by part as questions are put regarding those same parts that constitute the whole, which originally he was not able to see in its entirety. If in this case he is led on by the words of the questioner, still it is not that the words teach him, but they represent questions put to him in such a way as to correspond to his capacity for learning from his own inner self.

To illustrate: if I were to ask you whether it is true that nothing can be taught by means of words—the very topic we are discussing now—you would at first think the question absurd, because you could not see the problem in its entirety. Then I should have to question you in a way adapted to your capacity for hearing that Teacher within you. So I should say: "Those things which I stated and you granted as true, and of which you are certain and which you are sure you know—where did you learn them?" You would perhaps answer that I had taught them to you. Then I would rejoin: "Let us suppose I told you that I saw a man flying. Would my words give you the same certitude as if you heard that wise men are superior to fools?" You would, of course, answer in the negative and would tell me that you do not believe the former statement, or even if you did believe it, that you did not know it; whereas you knew the other statement to be absolutely certain. Certainly, the upshot of this would be that you would then realize that you had not learned anything from my words; neither in the case where you were not aware of the thing that I affirmed, nor in the case of that which you knew very well. For if you were asked about each case, you would even swear that you were unaware of the former and that you did know the latter. But then you would actually be admitting the entire proposition which you had denied, since you would now know clearly and certainly what it implies: namely, that whatever we say, the hearer either does not know whether it is true, or knows it is false, or knows that it is true. In the first of these three cases he either believes, or has an opinion, or is in doubt; in the second, he opposes and rejects the statement; in the third, he bears witness to the truth. In none of the cases, therefore, does he learn. The obvious reason is that the one who on hearing my words does not know the reality, and the one who knows that what he has heard is false, and the one who, if he were asked, could have answered precisely what was said, demonstrate that they have learned nothing from my words.

Words Do Not Always Have the Power Even to Reveal the Mind of the Speaker

Therefore, also in regard to the things which are seen by the mind, it is of no avail for anyone who cannot perceive them to hear the words of another who does perceive them, except in so far as it is useful to believe them, so long as one is not acquainted with them. But anyone who is able to perceive them is in his innermost a pupil of truth and outside himself a judge of the speaker or, rather, of what he says. For often enough he has knowledge of what is said even when the speaker lacks such knowledge. For example, someone who is a follower of the Epicureans and thinks the soul is mortal, sets forth the arguments for its immortality as expounded by wiser men. If one who is able to contemplate spiritual things hears him, he judges that the other is expressing the truth, while the speaker does not know whether the arguments are true; indeed he even thinks them utterly false. Is he, then, to be considered as teaching what he does not know? Yet he is using the very same words which one who does have the knowledge could also use.

Hence, not even this function is left to words, that they at least manifest the mind of the one who speaks them, since it is even uncertain whether he knows as true what he expresses. Take also the liars and deceivers: you can readily see that they employ words not only not to reveal their minds, but even to conceal them. I do not at all doubt, of course, that the words of those who tell the truth represent efforts and, in a way, promises, to manifest the mind of the speaker; and they would be sustained in this and find acceptance by all, if liars were not allowed to speak.

Of course, we have often experienced both in ourselves and in others, that words are uttered which do not correspond to the things thought about. This, I see, can happen in two ways: either a piece of diction that has been committed to memory and frequently repeated passes the mouth of one actually thinking of other things—as often happens to us when we are singing a hymn; or, contrary to our intention and by a slip of the tongue, some words will rush out in the place of others; obviously, in this case, too, what is heard does not represent the things that are in the mind. In fact, those who tell lies also think of what they express, so that even though we do not know whether they are expressing the truth, we nevertheless know that they have in mind what they are saying, if neither of the two things I spoke of applies to them. If anyone contends that these latter things occur only occasionally and that it is apparent when they occur, I make no objection; though they frequently do escape notice and they have often deceived me when I heard them.

But in addition to these there is another class, certainly very extensive, and the source of countless disagreements and disputes: when the one who speaks signifies exactly what he is thinking, but generally only to himself and certain others, while he does not signify the same thing to the one to whom he speaks and to a number of other persons. For example, let someone say in our hearing that man is surpassed in virtue by certain brute animals. We resent that at once, and with great insistence we refute that statement as utterly false and harmful.

Yet he may be using the term "virtue" to designate physical strength, and expressing by it what he has in mind; and he would not be lying, nor is he in error regarding the realities, nor is he reeling off words he has memorized, while he ponders something else in his mind; nor does he express by a slip of the tongue something he did not intend to say. But he merely calls the reality of which he is thinking, by another name than we do; and we should at once agree with him regarding that reality, if we could see his thought, which he was not able to manifest to us by the words he had already spoken in proposing his opinion.

They say that a definition can correct this type of error; so that, if in the present case the speaker should define what "virtue" means, it would be made clear, they say, that the dispute concerns not the reality, but the term used. Even granting that this is so, how many are there who can give good definitions? Even with regard to the method of defining, there has been much discussion; but it is not opportune to treat of that here, nor am I entirely satisfied with it. . . .

But listen to this—I now yield and concede that when words have been heard by one to whom they are familiar, he can know that the speaker has been thinking about the realities which they signify. But does he for that reason also learn whether what is said is true, which is the present point of inquiry?

Christ Teaches Within the Mind. Man's Words Are External, and Serve Only to Give Reminders

Teachers do not claim, do they, that their own thoughts are perceived and grasped by the pupils, but rather the branches of learning that they think they transmit by speaking? For who would be so absurdly curious as to send his child to school to learn what the teacher thinks? But when they have explained, by means of words, all those subjects which they profess to teach, and even the science of virtue and of wisdom, then those who are called pupils consider within themselves whether what has been said is true. This they do by gazing attentively at that interior truth, so far as they are able. Then it is that they learn; and when within themselves they find that what has been said is true, they give praise, not realizing that they are praising not so much teachers as persons taught—provided that the teachers also know what they are saying. But people deceive themselves in calling persons "teachers" who are not such at all, merely because generally there is no interval between the time of speaking and the time of knowing. And because they are quick to learn internally following the prompting of the one who speaks, they think they have learned externally from the one who was only a prompter.

But at some other time, God willing, we shall investigate the entire problem of the utility of words, which, if considered properly, is not negligible. For the present, I have reminded you that we must not attribute to words more than is proper. Thus we should no longer merely believe, but also begin to understand how truly it has been written on divine authority that we should not call anyone on earth a teacher, since *there is One in heaven who is the teacher of all.* What "in heaven" means He Himself will teach us, who has also counselled us through the instrumentality of human beings—by means of signs, and externally—to turn to Him internally and be instructed. He will teach us, to know and love whom is happiness of life, and this is what all proclaim they are seeking, though there are but few who may rejoice in having really found it.

Questions

1. Why was Augustine impressed by "a certain book of Cicero"?
2. Why, ultimately, did he reject it?
3. Do you think the reason he offered for that rejection was sufficient?
4. What, for Augustine, is the role of the teacher?
5. Compare Augustine's teacher with the model provided by Socrates. Which one do you prefer? Why?
6. How should the teacher use language, according to Augustine?
7. For Augustine, is language important?
8. Augustine suggests that all meaningful speech is related to some experience. Do you agree?
9. If you do agree, how might you structure your classroom so that speech will be meaningful?
10. Religion plays a very important role in the discovery of truth, according to Augustine. In the United States, there is a clear separation between church and state. What would Augustine see as the educational implication of that separation?
11. For Augustine, who is the ultimate teacher?

chapter 4

Erasmus

TIME LINE FOR ERASMUS

1466	Is born in Rotterdam or Gouda, Holland, the illegitimate son of a priest.
1475–1483	Studies at Deventer with the Brethern of the Common Life.
1484–1491	Studies at Hertogenbosch.
	Becomes an Augustinian friar at St. Gregory.
1492	Is ordained a priest.
1494	Becomes the Latin secretary to the bishop of Cambria.
1495	Begins studying theology at University of Paris.
1499	Leaves university and goes to England. While in England he becomes interested in humanism and develops a close friendship with John Colet and Thomas More.
1500	Returns to the Continent.
1501	Publishes *Enchiredion Militis Christiani (Handbook for the Christian Soldier)*.
1506	Receives doctorate of divinity at Turin.
1509	Returns to England and writes *Encomium Moriae (The Praise of Folly)*.
1511	Is appointed Lady Margaret Professor at Cambridge University.
1516	Publishes Greek edition of New Testament.
1518	Publishes *Colloquies*.

| **1524** | Publishes *De Libero Arbitrio (On Free Will)*, a response to Martin Luther. |
| **1536** | Dies at Basel. |

Introduction

It has been suggested that Desiderius Erasmus was a *philosophe*—an Enlightenment thinker—before his time. An exemplar of the humanist revival of the fifteenth and sixteenth centuries, Erasmus stood apart. In the words of Martin Luther, Erasmus's younger contemporary, "No one can grasp him but Christ alone."[1] This uniqueness, this elusive quality stems, in part, from Erasmus's ability to understand and appreciate the many sides of an issue. He saw and commented on the faults of the church as clearly as Luther, but, to him, the Reformation meant more than just replacing one dogma with another.

Throughout his life, Erasmus struggled to reconcile reason and religion, scholarship and morality, into an acceptable synthesis. Always seeking that reasoned middle ground between the Scylla of abusive Catholic dogma on the one hand and the Charybdis of irrational fanaticism on the other, Erasmus's advocacy of "sweet reason" fell on deaf ears in an increasingly polarized world. His vision of a rational and moral world fell apart during the last half of his life as Luther's fanatical opposition to the church left little room for reasoned middle ground. Prior to Luther's posting of the 95 Theses, the church laughed along as Erasmus satirized the church fathers, but eventually that same church blamed Erasmus for laying the egg that Luther hatched.[2] While reconciling reason and religion had been his life's quest, Erasmus had lived beyond his time. Events were making a mockery of his belief in the life of the mind, that is, "that those who knew and loved the great writings of all ages must live more justly and happily in their own age."[3]

Though Erasmus lived during the final third of the fifteenth century and the first third of the next century, his life and thought raise questions of contemporary interest and significance. For example, in a world that is more diverse than the one inhabited by Erasmus, is the humanist ideal of the educated person a viable option? Does the ability to understand and appreciate the multiple sides of an issue facilitate the creation of common ground among diverse groups, or is one who seeks such understanding rendered impotent by that very knowledge, incapable of choosing and acting on one of these multiple sides? What is or should be the relationship between reason and action? When and what kind of knowledge empowers or enables us to act and how does knowledge impede or paralyze us from acting? Is it ever possible to navigate a reasoned course between dogmatic and authoritarian extremes? While answers to these questions cannot be gleaned from any one person's life and work, the life and thought of Erasmus bring these issues sharply into focus.

Erasmus offers his vision of the ideally educated person in two different yet related ways. The first is satire, *The Praise of Folly,* and the second is a beautiful portrait of the ideally educated man as personified by Sir Thomas More. Both are works of edification: the former by illustrating the comic yet tragic products of a misguided education, and the latter by demonstrating that Erasmus's vision of the ideally educated individual is attainable. Before briefly discussing these works and their connections to the questions identified above, we need to set the stage, to describe, albeit briefly, western Europe of the fifteenth and sixteenth centuries.

Though Erasmus's vision of a universal humanist society was rejected by many of his contemporaries during his later years, his writings offer us glimpses of what western Europe was like during this period. Though he was a native of the Netherlands and a member of the Roman Catholic clergy, Erasmus's allegiance was to the world of humanist ideas and ideals. Considering himself a citizen of the humanist world, Erasmus traveled widely throughout Europe and, as a clergyman and intellectual, had access to the centers of culture and power throughout the Christian world.

As he describes the Netherlands, Paris, Oxford and Cambridge, northern Italy, Rome, and the cities of the Rhineland, especially Basel, common threads or themes begin to appear. One of these is a growing sense of nationalism as peoples in various regions began to identify with and express allegiance to what would become the modern nation states. In Erasmus's day, this trend manifested itself through the emergence of increasingly centralized forms of civil government controlled by a Christian prince or king. Paralleling and often interconnected with such principalities was the administrative structure of the Catholic Church, which often wielded significant political, economic, and cultural power. Erasmus personally benefited from such a system since it was the patronage of such prominent church officials as the bishop of Cambria that freed him from his clerical duties and allowed him to become the prince of the humanists.

Though nationalism was on the rise and with it the emergence of powerful rulers such as Henry VIII of England, the Roman Catholic Church remained, as it had been for centuries, the most powerful force in western Europe. Through the centuries the church had become an arrogant and corrupt institution, often denying its original purpose or mission. Erasmus was one of the first to articulate these faults, but hoped to reform the church by uniting reason and morality into a universal Christian humanism. As already noted, a reformation did begin during Erasmus's lifetime but it was led by the fervor, if not fanaticism, of Martin Luther and other nationalists.

Erasmus was a prolific scholar, achieving worldwide recognition for his translation into Latin of the New Testament. He is also well known for two Latin textbooks, the *Adagia* and the *Colloquies*. As part of his lifelong goal of spreading Christian humanism throughout the world, he wrote educational treatises for the Christian prince, the Christian soldier, and the Christian priest. In his belief that Christianity and humanism could and should be blended into a powerful synthesis, Erasmus took the lead in applying "the skills of the Humanist to the editing and translating of sacred literature."[4] The collected works of Erasmus, including his letters, comprise 16 volumes.

In keeping with our intent to highlight various perspectives of the ideally educated individual, selections chosen for this volume are an excerpt from *The Praise of Folly* and a letter from Erasmus to Ulrich von Hutten. Writing *Folly* in ten days in

1509, Erasmus apparently conceptualized this work while returning to England from a very successful visit with the humanists of northern Italy. In reflecting upon his vision of what the world should be and comparing that vision to the world as he had experienced it, Erasmus seemed almost compelled to destroy—we might say deconstruct—the many false idols inhabiting his world. Such an act of deconstruction was necessary before laying out his own ideas on what education and society could and should be. In *The Praise of Folly*, Erasmus uses satire to illustrate the depravity and pomposity of the grammarians, lawyers, logicians, sophists, scientists, and theologians of his day. With wit and humor, Erasmus warns his generation and ours not to take ourselves or our professions too seriously. In dramatizing the professional products of erudition, Erasmus demonstrates how easily education can degenerate into pedantry.

Almost ten years later, Erasmus provides us with a positive statement of his ideally educated individual. In describing his friend and fellow humanist to von Hutten, Erasmus praises Sir Thomas More. As Paul Nash explains, Erasmus's ideally educated individual is

> somewhat simple and even austere in his personal habits; he is always considerate, selfless, thoughtful, and generous. He does not slavishly conform to conventional thinking but is full of sound common sense. Humble and quite free from conceit, he lacks any assumption of superiority or aloofness. Sincere and genuine in religion, he is faithful without superstition, pious without pomposity.[5]

As Erasmus wrote this letter praising Thomas More, perhaps a thin smile crossed his lips as he grasped the similarity between the Latin *Encomium Moriae (The Praise of Folly)* and *Mori encomium* (the praise of More). Perhaps this little irony made western Europe's preference for the religious and nationalistic fervor of Martin Luther a little more palatable. Perhaps this little witticism helped to sustain his faith in Mori Encomium as the whole world, his and ours, marches in step with Encomium Moriae.

Notes

1. Cornelius Augustijn, *Erasmus: His Life, Works, and Influence* (Toronto: University of Toronto Press, 1991), p. 3.
2. Ibid., p. 147.
3. J. Bronowski and Bruce Mazlish, *The Western Intellectual Tradition: From Leonardo to Hegel* (New York: Harper & Row, 1962), p. 75.
4. Paul Nash, Andreas M. Kazamias, and Henry J. Perkinson, eds., *The Educated Man: Studies in the History of Educational Thought* (New York: John Wiley & Sons, 1967), p. 140.
5. Paul Nash, *Models of Man: Exploration in the Western Educational Tradition* (New York: John Wiley & Sons, 1968), p. 175.

From *The Praise of Folly* (1509)

But I should be most foolish myself and worthy of the manifold laughter of Democritus, if I should go on counting forms of folly and madness among the folk. Let me turn to those who maintain among mortals an appearance of wisdom and, as the saying is, seek for the golden bough. Among these the grammarians hold first place. Nothing could be more calamity-stricken, nothing more afflicted, than this generation of men, nothing so hated of God, if I were not at hand to mitigate the pains of their wretched profession by a certain sweet infusion of madness. For they are not only liable to the five curses which the Greek epigram calls attention to in Homer, but indeed to six hundred curses; as being hunger-starved and dirty in their schools—I said "their schools," but it were better said "their knowledge-factories" or "their mills"—or even "their shambles"—among herds of boys. There they grow old with their labors, they are deafened by the noise, they sicken by reason of the stench and nastiness. Yet thanks to me, they see themselves as first among men; so greatly do they please themselves when they terrify the timorous band by a menacing look and tone; when they beat the little wretches with ferules, rods, or straps; and when, imitating the ass in Aesop, they storm fiercely in all directions, as whim may dictate. And do you know, all the dirtiness seems sheer elegance, the stench is perfume of sweet marjoram, and the miserable servitude considered to be a kingdom, such a one that they would not trade their tyranny for the empire of Phalaris or Dionysius. . . .

Among men of learned professions, the lawyers may claim first place for themselves, nor is there any other class quite so self-satisfied; for while they industriously roll up the stone of Sisyphus by dint of weaving together six hundred laws in the same breath, no matter how little to the purpose, and by dint of piling glosses upon glosses and opinions upon opinions, they contrive to make their profession seem the most difficult of all. What is really tedious commends itself to them as brilliant. Let us put in with them the logicians and sophists, a breed of men more loquacious than the famed brass kettles at Dodona; any one of them can out-chat twenty picked women. They would be happier, however, if they were merely talkative, and not quarrelsome as well, to such a degree that they will stubbornly cut and thrust over a lock of goat's wool, quite losing track of the truth in question while they go on disputing. Their self-love makes them happy, and equipped with three syllogisms they will unhesitatingly dare to join battle upon any subject with any man. Mere frowardness brings them back unbeaten, though you match Stentor against them.

Near these march the scientists, reverenced for their beards and the fur on their gowns, who teach that they alone are wise while the rest of mortal men flit about as shadows. How pleasantly they dote, indeed, while they construct their numberless worlds, and measure the sun, moon, stars, and spheres as with thumb and line. They assign causes for lightning, winds, eclipses, and other inexplicable things, never hesitating a whit, as if they were privy to the secrets of

---

Erasmus, *The Praise of Folly,* translated by Hoyt Hopewell Hudson. Copyright © 1941 by PUP. Renewed 1969. Reprinted by permission of Princeton University Press.

nature, artificer of things, or as if they visited us fresh from the council of the gods. Yet all the while nature is laughing grandly at them and their conjectures. For to prove that they have good intelligence of nothing, this is a sufficient argument: they can never explain why they disagree with each other on every subject. Thus knowing nothing in general, they profess to know all things in particular; though they are ignorant even of themselves, and on occasion do not see the ditch or the stone lying across their path, because many of them are blear-eyed or absent-minded; yet they proclaim that they perceive ideas, universals, forms without matter, primary substances, quiddities, and ecceities— things so tenuous, I fear, that Lynceus himself could not see them. When they especially disdain the vulgar crowd is when they bring out their triangles, quadrangles, circles, and mathematical pictures of the sort, lay one upon the other, intertwine them into a maze, then deploy some letters as if in line of battle, and presently do it over in reverse order—and all to involve the uninitiated in darkness. Their fraternity does not lack those who predict future events by consulting the stars, and promise wonders even more magical; and these lucky scientists find people to believe them.

Perhaps it were better to pass over the theologians in silence, and not to move such a Lake Camarina, or to handle such an herb *Anagyris foetida*, as that marvelously supercilious and irascible race. For they may attack me with six hundred arguments, in squadrons, and drive me to make a recantation; which if I refuse, they will straightway proclaim me an heretic. By this thunderbolt they are wont to terrify any toward whom they are ill-disposed. No other people are so loth to acknowledge my favors to them; yet the divines are bound to me by no ordinary obligations. They are happy in their self-love, and as if they already inhabited the third heaven they look down from a height on all other mortal men as on creatures that crawl on the ground, and they come near to pitying them. They are protected by a wall of scholastic definitions, arguments, corollaries, implicit and explicit propositions; they have so many hideaways that they could not be caught even by the net of Vulcan; for they slip out on their distinctions, by which also they cut through all knots as easily as with a double-bitted axe from Tenedos; and they abound with newly-invented terms and prodigious vocables. Furthermore, they explain as pleases them the most arcane matters, such as by what method the world was founded and set in order, through what conduits original sin has been passed down along the generations, by what means, in what measure, and how long the perfect Christ was in the Virgin's womb, and how accidents subsist in the Eucharist without their subject. . . .

Coming nearest to these in felicity are the men who generally call themselves "the religious" and "monks"—utterly false names both, since most of them keep as far away as they can from religion and no people are more in evidence in every sort of place. But I do not see how anything could be more dismal than these monks if I did not succor them in many ways. For though people as a whole so detest this race of men that meeting one by accident is supposed to be bad luck, yet they flatter themselves to the queen's taste. For one thing, they reckon it the highest degree of piety to have no contact with literature, and hence they see to it that they do not know how to read. For another, when with asinine voices they bray out in church those psalms they have learned, by rote rather than by heart, they are convinced that they are anointing God's ears with the blandest of oil. Some of them make a good profit from their dirtiness and mendicancy, collecting their food from door to door with importunate bellowing; nay, there is not an inn, public conveyance, or ship where they do not intrude, to the great disadvantage of the other common beggars. Yet according to their account, by their very dirtiness, ignorance, want of manners, and insolence, these delightful fellows are representing to us the lives of the apostles.

Letter from Erasmus to Ulrich von Hutten (1516)

Most illustrious Hutten, your love, I had almost said your passion for the genius of Thomas More,—kindled as it is by his writings, which, as you truly say, are as learned and witty as anything can possibly be,—is I assure you, shared by many others; and moreover the feeling in this case is mutual; since More is so delighted with what you have written, that I am myself almost jealous of you. . . .

As to your asking me to paint you a full-length portrait of More, I only wish my power of satisfying your request were equal to your earnestness in pressing it. For to me too, it will be no unpleasant task to linger awhile in the contemplation of a friend who is the most delightful character in the world. But, in the first place, it is not given to every man to be aware of all More's accomplishments; and in the next place, I know not whether he will himself like to have his portrait painted by any artist that chooses to do so. For indeed I do not think it more easy to make a likeness of More than of Alexander the Great, or of Achilles; neither were those heroes more worthy of immortality. . . .

I have never seen any person less fastidious in his choice of food. As a young man, he was by preference a water-drinker, a practice he derived from his father. But, not to give annoyance to others, he used at table to conceal this habit from his guests by drinking, out of a pewter vessel, either small beer almost as weak as water, or plain water. As to wine, it being the custom, where he was, for the company to invite each other to drink in turn out of the same cup, he used sometimes to sip a little of it, to avoid appearing to shrink from it altogether, and to habituate himself to the common practice. . . .

He likes to be dressed simply, and does not wear silk, or purple, or gold chains, except when it is not allowable to dispense with them. He cares marvelously little for those formalities, which with ordinary people are the test of politeness; and as he does not exact these ceremonies from others, so he is not scrupulous in observing them himself, either on occasions of meeting or at entertainments, though he understands how to use them, if he thinks proper to

From Vol III *The Epistles of Erasmus*, translated by Francis Morgan Nichols, published in three volumes (1918) in New York in 1962 in London by Russell and Russell, Inc., pp. 387–392, 395, 397, 399.

do so; but he holds it to be effeminate and unworthy of a man to waste much of his time on such trifles. . . .

He seems to be born and made for friendship, of which he is the sincerest and most persistent devotee. Neither is he afraid of that multiplicity of friends, of which Hesiod disapproves. Accessible to every tender of intimacy, he is by no means fastidious in choosing his acquaintance, while he is most accommodating in keeping it on foot, and constant in retaining it. If he has fallen in with anyone whose faults he cannot cure, he finds some opportunity of parting with him, untying the knot of intimacy without tearing it; but when he has found any sincere friends, whose characters are suited to his own, he is so delighted with their society and conversation, that he seems to find in these the chief pleasure of life, having an absolute distaste for tennis and dice and cards, and the other games with which the mass of gentlemen beguile the tediousness of Time. It should be added that, while he is somewhat neglectful of his own interest, no one takes more pains in attending to the concerns of his friends. What more need I say? If anyone requires a perfect example of true friendship, it is in More that he will best find it. . . .

There is nothing that occurs in human life, from which he does not seek to extract some pleasure, although the matter may be serious in itself. If he has to do with the learned and intelligent, he is delighted with their cleverness, if with unlearned or stupid people, he finds amusement in their folly. He is not offended even by professed clowns, as he adapts himself with marvellous dexterity to the tastes of all; while with ladies generally, and even with his wife, his conversation is made up of humour and playfulness. You would say it was a second Democritus, or rather that Pythagorean philosopher, who strolls in leisurely mood through the market-place, contemplating the turmoil of those who buy and sell. There is no one less guided by the opinion of the multitude, but on the other hand no one sticks more closely to common sense. . . .

His character is entirely free from any touch of avarice. He has set aside out of his property what he thinks sufficient for his children, and spends the rest in a liberal fashion. When he was still dependent on his profession, he gave every client true and friendly counsel with an eye to their advantage rather than his own, generally advising them, that the cheapest thing they could do was to come to terms with their opponents. If he could not persuade them to do this, he pointed out how they might go to law at least expense; for there are some people whose character leads them to delight in litigation. . . .

Meanwhile there is no assumption of superiority. In the midst of so great a pressure of business he remembers his humble friends; and from time to time he returns to his beloved studies. Whatever authority he derives from his rank, and whatever influence he enjoys by the favour of a powerful sovereign, are employed in the service of the public, or in that of his friends. It has always been part of his character to be most obliging to every body, and marvelously ready with his sympathy; and this disposition is more conspicuous than ever, now that his power of doing good is greater. Some he relieves with money, some he protects by his authority, some he promotes by his recommendation, while those whom he cannot otherwise assist are benefited by his advice. No one is sent away in distress, and you might call him the general patron of all poor people. He counts it a great gain to himself, if he has relieved some oppressed person, made the path clear for one that was in difficulties, or brought back into favour one that was in disgrace. No man more readily confers a benefit, no man expects less in return. And successful as he is in so many ways,—while success is generally accompanied by self-conceit,—I have never seen any mortal being more free from this failing. . . .

However averse he may be from all superstition, he is a steady adherent of true piety; having regular hours for his prayers, which are not uttered by rote, but from the heart. He talks with his friends about a future life in such a way as to make you feel that he believes what he says, and does not speak without the best hope. Such is More, even at Court; and there are still people who think that Christians are only to be found in monasteries!

From "On the Right Method of Instruction" (1518)

1. Thought and Expression Form the Two-Fold Material of Instruction

All knowledge falls into one of two divisions: the knowledge of "truths" and the knowledge of "words": and if the former is first in importance the latter is acquired first in order of time. They are not to be commended who, in their anxiety to increase their store of truths, neglect the necessary art of expressing them. For ideas are only intelligible to us by means of the words which describe them; wherefore defective knowledge of language reacts upon our apprehension of the truths expressed. We often find that no one is so apt to lose himself in verbal arguments as the man who boasts that facts, not words, are the only things that interest him. This goes to prove that true education includes what is *best* in both kinds of knowledge, taught, I must add, under the *best* guidance. For, remembering how difficult it is to eradicate early impressions, we should aim from the first at learning what need never be unlearnt, and that only.

2. Expression Claims the First Place in Point of Time. Both the Greek and Latin Languages Needful to the Educated Man

Language thus claims the first place in the order of studies and from the outset should include both Greek and Latin. The argument for this is two-fold. First, that within these two literatures are contained all the knowledge which we recognise as of vital importance to mankind. Secondly, that the natural affinity of the two tongues renders it more profitable to study them side by side than

Reprinted by permission of the publisher from Woodward, W. H., *DESIDERIUS ERASMUS CONCERNING THE AIM AND METHOD OF EDUCATION* (New York: Teachers College Press, c.1964 by Teachers College, Columbia University. All rights reserved.), pp. 162–164.

apart. Latin particularly gains by this method. Quintilian advised that a beginning should be made with Greek before systematic work in Latin is taken in hand. Of course he regarded proficiency in both as essential. The elements, therefore, of Greek and Latin should be acquired early, and should a thoroughly skilled master not be available, then—but only then—let the learner fall back upon self-teaching by means of the study of classical masterpieces.

3. The Right Method of Acquiring Grammar Rests Upon Reading and Not Upon Definitions and Rules

. . . Whilst a knowledge of the rules of accidence and syntax is most necessary to every student, still they should be as few, as simple, and as carefully framed as possible. I have no patience with the stupidity of the average teacher of grammar who wastes precious years in hammering rules into children's heads. For it is not by learning rules that we acquire the power of speaking a language, but by daily intercourse with those accustomed to express themselves with exactness and refinement, and by the copious reading of the best authors. . . .

Some proficiency in expression being . . . attained the student devotes his attention to the *content* of the ancient literatures. It is true, of course, that in reading an author for purposes of vocabulary and style the student cannot fail to gather something besides. But I have in my mind much more than this when I speak of studying "contents." For I affirm that with slight qualification the whole of attainable knowledge lies enclosed within the literary monuments of ancient Greece. This great inheritance I will compare to a limpid spring of whose undefiled waters it behoves all who truly thirst to drink and be restored.

Questions

1. What is the humanist ideal of the educated person?
2. What does Erasmus mean by "sweet reason"?
3. What is or what should be the relationship between knowing and doing?
4. Why was Erasmus more at home in the company of the Italian humanists or with his English friends than in his native Rotterdam?
5. How would Erasmus distinguish between pedantry and education?
6. Describe in your own words Erasmus's vision of the ideally educated individual.
7. Using Erasmus's criticism of the grammarians, lawyers, scientists, theologians, and monks, distinguish between a genuinely wise individual and one who maintains only an appearance of wisdom.
8. In your own words, describe Thomas More, Erasmus's friend and the embodiment of his ideally educated human being.
9. How does Erasmus distinguish among wisdom, truths, and words?

10. Why does Erasmus consider knowledge of Greek and Latin more important than knowledge of content?
11. What do you think of his argument about Greek and Latin?
12. Do you think that Erasmus's ideal of an educated person is possible today? Why or why not?
13. Is it possible, in today's world, to reconcile reason and religion? Why or why not?

chapter 5

John Locke

TIME LINE FOR LOCKE

1632	Is born in Wrington, Somerset, England, to a Puritan home.
1646	Enters the Westminister School, where he studies the classics.
1652	Is elected to a studentship at Christ's Church, Oxford.
1656	Receives his bachelor's degree and continues in residence for the master's degree.
1661	Receives small inheritance from father's estate and decides to study medicine.
1664	Is appointed censor of moral philosophy.
1667	Is appointed personal physician to Lord Ashley, Earl of Shaftesbury, who is the leader of the parliamentary opposition to the Stuarts.
1674	Is awarded medical degree and is licensed to practice medicine.
1675	Travels to France.
1679	Returns to England.
1683	Is denounced as a traitor and flees England for Holland.
1683–1688	Is involved in activities to place William of Orange on the throne of England.
1689	Publishes *First Letter Concerning Toleration* and *Essay Concerning Human Understanding*.

1689	Returns to England escorting the princess of Orange, who later becomes Queen Mary.
1690	Publishes *Two Treatises of Government.*
1691	Accepts position as commissioner on the Board of Trade and Plantations.
1693	Publishes *Some Thoughts Concerning Education.*
1695	Publishes *Reasonableness of Christianity,* followed by a response to its critics, *Vindiction of Reasonableness of Christianity.*
1697	Publishes second *Vindiction of Reasonableness of Christianity.*
1704	Dies at the home of Sir Francis and Lady Masham (October 28).

Introduction

John Locke (1632–1704) is one of the most influential philosophers of the modern era. His empiricism, which included an attack on innate ideas—ideas, say, of truth, beauty, and goodness—which were thought of as part of one's birthright as a human being, and his subsequent claim that all knowledge comes through the senses, set the stage not only for Anglo-American philosophy for the next two or three hundred years, but also for the flowering of the scientific method throughout the world.

His political writing, as presented in *Two Treatises of Government,* reads in many ways as a precursor of the revolutionary events in America during the eighteenth century. Locke was concerned with uncovering the sources and limits of political rights and responsibilities. To do this, he assumed a fictional place called a "state of nature," a place where the philosopher could imagine people in their natural condition and from that generate a theory of political rights and responsibilities

In that "state," natural laws governed people's behavior and reasonable people would follow those laws. Unfortunately, not all people were reasonable. And, in this fictional state, there was no power of enforcement. To deal with these problems, people banded together and created civil society. They *contracted,* each with everyone, to create a sovereign power who would be in charge of protecting their rights (rights which were given by the natural law).

> Locke explicitly recognized, as the events during his lifetime had shown, that men may become tyrants to those whom they were bound to serve. It may be a king, an assembly, or a usurper that claims absolute power. In such cases the people have a right to rebellion if no other redress is possible. Locke was not unmindful of the fact that the executive needs latitude and prerogatives so that he may govern, and that the legislative body must be in the public good. The right to rebellion is warranted only in the most extreme conditions, where all other means fail. Locke did not believe that

men would lightly avail themselves of this power, for men will suffer and endure much before they resort to rebellion.[1]

It is not hard to see why Locke would be so influential, why he would strike such a chord with colonists such as Thomas Jefferson and Alexander Hamilton. Locke was not a wide-eyed radical advocating revolution. There is something very bourgeois, very middle class, at the core of his thought. His argument goes something like: We have created a sovereign to protect our rights. That sovereign must have the latitude to do what she or he thinks best. It is unreasonable to expect the sovereign to report to citizens in all matters. Still if, over an extended period of time, the sovereign does not live up to the demands of the contract, if, over an extended period of time, the sovereign does not protect our rights, then we, the citizens, have the right to rebel. We have the right to dump the tea in Boston Harbor.

Given the fact that Locke does strike such a resonant chord in the American political psyche, and given the fact that many of Locke's educational claims and arguments, as found in *Some Thoughts Concerning Education,* are now accepted as near commonplaces of contemporary educative thought, it is at least curious that Locke's understanding of the educated person should receive such little attention.

Consider, first, some of the "commonplaces":

1. Education is something that adults do to children. As such, the educative process is, at heart, hierarchical, with authority residing in the hands of the adult.
2. Education is dependent on the securing of right habits of thought and action. Children, especially young children, have not developed enough, intellectually and morally, to understand why they must perform certain activities. Indeed, the habitual performing of those is a necessary condition for children's, one day, understanding.
3. Children learn more by example than by mere telling. Thus, it is crucial to create an environment in which children can learn from the example of their elders. In effect, the teacher models correct behavior for her or his students.
4. Cognitive development in children tends to proceed from part to whole and from the concrete to the abstract. The curriculum, in turn, should mirror this developmental sequence, moving from part to whole, from the concrete to the abstract.

These commonplaces, of course, come under occasional review by critics, who have pointed out, for example, that children's most efficient learning seems to occur in the earliest years of their lives, and it is not at all clear that learning always proceeds from the concrete to the abstract. For example, children typically master a highly complex concept like "Mommy" or "Daddy" well before, say, they memorize the alphabet. Still, the commonplaces have a staying power, which makes all the more curious the fact that Locke's understanding of the educated person is largely ignored when it comes to the contemporary debate regarding education in the United States.

Locke was quite explicit regarding the nature of education. The first part of education Locke called "virtue." It was concerned, for the most part, with a twofold relationship, namely, a relationship with God and a relationship with other people. A virtuous person was one who believed in and worshiped God and who treated other people with respect, dignity, care, and so on. For Locke, this was the most important part of education.

The second most important part of education Locke called "wisdom." Here, it is helpful to recall Locke's affinity with the middle class. A wise person was one who could manage her or his affairs, primarily business affairs, in a fair and prudent manner. The wise person is that individual who can manage affairs in such a way that both family and community will prosper.

The third part of education Locke claimed for breeding, the ability to handle oneself in social situations. The well-bred person is the person who behaves fairly and without condescension to "inferiors" and honestly and without obsequiousness toward "superiors."

Finally, and Locke is explicit about this, is what is called "learning."

> You will wonder, perhaps, that I put learning last, especially if I tell you I think it the least part. This may seem strange in the mouth of a bookish man, and this making usually the chief, if not only, bustle and stir about children, this being almost that alone which is thought on when people talk of education, makes it the greater paradox. When I consider what ado is made about a little Latin and Greek, how many years are spent on it and what a noise and business it makes to no purpose, I can hardly forbear thinking that the parents of children still live in fear of the schoolmaster's rod, which they look on as the only instrument of education, as a language or two to be its whole business. How else is it possible that a child should be chained to the oar seven, eight or ten of the best years of his life to get a language or two which, I think, might be had at a great deal cheaper rate of pains and time, and be learned almost in playing.[2]

Again, it is very curious that the philosopher who, in many ways, sets the contemporary educational agenda is ignored at precisely the moment he speaks about the characteristics of the educated person. Focus on the ethical and aesthetic qualities, try to create a person of decency, resourcefulness, and style, and the cognitive qualities can be developed "almost in playing." In an era dominated by the contemporary equivalent of the schoolmaster's rod—standardized tests—it may be the appropriate time to return to John Locke.

Notes

1. James Gordon Clapp, "John Locke" in *Encyclopedia of Philosophy*, vol. 4., ed. Paul Edwards (New York: Macmillan Publishing, 1967), p. 500.
2. John Locke, *Some Thoughts Concerning Education*, ed. F. W. Garforth (London: Heinemann, 1925), pp. 129-130.

From *Some Thoughts Concerning Education* (1693)

The well educating of their children is so much the duty and concern of parents, and the welfare and prosperity of the nation so much depends on it, that I would have everyone lay it seriously to heart; and after having well examined and distinguished what fancy, custom or reason advises in the case, set his helping hand to promote everywhere that way of training up youth, with regard to their several conditions, which is the easiest, shortest and likeliest to produce virtuous, useful and able men in their distinct callings; though that most to be taken care of is the gentleman's calling. For if those of that rank are by their education once set right, they will quickly bring all the rest into order.

A sound mind in a sound body is a short but full description of a happy state in this world. He that has these two has little more to wish for; and he that wants either of them will be but little the better for anything else. Men's happiness or misery is most part of their own making. He whose mind directs not wisely will never take the right way; and he whose body is crazy and feeble will never be able to advance in it. I confess there are some men's constitutions of body and mind so vigorous and well framed by nature that they need not much assistance from others; but by the strength of their natural genius they are from their cradles carried towards what is excellent, and by the privilege of their happy constitutions are able to do wonders. But examples of this kind are but few; and I think I may say that of all the men we meet with nine part of ten are what they are, good or evil, useful or not, by their education. 'Tis that which makes the great difference in mankind. The little or almost insensible impressions on our tender infancies have very important and lasting consequences; and there 'tis, as in the fountains of some rivers, where a gentle application of the hand turns the flexible waters in channels that make them take quite contrary courses; and by this direction given them at first in the source they receive different tendencies and arrive at last at very remote and distant places. . . .

That which every gentleman (that takes any care of his education) desires for his son, besides the estate he leaves him, is contained, I suppose, in these four things, virtue, wisdom, breeding and learning. I will not trouble myself whether these names do not some of them sometimes stand for the same thing, or really include one another. It serves my turn here to follow the popular use of these words, which, I presume, is clear enough to make me be understood, and I hope there will be no difficulty to comprehend my meaning.

I place virtue as the first and most necessary of those endowments that belong to a man or a gentleman, as absolutely requisite to make him valued and beloved by others, acceptable or tolerable to himself. Without that, I think, he will be happy neither in this nor the other world.

As the foundation of this there ought very early to be imprinted on his mind a true notion of God, as of the independent Supreme Being, Author and

From *Some Thoughts Concerning Education*, John Locke, edited by F. W. Garforth © 1925 by Heinemann Educational Books Ltd., Oxford, England, pp. 25–26, 122–127, 129–130.

Maker of all things, from whom we receive all our good, who loves us and gives us all things. And consequent to this, instil into him a love and reverence of this Supreme Being. This is enough to begin with, without going to explain this matter any farther, for fear lest, by talking too early to him of spirits and being unseasonably forward to make him understand the incomprehensible nature of that Infinite Being, his head be either filled with false or perplexed with unintelligible notions of him. Let him only be told upon occasion that God made and governs all things, hears and sees everything, and does all manner of good to those that love and obey him; you will find that, being told of such a God, other thoughts will be apt to rise up fast enough in his mind about him, which, as you observe them to have any mistakes, you must set right. And I think it would be better if men generally rested in such an idea of God, without being too curious in their notions about a Being which all must acknowledge incomprehensible; whereby many, who have not strength and clearness of thought to distinguish between what they can and what they cannot know, run themselves in superstition or atheism, making God like themselves or, because they cannot comprehend anything else, none at all. And I am apt to think the keeping children constantly morning and evening to acts of devotion to God, as to their Maker, Preserver and Benefactor, in some plain and short form of prayer suitable to their age and capacity will be of much more use to them in religion, knowledge and virtue than to distract their thoughts with curious enquiries into his inscrutable essence and being.

Having laid the foundations of virtue in a true notion of God, such as the creed wisely teaches, as far as his age is capable, and by accustoming him to pray to him, the next thing to be taken care of is to keep him exactly to speaking of truth and by all the ways imaginable inclining him to be good-natured. Let him know that twenty faults are sooner to be forgiven than the straining of truth to cover anyone by an excuse. And to teach him betimes to love and be good-natured to others is to lay early the true foundation of an honest man; all injustice generally springing from too great love of ourselves and too little of others.

Wisdom I take in the popular acceptation for a man's managing his business ably and with foresight in this world. This is the product of a good natural temper, application of mind and experience together, and so above the reach of children. The greatest thing that in them can be done towards it is to hinder them as much as may be from cunning, which, being the ape of wisdom, is the most distant from it that can be. . . . Cunning is only the want of understanding, which, because it cannot compass its ends by direct ways, would do it by a trick and circumvention; and the mischief of it is, a cunning trick helps but once, but hinders ever after. No cover was ever made so big or so fine as to hide itself; nobody was ever so cunning as to conceal their being so; and when they are once discovered, everybody is shy, everybody distrustful of crafty men; and all the world forwardly join to oppose and defeat them, whilst the open, fair, wise man has everybody to make way for him and goes directly to his business. To accustom a child to have true notions of things and not to be satisfied till he has them, to raise his mind to great and worthy thoughts and to keep him at a distance from falsehood and cunning, which has always a broad mixture of falsehood in it, is the fittest preparation of a child for wisdom. The rest, which is to be learned from time, experience and observation and an acquaintance with men, their tempers and designs, is not to be expected in the ignorance and inadvertency of childhood or the inconsiderate heat and unwariness of youth. All that can be done towards it during this unripe age is, as I have said, to accustom them to truth and sincerity, to a submission to reason and, as much as may be, to reflection on their own actions.

The next good quality belonging to a gentleman is good breeding. There are two sorts of ill breeding, the one a sheepish bashfulness, and the other a misbecoming negligence and disrespect in our carriage; both which are avoided by duly observing this one rule, not to think meanly of ourselves and not to think meanly of others.

The first part of this rule must not be understood in opposition to humility but to assurance. We ought not to think so well of ourselves as to stand upon our own value and assume to ourselves a preference before others because of any advantage we may imagine we have over them, but modestly to take what is offered when it is our due. But yet we ought to think so well of ourselves as to perform those actions which are incumbent on and expected of us without discomposure or disorder in whose presence soever we are, keeping that respect and distance which is due to everyone's rank and quality. There is often in people, especially children, a clownish shamefacedness before strangers or those above them; they are confounded in their thoughts, words and looks, and so lose themselves in that confusion as not to be able to do anything, or at least not to do it with that freedom and gracefulness which pleases and makes them acceptable. The only cure for this, as for any other miscarriage, is by use to introduce the contrary habit. But since we cannot accustom ourselves to converse with strangers and persons of quality without being in their company, nothing can cure this part of ill breeding but change and variety of company and that of persons above us.

As the before-mentioned consists in too great a concern how to behave ourselves towards others, so the other part of ill breeding lies in the appearance of too little care of pleasing or showing respect to those we have to do with. To avoid this, these two things are requisite: first, a disposition of the mind not to offend others; and secondly, the most acceptable and agreeable way of expressing that disposition. From the one men are called civil; from the other well-fashioned. The latter of these is that decency and gracefulness of looks, voice, words, motions, gestures and of all the whole outward demeanor, which takes in company and makes those with whom we may converse easy and well pleased. This is, as it were, the language whereby that internal civility of the mind is expressed; which, as other languages are, being very much governed by the fashion and custom of every country, must, in the rules and practice of it, be learned chiefly from observation and the carriage of those who are allowed to be exactly well-bred. The other part, which lies deeper than the outside, is that general good will and regard for all people, which makes anyone have a care not to show in his carriage any contempt, disrespect or neglect of them, but to express, according to the fashion and way of that country, a respect and value for them according to their rank and condition. It is a disposition of mind that shows itself in the carriage, whereby a man avoids making anyone uneasy in conversation. . . .

You will wonder, perhaps, that I put learning last, especially if I tell you I think it the least part. This may seem strange in the mouth of a bookish man; and this making usually the chief, if not only, bustle and stir about children, this being almost that alone which is thought on when people talk of education, makes it the greater paradox. When I consider what ado is made about a little Latin and Greek, how many years are spent in it and what a noise and business it makes to no purpose, I can hardly forbear thinking that the parents of children still live in fear of the schoolmaster's rod, which they look on as the only instrument of education, as a language or two to be its whole business. How else is it possible that a child should be chained to the oar seven, eight or ten of the best years of his life to get a language or two which, I think, might be had at a great deal cheaper rate of pains and time, and be learned almost in playing?

Forgive me, therefore, if I say I cannot with patience think that a young gentleman should be put into the herd and be driven with a whip and scourge, as if he were to run the gauntlet through the several classes *ad capiendum ingenti cultum*. What then, say you, would you not have him write and read? . . . Not so, not so fast, I beseech you. Reading and writing and learning I allow to be necessary, but yet not the chief business. I imagine you would think him a very foolish fellow that shall not value a virtuous or a wise man infinitely before a great scholar. Not but that I think learning a great help to both in well-disposed minds; but yet it must be confessed also that in others not so disposed it helps them only to be the more foolish or worse men. I say this that when you consider the breeding of your son and are looking out for a schoolmaster or a tutor, you would not have (as is usual) Latin and logic only in your thoughts. Learning must be had, but in the second place, as subservient only to greater qualities. Seek out somebody that may know how discreetly to frame his manners; place him in hands where you may, as much as possible, secure his innocence, cherish and nurse up the good, and gently correct and weed out any bad inclinations and settle in him good habits. This is the main point, and this being provided for, learning may be had into the bargain, and that, as I think, at a very easy rate by methods that may be thought on.

Questions

1. Why, for Locke, should "errors in education be less indulged in than any"?
2. For Locke, how important is education?
3. Locke is concerned with the education of gentlemen. Do you think that what he says is applicable to the education of gentlewomen?
4. Why do you think Locke focuses on the education of one part of the population?
5. What are the four parts of education?
6. Why is learning the least important part of education for Locke?
7. Do you think Locke's criticisms are applicable to contemporary American educational practices?

8. Describe a Lockean classroom.

9. Respond to the teacher who says she or he has neither the time nor the right to do all of the things Locke recommends.

10. Locke uses the metaphor of the child being "chained to the oar." Do you think that is an appropriate metaphor for describing schooling? Can you think of others?

11. Do you think that a person can be learned but not educated? Do you think that a person can be educated but not learned?

chapter **6**

Jean-Jacques Rousseau

TIME LINE FOR ROUSSEAU

1712	Is born in Geneva. His mother dies following his birth and he is brought up by his father and an aunt.
1712–1728	Receives little formal education.
	Lives two years with a country minister at Bossey.
	Returns to Geneva and lives with an uncle.
	Is apprenticed to a notary and then to an engraver who treats him badly.
1728	Leaves Geneva.
	Befriended by Mme. de Warens.
	Serves as a lackey.
	Converts to Catholicism.
1729	Returns to Mme. de Warens.
1730–1742	Travels widely.
1742	Arrives in Paris to introduce a new system of musical notation.
1743	Is appointed secretary to French ambassador at Venice.
1750	Publishes *Discours sur les sciences et les arts (Discourse on the Sciences and the Arts)*.
1754	Travels to Geneva and is reconciled with the republic and returns to Protestantism.
1755	Publishes *Discours sur l'origine de l'inégalité (Discourse on the Origin of Inequality)*.

1762	Publishes *Emile* and *Contrat social (The Social Contract)*.
1766	Arrives in England at the invitation of the philosopher David Hume.
1767	Leaves England following an argument with Hume.
1767–1770	Travels widely, spurred by the assumption that he is universally persecuted.
1770	Settles in Paris.
1770–1778	Writes a series of personal works: *Confessions, Rousseau juge de Jean-Jacques (Confessions: Rousseau Judges Himself)* and *Reveries do promeneur solitaire* (unfinished) *(Reveries of a Solitary Walker)*.
1778	Dies suddenly on July 2 at the estate of the marquis de Girardin at Ermenonville.

Introduction

Jean-Jacques Rousseau remains, on the surface at least, an enigmatic figure in the history of modern thought. In spite of or perhaps because of his enigmatic nature, Rousseau's ideas are as relevant today as they ever were. In challenging the *philosophes* and other Enlightenment thinkers' faith in progress through reason, Rousseau anticipated much of the contemporary postmodernists' critique. At times Rousseau presents himself as the unabashed champion of the individual in the inevitable clash with more powerful societal forces. At other times, he seems to favor a dominating if not totalitarian societal structure that all but eclipses individual freedom. In reality, what Rousseau has done is to attack the individual-collectivity problem head on. With such statements as "Man is born free; and everywhere he is in chains" and "Everything is good as it comes from the hands of the Maker of the World but degenerates once it gets into the hands of man," he seems to be calling for a return to a primitive life. A more careful reading suggests Rousseau believed that, by properly educating future generations, a society could be created that resolved the conflict between individual needs and societal demands. Recognizing that in the corrupt society of his time it was impossible to transform the boy into both a man and a citizen, Rousseau, when faced with the opportunity of reforming a society, did not hesitate in proposing an educational system aimed at making a good citizen.

To assist the reader to better understand this enigmatic figure and his contributions to contemporary educational philosophy, his life and thought are discussed briefly below. Following this discussion is a selection from Rousseau's *Emile*, a work characterized by Allan Bloom as "a truly great book," for it describes the education of democratic man.

Born in 1712 to a watchmaker in Geneva, Switzerland, Jean-Jacques Rousseau was not blessed with a stable childhood. When his mother died shortly after

Rousseau was born, his father, with the aid of an incompetent aunt, assumed responsibility for raising him. He learned to read on his father's knee, but neither his father nor his aunt provided much discipline for the young child. While still an adolescent, Rousseau's father abandoned him: Finding himself in trouble with a local patrician, the elder Rousseau left town never to return.

Rousseau was left with one of his uncles and over the next few years was apprenticed to a town clerk, to an engraver, and to a religious cleric. After failing miserably in each of these endeavors, Rousseau fled Geneva some three years later. For the next 20 years, Rousseau pursued many vocations, but achieved little success in any of them. He converted to Catholicism—only to renounce it later in life—even studying for the priesthood, practiced music, worked as a secretary, and on occasion found work as a tutor.

There was little if any hint of genius until, at the age of 37, Rousseau entered and won an essay contest on the topic "Has the Progress of the Arts and Sciences Contributed More to the Corruption or Purification of Morals?" Emotionally unstable, often violating his own sense of duty and right, winning the prize for the best essay in this contest sponsored by the Academy of Dijon catapulted Rousseau into intellectual stardom. Though suffering from inadequacies in logic and historical accuracy, Rousseau's wild, impassioned rhetoric won the day. With the victory came entry into the intellectual salons of the time, and recognition, if not acceptance, by the *philosophes*. Following this initial success came the more significant and better known *Discourse on the Origin of Inequality, The Social Contract*, and *Emile*. Rousseau completed what is arguably his most famous work, his autobiographical *Confessions*, just before his death in 1778.

In studying the ideas of Jean-Jacques Rousseau, one encounters what appear to be many contradictions or inconsistencies in his thought. Rousseau denies this, arguing in his *Confessions* that his writings taken as a whole reveal a "consistent and coherent philosophy." As noted earlier and as we shall see in the brief discussion of his works that follows, the theme that binds all the many apparent discrepancies together is Rousseau's attempt to account for and resolve the conflict between the individual and the collectivity.

In the summer of 1749, while walking from Paris to Vincennes, Rousseau learned of the essay contest sponsored by the Academy of Dijon. Experiencing a vision in response to the question concerning the efficacy of the arts and sciences in promoting humankind's moral development, Rousseau responded in the negative, denying that progress in the arts and sciences translates into moral progress. His basic theme is perhaps best captured by a hypothetical prayer for the future of humankind:

> Almighty God! thou holdest in Thy hand the minds of men, deliver us from the fatal arts and sciences of our forefathers; give us back ignorance, innocence, and poverty, which alone can make us happy and precious in thy sight.

In short, Rousseau argued that human civilization, that is, the product of progress in the arts and sciences, had done little to advance the happiness of humankind. As such, he was attacking one of the basic tenets or faiths of the *philosophes* in particular and of the Enlightenment in general, that is, the equating of knowledge with goodness. In this sense, Rousseau was one of the first postmodernists. Rousseau argued that increased knowledge in the arts and sciences, rather than contributing to the moral improvement of humankind, tended to corrupt humankind by taking away their natural innocence. In juxtaposing natural or primitive human beings with civilized or learned ones, Rousseau suggested that the primitive or natural human being is free and happy, not due to the absence of boundaries or constraints, but because primitive or natural human beings have learned to live in accordance with the limitations or constraints found in nature. For Rousseau, progress in the arts and sciences meant the creation of unnatural and evil boundaries and restraints on human freedom.

Herein lies the crucial point, or what Rousseau would subsequently identify as "the origin of inequality." Simply put, Rousseau believed that natural or primitive humankind has, through the impulses and instincts of nature, the ability to learn about and live within the world they inhabit. Rather than enhance or support this natural ability, advancements in the arts and sciences have tended to deny and thus alienate modern beings from this natural capacity.

Rousseau offers us more than just a lament over the lost innocence of the natural or primitive human beings. Realizing that we cannot "return again to the forests to live among bears," that we "can no longer subsist on plants or acorns," that we "must remain in society and respect the sacred bonds of the community, loving [our] fellow-citizens, obeying the laws, honoring the wise and good princes," the task becomes one of creating a human society that emulates the natural restraints primitive human beings once encountered. At the very least such a society must be grounded in what Rousseau identified as the general will, which the members of the society knowingly defer to and accept.

It is at this point that Rousseau's *Social Contract* and *Emile* come into play. Rousseau introduces *The Social Contract* with the assertion that "Man is born free and everywhere he is in chains." Every and any society has chains for they are the necessary restraints or coercions that hold the separate parts together. As stated earlier, the problem becomes one of finding or creating some form of society so consistent with humankind's natural capacities that all will willingly accept its laws and restrictions. Establishing such a society requires negotiating a "social contract" in which the individual freely gives up natural freedom, but gains civil freedom in return. This means sublimating one's individual will to the will of the group or *general will*.

Rousseau's concept of the general will is different from and superior to the will of all in that it concerns common, as opposed to individual, interests. Rousseau's notion of the general will is elusive and apparently understandable only by those properly educated. Our only hope of developing individuals capable of sublimating their own private wills to the common or general will is to educate future generations in accordance with the laws or restraints of nature. To explain how this could and should be done, Rousseau wrote *Emile* and *The Social Contract* concurrently publishing *Emile* six months after publishing *The Social Contract*.

Reminiscent of *The Social Contract, Emile* begins by suggesting that "God makes all things good; man meddles with them and they become evil." Remember, from Rousseau's perspective, since his society—the one corrupted by the arts and sciences—is evil, for Emile to be properly educated he must be isolated from such a corrupt society. Such isolation is necessary if Emile is to recapture his natural state. Recapturing this natural state is necessary if Emile is to "see with his own eyes and feel with his own heart." Once this natural state has been recaptured and properly nurtured, Emile will, or so Rousseau suggests, make the right moral decision. Emile will knowingly and willingly subjugate himself to the general will and seek the common good.

Nature is the key to Rousseau's educational process. According to Rousseau, a young child is apolitical, asocial, and amoral. Initially the child knows only that she or he inhabits a physical world and quickly learns to abide by the law of necessity. Rousseau suggests the young child should never act from obedience but only from necessity. In the early stages of her or his development, the child should be dependent only on things. As Emile develops under the skillful manipulation of his tutor (Rousseau himself), he internalizes the notion that restraints are natural and inevitable. Once this lesson is learned, and as Emile develops an appreciation for the moral, political, and social worlds he inhabits and the laws that govern these worlds, this properly educated individual comes to understand and appreciate the general will or common good. In short, what Rousseau offers us in *Emile* is the prototype of what human beings could and should be. Through an educational process that follows nature, Rousseau creates for us an exemplar, that is, a just human being in an unjust world. By emulating nature in the education of our children and youth, Rousseau is suggesting that it is possible to develop a society of Emiles who willingly sublimate their own desires to those of the common or general will. It is these individuals who will establish the just or good society by creating the social contract, in the process resolving once and for all the conflict between individual needs and societal demands.

From *Emile* (1762)

Consistency is plainly impossible when we seek to educate a man for others, instead of for himself. If we have to combat either nature or society, we must choose between making a man or making a citizen. We cannot make both. There is an inevitable conflict of aims, from which come two opposing forms of education: the one communal and public, the other individual and domestic.

To get a good idea of communal education, read Plato's *Republic*. It is not a political treatise, as those who merely judge books by their titles think. It is the

Reprinted by permission of the publisher from Boyd, W. E. (ed. & trans.), *THE EMILE OF JEAN JACQUES ROUSSEAU: SELECTIONS* (New York: Teachers College Press, c 1962 by Teachers College, Columbia University. All rights reserved.)

finest treatise on education ever written. Communal education in this sense, however, does not and can not now exist. There are no longer any real father-lands and therefore no real citizens. The words "fatherland" and "citizen" should be expunged from modern languages. . . .

There remains then domestic education, the education of nature. But how will a man who has been educated entirely for himself get on with other people? If there were any way of combining in a single person the twofold aim, and removing the contradictions of life, a great obstacle to happiness would be removed. But before passing judgment on this kind of man it would be neces-sary to follow his development and see him fully formed. It would be necessary, in a word, to make the acquaintance of the natural man. This is the subject of our quest in this book. . . .

In the natural order where all men are equal, manhood is the common voca-tion. One who is well educated for that will not do badly in the duties that per-tain to it. The fact that my pupil is intended for the army, the church or the bar does not greatly concern me. Before the vocation determined by his parents comes the call of nature to the life of human kind. Life is the business I would have him learn. When he leaves my hands, I admit he will not be a magistrate, or a soldier, or a priest. First and foremost, he will be a man. All that a man must be he will be when the need arises, as well as anyone else. Whatever the changes of fortune he will always be able to find a place for himself. . . .

Instead of the difficult task of educating a child, I now undertake the easier task of writing about it. To provide details and examples in illustration of my views and to avoid wandering off into airy speculations, I propose to set forth the education of Emile, an imaginary pupil, from birth to manhood. I take for granted that I am the right man for the duties in respect of age, health, knowl-edge and talents.

A tutor is not bound to his charge by the ties of nature as the father is, and so is entitled to choose his pupil, especially when as in this case he is providing a model for the education of other children. I assume that Emile is no genius, but a boy of ordinary ability; that he is the inhabitant of some temperate climate, since it is only in temperate climates that human beings develop completely; that he is rich, since it is only the rich who have need of the natural education that would fit them to live under all conditions; that he is to all intents and purposes an orphan, whose tutor having undertaken the parents' duties will also have their right to control all the circumstances of his upbringing; and, finally, that he is a vigorous, healthy, well-built child. . . .

True happiness comes with equality of power and will. The only man who gets his own way is the one who does not need another's help to get it: from which it follows that the supreme good is not authority, but freedom. The true free-man wants only what he can get, and does only what pleases him. This is my fundamental maxim. Apply it to childhood and all the rules of education follow.

There are two kinds of dependence: dependence on things, which is natural, and dependence on men, which is social. Dependence on things being non-moral is not prejudicial to freedom and engenders no vices: dependence on men being capricious engenders them all. The only cure for this evil in society would be to put the law in place of the individual, and to arm the general will with a real power that made it superior to every individual will.

Keep the child in sole dependence on things and you will follow the natural order in the course of his education. Put only physical obstacles in the way of indiscreet wishes and let his punishments spring from his own actions. Without forbidding wrong-doing, be content to prevent it. Experience or impotence apart from anything else should take the place of law for him. Satisfy his desires, not because of his demands but because of his needs. He should have no consciousness of obedience when he acts, nor of mastery when someone acts for him. Let him experience liberty equally in his actions and in yours. . . .

Let us lay it down as an incontestable principle that the first impulses of nature are always right. There is no original perversity in the human heart. Of every vice we can say how it entered and whence it came. The only passion natural to man is self-love, or self-esteem in a broad sense. This self-esteem has no necessary reference to other people. In so far as it relates to ourselves it is good and useful. It only becomes good or bad in the social application we make of it. Until reason, which is the guide of self-esteem, makes its appearance, the child should not do anything because he is seen or heard by other people, but only do what nature demands of him. Then he will do nothing but what is right. . . .

May I set forth at this point the most important and the most useful rule in all education? It is not to save time but to waste it. The most dangerous period in human life is that between birth and the age of twelve. This is the age when errors and vices sprout, before there is any instrument for their destruction. When the instrument is available the roots have gone too deep to be extracted. The mind should remain inactive till it has all its faculties.

It follows from this that the first education should be purely negative. It consists not in teaching virtue and truth, but in preserving the heart from vice and the mind from error. If you could do nothing and let nothing be done, so that your pupil came to the age of twelve strong and healthy but unable to distinguish his right hand from his left, the eyes of this understanding would be open to reason from your very first lessons. In the absence of both prejudices and habits there would be nothing in him to oppose the effects of your teaching and care. . . .

Assuming that my method is that of nature and that I have not made any mistakes in putting it into practice, I have now brought my pupil through the land of the sensations right up to the bounds of childish reason. The first step beyond this should take him towards manhood. But before entering on this new stage let us cast our eyes backward for a moment on the one we have traversed. Each age and state of life has its own proper perfection, its own distinctive maturity. People sometimes speak about a complete man. Let us think rather of a complete child. This vision will be new for us and perhaps not less agreeable.

When I picture to myself a boy of ten or twelve, healthy, strong and well built for his age, only pleasant thoughts arise in me, whether for his present or for his future. I see him bright, eager, vigorous, carefree, completely absorbed in the present, rejoicing in abounding vitality. I see him in the years ahead using senses, mind and power as they develop from day to day. I view him as a child and he pleases me. I think of him as a man and he pleases me still more. His warm blood seems to heat my own. I feel as if I were living in his life and am rejuvenated by his vivacity.

The clock strikes and all is changed. In an instant his eye grows dull and his merriment disappears. No more mirth, no more games! A severe, hard-faced man takes him by the hand, says gravely, "Come away, sir," and leads him off. In the room they enter I get a glimpse of books. Books! What a cheerless equipment for his age. As he is dragged away in silence, he casts a regretful look around him. His eyes are swollen with tears he dare not shed, his heart heavy with sighs he dare not utter.

Come, my happy pupil, and console us for the departure of the wretched boy. Here comes Emile, and at his approach I have a thrill of joy in which I see he shares. It is his friend and comrade, the companion of his games to whom he comes. His person, his bearing, his countenance reveal assurance and contentment. Health glows in his face. His firm step gives him an air of vigour. His complexion is refined without being effeminate; sun and wind have put on it the honourable imprint of his sex. His eyes are still unlighted by the fires of sentiment and have all their native serenity. His manner is open and free without the least insolence or vanity.

His ideas are limited but precise. If he knows nothing by heart, he knows a great deal by experience. If he is not as good a reader in books as other children, he reads better in the book of nature. His mind is not in his tongue but in his head. He has less memory but more judgment. He only knows one language, but he understands what he says and if he does not talk as well as other children he can do things better than they can.

Habit, routine and custom mean nothing to him. What he did yesterday has no effect on what he does today. He never follows a fixed rule and never accepts authority or example. He only does or says what seems good to himself. For this reason you must not expect stock speeches or studied manners from him but just the faithful expression of his ideas and the conduct that comes from his inclinations.

You will find in him a few moral notions relating to his own situation, but not being an active member of society he has none relating to manhood. Talk to him about liberty, property and even convention, and he may understand you thus far. But speak to him about duty and obedience, and he will not know what you mean. Command him to do something, and he will pay no heed. But say to him: "If you will do me this favour, I will do the same for you another time," and immediately he will hasten to oblige. For his part, if he needs any help he will ask the first person he meets as a matter of course. If you grant his request he will not thank you, but will feel that he has contracted a debt. If you refuse, he will neither complain nor insist. He will only say: "It could not be done." He does not rebel against necessity once he recognizes it.

Work and play are all the same to him. His games are his occupations: he is not aware of any difference. He goes into everything he does with a pleasing interest and freedom. It is indeed a charming spectacle to see a nice boy of this age with open smiling countenance, doing the most serious things in his play or profoundly occupied with the most frivolous amusements.

Emile has lived a child's life and has arrived at the maturity of childhood, without any sacrifice of happiness in the achievement of his own perfection. He has acquired all the reason possible for his age, and in doing so has been as free and as happy as his nature allowed him to be. If by chance the fatal scythe were to cut down the flower of our hopes we would not have to bewail at the same time his life and his death, nor add to our griefs the memory of those we caused him. We would say that at any rate he had enjoyed his childhood and that nothing we had done had deprived him of what nature gave. . . .

The passions are the chief instruments for our preservation. The child's first sentiment is self-love, the only passion that is born with man. The second, which is derived from it, is the love he has for the people he sees ready to help him, and from this develops a kindly feeling for mankind. But with fresh needs and grow-ing dependence on others comes the consciousness of social relations and with it the sense of duties and preference. It is at this point that the child may become domineering, jealous, deceitful, vindictive. Self-love being concerned only with ourselves is content when our real needs are satisfied, but self-esteem which involves comparisons with other people never is and never can be content because it makes the impossible demand that others should prefer us to them-selves. That is how it comes that the gentle kindly passions issue from self-love, while hate and anger spring from self-esteem. Great care and skill are required to prevent the human heart being depraved by the new needs of social life. . . .

My readers, I foresee, will be surprised to see me take my pupil through the whole of the early years without mentioning religion. At fifteen he was not aware that he had a soul, and perhaps at eighteen it is not yet time for him to learn. For if he learns sooner than is necessary he runs the risk of never knowing.

My picture of hopeless stupidity is a pedant teaching the catechism to chil-dren. If I wanted to make a child dull I would compel him to explain what he says when he repeats his catechism. It may be objected that since most of the Christian doctrines are mysteries it would be necessary for the proper under-standing of them to wait, not merely till the child becomes a man but till the man is no more. To that I reply, in the first place, that there are mysteries man can neither conceive nor believe and that I see no purpose in teaching them to children unless it be to teach them to lie. I say, further, that to admit there are mysteries one must understand that they are incomprehensible, and that this is an idea which is quite beyond children. For an age when all is mystery, there can be no mysteries, properly so-called.

Let us be on guard against presenting the truth to those unable to compre-hend it. The effect of that is to substitute error for truth. It would be better to have no idea of the Divine Being than to have ideas that are mean, fantastic and unworthy. . . .

Sophie should be as typically woman as Emile is man. She must possess all the characteristics of humanity and of womanhood which she needs for playing her part in the physical and the moral order. Let us begin considering in what respects her sex and ours agree and differ.

In the mating of the sexes each contributes in equal measure to the common end but not in the same way. From the diversity comes the *first* difference which has to be noted in their personal relations. It is the part of the one to be active and strong, and of the other to be passive and weak. Accept this principle and it follows in the *second* place that woman is intended to please man. If the man requires to please the woman in turn the necessity is less direct. Masterfulness is his special attribute. He pleases by the very fact that he is strong. This is not the law of love, I admit. But it is the law of nature, which is more ancient than love.

The faculties common to the sexes are not equally shared between them; but take them all in all, they are well balanced. The more womanly a woman is, the better. Whenever she exercises her own proper powers she gains by it: when she tries to usurp ours she becomes our inferior. Believe me, wise mother, it is a mistake to bring up your daughter to be like a good man. Make her a good woman, and you can be sure that she will be worth more for herself and for us. This does not mean that she should be brought up in utter ignorance and confined to domestic tasks. A man does not want to make his companion a servant and deprive himself of the peculiar charms of her company. That is quite against the teaching of nature, which has endowed women with quick pleasing minds. Nature means them to think, to judge, to love, to know and to cultivate the mind as well as the countenance. This is the equipment nature has given them to compensate for their lack of strength and enable them to direct the strength of men.

As I see it, the special functions of women, their inclinations and their duties, combine to suggest the kind of education they require. Men and women are made for each other but they differ in the measure of their dependence on each other. We could get on better without women than women could get on without us. To play their part in life they must have our willing help, and for that they must earn our esteem. By the very law of nature women are at the mercy of men's judgments both for themselves and for their children. It is not enough that they should be estimable: they must be esteemed. It is not enough that they should be beautiful: they must be pleasing. It is not enough that they should be wise: their wisdom must be recognised. Their honour does not rest on their conduct but on their reputation. Hence the kind of education they get should be the very opposite of men's in this respect. Public opinion is the tomb of a man's virtue but the throne of a woman's.

On the good constitution of the mothers depends that of the children and the early education of men is in their hands. On women too depend the morals, the passions, the tastes, the pleasures, aye and the happiness of men. For this reason their education must be wholly directed to their relations with men. To give them pleasure, to be useful to them, to win their love and esteem, to train them in their childhood, to care for them when they grow up, to give them counsel and consolation, to make life sweet and agreeable for them: these are the tasks of women in all times for which they should be trained from childhood.

Questions

1. What is the individual-collectivity problem?
2. How does Rousseau attack it head on?
3. Do you agree with Rousseau's position that the arts and sciences have done little to advance the happiness of humankind? Explain.
4. Why is Rousseau's view of education characterized as negative education?
5. Is such a characterization justified? Explain.
6. From Rousseau's perspective, can human beings improve upon nature? Explain.
7. Have human beings improved upon nature? Explain.
8. What is Rousseau's solution to the social malaise he sees all around him?
9. Emile's tutor clearly manipulates the environment to ensure that Emile responds properly or learns the desired principle. Is there anything morally wrong with such manipulation? In pedagogy, does the end justify the means? Explain.
10. Given what you know about Rousseau and his times, why do you think he was so openly critical of the harshness with which children were treated in his day?
11. How does Rousseau define freedom?
12. What, for Rousseau, should be the role of the teacher?
13. How does Rousseau suggest that we teach someone to read?
14. What does Rousseau have to say about competition in education?
15. What are Rousseau's views on the use of books in the education of our children?
16. Why was *Robinson Crusoe* Rousseau's favorite book?
17. Do you think that Rousseau succeeded in resolving the individual-collectivity dilemma? Explain.
18. Is the kind of education Rousseau advocates feasible in a democracy? Explain.
19. Does such education promote or sustain democracy? Explain.
20. To what extent is the education advocated by Rousseau a kind of moral education?
21. Describe in your own words Rousseau's vision of the ideally educated individual.
22. How, for Rousseau, would an ideally educated woman be different from an ideally educated man?

chapter 7

William James

TIME LINE FOR JAMES

1842	Is born on January 11 in New York City, the eldest of five children.
1855–1860	Attends schools in England, France, Switzerland, and Germany.
1860–1861	Studies painting with William M. Hunt in Newport.
1861	Enters the Lawrence Scientific School, Harvard, studying first chemistry then comparative anatomy and physiology.
1863	Enters Harvard Medical School.
1865–1866	Assists Louis Agassiz with a biological expedition along the Amazon.
1867–1868	Studies medicine in Germany.
1869	Receives his M.D. from Harvard.
1869–1870	Suffers a nervous breakdown.
1873–1876	Teaches anatomy and physiology at Harvard.
1875	Teaches psychology at Harvard.
1878	Begins work on a treatise on psychology. Marries Alice Howe Gibbens. They have five children.
1882–1883	Travels to Europe.
1885	Is appointed professor of philosophy.
1889	Is appointed professor of psychology.
1890	Publishes *Principles of Psychology*.

1892–1893	Travels to Europe.
1897	Publishes *The Will to Believe and Other Essays on Popular Psychology.*
1899	Publishes *Talks to Teachers.*
1899–1902	Travels to Europe to try to regain his health.
1901–1902	Gives Gifford Lectures, published as *The Varieties of Religious Experience.*
1906	Gives the Lowell Institute Lectures, published as *Pragmatism.*
1907	Retires from Harvard.
1908	Presents papers at the Hibbert Lectures at Manchester College, Oxford, published as *A Pluralistic Universe.*
1910	Dies August 26, at Chocorua, New Hampshire.
1912	*Essays in Radical Empiricism* are published.

Introduction

In his introduction to *The Writings of William James: A Comprehensive Edition,* John McDermott reminds the reader of Julius Seelye Bixler's famous warning against excerpting James: "The isolated reference from James is always unreliable." It is easy, far too easy, to take James's own words, wrest them from their context and turn James into a raving, easily duped mystic or into a narrow-minded entrepreneur who equated truth with utility. James was interested in the varieties of religious experience, including extrasensory perception, and he was concerned with what he called the "cash value" of an idea, but a careful reading of his work will show that his thinking is far richer, far more complex than the labels mentioned above suggest.

William James was born into a family that prized and produced genius. It is hard to imagine a more famous nineteenth-century family than the Jameses. The father, Henry Sr., was perhaps the preeminent theologian of his day. Henry Jr., with his wonderfully elaborate sentences and his disdain for things American, became the embodiment of the expatriate novelist, finding aesthetic salvation in England and on the Continent. In addition, recent biographies—and no American family this side of the Kennedys has been subject to as many biographical accounts as the James clan—suggest that in this family of geniuses, the most powerful may have been also the most fragile: Had Alice James received the same support as her more fortunate brothers, there is reason to believe that her intellectual star would now shine as brightly as her brothers' or her father's.

Of the three major American pragmatists—Charles Sanders Peirce, William James, and John Dewey—James's reputation has suffered the deepest and most significant shifts. Peirce (1839–1914), as the philosopher most concerned with the logic of pragmatism and with its theoretical underpinnings, has always been esteemed by the philosophical community. Dewey's reputation has ebbed and flowed, but his work has always been in print, and even when his reputation was at its lowest, he was always considered a philosopher, although his detractors would attach "muddle-headed" to the noun. William James, however, is quite another story. During his glory days at Harvard (1876–1907) no philosopher was held in higher esteem. The publication of his most technical work, *The Principles of Psychology,* was one of the major events of intellectual history of the nineteenth century. While it may not have had the dramatic impact on popular life that Darwin's *Origin of Species* had, it certainly helped revolutionize thinking in psychology and philosophy. After his death, however, James's reputation suffered a decline. His books went out of print, and academicians, when they could refrain from snickering at him, treated him as hopelessly naive, lacking all philosophical rigor, and unrelentingly eccentric. Recently, in large part due to John McDermott's masterful collection of James's work but also due to changes in philosophy itself—changes including the entrance of minorities into the profession of philosophy and the expansion of philosophy into applied areas such as education and environmental issues—James's reputation has been restored. History suggests it would be foolhardy to think that further shifts will not occur.

Part of the difficulty with James, one of the reasons that his reputation has suffered such violent change, is that James presented his work in two distinct forms. His theoretical work, especially as it appears in *Principles of Psychology* and *Essays in Radical Empiricism,* has the tightness and rigor one would normally expect from a philosophical document. Unfortunately, the writing is frequently inaccessible to educators who have an interest in the philosophical dimensions of education. Simply, the bridge from philosophical theory to educational practice is not apparent. Thus James's technical work tends to get ignored.

On the other hand, much of James's nontechnical writing is comprised of speeches that he gave to popular audiences—teachers, ministers, and so on. They are frequently pithy and invariably evocative, but it is a stretch to suggest that they are rigorous. They read exactly as what they are—chatty speeches about matters of popular interest.

The difficulty, then, is how to present James so that the reader can see his educational importance. To solve this difficulty, we, as editors, will be a bit more prescriptive than we have been in previous sections and urge the reader to keep in mind, when reading James, two basic points: (1) James's world, the world of the pragmatists in general, is unfinished and open. It is a world both precarious and stable—a world in which we can predict, frequently accurately, but a world that, at crucial moments, tends to slip outside our theories and preconceived notions. (2) In order to make one's way in this world, in order to achieve one's end, one must be sensitive to the varieties of experience. The educated person must listen and look hard: She or he must look at things, even the most mundane things, with a "'fresh eye," with the eye of a poet or an artist. This sensitivity to experience, this willingness to look and listen hard is at the very heart of James's educational theory and is constitutive of the educated person.

The following excerpts are all taken from what is considered to be James's popular writing. Embrace, if you will, the two points, remember Bixler's remark about

Jamesian excerpts, and mentally "complete" James' popular thought with its technical foundation. Finally, James' "What Pragmatism Means" might serve as a prism through which the careful reader can examine the works of later pragmatists such as John Dewey, Cornel West, and Richard Rorty.

From *Talks to Teachers* (1899)

"On a Certain Blindness in Human Beings"

Our judgments concerning the worth of things, big or little, depend on the *feelings* the things arouse in us. Where we judge a thing to be precious in consequence of the *idea* we frame of it, this is only because the idea is itself associated already with a feeling. If we were radically feelingless, and if ideas were the only things our mind could entertain, we should lose all our likes and dislikes at a stroke, and be unable to point to any one situation or experience in life more valuable or significant than any other.

Now the blindness in human beings, of which this discourse will treat, is the blindness with which we all are afflicted in regard to the feelings of creatures and people different from ourselves.

We are practical beings, each of us with limited functions and duties to perform. Each is bound to feel intensely the importance of his own duties and the significance of the situations that call these forth. But this feeling is in each of us a vital secret, for sympathy with which we vainly look to others. The others are too much absorbed in their own vital secrets to take an interest in ours. Hence the stupidity and injustice of our opinions, so far as they deal with the significance of alien lives. Hence the falsity of our judgments, so far as they presume to decide in an absolute way on the value of other persons' conditions or ideals.

Take our dogs and ourselves, connected as we are by a tie more intimate than most ties in this world; and yet, outside of that tie of friendly fondness, how insensible, each of us, to all that makes life significant for the other!—we to the rapture of bones under hedges, or smells of trees and lamp-posts, they to the delights of literature and art. As you sit reading the most moving romance you ever fell upon, what sort of a judge is your fox-terrier of your behavior? With all his good will toward you, the nature of your conduct is absolutely excluded from his comprehension. To sit there like a senseless statue, when you might be taking him to walk and throwing sticks for him to catch! What queer disease is this that comes over you every day, of holding things and staring at them like that for hours together, paralyzed of motion and vacant of all conscious life? The African savages came nearer the truth; but they, too, missed it, when they gathered wonderingly round one of our American travellers who, in the interior, had

From *The Writings of William James,* edited by John J. McDermott © 1977 University of Chicago Press, pp. 629–635.

just come into possession of a stray copy of the New York *Commercial Advertiser,* and was devouring it column by column. When he got through, they offered him a high price for the mysterious object; and, being asked for what they wanted it, they said: "For an eye medicine,"—that being the only reason they could conceive of for the protracted bath which he had given his eyes upon its surface.

The spectator's judgment is sure to miss the root of the matter, and to possess no truth. The subject judged knows a part of the world of reality which the judging spectator fails to see, knows more while the spectator knows less; and, whenever there is conflict of opinion and difference of vision, we are bound to believe that the truer side is the side that feels the more, and not the side that feels the less.

Let me take a personal example of the kind that befalls each one of us daily:—

Some years ago, while journeying in the mountains of North Carolina, I passed by a large number of "coves," as they call them there, or heads of small valleys between the hills, which had been newly cleared and planted. The impression on my mind was one of unmitigated squalor. The settler had in every case cut down the more manageable trees, and left their charred stumps standing. The larger trees he had girdled and killed, in order that their foliage should not cast a shade. He had then built a log cabin, plastering its chinks with clay, and had set up a tall zigzag rail fence around the scene of his havoc, to keep the pigs and cattle out. Finally, he had irregularly planted the intervals between the stumps and trees with Indian corn, which grew among the chips; and there he dwelt with his wife and babes—an axe, a gun, a few utensils, and some pigs and chickens feeding in the woods, being the sum total of his possessions.

The forest had been destroyed; and what had "improved" it out of existence was hideous, a sort of ulcer, without a single element of artificial grace to make up for the loss of Nature's beauty. Ugly, indeed, seemed the life of the squatter, scudding, as the sailors say, under bare poles, beginning again away back where our first ancestors started, and by hardly a single item the better off for all the achievements of the intervening generations.

Talk about going back to nature! I said to myself, oppressed by the dreariness, as I drove by. Talk of a country life for one's old age and for one's children! Never thus, with nothing but the bare ground and one's bare hands to fight the battle! Never, without the best spoils of culture woven in! The beauties and commodities gained by the centuries are sacred. They are our heritage and birthright. No modern person ought to be willing to live a day in such a state of rudimentariness and denudation.

Then I said to the mountaineer who was driving me, "What sort of people are they who have to make these new clearings?" "All of us," he replied. "Why, we ain't happy here, unless we are getting one of these coves under cultivation." I instantly felt that I had been losing the whole inward significance of the situation. Because to me the clearings spoke of naught but denudation, I thought that to those whose sturdy arms and obedient axes had made them they could tell no other story. But, when *they* looked on the hideous stumps, what they thought of was personal victory. The chips, the girdled trees, and the vile split rails spoke of honest sweat, persistent toil and final reward. The cabin was a warrant of safety for self and wife and babes. In short, the clearing, which to me was a mere ugly picture on the retina, was to them a symbol redolent with moral memories and sang a very pæan of duty, struggle, and success.

I had been as blind to the peculiar ideality of their conditions as they certainly would also have been to the ideality of mine, had they had a peep at my strange indoor academic ways of life at Cambridge.

Wherever a process of life communicates an eagerness to him who lives it, there the life becomes genuinely significant. Sometimes the eagerness is more knit up with the motor activities, sometimes with the perceptions, sometimes with the imagination, sometimes with reflective thought. But, wherever it is found, there is the zest, the tingle, the excitement of reality; and there *is* "importance" in the only real and positive sense in which importance ever anywhere can be.

Robert Louis Stevenson has illustrated this by a case, drawn from the sphere of the imagination, in an essay which I really think deserves to become immortal, both for the truth of its matter and the excellence of its form.

"Toward the end of September," Stevenson writes, "when school-time was drawing near, and the nights were already black, we would begin to sally from our respective villas, each equipped with a tin bull's-eye lantern. The thing was so well known that it had worn a rut in the commerce of Great Britain; and the grocers, about the due time, began to garnish their windows with our particular brand of luminary. We wore them buckled to the waist upon a cricket belt, and over them, such was the rigor of the game, a buttoned top-coat. They smelled noisomely of blistered tin. They never burned aright, though they would always burn our fingers. Their use was naught, the pleasure of them merely fanciful, and yet a boy with a bull's-eye under his top-coat asked for nothing more. The fishermen used lanterns about their boats, and it was from them, I suppose, that we had got the hint; but theirs were not bull's-eyes, nor did we ever play at being fishermen. The police carried them at their belts, and we had plainly copied them in that; yet we did not pretend to be policemen. Burglars, indeed, we may have had some haunting thought of; and we had certainly an eye to past ages when lanterns were more common, and to certain story-books in which we had found them to figure very largely. But take it for all in all, the pleasure of the thing was substantive; and to be a boy with a bull's-eye under his top-coat was good enough for us.

"When two of these asses met, there would be an anxious 'Have you got your lantern?' and a gratified 'Yes!' That was the shibboleth, and very needful, too; for, as it was the rule to keep our glory contained, none could recognize a lantern-bearer unless (like the polecat) by the smell. Four or five would sometimes climb into the belly of a ten-man lugger, with nothing but the thwarts above them,—for the cabin was usually locked,—or chose out some hollow of the links where the wind might whistle overhead. Then the coats would be unbuttoned, and the bull's-eyes discovered; and in the chequering glimmer, under the huge, windy hall of the night, and cheered by a rich steam of toasting tinware, these fortunate young gentlemen would crouch together in the cold sand of the links, or on the scaly bilges of the fishing-boat, and delight them with inappropriate talk. Woe is me that I cannot give some specimens! . . . But the talk was but a condiment, and these gatherings themselves only accidents in the career of the lantern-bearer. The essence of this bliss was to walk by yourself in the black night, the slide shut, the top-coat buttoned, not a ray escaping, whether to conduct your footsteps or to make your glory public,—a mere pillar of darkness in the dark; and all the while, deep down in the privacy of your fool's heart, to know you had a bull's-eye at your belt, and to exult and sing over the knowledge.

"It is said that a poet has died young in the breast of the most stolid. It may be contended rather that a (somewhat minor) bard in almost every case survives, and is the spice of life to his possessor. Justice is not done to the versatility and the unplumbed childishness of man's imagination. His life from without may seem but a rude mound of mud: there will be some golden chamber at the heart of it, in which he dwells delighted; and for as dark as his pathway seems to the observer, he will have some kind of bull's-eye at his belt. . . .

"There is one fable that touches very near the quick of life,—the fable of the monk who passed into the woods, heard a bird break into song, hearkened for a trill or two, and found himself at his return a stranger at his convent gates; for he had been absent fifty years, and of all his comrades there survived but one to recognize him. It is not only in the woods that this enchanter carols, though perhaps he is native there. He sings in the most doleful places. The miser hears him and chuckles, and his days are moments. With no more apparatus than an evil-smelling lantern, I have evoked him on the naked links. All life that is not merely mechanical is spun out of two strands,—seeking for that bird and hearing him. And it is just this that makes life so hard to value, and the delight of each so incommunicable. And it is just a knowledge of this, and a remembrance of those fortunate hours in which the bird *has* sung to *us*, that fills us with such wonder when we turn to the pages of the realist. There, to be sure, we find a picture of life in so far as it consists of mud and of old iron, cheap desires and cheap fears, that which we are ashamed to remember and that which we are careless whether we forget; but of the note of that time-devouring nightingale we hear no news. . . .

"Say that we came [in such a realistic romance] on some such business as that of my lantern-bearers on the links, and described the boys as very cold, spat upon by flurries of rain, and drearily surrounded, all of which they were; and their talk as silly and indecent, which it certainly was. To the eye of the observer they *are* wet and cold and drearily surrounded; but ask themselves, and they are in the heaven of a recondite pleasure, the ground of which is an ill-smelling lantern.

"For, to repeat, the ground of a man's joy is often hard to hit. It may hinge at times upon a mere accessory, like the lantern; it may reside in the mysterious inwards of psychology. . . . It has so little bond with externals . . . that it may even touch them not, and the man's true life, for which he consents to live, lie together in the field of fancy. . . . In such a case the poetry runs underground. The observer (poor soul, with his documents!) is all abroad. For to look at the man is but to count deception. We shall see the trunk from which he draws his nourishment; but he himself is above and abroad in the green dome of foliage, hummed through by winds and nested in by nightingales. And the true realism were that of the poets, to climb after him like a squirrel, and catch some glimpse of the heaven in which he lives. And the true realism, always and everywhere, is that of the poets: to find out where joy resides, and give it a voice far beyond singing.

"For to miss the joy is to miss all. In the joy of the actors lies the sense of any action. That is the explanation, that the excuse. To one who has not the secret of the lanterns the scene upon the links is meaningless. And hence the haunting and truly spectral unreality of realistic books. . . . In each we miss the personal poetry, the enchanted atmosphere, that rainbow work of fancy that clothes what is naked and seems to ennoble what is base; in each, life falls dead like dough, instead of soaring away like a balloon into the colors of the sunset; each is true, each inconceivable; for no man lives in the external truth among salts and acids, but in the warm, phantasmagoric chamber of his brain, with the painted windows and the storied wall."[1]

These paragraphs are the best thing I know in all Stevenson. "To miss the joy is to miss all." Indeed, it is. Yet we are but finite, and each one of us has some single specialized vocation of his own. And it seems as if energy in the service of its particular duties might be got only by hardening the heart toward everything unlike them. Our deadness toward all but one particular kind of joy would thus be the price we inevitably have to pay for being practical creatures. Only in some pitiful dreamer, some philosopher, poet, or romancer, or when the common practical man becomes a lover, does the hard externality give way, and a gleam of insight into the ejective world, as Clifford called it, the vast world of inner life beyond us, so different from that of outer seeming, illuminate our mind. Then the whole scheme of our customary values gets confounded, then our self is riven and its narrow interests fly to pieces, then a new centre and a new perspective must be found.

The change is well described by my colleague, Josiah Royce:—

"What, then, is our neighbor? Thou hast regarded his thought, his feeling, as somehow different from thine. Thou hast said, 'A pain in him is not like a pain in me, but something far easier to bear.' He seems to thee a little less living than thou; his life is dim, it is cold, it is a pale fire beside thy own burning desires. . . . So, dimly and by instinct hast thou lived with thy neighbor, and hast known him not, being blind. Thou hast made [of him] a thing, no Self at all. Have done with this illusion, and simply try to learn the truth. Pain is pain, joy is joy, everywhere, even as in thee. In all the songs of the forest birds; in all the cries of the wounded and dying, struggling in the captor's power; in the boundless sea where the myriads of water-creatures strive and die; amid all the countless hordes of savage men; in all sickness and sorrow; in all exultation and hope, everywhere, from the lowest to the noblest, the same conscious, burning, wilful life is found, endlessly manifold as the forms of the living creatures, unquenchable as the fires of the sun, real as these impulses that even now throb in thine

---

[1] "The Lantern-bearers," in the volume entitled *Across the Plains*. Abridged in the quotation.

own little selfish heart. Lift up thy eyes, behold that life, and then turn away, and forget it as thou canst; but, if thou hast *known* that, thou hast begun to know thy duty."[2]

From *Pragmatism* (1906)

"What Pragmatism Means"

Some years ago, being with a camping party in the mountains, I returned from a solitary ramble to find every one engaged in a ferocious metaphysical dispute. The *corpus* of the dispute was a squirrel—a live squirrel supposed to be clinging to one side of a tree-trunk; while over against the tree's opposite side a human being was imagined to stand. This human witness tries to get sight of the squirrel by moving rapidly round the tree, but no matter how fast he goes, the squirrel moves as fast in the opposite direction, and always keeps the tree between himself and the man, so that never a glimpse of him is caught. The resultant metaphysical problem now is this: *Does the man go round the squirrel or not?* He goes round the tree, sure enough, and the squirrel is on the tree; but does he go round the squirrel? In the unlimited leisure of the wilderness, discussion had been worn threadbare. Everyone had taken sides, and was obstinate; and the numbers on both sides were even. Each side, when I appeared, therefore appealed to me to make it a majority. Mindful of the scholastic adage that whenever you meet a contradiction you must make a distinction, I immediately sought and found one, as follows: "Which party is right," I said," depends on what you *practically mean* by 'going round' the squirrel. If you mean passing from the north of him to the east, then to the south, then to the west, and then to the north of him again, obviously the man does go round him, for he occupies these successive positions. But if on the contrary you mean being first in front of him, then on the right of him, then behind him, then on his left, and finally in front again, it is quite as obvious that the man fails to go round him, for by the compensating movements the squirrel makes, he keeps his belly turned towards the man all the time, and his back turned away. Make the distinction, and there is no occasion for any farther dispute. You are both right and both wrong according as you conceive the verb 'to go round' in one practical fashion or the other."

Although one or two of the hotter disputants called my speech a shuffling evasion, saying they wanted no quibbling or scholastic hair-splitting, but meant just plain honest English "round," the majority seemed to think that the distinction had assuaged the dispute.

I tell this trivial anecdote because it is a peculiarly simple example of what I wish now to speak of as *the pragmatic method*. The pragmatic method is primarily a method of settling metaphysical disputes that otherwise might be interminable. Is the world one or many?—fated or free?—material or spiritual?—here are

---

[2] *The Religious Aspect of Philosophy,* pp. 157–162 (abridged).

From *The Writings of William James,* edited by John J. McDermott, © 1977 University of Chicago Press, pp. 376–380.

notions either of which may or may not hold good of the world; and disputes over such notions are unending. The pragmatic method in such cases is to try to interpret each notion by tracing its respective practical consequences. What difference would it practically make to any one if this notion rather than that notion were true? If no practical difference whatever can be traced, then the alternatives mean practically the same thing, and all dispute is idle. Whenever a dispute is serious, we ought to be able to show some practical difference that must follow from one side or the other's being right.

A glance at the history of the idea will show you still better what pragmatism means. The term is derived from the same Greek word $\pi\rho\alpha\gamma\mu\alpha$, meaning action, from which our words "practice" and "practical" come. It was first introduced into philosophy by Mr. Charles Peirce in 1878. In an article entitled "How to Make Our Ideas Clear," in the *Popular Science Monthly* for January of that year[1] Mr. Peirce, after pointing out that our beliefs are really rules for action, said that, to develop a thought's meaning, we need only determine what conduct it is fitted to produce: that conduct is for us its sole significance. And the tangible fact at the root of all our thought-distinctions, however subtle, is that there is no one of them so fine as to consist in anything but a possible difference of practice. To attain perfect clearness in our thoughts of an object, then, we need only consider what conceivable effects of a practical kind the object may involve—what sensations we are to expect from it, and what reactions we must prepare. Our conception of these effects, whether immediate or remote, is then for us the whole of our conception of the object, so far as that conception has positive significance at all.

This is the principle of Peirce, the principle of pragmatism. It lay entirely unnoticed by any one for twenty years, until I, in an address before Professor Howison's philosophical union at the University of California, brought it forward again and made a special application of it to religion. By that date (1898) the times seemed ripe for its reception. The word "pragmatism" spread, and at present it fairly spots the pages of the philosophic journals. On all hands we find the "pragmatic movement" spoken of, sometimes with respect, sometimes with contumely, seldom with clear understanding. It is evident that the term applies itself conveniently to a number of tendencies that hitherto have lacked a collective name, and that it has "come to stay."

To take in the importance of Peirce's principle, one must get accustomed to applying it to concrete cases. I found a few years ago that Ostwald, the illustrious Leipzig chemist, had been making perfectly distinct use of the principle of pragmatism in his lectures on the philosophy of science, though he had not called it by that name.

"All realities influence our practice," he wrote me, "and that influence is their meaning for us. I am accustomed to put questions to my classes in this way: In what respects would the world be different if this alternative or that

---

[1] Translated in the *Revue Philosophique* for January, 1879 (vol. vii).

were true? If I can find nothing that would become different, then the alternative has no sense."

That is, the rival views mean practically the same thing, and meaning, other than practical, there is for us none. Ostwald in a published lecture gives this example of what he means. Chemists have long wrangled over the inner constitution of certain bodies called "tautomerous." Their properties seemed equally consistent with the notion that an instable hydrogen atom oscillates inside of them, or that they are instable mixtures of two bodies. Controversy raged, but never was decided. "It would never have begun," says Ostwald, "if the combatants had asked themselves what particular experimental fact could have been made different by one or the other view being correct. For it would then have appeared that no difference of fact could possibly ensue; and the quarrel was as unreal as if, theorizing in primitive times about the raising of dough by yeast, one party should have invoked a 'brownie,' while another insisted on an 'elf' as the true cause of the phenomenon."[2]

It is astonishing to see how many philosophical disputes collapse into insignificance the moment you subject them to this simple test of tracing a concrete consequence. There can *be* no difference anywhere that doesn't *make* a difference elsewhere—no difference in abstract truth that doesn't express itself in a difference in concrete fact and in conduct consequent upon that fact, imposed on somebody, somehow, somewhere, and somewhen. The whole function of philosophy ought to be to find out what definite difference it will make to you and me, at definite instants of our life, if this world-formula or that world-formula be the true one.

There is absolutely nothing new in the pragmatic method. Socrates was an adept at it. Aristotle used it methodically. Locke, Berkeley, and Hume made momentous contributions to truth by its means. Shadworth Hodgson keeps insisting that realities are only what they are "known as." But these forerunners of pragmatism used it in fragments: they were preluders only. Not until in our time has it generalized itself, become conscious of a universal mission, pretended to a conquering destiny. I believe in that destiny, and I hope I may end by inspiring you with my belief.

Pragmatism represents a perfectly familiar attitude in philosophy, the empiricist attitude, but it represents it, as it seems to me, both in a more radical and in a less objectionable form than it has ever yet assumed. A pragmatist turns his back resolutely and once for all upon a lot of inveterate habits dear to professional philosophers. He turns away from abstraction and insufficiency, from verbal solutions, from bad *a priori* reasons, from fixed principles, closed systems, and pretended absolutes and origins. He turns towards concreteness

---

[2] "Theorie und Praxis," *Zeitsch. des Oesterreichischen Ingenieur u. Architecten-Vereines,* 1905, Nr. 4 u. 6. I find a still more radical pragmatism than Ostwald's in an address by Professor W. S. Franklin: "I think that the sickliest notion of physics, even if a student gets it, is that it is 'the science of masses, molecules, and the ether.' And I think that the healthiest notion, even if a student does not wholly get it, is that physics is the science of the ways of taking hold of bodies and pushing them!" (*Science,* January 2, 1903.)

and adequacy, towards facts, towards action and towards power. That means the empiricist temper regnant and the rationalist temper sincerely given up. It means the open air and possibilities of nature, as against dogma, artificiality, and the pretense of finality in truth.

At the same time it does not stand for any special results. It is a method only. But the general triumph of that method would mean an enormous change in what I called in my last lecture the "temperament" of philosophy. Teachers of the ultra-rationalistic type would be frozen out, much as the courtier type is frozen out in republics, as the ultra-montane type of priest is frozen out in protestant lands. Science and metaphysics would come much nearer together, would in fact work absolutely hand in hand.

Metaphysics has usually followed a very primitive kind of quest. You know how men have always hankered after unlawful magic, and you know what a great part in magic *words* have always played. If you have his name, or the formula of incantation that binds him, you can control the spirit, genie, afrite, or whatever the power may be. Solomon knew the names of all the spirits and having their names, he held them subject to his will. So the universe has always appeared to the natural mind as a kind of enigma, of which the key must be sought in the shape of some illuminating or power-bringing word or name. That word names the universe's *principle,* and to possess it is after a fashion to possess the universe itself. "God," "Matter," "Reason," "the Absolute," "Energy," are so many solving names. You can rest when you have them. You are at the end of your metaphysical quest.

But if you follow the pragmatic method, you cannot look on any such word as closing your quest. You must bring out of each word its practical cash-value, set it at work within the stream of your experience. It appears less as a solution, then, than as a program for more work, and more particularly as an indication of the ways in which existing realities may be *changed.*

Theories thus become instruments, not answers to enigmas, in which we can rest. We don't lie back upon them, we move forward, and, on occasion, make nature over again by their aid. Pragmatism unstiffens all our theories, limbers them up and sets each one at work. Being nothing essentially new, it harmonizes with many ancient philosophic tendencies. It agrees with nominalism for instance, in always appealing to particulars; with utilitarianism in emphasizing practical aspects; with positivism in its disdain for verbal solutions, useless questions and metaphysical abstractions.

All these, you see, are *anti-intellectualist* tendencies. Against rationalism as a pretension and a method pragmatism is fully armed and militant. But, at the outset, at least, it stands for no particular results. It has no dogmas, and no doctrines save its method. As the young Italian pragmatist Papini has well said, it lies in the midst of our theories, like a corridor in a hotel. Innumerable chambers open out of it. In one you may find a man writing an atheistic volume; in the next some one on his knees praying for faith and strength; in a third a chemist investigating a body's properties. In a fourth a system of idealistic metaphysics is being excogitated; in a fifth the impossibility of metaphysics is being shown.

But they all own the corridor, and all must pass through it if they want a practicable way of getting into or out of their respective rooms.

No particular results then, so far, but only an attitude of orientation, is what the pragmatic method means. *The attitude of looking away from first things, principles, "categories," supposed necessities: and of looking towards last things, fruits, consequences, facts.*

Questions

1. What is the blindness to which William James alludes?
2. What is the difference between the spectator's judgment and the subject's judgment?
3. James suggests that merely mechanical actions are meaningless. Do you agree? Explain.
4. How would you structure things in a classroom so that they would not be merely mechanical?
5. What does pragmatism mean?
6. Is James's view of reality consistent with the view implicit in the discipline of science as you have experienced it in school? Explain.
7. What, for James, is a theory?
8. Do you agree with James's understanding of theory? Explain.
9. What is Peirce's principle?
10. Why is pragmatism such a radical empiricism?

chapter **8**

John Dewey

TIME LINE FOR DEWEY

1859	Is born October 20 in Burlington, Vermont.
1875	Enters the University of Vermont.
1879	Receives Bachelor's degree.
1879–1881	Teaches high school at Oil City, Pennsylvania.
1881	Studies philosophy with H. A. P. Torrey at Johns Hopkins University.
1882	Enters graduate school.
1884	Receives Ph.D. from Johns Hopkins.
1884–1894	Teaches philosophy at the University of Michigan.
1886	Marries Alice Chipman.
1894	Is appointed chairman of the Department of Philosophy, Psychology, and Pedagogy at the University of Chicago.
	Starts Lab School at University of Chicago.
1895	Suffers loss of son, Morris, from diphtheria while in Milan. The Deweys later return to Italy and adopt an orphan boy, Sabino.
1897	Publishes "My Pedagogic Creed."
1900	Publishes *The School and Society.*
1902	Publishes *The Child and the Curriculum.*
1904	Is appointed professor of philosophy at Columbia University.

87

1904	Suffers the loss of son, Gordon, from typhoid fever while vacationing in Ireland.
1910	Publishes *How We Think*.
1915	Establishes and is the first president of the American Association of University Professors.
1916	Publishes *Democracy and Education*.
1919–1928	Gives lectures in Japan, China, Turkey, Mexico, and Russia.
1920	Publishes *Reconstruction of Philosophy*, based on lectures given at the Imperial University, Japan.
1922	Publishes *Human Nature and Conduct*.
1925	Publishes *Experience and Nature*.
1927	Suffers loss of his wife, Alice.
1930	Is named professor emeritus at Columbia University.
1934	Publishes *Art as Experience* and *A Common Faith*.
1937	Serves as chairman of the commission of inquiry into the charges made against Leon Trotsky (Mexico City).
1938	Publishes *Experience and Education*.
1939	Publishes *Freedom and Culture*.
1946	Marries Roberta Lowitz Grant. They adopt two children. Publishes *Problems of Men*.
1949	Publishes, with Arthur Bentley, *Knowing and the Known*.
1952	Dies June 1 in New York City.

Introduction

Born in 1859—the same year that Horace Mann died and that saw the publication of Charles Darwin's *Origin of Species*—Dewey lived through the Civil War, two world wars, the Great Depression, and numerous lesser conflicts, and died as the cold war emerged full blown on the global scene. During his lifetime, the United States was transformed from a largely agrarian, experimental republic into the major industrial and military power in the world. Growing up in Puritan New England, Dewey would gradually abandon his religious foundations, moving, as he explains, "from absolutism to experimentalism." Attaining his undergraduate degree from the University of Vermont and eventually his Ph.D. from Johns Hopkins University, Dewey retained his religious commitment through his professorship at the University of Michigan in the 1880s and 1890s. As a young man, Dewey embraced the Social Gospel movement in hopes of connecting his commitment to democracy to an absolutist metaphysics—Hegelian idealism.

His commitment to social justice and democratic principles never waned, but by the early 1890s, Dewey had begun to distance himself from otherworldly metaphysics. Upon moving to Chicago in 1894 to chair the Department of Philosophy, Psychology, and Pedagogy at the University of Chicago, Dewey stopped participating in religious activities. By this time he had transformed his metaphysical idealism into pragmatic naturalism. Finally, feeling comfortable that his commitment to democratic principles could be sustained by grounding them in experience, Dewey spent much of the remainder of his life working out the implications of this philosophical shift for his social, political, and educational ideas.

The years Dewey lived in Chicago were productive ones. Here he continued his commitment to social justice by working with Jane Addams at Hull House, experiencing firsthand the dehumanizing effects that America's transformation into an industrialized and urbanized oligarchy produced. Here, too, Dewey established his famous Lab School, a living, self-correcting community, as a testing ground for his evolving educational ideas. Here, too, he emerged, along with William James and Charles S. Peirce, as a founder of that uniquely American brand of philosophy known as pragmatism.

Leaving Chicago in 1904, Dewey assumed a professorship of philosophy at Columbia University in New York City, a position he held until his retirement in 1929. In addition to teaching, writing, and numerous other academic responsibilities, Dewey struggled to find ways to construct "the Great Community" and to make the world "safe for democracy." Initially supportive of Wilson's war policy—for which his former student, Randolph Bourne, criticized him for falling "prey to the very mistakes his philosophy was designed to prevent"[1]—Dewey participated in the quixotic Outlaw War movement during the postwar period. During these years and throughout his life, "Dewey was the most important advocate of participatory democracy, that is of the belief that democracy as an ethical ideal calls upon men and women to build communities in which the necessary opportunities and resources are available for every individual to fully realize his or her particular capacities and powers through participation in political, social, and cultural life."[2]

Though officially retired, Dewey remained remarkably active during the last 23 years of his life. He continued his prolific writing, publishing major works on aesthetics, religion, politics, education, logic, and epistemology. He remained active in social causes, including traveling to Mexico to chair the commission of inquiry investigating the charges leveled against Leon Trotsky. Maintaining an active lifestyle until his death in 1952, Dewey married in 1946 a woman almost half his age and with her adopted two Belgian war orphans.[3]

As suggested earlier, Dewey was a prolific scholar throughout his life; he published scores of books and pamphlets, hundreds of articles for scholarly and popular journals and magazines, and gave innumerable speeches and lectures—public as well as academic—on topics ranging from Hegelian metaphysics to woman's suffrage. Indeed, it is not an exaggeration to suggest that from 1900 to 1940, Dewey published more each year than many small college faculties produced during all of these years. Unfortunately, Dewey did not always write well. As Justice Oliver Wendell Holmes charges: "Dewey writes as the creator would write, if he were intent on explaining all of his creation but was hopelessly inarticulate." Dewey's works are often misunderstood, but more frequently Dewey is not read. As John

Novak explains, "John Dewey is like the Bible—often alluded to (both by his supporters and detractors) but seldom read...."[4]

Students who might be interested in Dewey's work, and who clearly could benefit from it, are often overwhelmed by the sheer volume of it. Those ambitious enough to dive into one of Dewey's works are likely to find his prose stiff and lacking in imagination. In addition, while there is an abundance of literature about Dewey, much of it treats him either as a saint or a villain. In this secondary literature, most of it published during this century, Dewey has been reviled and praised, criticized and attacked for being the father of progressive education, a communist dupe and a hopeless anticommunist, a pacifist and a turncoat to pacifist ideals, a secular humanist, and the founder of all things good (and bad) in American education.

A work like this one can do little to answer all the questions about Dewey and his influence on education other than to suggest that Dewey was a highly complex thinker whose thought could never be captured by any reductionist label. What this work can do—by introducing the reader to carefully selected excerpts from Dewey's works—is whet the reader's appetite for more information about this remarkable figure in American educational thought. If this work is successful, you will be motivated to further investigate both the man and his thought by reading Dewey's autobiographical essay "From Absolutism to Experimentalism"; George Dykhuizen's *The Life and Mind of John Dewey,* a work already quoted in this brief introduction; Robert B. Westbrook's recently published *John Dewey and American Democracy;* as well as the many seminal works Dewey published during his long and distinguished life.

Here we will focus on three works of John Dewey: "My Pedagogic Creed," published in 1897; an excerpt from *Democracy and Education* (1916), which for most of his career Dewey claimed to be the work in which his philosophy was best developed; and an excerpt from *Experience and Education* (1938), which might be read as a corrective to Dewey's followers in the progressive education movement.

"My Pedagogic Creed" is, in many way, Dewey's gift to scholars. Over the course of a few pages he tells what he believes about education, the school, subject matter, the nature of method, and the relation of the school to social progress. Dewey writes of the psychological and sociological sides of education, the child's cultural inheritance, discipline and interest, the relationship of the school to the neighborhood, activity and images in teaching, the connection between immediate experience and traditional school subject matters and disciplines, and finally the school as an instrument of social progress and the teacher as the "harbinger" of a new social order. In the middle of all that, Dewey defines education as "a continual process of reconstruction of experience." At heart, the educated person is a sense-maker, that is, one who can wrest as much meaning as possible from her or his experiences.

It is amazing that Dewey can cover so many topics in such a small space. Reading "Creed" is like looking at a far-off star through a telescope. The telescope gives one a relatively clear view of the star, but shows little of the evening sky. In effect, "Creed" is a statement, written before the fact, of the conclusions of Dewey's argument. "Creed" tells what Dewey thinks but omits the "sky" that frames those conclusions.

In order to see that sky, in order to deal with Dewey's arguments for his educational conclusions, one should look at Dewey's magnum opus, *Democracy and Education*. Here, Dewey unpacks what he means by education and relates education to democracy. In a move typical of Dewey, he suggests that as much as we educate for democracy, we should democratize for education.

Finally, it is hard to overstate Dewey's influence in American schooling from the turn of the twentieth century through the 1930s. During that period, all sorts of progressive educational experiments and programs were espoused and tried. In New York, people set up schools where children were allowed to do as they pleased and to devise their own curricula. At the same time, progressive educators like George S. Counts were urging teachers to indoctrinate children with proper social ideals and values. Everybody, however, claimed John Dewey as a special influence. This led a somewhat exasperated Dewey to publish, in 1937, *Experience and Education*. There he tried to make explicit his own brand of progressivism and to correct the excesses of many of his followers.

In *Experience and Education*, Dewey reiterates his opposition to either/or thinking. Specifically, Dewey rejects the either/or (Platonic/Aristotelian) worldview that dominated the Western world for so long. From this rather traditional perspective, knowledge is either innate—inside the individual at birth awaiting the right mnemonic device to bring it to consciousness—or external to human beings, awaiting our discovery. In either case, an absolute is implied, resulting in the imposition of knowledge and values upon each new generation. Such a worldview may be appropriate for a monarchy or some other form of autocracy, but it is antithetical to education in a democracy.

Is rejection enough? Is the urge to destroy really—as Bakunin suggests—a creative urge? Dewey realizes that if the so-called new education is developed as a negative reaction to traditional beliefs, then its advocates have fallen into the trap of either/or thinking. All too often what occurred in Dewey's name and under the rubric of progressivism was nothing more than mere reaction to the authorities of the past, with little or no attempt to reconstruct that which had been torn down. While such deconstruction may be necessary, it is not sufficient. For Dewey, there must be a vision of a better way, a more appropriate way for improving the individual within the collective, the human being in society.

In writing *Experience and Education*, Dewey suggested that many so-called progressives built their "new education" as a negative reaction to that which they did not like or with which they did not agree. Rather than just rebelling against the traditional version of either/or thinking, Dewey based his "new education" on experience. In distinguishing good or educative experiences from bad or miseducative experiences, Dewey suggests that good experience is characterized by both interaction and continuity. An educative experience is one in which an active mind interacts with a wide-open world to solve genuine problems that are continuous with, yet different from, previous experiences. Recognizing that we are creatures of habit,

Dewey suggests that it is our unique ability to stop, reflect, and then act—that is, to respond intelligently to a problematic situation requiring more than a mere habitual reaction—that distinguishes humans from less intelligent animals. In *Experience and Education,* Dewey offers the reader a succinct yet clear explanation of what he means by experience and how the key elements of interaction and continuity complement one another in good or educative experiences.

A careful reading of *Experience and Education* offers insights into Dewey's view of democracy. As already noted, Dewey championed democracy throughout his long life, and democracy for Dewey was more than opposition to authoritarian rule. Dewey was no anarchist. The basis for authority in a democracy is experience. Dewey suggests that in a true democracy, "it is not the will or desire of any one person (a philosopher-king or scientist) which establishes order but the moving spirit of the whole group." Creating and sustaining such a "moving spirit" is in Dewey's mind what education and philosophy should be about.

The poet Allen Ginsberg urged readers to "be not too quick to understand" his friend, the novelist Jack Kerouac. A similar caution ought to be adopted with John Dewey. A superficial reading of Article I of "Creed" might suggest that Dewey is trying to "adjust" the student to society. An equally superficial reading of Article V might suggest that Dewey is trying to overthrow the existing society. Dewey, unless he contradicts himself cannot be doing both. The excerpts from *Democracy and Education* and *Experience and Education* are meant to be the first steps in helping the reader to discover what Dewey meant and to formulate for herself or himself what education is.

Notes

1. Robert B. Westbrook, *John Dewey and American Democracy* (Ithaca: Cornell University Press, 1991), p. 203.
2. Ibid., p. vi.
3. Ibid., p. 536.
4. This quotation as well as much of the information in this brief introduction were derived from John Novak's review (distributed by the John Dewey Society) of John Westbrook's *John Dewey and American Democracy.*

"My Pedagogic Creed" (1897)

Article I—*What Education Is*

I believe that

—all education proceeds by the participation of the individual in the social consciousness of the race. This process begins unconsciously almost at birth,

From *John Dewey: The Early Works 1895–1898, vol. 5,* Jo Ann Boydston (Ed.) (Carbondale, IL: Southern Illinois University Press, © 1972), pp. 84–95. Reprinted by permission of Southern Illinois University Press.

and is continually shaping the individual's powers, saturating his consciousness, forming his habits, training his ideas, and arousing his feelings and emotions. Through this unconscious education the individual gradually comes to share in the intellectual and moral resources which humanity has succeeded in getting together. He becomes an inheritor of the funded capital of civilization. The most formal and technical education in the world cannot safely depart from this general process. It can only organize it or differentiate it in some particular direction.

—the only true education comes through the stimulation of the child's powers by the demands of the social situations in which he finds himself. Through these demands he is stimulated to act as a member of a unity, to emerge from his original narrowness of action and feeling, and to conceive of himself from the standpoint of the welfare of the group to which he belongs. Through the responses which others make to his own activities he comes to know what these mean in social terms. The value which they have is reflected back into them. For instance, through the response which is made to the child's instinctive babblings the child comes to know what those babblings mean; they are transformed into articulate language, and thus the child is introduced into the consolidated wealth of ideas and emotions which are now summed up in language.

—this educational process has two sides—one psychological and one sociological—and that neither can be subordinated to the other, or neglected, without evil results following. Of these two sides, the psychological is the basis. The child's own instincts and powers furnish the material and give the starting-point for all education. Save as the efforts of the educator connect with some activity which the child is carrying on of his own initiative independent of the educator, education becomes reduced to a pressure from without. It may, indeed, give certain external results, but cannot truly be called educative. Without insight into the psychological structure and activities of the individual, the educative process will, therefore, be haphazard and arbitrary. If it chances to coincide with the child's activity it will get a leverage; if it does not, it will result in friction, or disintegration, or arrest of the child nature.

—knowledge of social conditions, of the present state of civilization, is necessary in order properly to interpret the child's powers. The child has his own instincts and tendencies, but we do not know what these mean until we can translate them into their social equivalents. We must be able to carry them back into a social past and see them as the inheritance of previous race activities. We must also be able to project them into the future to see what their outcome and end will be. In the illustration just used, it is the ability to see in the child's babblings the promise and potency of a future social intercourse and conversation which enables one to deal in the proper way with that instinct.

—the psychological and social sides are organically related, and that education cannot be regarded as a compromise between the two, or a superimposition of one upon the other. We are told that the psychological definition of education is barren and formal—that it gives us only the idea of a development of all the mental powers without giving us any idea of the use to which these powers are put. On the other hand, it is urged that the social definition of education, as getting adjusted to civilization, makes of it a forced and external process, and results in subordinating the freedom of the individual to a preconceived social and political status.

—each of these objections is true when urged against one side isolated from the other. In order to know what a power really is we must know what its end, use, or function is, and this we cannot know save as we conceive of the individual as active in social relationships. But, on the other hand, the only possible adjustment which we can give to the child under existing conditions is that which arises through putting him in complete possession of all his powers. With the advent of democracy and modern industrial conditions, it is impossible to foretell definitely just what civilization will be twenty years from now. Hence it is impossible to prepare the child for any precise set of conditions. To prepare him for the future life means to give him command of himself; it means so to train him that he will have the full and ready use of all his capacities; that his eye and ear and hand may be tools ready to command, that his judgment may be capable of grasping the conditions under which it has to work, and the executive forces be trained to act economically and efficiently. It is impossible to reach this sort of adjustment save as constant regard is had to the individual's own powers, tastes, and interests—that is, as education is continually converted into psychological terms.

In sum, I believe that the individual who is to be educated is a social individual, and that society is an organic union of individuals. If we eliminate the social factor from the child we are left only with an abstraction; if we eliminate the individual factor from society, we are left only with an inert and lifeless mass. Education, therefore, must begin with a psychological insight into the child's capacities, interests, and habits. It must be controlled at every point by reference to these same considerations. These powers, interests, and habits must be continually interpreted—we must know what they mean. They must be translated into terms of their social equivalents—into terms of what they are capable of in the way of social service.

Article II—*What The School Is*

I believe that

—the school is primarily a social institution. Education being a social process, the school is simply that form of community life in which all those agencies are concentrated that will be most effective in bringing the child to share in the inherited resources of the race, and to use his own powers for social ends.

—education, therefore, is a process of living and not a preparation for future living.

—the school must represent present life—life as real and vital to the child as that which he carries on in the home, in the neighborhood, or on the playground.

—that education which does not occur through forms of life, forms that are worth living for their own sake, is always a poor substitute for the genuine reality, and tends to cramp and to deaden.

—the school, as an institution, should simplify existing social life; should reduce it, as it were, to an embryonic form. Existing life is so complex that the child cannot be brought into contact with it without either confusion or distraction; he is either overwhelmed by the multiplicity of activities which are going on, so that he loses his own power of orderly reaction, or he is so stimulated by these various activities that his powers are prematurely called into play and he becomes either unduly specialized or else disintegrated.

—as such simplified social life, the school life should grow gradually out of the home life; that it should take up and continue the activities with which the child is already familiar in the home.

—it should exhibit these activities to the child, and reproduce them in such ways that the child will gradually learn the meaning of them, and be capable of playing his own part in relation to them.

—this is a psychological necessity, because it is the only way of securing continuity in the child's growth, the only way of giving a background of past experience to the new ideas given in school.

—it is also a social necessity because the home is the form of social life in which the child has been nurtured and in connection with which he has had his moral training. It is the business of the school to deepen and extend his sense of the values bound up in his home life.

—much of present education fails because it neglects this fundamental principle of the school as a form of community life. It conceives the school as a place where certain information is to be given, where certain lessons are to be learned, or where certain habits are to be formed. The value of these is conceived as lying largely in the remote future; the child must do these things for the sake of something else he is to do; they are mere preparations. As a result they do not become a part of the life experience of the child and so are not truly educative.

—the moral education centers upon this conception of the school as a mode of social life, that the best and deepest moral training is precisely that which one gets through having to enter into proper relations with others in a unity of work and thought. The present educational systems, so far as they destroy or neglect this unity, render it difficult or impossible to get any genuine, regular moral training.

—the child should be stimulated and controlled in his work through the life of the community.

—under existing conditions far too much of the stimulus and control proceeds from the teacher, because of neglect of the idea of the school as a form of social life.

—the teacher's place and work in the school is to be interpreted from this same basis. The teacher is not in the school to impose certain ideas or to form certain habits in the child, but is there as a member of the community to select the influences which shall affect the child and to assist him in properly responding to these influences.

—the discipline of the school should proceed from the life of the school as a whole and not directly from the teacher.

—the teacher's business is simply to determine, on the basis of larger experience and riper wisdom, how the discipline of life shall come to the child.

—all questions of the grading of the child and his promotion should be determined by reference to the same standard. Examinations are of use only so far as they test the child's fitness for social life and reveal the place in which he can be of the most service and where he can receive the most help.

Article III—*The Subject-Matter of Education*

I believe that

—the social life of the child is the basis of concentration, or correlation, in all his training or growth. The social life gives the unconscious unity and the background of all his efforts and of all his attainments.

—the subject-matter of the school curriculum should mark a gradual differentiation out of the primitive unconscious unity of social life.

—we violate the child's nature and render difficult the best ethical results by introducing the child too abruptly to a number of special studies, of reading, writing, geography, etc., out of relation to this social life.

—the true center of correlation on the school subjects is not science, nor literature, nor history, nor geography, but the child's own social activities.

—education cannot be unified in the study of science, or so-called nature study, because apart from human activity, nature itself is not a unity; nature in itself is a number of diverse objects in space and time, and to attempt to make it the center of work by itself is to introduce a principle of radiation rather than one of concentration.

—literature is the reflex expression and interpretation of social experience; that hence it must follow upon and not precede such experience. It, therefore, cannot be made the basis, although it may be made the summary of unification.

—once more that history is of educative value in so far as it presents phases of social life and growth. It must be controlled by reference to social life. When taken simply as history it is thrown into the distant past and becomes dead and inert. Taken as the record of man's social life and progress it becomes full of meaning. I believe, however, that it cannot be so taken excepting as the child is also introduced directly into social life.

—the primary basis of education is in the child's powers at work along the same general constructive lines as those which have brought civilization into being.

—the only way to make the child conscious of his social heritage is to enable him to perform those fundamental types of activity which make civilization what it is.

—in the so-called expressive or constructive activities as the center of correlation.

—this gives the standard for the place of cooking, sewing, manual training, etc., in the school.

—they are not special studies which are to be introduced over and above a lot of others in the way of relaxation or relief, or as additional accomplishments. I believe rather that they represent, as types, fundamental forms of social activity; and that it is possible and desirable that the child's introduction into the more formal subjects of the curriculum be through the medium of these activities.

—the study of science is educational in so far as it brings out the materials and processes which make social life what it is.

—one of the greatest difficulties in the present teaching of science is that the material is presented in purely objective form, or is treated as a new peculiar kind of experience which the child can add to that which he has already had. In reality, science is of value because it gives the ability to interpret and control the experience already had. It should be introduced, not as so much new subject-matter, but as showing the factors already involved in previous experience and as furnishing tools by which that experience can be more easily and effectively regulated.

—at present we lose much of the value of literature and language studies because of our elimination of the social element. Language is almost always treated in the books of pedagogy simply as the expression of thought. It is true that language is a logical instrument, but it is fundamentally and primarily a social instrument. Language is the device for communication; it is the tool through which one individual comes to share the ideas and feelings of others. When treated simply as a way of getting individual information, or as a means of showing off what one has learned, it loses its social motive and end.

—there is, therefore, no succession of studies in the ideal school curriculum. If education is life, all life has, from the outset, a scientific aspect, an aspect of art and culture, and an aspect of communication. It cannot, therefore, be true that the proper studies for one grade are mere reading and writing, and that at a later grade, reading, or literature, or science, may be introduced. The progress is not in the succession of studies, but in the development of new attitudes towards, and new interests in, experience.

—education must be conceived as a continuing reconstruction of experience; that the process and the goal of education are one and the same thing.

—to set up any end outside of education, as furnishing its goal and standard, is to deprive the educational process of much of its meaning, and tends to make us rely upon false and external stimuli in dealing with the child.

Article IV—*The Nature of Method*

I believe that

—the question of method is ultimately reducible to the question of the order of development of the child's powers and interests. The law for presenting and treating material is the law implicit within the child's own nature. Because this is so I believe the following statements are of supreme importance as determining the spirit in which education is carried on:

—the active side precedes the passive in the development of the child-nature; that expression comes before conscious impression; that the muscular development precedes the sensory; that movements come before conscious sensations; I believe that consciousness is essentially motor or impulsive; that conscious states tend to project themselves in action.

—the neglect of this principle is the cause of a large part of the waste of time and strength in school work. The child is thrown into a passive, receptive, or absorbing attitude. The conditions are such that he is not permitted to follow the law of his nature; the result is friction and waste.

—ideas (intellectual and rational processes) also result from action and devolve for the sake of the better control of action. What we term reason is primarily the law of orderly or effective action. To attempt to develop the reasoning powers, the powers of judgment, without reference to the selection and arrangement of means in action, is the fundamental fallacy in our present methods of dealing with this matter. As a result we present the child with arbitrary symbols. Symbols are a necessity in mental development, but they have their place as tools for economizing effort; presented by themselves they are a mass of meaningless and arbitrary ideas imposed from without.

—the image is the great instrument of instruction. What a child gets out of any subject presented to him is simply the images which he himself forms with regard to it.

—if nine-tenths of the energy at present directed towards making the child learn certain things were spent in seeing to it that the child was forming proper images, the work of instruction would be indefinitely facilitated.

—much of the time and attention now given to the preparation and presentation of lessons might be more wisely and profitably expended in training the child's power of imagery and in seeing to it that he was continually forming definite, vivid, and growing images of the various subjects with which he comes in contact in his experience.

—interests are the signs and symptoms of growing power. I believe that they represent dawning capacities. Accordingly the constant and careful observation of interests is of the utmost importance for the educator.

—these interests are to be observed as showing the state of development which the child has reached.

—they prophesy the stage upon which he is about to enter.

—only through the continual and sympathetic observation of childhood's interests can the adult enter into the child's life and see what it is ready for, and upon what material it could work most readily and fruitfully.

—these interests are neither to be humored nor repressed. To repress interest is to substitute the adult for the child, and so to weaken intellectual curiosity and alertness, to suppress initiative, and to deaden interest. To humor the interests is to substitute the transient for the permanent. The interest is always the sign of some power below; the important thing is to discover this power. To humor the interest is to fail to penetrate below the surface, and its sure result is to substitute caprice and whim for genuine interest.

—the emotions are the reflex of actions.

—to endeavor to stimulate or arouse the emotions apart from their correspond- ing activities is to introduce an unhealthy and morbid state of mind.

—if we can only secure right habits of action and thought, with reference to the good, the true, and the beautiful, the emotions will for the most part take care of themselves.

—next to deadness and dullness, formalism and routine, our education is threat- ened with no greater evil than sentimentalism.

—this sentimentalism is the necessary result of the attempt to divorce feeling from action.

Article V—*The School and Social Progress*

I believe that

—education is the fundamental method of social progress and reform.

—all reforms which rest simply upon the enactment of law, or the threatening of certain penalties, or upon changes in mechanical or outward arrangements, are transitory and futile.

—education is a regulation of the process of coming to share in the social con- sciousness; and that the adjustment of individual activity on the basis of this social consciousness is the only sure method of social reconstruction.

—this conception has due regard for both the individualistic and socialistic ideals. It is duly individual because it recognizes the formation of a certain char- acter as the only genuine basis of right living. It is socialistic because it recog- nizes that this right character is not to be formed by merely individual precept, example, or exhortation, but rather by the influence of a certain form of institu- tional or community life upon the individual, and that the social organism through the school, as its organ, may determine ethical results.

—in the ideal school we have the reconciliation of the individualistic and the institutional ideals.

—the community's duty to education is, therefore, its paramount moral duty. By law and punishment, by social agitation and discussion, society can regulate and form itself in a more or less haphazard and chance way. But through edu- cation society can formulate its own purposes, can organize its own means and resources, and thus shape itself with definiteness and economy in the direction in which it wishes to move.

—when society once recognizes the possibilities in this direction, and the obligations which these possibilities impose, it is impossible to conceive of the resources of time, attention, and money which will be put at the disposal of the educator.

—it is the business of every one interested in education to insist upon the school as the primary and most effective interest of social progress and reform in order that society may be awakened to realize what the school stands for, and aroused to the necessity of endowing the educator with sufficient equipment properly to perform his task.

—education thus conceived marks the most perfect and intimate union of science and art conceivable in human experience.

—the art of thus giving shape to human powers and adapting them to social service is the supreme art; one calling into its service the best of artists; that no insight, sympathy, tact, executive power, is too great for such service.

—with the growth of psychological service, giving added insight into individual structure and laws of growth; and with growth of social science, adding to our knowledge of the right organization of individuals, all scientific resources can be utilized for the purposes of education.

—when science and art thus join hands the most commanding motive for human action will be reached, the most genuine springs of human conduct aroused, and the best service that human nature is capable of guaranteed.

—the teacher is engaged, not simply in the training of individuals, but in the formation of the proper social life.

—every teacher should realize the dignity of his calling; that he is a social servant set apart for the maintenance of proper social order and the securing of the right social growth.

—in this way the teacher always is the prophet of the true God and the usherer in of the true kingdom of God.

From *Democracy and Education* (1916)

For the most part, save incidentally, we have hitherto been concerned with education as it may exist in any social group. We have now to make explicit the differences in the spirit, material, and method of education as it operates in different types of community life. To say that education is a social function, securing direction and development in the immature through their participation in the life of the group to which they belong, is to say in effect that education will vary with the quality of life which prevails in a group. Particularly is it true that a society which not only changes but which has the ideal of such

From *Democracy and Education* by John Dewey (NY: Macmillan Publishing, 1916).

change as will improve it, will have different standards and methods of education from one which aims simply at the perpetuation of its own customs. To make the general ideas set forth applicable to our own educational practice, it is, therefore, necessary to come to closer quarters with the nature of present social life.

1. The Implications of Human Association. Society is one word, but many things. Men associate together in all kinds of ways and for all kinds of purposes. One man is concerned in a multitude of diverse groups, in which his associates may be quite different. It often seems as if they had nothing in common except that they are modes of associated life. Within every larger social organization there are numerous minor groups: not only political subdivisions, but industrial, scientific, religious associations. There are political parties with differing aims, social sets, cliques, gangs, corporations, partnerships, groups bound closely together by ties of blood, and so on in endless variety. In many modern states and in some ancient, there is great diversity of populations, of varying languages, religions, moral codes, and traditions. From this standpoint, many a minor political unit, one of our large cities, for example, is a congeries of loosely associated societies, rather than an inclusive and permeating community of action and thought.

The terms of society, community, are thus ambiguous. They have both a eulogistic or normative sense, and a descriptive sense; a meaning *de jure* and a meaning *de facto*. In social philosophy, the former connotation is almost always uppermost. Society is conceived as one by its very nature. The qualities which accompany this unity, praiseworthy community of purpose and welfare, loyalty to public ends, mutuality of sympathy, are emphasized. But when we look at the facts which the term *denotes* instead of confining our attention to its intrinsic *connotation,* we find not unity, but a plurality of societies, good and bad. Men banded together in a criminal conspiracy, business aggregations that prey upon the public while serving it, political machines held together by the interest of plunder, are included. If it is said that such organizations are not societies because they do not meet the ideal requirements of the notion of society, the answer, in part, is that the conception of society is then made so "ideal" as to be of no use, having no reference to facts; and in part, that each of these organizations, no matter how opposed to the interests of other groups, has some thing of the praiseworthy qualities of "Society" which hold it together. There is honor among thieves, and a band of robbers has a common interest as respects its members. Gangs are marked by fraternal feeling, and narrow cliques by intense loyalty to their own codes. Family life may be marked by exclusiveness, suspicion, and jealousy as to those without, and yet be a model of amity and mutual aid within. Any education given by a group tends to socialize its members, but the quality and value of the socialization depends upon the habits and aims of the group.

Hence, once more, the need of a measure for the worth of any given mode of social life. In seeking this measure, we have to avoid two extremes. We can not set up, out of our heads, something we regard as an ideal society. We must base our conception upon societies which actually exist, in order to have any assurance that our ideal is a practicable one. But, as we have just seen, the ideal cannot simply repeat the traits which are actually found. The problem is to extract the desirable traits of forms of community life which actually exist, and employ them to criticize undesirable features and suggest improvement. Now in any social group whatever, even in a gang of thieves, we find some interest held in common, and we find a certain amount of interaction and coöperative intercourse with other groups. From these two traits we derive our standard. How numerous and varied are the interests which are consciously shared? How full and free is the interplay with other forms of association? If we apply these considerations to, say, a criminal band, we find that the ties which consciously hold the members together are few in number, reducible almost to a common interest in plunder; and that they are of such a nature as to isolate the group from other groups with respect to give and take of the values of life. Hence, the education such a society gives is partial and distorted. If we take, on the other hand, the kind of family life which illustrates the standard, we find that there are material, intellectual, aesthetic interests in which all participate and that the progress of one member has worth for the experience of other members—it is readily communicable—and that the family is not an isolated whole, but enters intimately into relationships with business groups, with schools, with all the agencies of culture, as well as with other similar groups, and that it plays a due part in the political organization and in return receives support from it. In short, there are many interests consciously communicated and shared; and there are varied and free points of contact with other modes of association.

I. Let us apply the first element in this criterion to a despotically governed state. It is not true there is no common interest in such an organization between governed and governors. The authorities in command must make some appeal to the native activities of the subjects, must call some of their powers into play. Talleyrand said that a government could do everything with bayonets except sit on them. This cynical declaration is at least a recognition that the bond of union is not merely one of coercive force. It may be said, however, that the activities appealed to are themselves unworthy and degrading—that such a government calls into functioning activity simply capacity for fear. In a way, this statement is true. But it overlooks the fact that fear need not be an undesirable factor in experience. Caution, circumspection, prudence, desire to foresee future events so as to avert what is harmful, these desirable traits are as much a product of calling the impulse of fear into play as is cowardice and abject submission. The real difficulty is that the appeal to fear is *isolated*. In evoking dread and hope of specific tangible reward—say comfort and ease—many other capacities are left untouched. Or rather, they are affected, but in such a way as to pervert them. Instead of operating on their own account they are reduced to mere servants of attaining pleasure and avoiding pain.

This is equivalent to saying that there is no extensive number of common interests; there is no free play back and forth among the members of the social group. Stimulation and response are exceedingly one-sided. In order to have a larger number of values in common, all the members of the group must have an equable opportunity to receive and to take from others. There must be a large variety of shared undertakings and experiences. Otherwise, the influences

which educate some into masters, educate others into slaves. And the experience of each party loses in meaning, when the free interchange of varying
modes of life-experience is arrested. A separation into a privileged and a subject-
class prevents social endosmosis. The evils thereby affecting the superior class
are less material and less perceptible, but equally real. Their culture tends to be
sterile, to be turned back to feed on itself; their art becomes a showy display and
artificial; their wealth luxurious; their knowledge overspecialized; their manners
fastidious rather than humane.

Lack of the free and equitable intercourse which springs from a variety of
shared interests makes intellectual stimulation unbalanced. Diversity of stimulation means novelty, and novelty means challenge to thought. The more activity is restricted to a few definite lines—as it is when there are rigid class lines
preventing adequate interplay of experiences—the more action tends to become
routine on the part of the class at a disadvantage, and capricious, aimless, and
explosive on the part of the class having the materially fortunate position. Plato
defined a slave as one who accepts from another the purposes which control his
conduct. This condition obtains even where there is no slavery in the legal sense.
It is found wherever men are engaged in activity which is socially serviceable,
but whose service they do not understand and have no personal interest in.
Much is said about scientific management of work. It is a narrow view which
restricts the science which secures efficiency of operation to movements of the
muscles. The chief opportunity for science is the discovery of the relations of a
man to his work—including his relations to others who take part—which will
enlist his intelligent interest in what he is doing. Efficiency in production often
demands division of labor. But it is reduced to a mechanical routine unless
workers see the technical, intellectual, and social relationships involved in what
they do, and engage in their work because of the motivation furnished by such
perceptions. The tendency to reduce such things as efficiency of activity and scientific management to purely technical externals is evidence of the one-sided
stimulation of thought given to those in control of industry—those who supply
its aims. Because of their lack of all-round and well-balanced social interest,
there is not sufficient stimulus for attention to the human factors and relationships in industry. Intelligence is narrowed to the factors concerned with technical production and marketing of goods. No doubt, a very acute and intense
intelligence in these narrow lines can be developed, but the failure to take into
account the significant social factors means none the less an absence of mind,
and a corresponding distortion of emotional life.

II. This illustration (whose point is to be extended to all associations lacking
reciprocity of interest) brings us to our second point. The isolation and exclusiveness of a gang or clique brings its antisocial spirit into relief. But this same
spirit is found wherever one group has interests "of its own" which shut it out
from full interaction with other groups, so that its prevailing purpose is the
protection of what it has got, instead of reorganization and progress through
wider relationships. It marks nations in their isolation from one another; families
which seclude their domestic concerns as if they had no connection with a larger

life; schools when separated from the interest of home and community; the divisions of rich and poor; learned and unlearned. The essential point is that isolation makes for rigidity and formal institutionalizing of life, for static and selfish ideals within the group. That savage tribes regard aliens and enemies as synonymous is not accidental. It springs from the fact that they have identified their experience with rigid adherence to their past customs. On such a basis it is wholly logical to fear intercourse with others, for such contact might dissolve custom. It would certainly occasion reconstruction. It is a commonplace that an alert and expanding mental life depends upon an enlarging range of contact with the physical environment. But the principle applies even more significantly to the field where we are apt to ignore it—the sphere of social contacts.

Every expansive era in the history of mankind has coincided with the operation of factors which have tended to eliminate distance between peoples and classes previously hemmed off from one another. Even the alleged benefits of war, so far as more than alleged, spring from the fact that conflict of peoples at least enforces intercourse between them and thus accidentally enables them to learn from one another, and thereby to expand their horizons. Travel, economic and commercial tendencies, have at present gone far to break down external barriers; to bring peoples and classes into closer and more perceptible connection with one another. It remains for the most part to secure the intellectual and emotional significance of this physical annihilation of space.

2. The Democratic Ideal. The two elements in our criterion both point to democracy. The first signifies not only more numerous and more varied points of shared common interest, but greater reliance upon the recognition of mutual interests as a factor in social control. The second means not only freer interaction between social groups (once isolated so far as intention could keep up a separation) but change in social habit—its continuous readjustment through meeting the new situations produced by varied intercourse. And these two traits are precisely what characterize the democratically constituted society.

Upon the educational side, we note first that the realization of a form of social life in which interests are mutually interpenetrating, and where progress, or readjustment, is an important consideration, makes a democratic community more interested than other communities have cause to be in deliberate and systematic education. The devotion of democracy to education is a familiar fact. The superficial explanation is that a government resting upon popular suffrage cannot be successful unless those who elect and who obey their governors are educated. Since a democratic society repudiates the principle of external authority, it must find a substitute in voluntary disposition and interest; these can be created only by education. But there is a deeper explanation. A democracy is more than a form of government; it is primarily a mode of associated living, of conjoint communicated experience. The extension in space of the number of individuals who participate in an interest so that each has to refer his own action to that of others, and to consider the action of others to give point and direction to his own, is equivalent to the breaking down of those barriers of class, race, and national territory which kept men from perceiving the full import of their activity. These more numerous and more varied points of contact denote a greater diversity of stimuli to which an individual has to respond; they consequently put a premium on variation in his action. They secure a liberation of powers which remain suppressed as long as the incitations to action are partial, as they must be in a group which in its exclusiveness shuts out many interests.

The widening of the area of shared concerns, and the liberation of a greater diversity of personal capacities which characterize a democracy, are not of course the product of deliberation and conscious effort. On the contrary, they were caused by the development of modes of manufacture and commerce, travel, migration, and intercommunication which flowed from the command of science over natural energy. But after greater individualization on one hand and a broader community of interest on the other have come into existence it is a matter of deliberate effort to sustain and extend them. Obviously a society to which stratification into separate classes would be fatal, must see to it that intellectual opportunities are accessible to all on equable anal easy terms. A society marked off into classes need be specially attentive only to the education of its ruling elements. A society which is mobile, which is full of channels for the distribution of a change occurring anywhere, must see to it that its members are educated to personal initiative and adaptability. Otherwise they will be overwhelmed by the changes in which they are caught and whose significance or connections they do not perceive. The result will be a confusion in which a few will appropriate to themselves the results of the blind and externally directed activities of others.

From *Experience and Education* (1938)

If there is any truth in what has been said about the need of forming a theory of experience in order that education may be intelligently conducted upon the basis of experience, it is clear that the next thing in order in this discussion is to present the principles that are most significant in framing this theory. I shall not, therefore, apologize for engaging in a certain amount of philosophical analysis, which otherwise might be out of place. I may, however, reassure you to some degree by saying that this analysis is not an end in itself but is engaged in for the sake of obtaining criteria to be applied later in discussion of a number of concrete and, to most persons, more interesting issues.

I have already mentioned what I called the category of continuity, or the experiential continuum. This principle is involved, as I pointed out, in every attempt to discriminate between experiences that are worth while educationally and those that are not. It may seem superfluous to argue that this discrimination is necessary not only in criticizing the traditional type of education but

From *Experience and Education* by John Dewey (IN: Kappa Delta Pi, © 1938), pp. 33–50. Reprinted by permission of Kappa Delta Pi, an International Honor Society in Education.

also in initiating and conducting a different type. Nevertheless, it is advisable to pursue for a little while the idea that it is necessary. One may safely assume, I suppose, that one thing which has recommended the progressive movement is that it seems more in accord with the democratic ideal to which our people is committed than do the procedures of the traditional school, since the latter have so much of the autocratic about them. Another thing which has contributed to its favorable reception is that its methods are humane in comparison with the harshness so often attending the policies of the traditional school.

The question I would raise concerns why we prefer democratic and humane arrangements to those which are autocratic and harsh. And by "why," I mean the *reason* for preferring them, not just the *causes* which lead us to the preference. One *cause* may be that we have been taught not only in the schools but by the press, the pulpit, the platform, and our laws and law-making bodies that democracy is the best of all social institutions. We may have so assimilated this idea from our surroundings that it has become an habitual part of our mental and moral make-up. But similar causes have led other persons in different surroundings to widely varying conclusions—to prefer fascism, for example. The cause for our preference is not the same thing as the reason why we *should* prefer it.

It is not my purpose here to go in detail into the reason. But I would ask a single question: Can we find any reason that does not ultimately come down to the belief that democratic social arrangements promote a better quality of human experience, one which is more widely accessible and enjoyed, than do non-democratic and anti-democratic forms of social life? Does not the principle of regard for individual freedom and for decency and kindliness of human relations come back in the end to the conviction that these things are tributary to a higher quality of experience on the part of a greater number than are methods of repression and coercion or force? Is it not the reason for our preference that we believe that mutual consultation and convictions reached through persuasion make possible a better quality of experience than can otherwise be provided on any wide scale?

If the answer to these questions is in the affirmative (and personally I do not see how we can justify our preference for democracy and humanity on any other ground), the ultimate reason for hospitality to progressive education, because of its reliance upon and use of humane methods and its kinship to democracy, goes back to the fact that discrimination is made between the inherent values of different experiences. So I come back to the principle of continuity of experience as a criterion of discrimination.

At bottom, this principle rests upon the fact of habit, when *habit* is interpreted biologically. The basic characteristic of habit is that every experience enacted and undergone modifies the one who acts and undergoes, while this modification affects, whether we wish it or not, the quality of subsequent experiences. For it is a somewhat different person who enters into them. The principle of habit so understood obviously goes deeper than the ordinary conception of *a* habit as a more or less fixed way of doing things, although it includes the latter as one of its special cases. It covers the formation of attitudes, attitudes that are emotional and intellectual; it covers our basic sensitivities and ways of meeting and responding to all the conditions which we meet in living. From this point of view, the principle of continuity of experience means that every experience both takes up something from those which have gone before and modifies in some way the quality of those which come after. As the poet states it,

> . . . all experience is an arch wherethro'
> Gleams that untraveled world, whose margin fades
> For ever and for ever when I move.

So far, however, we have no ground for discrimination among experiences. For the principle is of universal application. There is *some* kind of continuity in every case. It is when we note the different forms in which continuity of experience operates that we get the basis of discriminating among experiences. I may illustrate what is meant by an objection which has been brought against an idea which I once put forth—namely, that the educative process can be identified with growth when that is understood in terms of the active participle, *growing.*

Growth, or growing as developing, not only physically but intellectually and morally, is one exemplification of the principle of continuity. The objection made is that growth might take many different directions: a man, for example, who starts out on a career of burglary may grow in that direction, and by practice may grow into a highly expert burglar. Hence it is argued that "growth" is not enough; we must also specify the direction in which growth takes place, the end towards which it tends. Before, however, we decide that the objection is conclusive we must analyze the case a little further.

That a man may grow in efficiency as a burglar, as a gangster, or as a corrupt politician, cannot be doubted. But from the standpoint of growth as education and education as growth the question is whether growth in this direction promotes or retards growth in general. Does this form of growth create conditions for further growth, or does it set up conditions that shut off the person who has grown in this particular direction from the occasions, stimuli, and opportunities for continuing growth in new directions? What is the effect of growth in a special direction upon the attitudes and habits which alone open up avenues for development in other lines? I shall leave you to answer these questions, saying simply that when and *only* when development in a particular line conduces to continuing growth does it answer to the criterion of education as growing. For the conception is one that must find universal and not specialized limited application.

I return now to the question of continuity as a criterion by which to discriminate between experiences which are educative and those which are miseducative. As we have seen, there is some kind of continuity in any case since every experience affects for better or worse the attitudes which help decide the quality of further experiences, by setting up certain preference and aversion, and making it easier or harder to act for this or that end. Moreover, every experience influences in some degree the objective conditions under which further experiences are had. For example, a child who learns to speak has a new facility and new desire. But he has also widened the external conditions of subsequent learning. When he learns to read, he similarly opens up a new environment. If a person decides to become a teacher, lawyer, physician, or stockbroker, when he executes his intention he thereby necessarily determines to some extent the environment in which he will act in the future. He has rendered himself more sensitive and responsive to certain conditions, and relatively immune to those things about him that would have been stimuli if he had made another choice.

But, while the principle of continuity applies in some way in every case, the quality of the present experience influences the *way* in which the principle applies. We speak of spoiling a child and of the spoilt child. The effect of overindulging a child is a continuing one. It sets up an attitude which operates as an automatic demand that persons and objects cater to his desires and caprices in the future. It makes him seek the kind of situation that will enable him to do what he feels like doing at the time. It renders him averse to and comparatively incompetent in situations which require effort and perseverance in overcoming obstacles. There is no paradox in the fact that the principle of the continuity of experience may operate so as to leave a person arrested on a low plane of development, in a way which limits later capacity for growth.

On the other hand, if an experience arouses curiosity, strengthens initiative, and sets up desires and purposes that are sufficiently intense to carry a person over dead places in the future, continuity works in a very different way. Every experience is a moving force. Its value can be judged only on the ground of what it moves toward and into. The greater maturity of experience which should belong to the adult as educator puts him in a position to evaluate each experience of the young in a way in which the one having the less mature experience cannot do. It is then the business of the educator to see in what direction an experience is heading. There is no point in his being more mature if, instead of using his greater insight to help organize the conditions of the experience of the immature, he throws away his insight. Failure to take the moving force of an experience into account so as to judge and direct it on the ground of what it is moving into means disloyalty to the principle of experience itself. The disloyalty operates in two directions. The educator is false to the understanding that he should have obtained from his own past experience. He is also unfaithful to the fact that all human experience is ultimately social: that it involves contact and communication. The mature person, to put it in moral terms, has no right to withhold from the young on given occasions whatever capacity for sympathetic understanding his own experience has given him.

No sooner, however, are such things said than there is a tendency to react to the other extreme and take what has been said as a plea for some sort of disguised imposition from outside. It is worth while, accordingly, to say something about the way in which the adult can exercise the wisdom his own wider experience gives him without imposing a merely external control. On one side, it is his business to be on the alert to see what attitudes and habitual tendencies are being created. In this direction he must, if he is an educator, be able to judge what attitudes are actually conducive to continued growth and what are detrimental. He must, in addition, have that sympathetic understanding of individuals as individuals which gives him an idea of what is actually going on in the minds of those who are learning. It is, among other things, the need for these abilities on the part of the parent and teacher which makes a system of education based upon living experience a more difficult affair to conduct successfully than it is to follow the patterns of traditional education.

But there is another aspect of the matter. Experience does not go on simply inside a person. It does go on there, for it influences the formation of attitudes of desire and purpose. But this is not the whole of the story. Every genuine experience has an active side which changes in some degree the objective conditions under which experiences are had. The difference between civilization and savagery, to take an example on a large scale, is found in the degree in which previous experiences have changed the objective conditions under which subsequent experiences take place. The existence of roads, of means of rapid movement and transportation, tools, implements, furniture, electric light and power, are illustrations. Destroy the external conditions of present civilized experience, and for a time our experience would relapse into that of barbaric peoples.

In a word, we live from birth to death in a world of persons and things which in large measure is what it is because of what has been done and transmitted from previous human activities. When this fact is ignored, experience is treated as if it were something which goes on exclusively inside an individual's body and mind. It ought not to be necessary to say that experience does not occur in a vacuum. There are sources outside an individual which give rise to experience. It is constantly fed from these springs. No one would question that a child in a slum tenement has a different experience from that of a child in a cultured home; that the country lad has a different kind of experience from the city boy, or a boy on the seashore one different from the lad who is brought up on inland prairies. Ordinarily we take such facts for granted as too commonplace to record. But when their educational import is recognized, they indicate the second way in which the educator can direct the experience of the young without engaging in imposition. A primary responsibility of educators is that they not only be aware of the general principle of the shaping of actual experience by environing conditions, but that they also recognize in the concrete what surroundings are conducive to having experiences that lead to growth. Above all, they should know how to utilize the surroundings, physical and social, that exist so as to extract from them all that they have to contribute to building up experiences that are worth while.

Traditional education did not have to face this problem; it could systematically dodge this responsibility. The school environment of desks, blackboards, a small school yard, was supposed to suffice. There was no demand that the teacher should become intimately acquainted with the conditions of the local community, physical, historical, economic, occupational, etc., in order to utilize them as educational resources. A system of education based upon the necessary connection of education with experience must, on the contrary, if faithful to its principle, take these things constantly into account. This tax upon the educator is another reason why progressive education is more difficult to carry on than was ever the traditional system.

It is possible to frame schemes of education that pretty systematically subordinate objective conditions to those which reside in the individuals being educated. This happens whenever the place and function of the teacher, of books, of apparatus and equipment, of everything which represents the products of the more mature experience of elders, is systematically subordinated to the immediate inclinations and feelings of the young. Every theory which assumes that importance can be attached to these objective factors only at the expense of imposing external control and of limiting the freedom of individuals rests finally upon the notion that experience is truly experience only when objective conditions are subordinated to what goes on within the individuals having the experience.

I do not mean that it is supposed that objective conditions can be shut out. It is recognized that they must enter in: so much concession is made to the inescapable fact that we live in a world of things and persons. But I think that observation of what goes on in some families and some schools would disclose that some parents and some teachers are acting upon the idea of *subordinating* objective conditions to internal ones. In that case, it is assumed not only that the latter are primary, which in one sense they are, but that just as they temporarily exist they fix the whole educational process.

Let me illustrate from the case of an infant. The needs of a baby for food, rest, and activity are certainly primary and decisive in one respect. Nourishment must be provided; provision must be made for comfortable sleep, and so on. But these facts do not mean that a parent shall feed the baby at any time when the baby is cross or irritable, that there shall not be a program of regular hours of feeding and sleeping, etc. The wise mother takes account of the needs of the infant but not in a way which dispenses with her own responsibility for regulating the objective conditions under which the needs are satisfied. And if she is a wise mother in this respect, she draws upon past experiences of experts as well as her own for the light that these shed upon what experiences are in general most conducive to the normal development of infants. Instead of these conditions being subordinated to the immediate internal condition of the baby, they are definitely ordered so that a particular kind of *interaction* with these immediate internal states may be brought about.

The word "interaction," which has just been used, expresses the second chief principle for interpreting an experience in its educational function and force. It assigns equal rights to both factors in experience—objective and internal conditions. Any normal experience is an interplay of these two sets of conditions. Taken together, or in their interaction, they form what we call a *situation*. The trouble with traditional education was not that it emphasized the external conditions that enter into the control of the experiences but that it paid so little attention to the internal factors which also decide what kind of experience is had. It violated the principle of interaction from one side. But this violation is no reason why the new education should violate the principle from the other side—except upon the basis of the extreme *Either-Or* educational philosophy which has been mentioned.

The illustration drawn from the need for regulation of the objective conditions of a baby's development indicates, first, that the parent has responsibility for arranging the conditions under which an infant's experience of food, sleep, etc., occurs, and, secondly, that the responsibility is fulfilled by utilizing the funded experience of the past, as this is represented, say, by the advice of competent physicians and others who have made a special study of normal physical growth. Does it limit the freedom of the mother when she uses the body of knowledge thus provided to regulate the objective conditions of nourishment and sleep? Or does the enlargement of her intelligence in fulfilling her parental function widen her freedom? Doubtless if a fetish were made of the advice and directions so that they came to be inflexible dictates to be followed under every possible condition, then restriction of freedom of both parent and child would occur. But this restriction would also be a limitation of the intelligence that is exercised in personal judgment.

In what respect does regulation of objective conditions limit the freedom of the baby? Some limitation is certainly placed upon its immediate movements and inclinations when it is put in its crib, at a time when it wants to continue playing, or does not get food at the moment it would like it, or when it isn't picked up and dandled when it cries for attention. Restriction also occurs when mother or nurse snatches a child away from an open fire into which it is about to fall. I shall have more to say later about freedom. Here it is enough to ask whether freedom is to be thought of and adjudged on the basis of relatively momentary incidents or whether its meaning is found in the continuity of developing experience.

The statement that individuals live in a world means, in the concrete, that they live in a series of situations. And when it is said that they live *in* these situations, the meaning of the word "in" is different from its meaning when it is said that pennies are "in" a pocket or paint is "in" a can. It means, once more, that interaction is going on between an individual and objects and other persons. The conceptions of *situation* and of *interaction* are inseparable from each other. An experience is always what it is because of a transaction taking place between an individual and what, at the time, constitutes his environment, whether the latter consists of persons with whom he is talking about some topic or event, the subject talked about being also a part of the situation; or the toys with which he is playing; the book he is reading (in which his environing conditions at the time may be England or ancient Greece or an imaginary region); or the materials of an experiment he is performing. The environment, in other words, is whatever conditions interact with personal needs, desires, purposes, and capacities to create the experience which is had. Even when a person builds a castle in the air he is interacting with the objects which he constructs in fancy.

The two principles of continuity and interaction are not separate from each other. They intercept and unite. They are, so to speak, the longitudinal and lateral aspects of experience. Different situations succeed one another. But because of the principle of continuity something is carried over from the earlier to the later ones. As an individual passes from one situation to another, his world, his environment, expands or contracts. He does not find himself living in another world but in a different part or aspect of one and the same world. What he has learned in the way of knowledge and skill in one situation becomes an instrument of understanding and dealing effectively with the situations which follow. The process goes on as long as life and learning continue. Otherwise the course of experience is disorderly, since the individual factor that enters into making an experience is split. A divided world, a world whose parts and aspects do not hang together, is at once a sign and a cause of a divided personality. When the splitting-up reaches a certain point we call the person insane. A fully integrated personality, on the other hand, exists only when successive experiences are integrated with one another. It can be built up only as a world of related objects is constructed.

Continuity and interaction in their active union with each other provide the measure of the educative significance and value of an experience. The immediate and direct concern of an educator is then with the situations in which interaction takes place. The individual, who enters as a factor into it, is what he is at a given time. It is the other factor, that of objective conditions, which lies to some extent within the possibility of regulation by the educator. As has already been noted, the phrase "objective conditions" covers a wide range. It includes what is done by the educator and the way in which it is done, not only words spoken but the tone of voice in which they are spoken. It includes equipment, books, apparatus, toys, games played. It includes the materials with which an individual interacts, and, most important of all, the total *social* set-up of the situations in which a person is engaged.

When it is said that the objective conditions are those which are within the power of the educator to regulate, it is meant, of course, that his ability to influence directly the experience of others and thereby the education they obtain places upon him the duty of determining that environment which will interact with the existing capacities and needs of those taught to create a worth-while experience. The trouble with traditional education was not that educators took upon themselves the responsibility for providing an environment. The trouble was that they did not consider the other factor in creating an experience; namely, the powers and purposes of those taught. It was assumed that a certain set of conditions was intrinsically desirable, apart from its ability to evoke a certain quality of response in individuals. This lack of mutual adaptation made the process of teaching and learning accidental. Those to whom the provided conditions were suitable managed to learn. Others got on as best they could. Responsibility for selecting objective conditions carries with it, then, the responsibility for understanding the needs and capacities of the individuals who are learning at a given time. It is not enough that certain materials and methods have proved effective with other individuals at other times. There must be a reason for thinking that they will function in generating an experience that has educative quality with particular individuals at a particular time.

It is no reflection upon the nutritive quality of beefsteak that it is not fed to infants. It is not an invidious reflection upon trigonometry that we do not teach it in the first or fifth grade of school. It is not the subject *per se* that is educative or that is conducive to growth. There is no subject that is in and of itself, or without regard to the stage of growth attained by the learner, such that inherent educational value can be attributed to it. Failure to take into account adaptation to the needs and capacities of individuals was the source of the idea that certain subjects and certain methods are intrinsically cultural or intrinsically good for mental discipline. There is no such thing as educational value in the abstract. The notion that some subjects and methods and that acquaintance with certain facts and truths possess educational value in and of themselves is the reason why traditional education reduced the material of education so largely to a diet of predigested materials. According to this notion, it was enough to regulate the quantity and difficulty of the material provided, in a scheme of quantitative grading, from month to month and from year to year. Otherwise a pupil was expected to take it in the doses that were prescribed from without. If the pupil left it instead of taking it, if he engaged in physical truancy, or in the mental truancy of mind-wandering and finally built up an emotional revulsion against the subject, he was held to be at fault. No question was raised as to whether the trouble might not lie in the subject-matter or in the way in which it was offered. The principle of interaction makes it clear that failure of adaptation of material to needs and capacities of individuals may cause an experience to be non-educative quite as much as failure of an individual to adapt himself to the material.

The principle of continuity in its educational application means, nevertheless, that the future has to be taken into account at every stage of the educational process. This idea is easily misunderstood and is badly distorted in traditional education. Its assumption is, that by acquiring certain skills and by learning certain subjects which would be needed later (perhaps in college or perhaps in adult life) pupils are as a matter of course made ready for the needs and circumstances of the future. Now "preparation" is a treacherous idea. In a certain sense every experience should do something to prepare a person for later experiences of a deeper and more expansive quality. That is the very meaning of growth, continuity, reconstruction of experience. But it is a mistake to suppose that the mere acquisition of a certain amount of arithmetic, geography, history, etc., which is taught and studied because it may be useful at some time in the future, has this effect, and it is a mistake to suppose that acquisition of skills in reading and figuring will automatically constitute preparation for their right and effective use under conditions very unlike those in which they were acquired.

Almost everyone has had occasion to look back upon his school days and wonder what has become of the knowledge he was supposed to have amassed during his years of schooling, and why it is that the technical skills he acquired have to be learned over again in changed form in order to stand him in good stead. Indeed, he is lucky who does not find that in order to make progress, in order to go ahead intellectually, he does not have to unlearn much of what he learned in school. These questions cannot be disposed of by saying that the subjects were not actually learned, for they were learned at least sufficiently to enable a pupil to pass examinations in them. One trouble is that the subject-matter in question was learned in isolation; it was put, as it were, in a water-tight compartment. When the question is asked, then, what has become of it, where has it gone to, the right answer is that it is still there in the special compartment in which it was originally stowed away. If exactly the same conditions recurred as those under which it was acquired, it would also recur and be available. But it was segregated when it was acquired and hence is so disconnected from the rest of experience that it is not available under the actual conditions of life. It is contrary to the laws of experience that learning of this kind, no matter how thoroughly engrained at the time, should give genuine preparation.

Nor does failure in preparation end at this point. Perhaps the greatest of all pedagogical fallacies is the notion that a person learns only the particular thing he is studying at the time. Collateral learning in the way of formation of enduring attitudes, of likes and dislikes, may be and often is much more important than the spelling lesson or lesson in geography or history that is learned. For these attitudes are fundamentally what count in the future. The most important attitude that can be formed is that of desire to go on learning. If impetus in this direction is weakened instead of being intensified, something much more than mere lack of preparation takes place. The pupil is actually robbed of native capacities which otherwise would enable him to cope with the circumstances that he meets in the course of his life. We often see persons who have had little schooling and in whose case the absence of set schooling proves to be a positive asset. They have at least retained their native common sense and power of judgment, and its exercise in the actual conditions of living has given them the precious gift of ability to learn from the experiences they have. What avail is it to win prescribed amounts of information about geography and history, to win ability to read and write, if in the process the individual loses his own soul: loses his appreciation of things worth while, of the values to which these things are relative; if he loses desire to apply what he has learned and, above all, loses the ability to extract meaning from his future experiences as they occur?

What, then, is the true meaning of preparation in the educational scheme? In the first place, it means that a person, young or old, gets out of his present experience all that there is in it for him at the time in which he has it. When preparation is made the controlling end, then the potentialities of the present are sacrificed to a suppositious future. When this happens, the actual preparation for the future is missed or distorted. The ideal of using the present simply to get ready for the future contradicts itself. It omits, and even shuts out, the very conditions by which a person can be prepared for his future. We always live at the time we live and not at some other time, and only by extracting at each present time the full meaning of each present experience are we prepared for doing the same thing in the future. This is the only preparation which in the long run amounts to anything.

All this means that attentive care must be devoted to the conditions which give each present experience a worth-while meaning. Instead of inferring that it doesn't make much difference what the present experience is as long as it is enjoyed, the conclusion is the exact opposite. Here is another matter where it is easy to react from one extreme to the other. Because traditional schools tended to sacrifice the present to a remote and more or less unknown future, therefore it comes to be believed that the educator has little responsibility for the kind of present experiences the young undergo. But the relation of the present and the future is not an *Either-Or* affair. The present affects the future anyway. The persons who should have some idea of the connection between the two are those who have achieved maturity. Accordingly, upon them devolves the responsibility for instituting the conditions for the kind of present experience which has a favorable effect upon the future. Education as growth or maturity should be an ever-present process.

Questions

1. For Dewey, what are the two sides to education?
2. Is Dewey in favor of a child-centered curriculum? Explain.
3. In a time like ours, in which many homes and many families seem to be in disarray, would Dewey continue to argue that the school should exist on a continuum with the home? Explain.
4. Explain "reconstruction of experience."
5. If Dewey is right about reconstruction of experience, would you say that American schools today are trying to educate children? Explain.
6. What does Dewey mean in Article V of "My Pedagogic Creed"?
7. What is the difference between an aggregate and a community?
8. State "the democratic ideal" in your own words.
9. What is the relationship of democracy to education?
10. What are the two principles Dewey uses to evaluate experience?
11. How might you use those criteria in determining a curriculum or in determining how to treat your students?

chapter 9

George S. Counts

TIME LINE FOR COUNTS

1889	Is born December 9 in Baldwin, Kansas.
1911	Receives A.B. from Baker University in Baldwin.
1913	Marries Lois H. Bailey. They have two children.
1916	Receives Ph.D. from University of Chicago.
	Begins teaching at Delaware College.
1919–1920	Is professor of secondary education at the University of Washington (in Seattle).
1920–1924	Is associate professor of secondary education at Yale.
1924–1926	Is professor of education at the University of Chicago.
1926	Publishes *Senior High School Curriculum*.
1927–1956	Is professor of education at Columbia University.
1929	Publishes *Secondary Education and Industrialism*.
1932	Publishes *Dare the School Build a New Social Order?*
1934	Publishes *Social Foundations of Education*.
1935	Receives the Teachers College Medal for Distinguished Service.
1938	Publishes *Prospects of American Democracy*.
1949	Publishes *Country of the Blind: The Soviet System of Mind Control*.
1955–1960	Serves as chairman of the Liberal Party of New York.
1957	Publishes *The Soviet Challenge to American Education*.

1959	Publishes *Khrushchev and the Central Committee Speak on Education.*
1963	Publishes *Education and the Foundation of Human Freedom.*
1974	Dies November 10.

Introduction

In many ways, George S. Counts's life and intellectual development mirror that of John Dewey. Both spent crucial early periods of their intellectual lives at the University of Chicago: Dewey taught there from 1895 to 1905 and developed many of his educational theories at the university's Lab School. Counts (1889–1974) missed Dewey's tenure at the University of Chicago, but did receive his doctorate from Chicago in 1916. Later both were faculty members at Columbia University and, in their writing and teaching, dramatically widened a traditional understanding of the university and the professorate. They were, in a sense, public intellectuals—thinkers who were willing to deal with contemporary issues not necessarily related to their field, thinkers who were able to deal with the interdisciplinary nature of the problems affecting contemporary life, and, perhaps most significantly, thinkers who viewed some form of action as the normal outgrowth of theory.

To understand Counts, it is useful to recall two salient biographical facts. First, Counts, a Kansas farm boy, was born into an era that, in effect, was disappearing: The great American frontier was closing. The dreams that constituted a previous America—of expansion, finding new lands, going West—were becoming less and less tenable. America, of geographic necessity, was closing in on itself and new dreams, new goals would have to be discovered if America was to retain the vitality that previously characterized it.

The second fact is more a function of Counts's time of maturity. As a young intellectual, coming of age in the teens and twenties, Counts was at once intrigued by the experiment that was taking place in the Soviet Union and dismayed by the apparent lack of moral purpose and seriousness exhibited in America at the time. As the Russians embarked on the great revolution of the twentieth century, Americans danced and drank their way through the party that was the roaring twenties. That party, of course, ended with the stock market crash of 1929.

The thirties, as much as they were a time of economic crisis, were times of spiritual and ethical distress. If the twenties were about acquiring material wealth and having a good time, what does a nation do when those goals are no longer reachable?

Throughout his career, Counts always considered himself a follower of John Dewey, and although Dewey himself was not always happy with that claim, there is reason to believe that Counts is one of the few philosophers of education who really took to heart Dewey's concluding remarks in Article V of "My Pedagogic Creed." There Dewey said "I believe that"

—the teacher is engaged, not simply in the training of individuals, but in the formation of the proper social life.

—every teacher should realize the dignity of his calling; that he is a social servant set apart for the maintenance of proper social order and the securing of the right social growth.

—in this way the teacher always is the prophet of the true God and the usherer in of the true kingdom of God.

Counts may be viewed as trying to work out the implications of those remarks, especially as those remarks were played out during what is arguably the worst crisis of American democracy in the twentieth century. When Counts's classic *Dare the School Build a New Social Order?* appeared in 1934, there was a widespread belief that something significant would have to be done or else the country would continue to drift aimlessly or find itself prey to a Soviet-style revolution. Counts, as the title of his work suggests, argued that the school should take the lead in creating a new and better social order. This meant, as the selections will show, a reexamination of the role of the teacher and an expansion of the notion of the educated person.

Counts's argument is almost classic in its simplicity. He starts with a claim of fact, to wit: Although some people might argue that education is about the simple transmission of information, a closer examination will show that education, in large part, is about the formation of character (remember Dewey's remarks quoted above). When teachers choose this text and not some other, when some teachers choose to focus on this part of the culture's legacy and not some other, when, using contemporary language, teachers choose to focus on Western culture as opposed to, say, Eastern or African, they are making choices that will have an impact on what their students think and feel, on what they value, and, ultimately, on what sorts of persons they will become. Thus, for Counts, education is fundamentally about imposition.

Now this imposition, assuming Counts is right in his factual claim, can be done in a number of different ways. First, and one might argue that this is the most typical way, it can be done in a blind and unintelligent fashion. The teacher is guided by all sorts of unstated or unknown assumptions. Some of those assumptions come from her or his own background (Is the teacher a liberal? a conservative? Does the teacher trust or fear children? and so on), some come from the board of education, some come from the other teachers, some come from the larger culture and the business community, and so on. Precisely because the imposition is done in a blind fashion, the possibility is always there that teachers will create "incoherent" characters—students operating with value systems that are seriously askew, that are fraught with contradictions.

Secondly, I think the imposition can be done in a conscious fashion where the goal is to replicate the dominant cultural and political ideology in the individual child. Here the teacher in effect, does a survey of the dominant cultural values, extracts them from their sources in the culture, and then, using her or his pedagogical skill and expertise, engenders the appropriate character in the student. For example, in the racist society, the racist teacher will consciously "stack" the curriculum, using, for example, literature, art, and statistical studies that support the racist position.

Finally, and this is Counts's main point, the imposition can be done in a conscious fashion with an eye toward improving the existing society. Paraphrasing Dewey, teachers should recognize the moral nature of the enterprise and use their skills to create a more just society.

Again, it is helpful to remember the context in which Counts worked. Counts and Dewey and virtually all American intellectuals who were raised in the latter part of the nineteenth century had an enormous faith in science as a tool for ensuring social progress. To use the language of postmodernism, nineteenth-century scholars viewed science as a "privileged narrative," a methodology that gave special insight into the nature of things and that could be used to solve human problems. Simply, Counts *assumed* that there was a way, a scientific way, to adjudicate disputes that to our contemporary ears seem questionable, namely How do you tell what a better society is? What criteria are used in deciding that issue and issues like it? and, perhaps most significantly, Who gets to decide the issue? For Counts, the significant question was exactly the one he asked. Should the schools (or somebody else) be in the business of creating a better society? For contemporary thinkers, there may be a question that takes precedence over Counts's: What *is* a better society?

This is not to say that *Dare the School Build a New Social Order?* is of mere antiquarian interest. In his classic work, Counts expands the notion of the educated person (or perhaps emphasizes a part of the notion that is frequently ignored) to include not merely information and skills but the quality of belief and the values and actions that flow from those beliefs. Just as Plato suggested that a truly knowledgeable person would be a good person, Counts suggests that an educated person would exhibit all sorts of ethical qualities. To divorce education, say, from the cultivation of democratic sentiments is to create, for Counts, a nation of technocrats, that is, an uneducated citizenry.

From *Dare the School Build a New Social Order?* (1932)

There is a fallacy that the school should be impartial in its emphases, that no bias should be given instruction. We have already observed how the individual is inevitably molded by the culture into which he is born. In the case of the

school a similar process operates and presumably is subject to a degree of conscious direction. My thesis is that complete impartiality is utterly impossible,
that the school must shape attitudes, develop tastes, and even impose ideas. It is
obvious that the whole of creation cannot be brought into the school. This means
that some selection must be made of teachers, curricula, architecture, methods of
teaching. And in the making of the selection the dice must always be weighted
in favor of this or that. Here is a fundamental truth that cannot be brushed
aside as irrelevant or unimportant; it constitutes the very essence of the matter
under discussion. Nor can the reality be concealed beneath agreeable phrases.
Professor Dewey states in his *Democracy and Education* that the school should
provide a *purified* environment for the child. With this view I would certainly
agree; probably no person reared in our society would favor the study of
pornography in the schools. I am sure, however, that this means stacking the
cards in favor of the particular systems of value which we may happen to possess. It is one of the truisms of the anthropologist that there are no maxims of
purity on which all peoples would agree. Other vigorous opponents of imposition unblushingly advocate the "cultivation of democratic sentiments" in children or the promotion of child growth in the direction of "a better and richer
life." The first represents definite acquiescence in imposition; the second, if it
does not mean the same thing, means nothing. I believe firmly that democratic
sentiments should be cultivated and that a better and richer life should be the
outcome of education, but in neither case would I place responsibility on either
God or the order of nature. I would merely contend that as educators we must
make many choices involving the development of attitudes in boys and girls
and that we should not be afraid to acknowledge the faith that is in us or
mayhap the forces that compel us. . . .

As the possibilities in our society begin to dawn upon us, we are all, I think,
growing increasingly weary of the brutalities, the stupidities, the hypocrisies,
and the gross inanities of contemporary life. We have a haunting feeling that we
were born for better things and that the nation itself is falling far short of its
powers. The fact that other groups refuse to deal boldly and realistically with the
present situation does not justify the teachers of the country in their customary
policy of hesitation and equivocation. The times are literally crying for a new
vision of American destiny. The teaching profession, or at least its progressive
elements, should eagerly grasp the opportunity which the fates have placed in
their hands.

Such a vision of what America might become in the industrial age I would
introduce into our schools as the supreme imposition, but one to which our children are entitled—a priceless legacy which it should be the first concern of our
profession to fashion and bequeath. The objection will of course be raised that
this is asking teachers to assume unprecedented social responsibilities. But we
live in difficult and dangerous times—times when precedents lose their significance. If we are content to remain where all is safe and quiet and serene, we
shall dedicate ourselves, as teachers have commonly done in the past, to a role of
futility, if not of positive social reaction. Neutrality with respect to the great
issues that agitate society, while perhaps theoretically possible, is practically tan-

tamount to giving support to the forces of conservatism. As Justice Holmes has candidly said in his essay on Natural Law, "we all, whether we know it or not, are fighting to make the kind of world that we should like." If neutrality is impossible even in the dispensation of justice, whose emblem is the blindfolded goddess, how is it to be achieved in education? To ask the question is to answer it.

To refuse to face the task of creating a vision of a future America immeasurably more just and noble and beautiful than the America of today is to evade the most crucial, difficult, and important educational task. Until we have assumed this responsibility we are scarcely justified in opposing and mocking the efforts of so-called patriotic societies to introduce into the schools a tradition which, though narrow and unenlightened, nevertheless represents an honest attempt to meet a profound social and educational need. Only when we have fashioned a finer and more authentic vision than they will we be fully justified in our opposition to their efforts. Only then will we have discharged the age-long obligation which the older generation owes to the younger and which no amount of sophistry can obscure. Only through such a legacy of spiritual values will our children be enabled to find their place in the world, be lifted out of the present morass of moral indifference, be liberated from the senseless struggle for material success, and be challenged to high endeavor and achievement. And only thus will we as a people put ourselves on the road to the expression of our peculiar genius and to the making of our special contribution to the cultural heritage of the race.

Questions

1. Do you think schools should "wage war on behalf of principles or ideals"? If so, which principles? Which ideals?

2. Counts claims to be "in agreement" with Dewey. Do you believe he is?

3. Should "democratic sentiments" be cultivated? If so, how would you go about such a cultivation?

4. Do you think schools (contemporary American ones) are in the business of imposing beliefs and values? Do you think the schools *should be* in the business of imposing beliefs and values? If so, which ones?

5. Is there a difference between indoctrination and education?

6. Would Counts say there is a difference between the two?

7. Counts makes a very strong case regarding the relationship of economics to education. Do you agree with him? Why or why not?

8. If Counts is right, how, for example, would you go about trying to educate one of your students who is homeless?

chapter **10**

Maxine Greene

TIME LINE FOR GREENE

1917	Is born December 23 in New York City.
1938	Receives B.A. from Barnard College.
1949	Receives M.A. from New York University.
1955	Receives Ph.D. from New York University.
1956–1957	Is assistant professor of English at Montclair State College, New Jersey.
1957	Is named assistant professor at New York University.
1962	Is named assistant professor at Brooklyn College.
1965	Is named associate professor at Teachers College/Columbia University.
	Publishes *Public School and the Private Vision.*
1967	Is named professor at Teachers College.
	Publishes *Existential Encounters for Teachers.*
1973	Publishes *Teacher as Stranger: Educational Philosophy for a Modern Age.*
1975	Publishes *Education, Freedom, and Possibility.*
1978	Publishes *Landscapes of Learning.*
1988	Publishes *The Dialectic of Freedom.*
1994	Publishes *Composing a Culture: Inside a Summer Writing Program with High School Teachers.*
1995	Publishes *Releasing the Imagination.*

Introduction

A theme permeating much of Maxine Greene's work is her unyielding faith in humankind's willingness and ability to build on and transcend their lived worlds. Her own life exemplifies this human characteristic in that as one who loves literature and the ideas embodied there, Greene grew up in a world in which "intellectual adventure" was not encouraged. Having grown up in New York City, Greene describes "the opera and the Sunday concerts in the Brooklyn Museum Sculpture Court and the outdoor concerts in the summer" as "rebellions, breakthroughs, secret gardens." As a child Greene took refuge in her journal writing, using it "as a way of ridding myself of my perplexities and confusions, instead of really dealing with them."[1]

Consistent with her advocacy of multiple ways of knowing for much of her academic career, Greene experienced life from a variety of perspectives. Before graduating from Barnard with a degree in history and a minor in philosophy, Greene visited Europe in her late teens, becoming involved in the antifascist activities in support of Republican Spain. While still quite young, she married a medical doctor, worked in his office, and had a child. She remained active in politics, serving as legislative director of the American Labor Party in Brooklyn. Though she wrote "two and a half novels" and numerous articles as a young woman, little of this work was published. At this time, there was little to suggest that Greene's future lay in academia or that she would gain prominence for her unique contribution to the educational thought of the twentieth century. Following World War II and after a divorce and remarriage, Greene decided to go back to school and pursue a master's degree. With this move, she embarked on a journey that led to her becoming the William F. Russell Professor in the Foundations of Education at Teachers College, Columbia University.

As is true for many of us, Greene's professional development resulted from discovering and creating a match between rather fortuitous circumstances and her own personal talents and interests. Her decision to attend graduate school at New York University proved to be one such fortuitous circumstance. She chose NYU not for academic reasons but because she could attend classes there on her own time as a special student. Here she encountered a philosophy of education course team-taught by Adolphe Meyer, George Axtelle, and Theodore Brameld, offered at a time when her daughter was in school. She was fascinated by this first real exposure to educational thought and was suddenly and totally hooked. This professional troika recognized her talent and potential and asked her to assist in the teaching of the course the next time around. Greene's affiliation with NYU continued for several years as she earned there both her master's and doctorate in philosophy of education. As a graduate assistant, she taught philosophy of education courses and began developing courses in what has become her unique trademark: the union of educational philosophy and literature.

As a doctoral student at NYU, Greene taught for both the English and education foundations departments. Once she received her Ph.D., she accepted a position in English at Montclair State College in New Jersey, commuting there from Queens each day. She soon returned to NYU to teach courses in literature and educational theory. As her work began to be recognized, she moved on to Brooklyn College to teach philosophy of education courses. To her credit and surprise, the analytically oriented Philosophy of Education Society appreciated her work, and she eventually served as president of that professional association. Invited to Teachers College, Columbia University, in 1965 to edit *The Teachers College Record,* Greene found her academic home, remaining there for the remainder of her career and becoming the leading light among Teachers College's prominent social foundations of education faculty.[2]

More interested in the artistic or aesthetic mode of inquiry, Greene uses characters and ideas from both traditional and contemporary literature to help the reader connect with and personalize the philosophical question or issue under scrutiny. Her blurring of the fields of philosophy and literature characterizes her major works, which include *The Public School and the Private Vision, Existential Encounters for Teachers, Teacher as Stranger,* and *Landscapes of Learning.* This unique, signature way of doing educational philosophy is also present in a more recent work, *The Dialectic of Freedom.* Here, Greene explains how for most of her life she has been preoccupied with both a personal and professional pilgrimage:

> On the one hand, the quest has been deeply personal: that of a woman striving to affirm the feminine as wife, mother, and friend, while reaching, always reaching beyond the limits imposed by the obligations of a woman's life. On the other hand, it has been in some sense deeply public as well: that of a person struggling to connect the undertaking of education, with which she has been so long involved, to the making and remaking of a public space, a space of dialogue and possibility.[3]

As this personal statement suggests, to be free means to be engaged in searching for or creating "an authentic public space" where "diverse human beings can appear before one another as, to quote Hannah Arendt, 'the best they know how to be.'"[4] Freedom means the overcoming of obstacles or barriers that one encounters that impede or obstruct our struggle to define ourselves and fulfill our potential. If one does not understand the obstacle or recognize it as an impediment, or if one simply does not care, then genuine freedom is not possible. As Greene explains, such an individual is like the indifferent gentleman traveler in Dostoevsky's *Notes from Underground* who simply stops when he encounters a stone wall.[5]

Greene joins both the existentialists and the pragmatists in suggesting that the obstacles or "walls" we encounter are human constructs subject to mediation or removal and not objective, universal realities impervious to human action. From this perspective, the educator has the formidable task of promoting freedom in each individual. Since embracing it is a matter of choice, freedom—like virtue—cannot be taught. Still, by creating an atmosphere conducive to the development of freedom, students can be awakened to the realities of their lived worlds, and their belief that things do not have to remain as they are can be rekindled. Through education individuals can be provoked to reach beyond themselves in their intersubjective space. It is through and by means of education that they may be empowered to think about what they are doing, to become mindful, to share meanings, to conceptualize, to make varied sense of their lived worlds.[6]

This, according to Greene, is the role that education must play in any just and free social order. From her perspective the ideally educated person is one who cares, that is, one who both recognizes the "wall" as an obstacle and chooses to intelligently and persistently attack it. To foster the development of such individuals, Greene turns to literature. For example, she suggests encouraging students to experience vicariously the refusal of Tom Joad and other Okies to accept their "wall"—manifested in *The Grapes of Wrath* by "the banks and the monstrous shapes of tractors levelling the fields." As students identify with Tom Joad—or some equally poignant fictional or historical character—as "he moves out to what may be a new frontier of collective action, a people's movement that may (or may not) bring about the desperately needed change," they may be motivated to resist the tendency of our increasingly technocratic and bureaucratic societies to lull us into passivity.[7]

For Greene, the educated individual is one who poses critical questions about the worlds we inhabit, one who is engaged with others in dialogue about their shared worlds and how to improve them, and one who seeks and scrutinizes the explanations of the human condition offered by others. If freedom is to characterize the human condition, we all need to become more wide awake, but, as suggested in the essay that follows, it is a necessary prerequisite for those who have chosen teaching as their "fundamental project" in life.

Notes

1. Maxine Greene, "Curriculum and Consciousness," in William Pinar, ed., *Curriculum Theorizing: The Reconceptualists* (Berkeley, CA: McCutchan Publishing Corporation, 1975), p. 295.
2. Ibid., pp. 295–298.
3. Maxine Greene, *The Dialectic of Freedom* (New York: Teachers College Press, 1988), p. xi.
4. Ibid.
5. Ibid., p. 5.
6. Ibid., p. 12.
7. Ibid., p. 49.

From *The Dialectic of Freedom* (1988)

Our exploration began in an awareness of a taken-for-grantedness and a void where present-day thinking is concerned, of a lassitude and a lack of care. The void exists with regard to the question of freedom, the givenness of which is taken for granted. We have, in the course of this inquiry, distinguished freedom from liberty for the purpose of highlighting the tension and the drama of personal choosing in an intersubjective field—choosing among others in a conditioned world. Liberty may be conceived of in social or political terms: Embodied in laws or contracts or formulations of human rights, it carves out a domain where free choices can be made. For Isaiah Berlin, the sense of freedom entails "the absence of obstacles to possible choices and activities—absence of obstructions on roads along which a man can decide to walk" (1970, p. xxxix). We recognize, as he did, that among the obstructions to be removed (and preferably through social action) are those raised by poverty, sickness, even ignorance. We recognize as well that the removal of obstacles to "possible choices and activities" may, in many cases, lead to domination by the few and the closing off of opportunities for the many. We know too that, even given conditions of liberty, many people do not act on their freedom; they do not risk becoming different; they accede; often, they submit.

The problems for education, therefore, are manifold. Certain ones cluster around the presumed connection between freedom and autonomy; certain ones have to do with the relation between freedom and community, most significantly moral community. Autonomy, many believe, is a prime characteristic of the educated person. To be autonomous is to be self-directed and responsible; it is to be capable of acting in accord with internalized norms and principles; it is to be insightful enough to know and understand one's impulses, one's motives, and the influences of one's past. There are those who ascribe to the autonomous person a free rational will, capable of making rational sense of an extended objective world. Values like independence, self-sufficiency, and authenticity are associated with autonomy, because the truly autonomous person is not supposed to be susceptible to outside manipulations and compulsions. Indeed, he/she can, by maintaining a calm and rational stance, transcend compulsions and complexes that might otherwise interfere with judgment and clarity.

As is well known, the attainment of autonomy characterizes the highest state in the developmental patterns devised by Jean Piaget (1977) and, later, by Lawrence Kohlberg (1971). Piaget saw autonomy as emergent from experience of mutual reciprocity and regard. A life plan, he wrote, is "an affirmation of autonomy"; and "a life plan is above all a scale of values which puts some ideals above others and subordinates the middle-range values to goals thought of as permanent" (p. 443). For Kohlberg, whose primary interest was in moral development, people who reach a high-enough cognitive stage of development become autonomous enough to guide their choices by universalizable principles of justice and benevolence. "That welfare and justice," he said, "are guiding principles of legislation as well as of individual moral action points to the fact that a principle is always a maxim or a rule for making rules or laws as well as a maxim of individual situational conduct" (p. 60). If the presumption is that autonomy is associated with "higher order" thinking and with the ability to conceptualize abstractions like human rights and justice, and if indeed such principles become maxims of individual conduct, many conclude that autonomous persons can be considered free persons. To abide by internalized principles, after all, is to acknowledge the rule of "ought" or "should." R. M. Hare has written that it is because we *can* act in this way or that, that we ask whether we ought to do this or that (1965, p. 51ff.). Granting the various usages of words like "ought" and "should," we can still understand why persons who are capable of principled action and who are responsive to ideals they have incarnated for themselves are considered self-determining and therefore free.

The implications for education have had to do with cognition—with logical thinking, the resolution of moral dilemmas, the mastery of interpersonal rules. For R. S. Peters, this kind of education involves the nurture of a "rational passion" associated with commitment to the worthwhile. Peters wrote: "Respect for truth is intimately connected with fairness, and respect for persons, which together with freedom, are fundamental principles which underlie our moral life and which are personalized in the form of the rational passions" (1970, p. 55). The problem with this highly cognitive focus in the classroom has in part to do with what it excludes. Also, it has to do with whether or not reasoning is enough when it comes to acting in a resistant world, or opening fields of possibilities among which people may choose to choose. There have been many reports on classroom discussions of issues ostensibly of moment to the students: cheating, betraying confidences, nonviolent resistance, sexual relations, discrimination. Not only has there been little evidence that the participants take such issues personally; there has been little sign of any transfer to situations in the "real world," even when there were opportunities (say, in a peace demonstration) to act on what were affirmed as guiding principles. We will touch, before long, on the importance of imagination and the exploration of alternative possibilities. It seems clear, as Oliver and Bane have said, that young people "need the opportunity to project themselves in rich hypothetical worlds created by their own imagination or those of dramatic artists. More important, they need the opportunity to test out new forms of social order—and only then to reason about their moral implications" (1971, p. 270).

Most of the writers to whom we have referred in these paragraphs are, of course, interested primarily in moral commitments, not freedom *per se*. It does appear, as has been said, that there is a presupposition linking autonomy to personal freedom, autonomy in the sense of rational and principled self-government. For many, a movement out of heteronomous existence, with all its conditioning and shaping factors, cannot but be a movement in the direction of a kind of rule-governed self-sufficiency and independence. And this (at least where qualified students are concerned) is viewed by numbers of educators as the most desirable end of pedagogy, to be achieved by liberal education and commitment to the worthwhile.

Such inquiries into women's moral development as Carol Gilligan's *In a Different Voice* (1981) and into women's distinctive modes of reflection as *Women's Ways of Knowing* by Mary Field Belenky and her colleagues (1986) have, at the very least, made problematic the focal emphasis on separateness and responsiveness to purely formal principle. Gilligan has pointed time and time again to the neglect of the patterns of women's development, whose "elusive mystery . . . lies in its recognition of the continuing importance of attachment in the human life cycle. Woman's place in man's life cycle is to protect this recognition while the developmental litany intones the celebration of separation, autonomy, individuation, and natural rights" (p. 23) Belenky's work emphasizes the relational thinking and the integration of voices that characterize women's life stories. Where freedom is concerned (and it is rarely mentioned in contemporary women's literature), it is taken to signify either liberation from domination or the provision of spaces where choices can be made. There is a general acknowledgment that the opening of such spaces depends on support and connectedness. "Connected teaching," for example, involves what Nel Noddings describes as "care" (1984, pp. 15–16). Rather than posing dilemmas to students or presenting models of expertise, the caring teacher tries to look through students' eyes, to struggle *with* them as subjects in search of their own projects, their own ways of making sense of the world. Reflectiveness, even logical thinking remain important; but the *point* of cognitive development is not to gain an increasingly complete grasp of abstract principles. It is to interpret from as many vantage points as possible lived experience, the ways there are of being in the world.

This recent attentiveness to mutuality and to responsiveness to others' wants and concerns cannot but recall the contextual thinking of Dewey, Merleau-Ponty, Hannah Arendt, Michel Foucault, and others. Dewey wrote of the habit of viewing sociality as a trait of an individual "isolated by nature, quite as much as, say, a tendency to combine with others in order to get protection against something threatening one's own private self" (1938/1963, p. 22). He believed it essential to consider the problem of freedom within the context of culture, surely within a context of multiple transactions and relationships. Part of the difficulty for him and those who followed him had to do with the positing of a "free will" associated with a mysterious interiority, even as it had to do with a decontextualization that denied the influences of associated life. Hannah Arendt found some of the century's worst contradictions in the distinction made between "inner" freedom and the kind of outward "unfreedom" or causality described by Immanuel Kant and his successors. The search for a freedom within, she said, denied notions of *praxis* and the public space. For her, as we have seen, freedom was identified with a space that provided room for human action and interaction. She believed that freedom was the major reason persons came together in political orders; it is, she wrote, "the *raison d'être* of politics" and the opposite of "inner freedom," which she called "the inward space into which we may escape from external coercion and *feel* free" (1961, pp. 141–146).

The relationships and responsibilities stressed by women inquirers are not to be identified entirely with the cultural matrix of such importance to Dewey; nor is either emphasis precisely the same as Arendt's concern with the public space. Nonetheless, all these strains of thought are significant responses to present calls, in philosophy and the human sciences, for some reconstitution of core values, some rebuilding of community today. Attention is being repeatedly called to the crucial good of "friendship" in the Aristotelian qualitative-moral sense (see *Nichomachean Ethics*, Bk. VIII)—the relation between those who desire the good of friends for their friends' sake, no matter how different that "good" may be from what a companion chooses and pursues. In some degree, this is a way of acknowledging and respecting another's freedom to choose among possibilities, as it involves a desire to foster that choosing, because the other is a friend. There is talk of "solidarity" as well, as in the case of Richard Rorty talking about human beings giving sense to their lives by placing them in a larger context. There are two ways of doing this, he says: "by telling the story of their contribution to a community" or "by describing themselves as standing in immediate relation to a nonhuman reality." He calls the first story an example of the desire for solidarity, the second an example of the desire for objectivity. "Insofar as a person is seeking solidarity, he or she does not ask about the relation between the practices of the chosen community and something outside that community" (1985, p. 3). Rorty associates the notion of solidarity with pragmatism, especially when the suggestion is made that the only foundation for the sense of community is "shared hope and the trust created by such sharing." This removes not only objectivism but absoluteness; it returns us to the ideas of relatedness, communication, and disclosure, which provide the context in which (according to the viewpoint of this book) freedom must be pursued.

It is because of people's embeddedness in memory and history, because of their incipient sense of community, that freedom in education cannot be conceived either as an autonomous achievement or as merely one of the principles underlying our moral life, personalized (as R. S. Peters said) "in the form of rational passions." It is because of the apparent normality, the givenness of young people's everyday lives, that intentional actions ought to be undertaken to bring things within the scope of students' attention, to make situations more palpable and visible. Only when they are visible and "at hand" are they likely to cry out for interpretation. And only when individuals are empowered to interpret the situations they live together do they become able to mediate between the object-world and their own consciousness, to locate themselves so that freedom can appear.

Aware of how living persons are enmeshed, engaged with what surrounds them, Merleau-Ponty wrote:

> It is because we are through and through compounded of relationships with the world that for us the only way to become aware of the fact is to suspend the resultant activity . . . to put it out of play. Not because we reject the certainties of common sense and a natural attitude to things— they are, on the contrary, the consistent theme of philosophy—but because, being the presupposed basis of any thought, they are taken for granted and go unnoticed, and because in order to arouse them and bring them into view we have to suspend for a moment our recognition of them. (1962/1967, p. xiii)

He was not talking about withdrawing into some interior domain. Nor was he calling for a deflection of attention from ordinary life. Rather, he was exploring the possibilities of seeing what was ordinarily obscured by the familiar, so much part of the accustomed and the everyday that it escaped notice entirely. We might think about the clocks that play such important parts in schoolrooms, or school bells, or loudspeakers blaring at the beginning and end of the day; about calling individual children "third graders" or "lower track"; about threats to summon the remote principal; even about the Pledge of Allegiance, and about the flags drooping in the public rooms. Why *should* these phenomena be presupposed as a "basis" for thought and self-identification? We might think of the way the chalkboard is placed, of the peculiar distancing of the teacher at the front desk, of books firmly shut before the reading is done. The point is to find a means of making all this an object of thought, of critical attention. And we may be reminded again of Foucault's remark that "thought is freedom in relation to what one does." Part of the effort might be to defamiliarize things, to make them strange. How would a Martian view what was there, a "boat person" newly arrived? What would happen if the hands were removed from the clock? (No one, for instance, who has read William Faulkner's *The Sound and the Fury* is likely to forget the strangeness of what happens when Quentin pulls the hands off his watch on the day of his suicide. "Hearing it, that is," thinks Quentin, "I don't suppose anybody ever deliberately listens to a watch or a clock. You don't have to. You can be oblivious to the sound for a long while, then in a second of ticking it can create in the mind unbroken the long diminishing parade of time you didn't hear" [1946, p. 96]. Later, he remembers that "Father said clocks slay time. He said time is dead as long as it is being clicked off by little wheels; only when the clock stops does time come to life" [p. 104]. Reading that, one cannot but find the clock-field, the clock-world, expanding. And the possibilities of thinking multiply.) What of paper? Why is there so much paper? So many files? (George Konrad's novel about a Hungarian social worker, called *The Caseworker*, also makes a reader see—and ask, and question. "I question, explain, prove, disprove, comfort, threaten, grant, deny, demand, approve. . . . The order I defend is brutal though fragile, it is unpleasant and austere; its ideas are impoverished and its style is lacking in grace. . . . I repudiate the high priests of individual salvation and the sob sisters of altruism, who exchange commonplace partial responsibility for the aesthetic transports of cosmohistorical guilt or the gratuitous slogans of universal love. I refuse to emulate these Sunday-school clowns and prefer—I know my limitations—to be the sceptical bureaucrat that I am. My highest aspiration is that a medium-rank, utterly insignificant civil servant should, as far as possible, live with his eyes open" [1974, p. 168]. Again, familiar bureaucratic orders in one's own world thrust themselves into visibility. Seeing more, feeling more, one reaches out for more to do.)

Walker Percy's narrator in *The Moviegoer* says it in another way. He is trying to relieve his own boredom, a boredom verging on despair; and the idea of a search suddenly occurs to him.

> What is the nature of the search? you ask.
>
> Really, it is very simple, at least for a fellow like me; so simple that it is easily overlooked.
>
> The search is what anyone would undertake if he were not sunk in the everydayness of his own life. This morning, for example, I felt as if I had come to myself on a strange island. And what does such a castaway do? Why, he pokes around the neighborhood and he doesn't miss a trick.

> To become aware of the possibility of the search is to be onto something. Not to be onto something is to be in despair. (1979, p. 13)

To undertake a search is, of course, to take an initiative, to refuse stasis and the flatness of ordinary life. Since the narrator says he was "sunk in everydayness," his search is clearly for another perspective, one that will disclose what he has never seen. Even to realize that he can be "onto something" is to begin perceiving lacks in his own life. The question as to what the "neighborhood" holds and implies remains open. He may be moved to "poke around" because others have taken heed of him, because he has appeared in the open for almost the first time. If this is so, he may acquire the space that will free him from his environment of everydayness. The experience may be one denoting a willingness "to learn again to see the world"—and to restore "a power to signify, a birth of meaning, or a wild meaning, an expression of experience by experience" (Merleau-Ponty, 1962/1967, p. 60). I am suggesting that there may be an integral relationship between reaching out to learn to learn and the "search" that involves a pursuit of freedom. Without being "onto something," young people feel little pressure, little challenge. There are no mountains they particularly want to climb, so there are few obstacles with which they feel they need to engage. They may take no heed of neighborhood shapes and events once they have become used to them—even the figures of homelessness, the wanderers who are mentally ill, the garbage-strewn lots, the burned-out buildings. It may be that no one communicates the importance of thinking about them or suggests the need to play with hypothetical alternatives. There may be no sense of identification with people sitting on the benches, with children hanging around the street corners after dark. There may be no ability to take it seriously, to take it personally. Visible or invisible, the world may not be problematized; no one aches to break through a horizon, aches in the presence of the question itself. So there are no tensions, no desires to reach beyond.

There is an analogy here for the passivity and the disinterest that prevent discoveries in classrooms, that discourage inquiries, that make even reading seem irrelevant. It is not simply a matter of motivation or interest. In this context, we can call it a question having to do with freedom or, perhaps, the absence of freedom in our schools. By that I do not necessarily mean the ordinary limits and constraints, or even the rules established to ensure order. I mean, in part, the apparent absence of concern for the ways in which young people feel conditioned, determined, even *fated* by prevailing circumstances. Members of minority groups, we are repeatedly informed, do not see the uses of commitment to schooling and studying. No matter how they yearn for success in society, they are convinced of inimical forces all around them, barricades that cannot be overcome. Poor children and others often experience the weight of what is called "cultural reproduction," although they cannot name it or resist it. By that is meant not only the reproduction of ways of knowing, believing, and valuing, but the maintenance of social patternings and stratifications as well. The young people may not chafe under the inequities being kept alive through schools, as inequities often are; they are likely to treat them as wholly "normal," as predictable as natural laws. The same might be said about advantaged children who grow up with a sense of entitlement and privilege, but still feel they have no choice.

The challenge is to engage as many young people as possible in the thought that is freedom—the mode of thought that moved Sarah Grimké, Elizabeth Cady Stanton, Septima Clark, Leonard Covello, the Reverend King, and so many others into action. Submergence and the inability to name what lies around interfere with questioning and learning. Dewey had something much like this in mind when he emphasized the dangers of "recurrence, complete uniformity," "the routine and mechanical" (1934, p. 272). What he sometimes called the "anaesthetic" in experience is what numbs people and prevents them from reaching out, from launching inquiries. For Dewey, experience becomes fully conscious only when meanings derived from earlier experience enter in through the exercise of the imaginative capacity, since imagination "is the only gateway through which these meanings can find their way into a present interaction; or rather . . . the conscious adjustment of the new and the old *is* imagination" (p. 272). The word, the concept "conscious" must be emphasized. Experience, for Dewey, becomes "human and conscious" only when what is "given here and now is extended by meanings and values drawn from what is absent in fact and present only imaginatively." Conscious thinking always involves a risk, a "venture into the unknown"; and it occurs against a background of funded or sedimented meanings that must themselves be tapped and articulated, so that the mind can continue dealing consciously and solicitously with lived situations, those situations (as Dewey put it) "in which we find ourselves" (p. 263).

Education for freedom must clearly focus on the range of human intelligences, the multiple languages and symbol systems available for ordering experience and making sense of the lived world. Dewey was bitterly opposed to the anti-intellectual tendencies in the culture and frequently gave voice to what he called "a plea for casting off that intellectual timidity which hampers the wings of imagination, a plea for speculative audacity, for more faith in ideas, sloughing off a cowardly reliance upon those partial ideas to which we are wont to give the name facts" (1931, p. 12). He spoke often as well about the kinds of inquiry that deliberately challenge desires for certainty, for fixity. He would undoubtedly have agreed with John Passmore's more recent call for "critico-creative thinking," the kind that is consciously norm-governed but at once willing to challenge rules that become irrelevant or stultifying. No principle, Passmore wrote, no person or text or work of art should be kept beyond the reach of rational criticism. There should nonetheless be a continuing initiation into the great traditions in which we are all, whether we are aware of it or not, embedded. Passmore went on:

> Critical thinking as it is exhibited in the great traditions conjoins imagination and criticism in a single form of thinking; in literature, science, history, philosophy or technology, the free flow of the imagination is controlled by criticism and criticisms are transformed into a new way of looking at things. Not that either the free exercise of the imagination or the raising of objections is in itself to be despised; the first can be suggestive of new ideas, the second can show the need for them. But certainly education tries to develop the two in combination. The educator

is interested in encouraging critical discussion as distinct from the mere raising of objections; and discussion is an exercise of the imagination. (1975, p. 33)

A concern for the critical and the imaginative, for the opening of new ways of "looking at things," is wholly at odds with the technicist and behaviorist emphases we still find in American schools. It represents a challenge, not yet met, to the hollow formulations, the mystifications so characteristic of our time. We have taken note of the forms of evangelism and fundamentalism, the confused uneasiness with modernism that so often finds expression in anti-intellectualism or an arid focus on "Great Books." Given the dangers of small-mindedness and privatism, however, I do not think it sufficient to develop even the most variegated, most critical, most imaginative, most "liberal" approach to the education of the young. If we are seriously interested in education for freedom as well as for the opening of cognitive perspectives, it is also important to find a way of developing a *praxis* of educational consequence that opens the spaces necessary for the remaking of a democratic community. For this to happen, there must of course be a new commitment to intelligence, a new fidelity in communication, a new regard for imagination. It would mean fresh and sometimes startling winds blowing through the classrooms of the nation. It would mean the granting of audibility to numerous voices seldom heard before and, at once, an involvement with all sorts of young people being provoked to make their own the multilinguality needed for structuring of contemporary experience and thematizing lived worlds. The languages required include many of the traditional modes of sensemaking: the academic disciplines, the fields of study. But none of them must ever be thought of as complete or all-encompassing, developed as they have been to respond to particular kinds of questions posed at particular moments in time. Turned, as lenses or per_____ ___ _he shared world of actualities, they cannot but continue resonati_ in the light of new undercurrents, new questions, new uncert_

Let us say young high school students are studying hist_ require some understanding of the rules of evidence where th_ is concerned. They need to distinguish among sources, to multiple determinants those forces that can be identified as places where chance cuts across necessity, to recognize whe appropriate and when they are not. All this takes reflective the norms governing the discipline of history. But this does not end or exc_ such study. There is a consciousness now, as there was not in time past, of the significance of doing history "from the ground up," of penetrating the so-called "cultures of silence" in order to discover what ordinary farmers and storekeepers and elementary schoolteachers and street children and Asian newcomers think and have thought about an event like the Holocaust or the Vietnam War or the bombing of Hiroshima or the repression in South Africa that continues to affect them directly or indirectly even as it recedes into the visualizable past. They need to be empowered to reflect on and talk about what happened in its varying connections with other events in the present as well as the past. And they may be brought to find out that a range of informed viewpoints may be just as important when it comes to understanding the Civil War, or the industrial revolution, or the slave trade, or the Children's Crusade. Clearly, if the voices of participants or near-participants (front-line soldiers, factory workers, slaves, crusaders) could be heard, whole dimensions of new understanding (and perplexity and uncertainty) would be disclosed. The same is true with respect to demographic studies, studies based on census rolls or tax collections, studies that include diaries and newspaper stories and old photographs. Turning the tools and techniques of history to resources of this kind often means opening up new spaces for study, metaphorical spaces sometimes, places for "speculative audacity." Such efforts may provide experiences of freedom in the study of history, because they unleash imagination in unexpected ways. They draw the mind to what lies beyond the accustomed boundaries and often to what is not yet. They do so as persons become more and more aware of the unanswered questions, the unexplored corners, the nameless faces behind the forgotten windows. These are the obstacles to be transcended if understanding is to be gained. And it is in the transcending, as we have seen, that freedom is often achieved.

The same can be said for the other disciplines and fields of study in the social and natural sciences; and, even among the exact sciences, a heightened curiosity may accompany the growth of feelings of connection between human hands and minds and the objects of study, whether they are rocks or stars or memory cores. Again, it is a matter of questioning and sense-making from a grounded vantage point, an interpretive vantage point, in a way that eventually sheds some light on the commonsense world, in a way that is always perspectival and therefore forever incomplete. The most potent metaphor for this can be found at the end of Melville's chapter called "Cetology" in the novel *Moby Dick*. The chapter deals with the essentially futile effort to provide a "systematized exhibition of the whale in his broad genera," or to classify the constituents of a chaos. And finally:

> It was stated at the outset, that this system would not be here, and at once, perfected. You cannot but plainly see that I have kept my word. But now I leave my cetological System standing thus unfinished, even as the great Cathedral of Cologne was left, with the crane still standing upon the top of the uncompleted tower. For small erections may be finished by their first architects; grand ones, true ones, ever leave the copestone to posterity. God keep me from ever completing anything. This whole book is but a draught—nay, but the draught of a draught. Oh, Time, Strength, Cash, and patience! (1851/1981, p. 148)

To recognize the role of perspective and vantage point, to recognize at the same time that there are always multiple perspectives and multiple vantage points, is to recognize that no accounting, disciplinary or otherwise, can ever be finished or complete. There is always more. There is always possibility. And this is where the space opens for the pursuit of freedom. Much the same can be said about experiences with art objects—not only literary texts, but music, painting, dance. They have the capacity, when authentically attended to, to enable persons to hear and to see what they would not ordinarily hear and see, to offer visions of consonance and dissonance that are unfamiliar and indeed abnormal, to disclose the incomplete profiles of the world. As importantly, in this context, they have the capacity to defamiliarize experience: to begin with the overly familiar and transfigure it into something different enough to make those who are awakened hear and see.

Generalizations with regard to what forms possess such potential for different people are tempting, but they must be set aside. Jazz and the blues have long had a transformative, often liberating effect on many populations, for example. We have only to read the musical history of our country, recall the stories of our great black musicians, heed such novels as *Invisible Man* (constructed, its author said, according to the patterns of the blues), take note of the importance of jazz in European art forms throughout the century, see how the Jazz Section of the Czech dissident movement has become the live center of dissent. The ways in which the blues have given rise to rock music and what are called "raps" testify as well to a power, not merely to embody and express the suffering of oppressed and constricted lives, but to name them somehow, to identify the gaps between what is and what is longed for, what (if the sphere of freedom is ever developed) will some day come to be.

Recent discoveries of women's novels, like discoveries of black literature, have certainly affected the vision of those reared in the traditions of so-called "great" literature, as they have the constricted visions of those still confined by outmoded ideas of gender. The growing ability to look at even classical works through new critical lenses has enabled numerous readers, of both genders, to apprehend previously unknown renderings of their lived worlds. Not only have many begun coming to literature with the intent of *achieving* it as meaningful through realization by means of perspectival readings. Many have begun engaging in what Mikhail Bakhtin called "dialogism," viewing literary texts as spaces where multiple voices and multiple discourses intersect and interact (1981, pp. 259–422). Even to confront what Bakhtin calls "heteroglossia" in a novel is to enlarge one's experience with multiplicity of perspectives and, at once, with the spheres that can open in the midst of pluralities.

With *Invisible Man* in mind, we might recall the point that invisibility represents a condition in the mind of the one who encounters the black person and draw implications for the ways we have looked at other strangers, and even for the ways we have looked at those posited as "other" or as enemies. We can find ourselves reading so-called canonical works like *Jane Eyre* and become astonished by a newly grasped interpretation of the "madwoman" imprisoned upstairs in Mr. Rochester's house. Shocked into a new kind of awareness, we find ourselves pushing back the boundaries again, hearing new voices, exploring new discourses, unearthing new possibilities. We can ponder such works as Tillie Olsen's "I Stand There Ironing" or "Tell Me a Riddle" and uncover dimensions of oppression, dream, and possibility never suspected before. We can look again at Gabriel Garcia Márquez's *One Hundred Years of Solitude* and find ourselves opening windows in our experience to startling renderings of time, death, and history that subvert more of our certainties. It is not only, however, in the domains of the hitherto "silent" cultures that transformations of our experience can take place. There is a sense in which the history of any art form carries with it a history of occasions for new visions, new modes of defamiliarization, at least in cases where artists thrust away the auras, and broke in some way with the past.

It has been clear in music, pushing back the horizons of silence for at least a century, opening new frequencies for ears willing to risk new sounds. It has been true of dance, as pioneers of movement and visual metaphor uncover new possibilities in the human body and therefore for embodied consciousnesses in the world. In painting, it has been dramatically the case. An example can be found in the work of the painter John Constable, who abandoned old paradigms of studio painting and studio light and began sketching his subjects in the open air. Breaking through "horizons of expectation," as the critic Ernst Gombrich writes (1965, p. 34), Constable enabled spectators to perceive green in the landscape, rather than rendering it in the traditional manner in gradations of brown. He defamiliarized the visible world, in effect, making accessible shadings and nuances never suspected before. We can say similar things about numerous visual artists, if we are enabled, say, to see them against their forerunners; moving through the "museums without walls," listening to those Merleau-Ponty called the "voices of silence," we can discover ourselves variously on an always-changing place on earth. Giotto, della Francesca, Botticelli, Michelangelo, Raphael, Poussin: The names sound, the doors open to vista after vista. Exemplary for moderns may be Claude Monet making visible the modelling effects of light on objects once seen as solidly and objectively *there*. Some can recall the multiple studies of haystacks in his garden at different seasons of the year or of Rouen Cathedral at different times of day. Recalling, we are reminded again how visions of fixity can be transformed, how time itself can take on new meanings for the perceiver, for the one choosing to journey through works of visual art. And we can (we ought to) recall Pablo Picasso's abrupt expansion of Western observers' conceptions of humanity and space with his "Demoiselles d'Avignon" and its African and Iberian visages, or his imaging of unendurable pain in the "Guernica."

Of course, such visions are unknown in most of our classrooms; and relatively few people are informed enough or even courageous enough actually to "see." And it must be acknowledged that, for all their emancipatory potential, the arts cannot be counted on to liberate, to ensure an education for freedom. Nonetheless, for those authentically concerned about the "birth of meaning," about breaking through the surfaces, about teaching others to "read" their own worlds, art forms must be conceived of as ever-present possibility. They ought not to be treated as decorative, as frivolous. They ought to be, if transformative teaching is our concern, a central part of curriculum, wherever it is devised. How can it be irrelevant, for example, to include such images as those of William Blake, with contraries and paradoxes that make it forever impossible to place the "lamb" and the "tiger" in distinctive universes, to separate the "marriage" from the "hearse"? How can it be of only extracurricular interest to turn to Emily Dickinson, for instance, and find normal views of experience disrupted and transformed? She wrote:

I stepped from plank to plank
   So slow and cautiously;
The stars about my head I felt,
   About my feet the sea.
I knew not but the next
   Would be my final inch,—
This gave me that precarious gait
   Some call experience.
             (1890/1959, p. 166)

The spaces widen in the poem—from plank to plank under an open sky. She identifies experience itself with a "precarious gait"; and the risk involved is emphasized. Reading such a work, we cannot but find our own world somehow defamiliarized. Defamiliarized, it discloses aspects of experience ordinarily never seen. Critical awareness may be somehow enhanced, as new possibilities open for reflection. Poetry does not offer us empirical or documentary truth, but it enables us to "know" in unique ways. So many poems come to mind, among them W. H. Auden's "Surgical Ward," which may emerge from memory because of the AIDS epidemic, or because of a concern about distancing and lack of care. He wrote of the remoteness of those who "are and suffer; that is all they do" and of the isolation of the sufferers compared with those who believe "in the common world of the uninjured and cannot imagine isolation—" (1970, pp. 44–45). Any one of a hundred others might have come to mind: the choice is arbitrary. A writer, like the writer of this book, can only hope to activate the memories of *her* readers, to awaken, to strike sparks.

The same is true, even more true, when it comes to novels and plays: The occasions for revelation and disclosure are beyond counting. In my train of thought (and readers will locate themselves in their own), I find Antigone, committed to her sense of what is moral and dying for her cause; King Lear, with all artifice and "superfluity" abandoned on the heath in the raging storm. I somehow see Lucifer falling in *Paradise Lost* and continually falling, reappearing at the end of James Joyce's *A Portrait of the Artist as a Young Man* when Stephen Dedalus says, "I will not serve." And then, remembering Joyce, I hear that resounding "Yes" at the end of Molly Bloom's soliloquy in *Ulysses*. In the background, softly, stubbornly, there is Bartleby's "I prefer not to" in the Melville story; there is the dying Ivan Ilyitch in the Tolstoy story, speaking of himself as "little Vanya" to the peasant holding his legs; there is the shadow of the little girl who hung herself in Dostoevsky's *The Possessed*. There are the soldiers described in Malraux's *Man's Fate*, young soldiers about to be executed on the Lithuanian front and forced to take off their trousers in the snow. They begin to sneeze, "and those sneezes were so intensely human in that dawn of execution, that the machine-gunners, instead of firing, waited—waited for life to become less indiscreet" (1936, p. 76). Indiscreet—and I see the house beaten by the storms and the dilapidations of time in the "Time Passes" section of Virginia Woolf's *To the Lighthouse;* Willa Cather's Paul (in "Paul's Case") and the winter roses and a boy's death on the railroad tracks. There are the spare, lace-curtained bedrooms and the slave women in red in Margaret Atwood's *The Handmaid's Tale;* and, in another future, there is the stark transcendence of the rocket in *Gravity's Rainbow* by Thomas Pynchon. There is Mark Helprin's white horse in the snow-bound city in *Winter's Tale,* the "air-borne toxic event" in Don DeLillo's *White Noise.*

Any reader might go on to recall how, as Herbert Marcuse has put it, "art is committed to that perception of the world which alienates individuals from their functional existence and performance in society" (1978, p. 9). An education for freedom must move beyond function, beyond the subordination of persons to external ends. It must move beyond mere performance to action, which entails the taking of initiatives. This is not meant to imply that aesthetic engagements, because they take place in domains of freedom, separate or alienate learners so fully from the tasks of the world that they become incapacitated for belonging or for membership or for work itself. Marcuse also spoke of an aesthetic transformation as a "vehicle of recognition," drawing the perceiver away from "the mystifying power of the given" (1978, p. 72). He was pointing to an emancipatory possibility of relevance for an education in and for freedom. Encounters with the arts alone will not realize it; but the arts will help open the situations that require interpretation, will help disrupt the walls that obscure the spaces, the spheres of freedom to which educators might some day attend.

With situations opening, students may become empowered to engage in some sort of *praxis,* engaged enough to name the obstacles in the way of their shared becoming. They may at first be identified with the school itself, with the neighborhood, with the family, with fellow-beings in the endangered world. They may be identified with prejudices, rigidities, suppressed violence: All these can petrify or impinge on the sphere of freedom. As Foucault would have it, persons may be made into subjects, docile bodies to be "subjected, used, transformed, and improved" (1977, p. 136). It is not merely the structures of class, race, and gender relations that embody such power and make it felt in classrooms. Much the same can happen through the differential distribution of knowledge, through a breaking of what is distributed into discrete particles, through an unwarranted classification of a "chaos."

Having attended to women's lives and the lives of many strangers, we are aware of the relation between the subjugation of voices and the silencing of memories. All these have often been due to the insidious workings of power or the maintenance of what has been called "hegemony" (Entwhistle, 1979, pp. 12–14). Hegemony, as explained by the Italian philosopher Antonio Gramsci, means direction by moral and intellectual persuasion, not by physical coercion. That is what makes it a matter of such concern for those interested in education for freedom. The persuasion is often so quiet, so seductive, so disguised that it renders young people acquiescent to power without their realizing it. The persuasion becomes most effective when the method used obscures what is happening in the learners' minds. Strangely, the acquiescence, the acceptance, may find expression through dropping out or other modes of alienation, as much as through a bland compliance to what is taken to be the given. This may be because the message or the direction emphasizes an opportunity system or a stratification system offering a limited range of possibilities, apparently attentive to but a few modes of being. This becomes most drastically clear in the case of youngsters whose IQs, according to current testing practices, are low. Ours is not a society that ponders fulfilling options for people with low IQs. Lacking an awareness of alternatives, lacking a vision of realizable possibilities, the young (left unaware of the messages they are given) have no hope of achieving freedom.

In the classroom opened to possibility and at once concerned with inquiry, critiques must be developed that uncover what masquerade as neutral frameworks, or what Rorty calls "a set of rules which will tell us how rational agreement can be reached on what would settle the issue on every point where statements seem to conflict" (1979, p. 315). Teachers, like their students, have to learn to love the questions, as they come to realize that there can be no final agreements or answers, no final commensurability. And we have been talking about stories that open perspectives on communities grounded in trust, flowering by means of dialogue, kept alive in open spaces where freedom can find a place.

Looking back, we can discern individuals in their we-relations with others, inserting themselves in the world by means of projects, embarking on new beginnings in spaces they open themselves. We can recall them—Thomas Jefferson, the Grimké sisters, Susan B. Anthony, Jane Addams, Frederick Douglass, W. E. B. DuBois, Martin Luther King, John Dewey, Carol Gilligan, Nel Noddings, Mary Daly—opening public spaces where freedom is the mainspring, where people create themselves by acting in concert. For Hannah Arendt, "power corresponds to the human ability . . . to act in concert. Power is never the property of an individual; it belongs to a group and remains in existence only so long as the group keeps together" (1972, p. 143). Power may be thought of, then, as "empowerment," a condition of possibility for human and political life and, yes, for education as well. But spaces have to be opened in the schools and around the schools; the windows have to let in the fresh air. The poet Mark Strand writes:

> It is all in the mind, you say, and has
> nothing to do with happiness. The coming of cold,
> The coming of heat, the mind has all the time in the world.
> You take my arm and say something will happen,
> something unusual for which we were always prepared,
> like the sun arriving after a day in Asia,
> like the moon departing after a night with us.
>   (1984, p. 126)

And Adrienne Rich, calling a poem "Integrity" and beginning, "A wild patience has taken me this far" (1981, p. 8). There is a need for a wild patience. And, when freedom is the question, it is always a time to begin.

Questions

1. What is the difference between liberty and freedom?
2. What is the relationship between autonomy and freedom?
3. How are freedom and autonomy related to women's ways of knowing?
4. What does Greene mean by suggesting that freedom must be pursued through relatedness, communication, and disclosure? How does this relate Rorty's notions of solidarity and objectivity?
5. What does Greene mean by the statement that "freedom in education cannot be conceived . . . as an autonomous achievement . . ."?
6. How does being "onto something" connect with the "search" that involves a pursuit of freedom?
7. What is meant by places for "speculative audacity" and how does speculative audacity relate to achieving freedom?
8. Why is it important to enable or empower persons to hear and see what they would not ordinarily see and hear?
9. Why is it important to "identify the gaps between what is and what is longed for, what will someday come to be?"
10. Why should the arts be a central, rather than frivolous, part of a curriculum?
11. How does a work of art, literature, music, etc., enhance our critical awareness?
12. Why are encounters with the arts insufficient for an education in and for freedom?
13. What is meant by *praxis* and how does it relate to freedom?
14. What does education have to do with unmasking neutral frameworks?

chapter 11

Jane Roland Martin

TIME LINE FOR MARTIN

1929	Is born July 20 in New York City. Her father, Charles, is a journalist, and her mother, Sarah, is a teacher.
1951	Receives A.B. from Radcliffe College.
1956	Receives Ed.M. from Harvard University.
1961	Receives Ph.D. from Radcliffe College.
1962	Marries Michael Martin on June 15. They have two sons.
1972–1981	Is associate professor of philosophy at University of Massachusetts, Boston.
1981–1994	Is professor of philosophy at University of Massachusetts, Boston.
1983–1984	Is Visiting Woman Scholar at the University of New Hampshire.
1985	Publishes *Reclaiming a Conversation: The Ideal of the Educated Woman*.
1992	Publishes *The Schoolhome*.
1994	Publishes *Changing the Educational Landscape: Philosophy, Women, and Curriculum*.
	Is named professor emerita of philosophy at the University of Massachusetts, Boston.
1995	Publishes *The Schoolhome* (paperback).

Introduction

Today it is hard to recapture the feeling of a vast theoretical shift that seemed to be taking place in philosophy, psychology, and education just a short decade ago. Carol Gilligan's deceptively slim but monumental *In a Different Voice* had just been published and, among other things, it suggested that women's ways of knowing might be radically different from men's, that a woman's hierarchy of values might be substantively distinct from a man's, and that previous ways of understanding persons, most notably the psychologist Lawrence Kohlberg's, might be seriously biased in favor of males and against females. Then, in 1984, appeared an equally slim but just as revolutionary work—Jane Roland Martin's *Reclaiming a Conversation*.

In many ways, Martin's work was the educational analogue to the work of art historians of the 1970s whose work, in turn, was precipitated by a deceptively "simple" question, namely, Why are there so few great women artists? Those historians responded in a number of different but related ways. They suggested that there are a number of great women artists but, for various reasons, the art forms they work in are considered "marginal," that is, more decorative than serious, producing pleasing designs rather than high art. They also suggested that many women are not allowed the same sort of access to the art world as men; for example, a woman first would have to meet obligations to family and hearth before she could take up the brush, while her male counterpart could ignore familial obligations. Finally, they suggested that there are a number of serious women painters whose works are largely ignored by the tradition precisely because the artists are women. The art historian's role became then, in large part, recovering those forgotten women artists.

In *Reclaiming a Conversation,* Martin suggests that, historically, women have typically been excluded from the "conversation" that constitutes the history of Western educational thought. There are three aspects to that exclusion: First, there has been very little written about the education of women. Either it was assumed that what was said about the education of men could, with equal justice, be said about the education of women and, hence, there was no real need to speak about the education of women, or it was assumed that issues surrounding the education of women were not as critical as those surrounding the education of men.

Second, what little writing there has been regarding the education of women by the important philosophers has been largely ignored, consigned, in effect, to the margins of their writing. Plato's writing about the education of women has been treated, within the history of philosophy, almost like Aristotle's views on various physical laws—quaint, of antiquarian interest, but hardly at the center of his philosophic discourse.

Finally, when women have written about the education of women, their work has quickly found a place on the edges of scholarship, where it can be safely ignored. By a curious stroke of logic, the argument goes something like this: Important philosophers do not write about the education of women. X wrote about the education of women. X was not an important philosopher and, so, can be safely ignored.

In *Reclaiming a Conversation,* Martin shows that the education of women is truly problematic and that questions regarding the education of women cannot be answered by simply reworking the answers to questions regarding the education of men. She does this, in large part, by unearthing a tradition of inquiry regarding the education of women that stretches back to Plato, leaps ahead to Jean-Jacques Rousseau, especially to his writing about the education of Emile and Sophie, and weaves through the works of Mary Wollstonecraft, Catherine Beecher, and Charlotte Perkins Gilman.

In addition to recovering a tradition of scholarship that was lost and/or trivialized, Martin recalls to mind one of the earliest understandings of the educated person available in the Western tradition. If one looks at the early dialogues of Plato, dialogues like the *Apology,* the *Crito,* and the *Phaedo,* one finds an implicit model of education as one of reasoned discourse, that is, intelligent, decent, well-meaning people, people of good faith, people who trust and like each other, people who might even be called friends, getting together and trying to talk themselves to a reasonable conclusion. They engage in a conversation, learn something from one another and from the conversation itself, and, if the gods smile on them, may even become wise.

For Martin, to be educated is to engage in a conversation that stretches back in time, that enables the student today to converse with previous scholars. In the words of Michael Oakeshott:

> We are all inheritors neither of an inquiry about ourselves and the world nor of an accumulating body of information, but of a conversation begun in the primeval forest and extended and made more articulate in the course of centuries. It is a conversation which goes on both in public and within each of ourselves. Of course there is argument and inquiry and information, but wherever these are profitable they are recognized as passages in this conversation. Education, properly speaking, is an initiation into the skill and partnership of this conversation in which we learn to recognize the voices, to distinguish the proper occasions of utterance, and in which we acquire the intellectual and moral habits appropriate to conversation. And it is this conversation which, in the end, gives place and character to every human activity and utterance.[1]

It does not hurt to underscore the significance of education for both Oakeshott and Martin. Education is not simply something that occurs in a specific building at a given time in one's life. It is not simply training in basic skills or the learning of essential elements. And it is not simply training or preparation for the next stage in one's life. For Martin and Oakeshott education *is* the development of intellectual and moral habits through the give and take of the conversation that ultimately gives "place and character to every human activity and utterance." Education—the conversation—is the place where one comes to learn what it is to be a person.

Cast in that light, the seriousness of Martin's charge is obvious. If the conversation, this discourse stretching back to the primeval forest is the place in which personhood is defined, to exclude women, or any group for that matter, from the conversation is to deny members of that group the right to become persons. It is to treat them as something less than human.

Finally, if the educational conversation is like more prosaic ones, it will depend for energy and vivacity on a multiplicity of perspectives and a diversity of voices. In ordinary conversations, if we all see things from the same vantage point, if we all look and sound and think alike, eventually the conversation will wind down to where we say the same old things in the same old ways, where, rather than learning from one another, we simply reaffirm our beliefs. As much as she is talking about who should have a voice in the conversation, Martin is talking about the health of the educational conversation itself.

Note

1. Michael Oakeshott, *Rationalism in Politics and Other Essays* (London: Methuen, 1962), p. 199.

From *Reclaiming a Conversation: The Ideal of the Educated Woman* (1985)

Contemporary philosophers of education ignore the subject of women. In the technical writings of the academy, as in popular polemical works, questions of gender simply do not arise. These theorists analyze the concept of education, discuss the nature and structure of liberal education, construct theories of teaching and learning, set forth criteria of excellence, and debate educational aims and methods without attending to the difference of sex. It has not always been this way. Plato—perhaps the greatest educational philosopher in the history of Western thought and certainly the first systematic one—wrote specifically about the education of females. So did Jean-Jacques Rousseau, one of the few Western philosophers whose educational thought rivals Plato's both in its depth of understanding and in its far-reaching influence. Indeed, throughout Western history both men and women have taken the subject of women's education sufficiently seriously to have written countless treatises about it.

The question arises, then, why educational theorists in our day take no notice of gender and why feminist theorists, in their turn, pay so little attention to questions of educational philosophy. Studies of sex differences in learning and sex bias in educational practices abound, research in the history of women's education flourishes, discussions of feminist pedagogy are numerous, and debates on the best way to incorporate the study of women into the liberal curriculum are commonplace. An examination of educational ideals, however, is seldom found in contemporary literature on women, and the construction of an adequate philosophy of women's education is rarely seen as relevant to the task of developing a comprehensive feminist theory.[1]

Feminist theory has not always been divorced from educational philosophy. Mary Wollstonecraft's *A Vindication of the Rights of Woman* (1792) is a treatise both on woman's place and on woman's education, and Charlotte Perkins Gilman's utopian novel *Herland* (1915) joins a well-developed theory of education to a feminist social vision. But that women now are receiving an education very much like the one Wollstonecraft urged for her daughters does not mean it is the one women *should* be receiving. Indeed, as Adrienne Rich, one of the few contemporary feminists who has written incisively and evocatively on the education of women, has pointed out, that women continue to *receive* an education is itself a matter of concern.

Addressing a group of female college students in 1977, Rich asked them to think of themselves as *claiming* rather than *receiving* an education. The difference between the two verbs is the difference between acting and being acted upon, she said, "and for women it can literally mean the difference between life and death."[2] Why is passivity toward learning a potentially fatal attitude? Rich was not merely echoing the psychologists who tell us that learning must be active if it is to be effective, although she might well accept the validity of the argument. Perceiving the extent to which education can promote or stunt women's growth and development, Rich grounded her thesis on a feminist vision of what women's lives can and should be. She was saying that in becoming mere receptacles for a university learning that excludes their experience and thought, women's lives can be damaged beyond repair.

Rich urged her audience to take charge not just of the manner in which they learn but of the content of their learning: "What you can learn here (and I mean not only at Douglass but any college in any university) is how *men* have perceived and organized their experience, their history, their ideas about social relationships, good and evil, sickness and health, etc. When you read or hear about 'great issues,' 'major texts,' 'the mainstream of Western thought,' you are hearing about what men, above all white men, in their male subjectivity, have decided is important."[3] She might have added that one should not expect to find included among those great issues or in the major texts her topic—the education of women. For although conversation on women's education began centuries before the birth of Christ and has continued into the present time, it has simply been ignored by the standard texts and anthologies in the history of educational thought.[4]

---

[1] I realize that although individual feminist thinkers have tended to neglect questions of educational philosophy, the women's studies movement is directly concerned with just such issues. The extent to which this movement has explored alternative educational *ideals* is a question that requires further investigation.

[2] Adrienne Rich, "Claiming an Education," in *On Lies, Secrets and Silence* (New York: W. W. Norton & Co., 1979), p. 231.

[3] Ibid., p. 232.

[4] Jane Roland Martin, "Excluding Women from the Educational Realm," *Harvard Educational Review* 52 (1982):133–48.

Does it matter that this conversation over time and space is missing? If females today have access to the same education as males—and in the United States to a great extent they do—what difference does it make that historians of educational thought neglect the topic of women, that Plato's, Rousseau's, Wollstonecraft's, and Gilman's discussions of women's education have not been incorporated into the mainstream of Western thought? Does the discovery in educational history of epistemological inequality—by which I mean inequality in knowledge itself: in this instance, in the representation of women in historical narratives and philosophical interpretations—have any practical significance for those who would follow Rich's advice and claim an education for and about themselves?[5]

Since the early 1970s research has documented the ways in which such intellectual disciplines as history and psychology, literature and the fine arts, sociology and biology are biased according to sex.[6] This work has revealed that on at least three counts the disciplines fall short of the ideal of epistemological equality for women: they exclude women from their subject matter, distort the female according to the male image of her, and deny value to characteristics the society considers feminine. When a discipline does not meet the standard of epistemological equality, not only women but the tasks and functions society associates with them are denigrated. The problem is compounded when the history of educational thought falls short of this ideal because so many parties to the ongoing conversation about female education are women.

To the extent that the major historical texts overlook Plato's female guardians and Rousseau's Sophie, women's lives and experiences are devalued. When the voices of Wollstonecraft and Gilman are unrecorded, students are denied contact with some of the great female minds of the past; the implicit message is that women have never thought systematically about education, that indeed, they may be incapable of serious philosophical reflection on the topic.

I do not mean to suggest that every female educational theorist has been interested primarily in the education of her own sex. Maria Montessori is a notable example of a woman who developed a philosophy of education without reference to sex or gender. Yet many women have focused on female education. For example, with *A Vindication of the Rights of Woman* Mary Wollstonecraft entered the ongoing conversation by questioning Rousseau's theory of the education of girls and women and presenting one of her own. She, in turn, was influenced by the contribution Catherine Macaulay had made to this conversa-

---

[5] To say that a discipline such as the history of educational thought has not achieved epistemological equality is to comment on the nature of the knowledge produced by that discipline, not on the nature of practitioners of the discipline and not on, for example, the hiring practices within the profession.

[6] This new scholarship on women is too extensive to be cited in its entirety here. For reviews of it, see the journal *Signs*. See also anthologies such as Julia A. Sherman and Evelyn Torton Beck, eds., *The Prism of Sex* (Madison: University of Wisconsin Press, 1979); Elizabeth Langland and Walter Gove, eds., *A Feminist Perspective in the Academy* (Chicago: University of Chicago Press, 1983); Sandra Harding and Merill B. Hintikka, eds., *Discovering Reality* (Dordrecht: D. Reidel Publishing Co., 1983).

tion in her *Letters on Education* (1790). In numerous books and articles written at a later date in another country, Catharine Beecher set forth a philosophy of the education of girls and women that presents interesting contrasts to Wollstonecraft's. And Beecher's grandniece, Charlotte Perkins Gilman, wove into her utopian novel, *Herland,* her educational philosophy for women.

Although these theorists of female education were well known in their own day, it is likely that until recently even Wollstonecraft's name would have been unfamiliar to historians of educational thought. I am able to cite them here because contemporary research on women is in the process of recovering the lives and works of so many who had been lost to history. Yet even if blame does not attach to the authors of the texts that silence women's voices, the fate of the contributions of Plato and Rousseau suggests that had the writings on female education of Macauley, Wollstonecraft, Beecher, and Gilman been known to exist, they too would have been ignored.

The devaluation of women is not the only unhappy consequence of the exclusion from the history of educational thought of all conversation about female education. The noted philosopher of education Israel Scheffler has said that the function of philosophy is to enlighten policy "by pressing its traditional questions of value, virtue, veracity, and validity."[7] These questions need to be pressed in relation to policies concerning the education of girls and women; yet as long as the conversation to which they belong is considered to fall outside the province of philosophy, they cannot be.

In inviting students to take responsibility for their own education, Rich beseeched them to reject those models of feminine weakness, self-denial, and subservience the culture holds up to them:

> Responsibility to yourself means that you don't fall for shallow and easy solutions—predigested books and ideas, weekend encounters guaranteed to change your life, taking 'gut' courses instead of ones you know will challenge you, bluffing at school and life instead of doing solid work, marrying early as an escape from real decisions, getting pregnant as an evasion of already existing problems. It means that you refuse to sell your talents and aspirations short, simply to avoid conflict and confrontation. And this, in turn, means resisting forces in society which say that women should be nice, play safe, have low professional expectations, drown in love and forget about work, live through others, and stay in the places assigned to us.[8]

Every woman has felt the pull of one or more of these negative models. She who is not attracted to the ideal of the self-denying wife and mother may become a woman who denies her intelligence; she who disdains the ideal of silent passivity may find the model of "the slapdash dilettante who never commits herself to anything the whole way" irresistible. Each of us will see mother

---

[7] Israel Scheffler, "Philosophy of Education: Some Recent Contributions," *Harvard Educational Review 50* (1980):402–06.

[8] Rich, "Claiming an Education," pp. 233–34.

or daughter, sister or friend, if not oneself, represented on Rich's list. Unfortunately, if a woman does what Rich asks—if she takes responsibility for her own education—she will find herself at a disadvantage. How can a woman avoid shallow solutions to the problems education poses if she never hears what has been said by those who have thought deeply on the subject? How can she know what education to claim if she has never entered into philosophical conversation about this education herself, indeed never even realized that such conversation existed?[9]

Not only women are led astray in this circumstance; men also suffer when they are denied knowledge of the range of educational ideals past philosophers have held up for half the population. In *A Vindication* Wollstonecraft makes clear the disastrous consequences for the man, Emile, of the faulty education Rousseau designs for Sophie. Sophie's case can be generalized. So long as men and women inhabit the same society and live overlapping lives, each sex will be affected by the education of the other. Unenlightened policies of female education will inevitably redound on males.

There is another reason men suffer when past conversation about women's education is ignored. Historians of educational thought are not antiquarians whose sole concern is to preserve the ideas of the past. They justify their inquiries by reference to the insights into contemporary education yielded by a study of past philosophies. "Philosophy, unlike the sciences, never fully outgrows its history," says Scheffler. "The arguments and conceptions of past thinkers retain a fundamental relevance for contemporary philosophy even as it struggles to find new ways for itself."[10] Historical study, then, illuminates educational practice today and guides the development, clarification, and testing of new theories about what education should be.[11]

How much illumination can be shed on the education of boys and men by a historical narrative that ignores girls and women? Philosophers do not construct theories of education in a vacuum. Viewing education as preparation for carrying on societal roles, they tie their proposals to some vision of the good society. And insofar as the society the philosopher pictures is peopled by both sexes, we cannot evaluate the educational ideal it holds up for males unless we know its expectations for females. We will not even know the right questions to ask. Do men and women in the envisioned society have reciprocal roles, with men carrying out the functions of citizenship and women those of domesticity? If so, we must ask not only if the education claimed for males will equip them to be good citizens but also if it will promote or frustrate the efforts of women to perform their own functions effectively. Alternatively, do men and women in

---

[9] Dale Spender says: "While men take it for granted that they can build on what has gone before, selecting, refining, adapting the knowledge they have inherited to meet their needs, women are constantly required to begin with a blank sheet (*Invisible Women: The Schooling Scandal* [London: Writers and Readers Publishing Cooperative Society, 1982], p. 17).

[10] Israel Scheffler, Preface to *Three Historical Philosophies of Education*, by William E Frankena (Chicago: Scott, Foresman & Co., 1965).

[11] Paul Nash, *Models of Man* (New York: John Wiley & Sons, 1968), p. vii; Henry J. Perkinson, *Since Socrates: Studies in the History of Western Educational Thought* (New York: Longman, 1980), p. xi.

this society share roles and the tasks and functions associated with them? If so, we must ask if the full complement of significant social roles is reflected in the education claimed for both men and women.

When history neglects past philosophical conversations about women's education, it follows that the tasks, functions, institutions, and traits of character that philosophy, as a part of our culture, has associated with women are neglected. Discussions about marriage, home, family are missing as are discussions about society's *reproductive* processes—a category I define broadly to include not simply conception and birth but the rearing of children to more or less maturity and associated activities such as tending the sick, taking care of family needs, and running a household.

We look to the history of educational thought for guidance. Because its narrative does not record conversation about female education, it is implied that the only valid questions about education have to do with its adequacy as preparation for citizenship and the workplace.[12] No one would deny the importance of education for society's *productive* processes—in which category I include political and cultural activities as well as economic ones—but other tasks and functions are just as compelling. In the United States in the late twentieth century, we may reject a sex-based division of labor, but we must not forget that many of the tasks and functions that have traditionally been assigned to women are essential to the existence of society and must be carried on well if we are to have any chance of creating a better world.[13]

The statistics on child abuse and domestic violence in our society today[14] belie the assumption that the knowledge, skills, attitudes, and traits of character necessary for effectively carrying out the reproductive processes of society occur naturally in people. Education for these processes is not only as essential as education for society's productive processes but also has an overarching political, social, and moral significance. Jonathan Schell has said that "the nuclear peril makes all of us, whether we happen to have children of our own or not, the parents of all future generations"; he has called the will to save the human species a form of love resembling "the generative love of parents."[15] A historical narrative that neglects conversation about the education of women has little, if anything, to say about this kind of love and cannot serve either sex well.

Men and women need to claim the best possible education for themselves and their sons and daughters. All must listen to and participate in conversation

---

[12] Recent reports on American education reflect this same focus. See, for example, Mortimer J. Adler, *The Paideia Proposal* (New York: Macmillan, 1982); Ernest L. Boyer, *High School* (New York: Harper & Row, 1983); John I. Goodlad, *A Place Called School* (New York: McGraw-Hill Book Co., 1984); Theodore R. Sizer, *Horace's Compromise* (Boston: Houghton Mifflin Co., 1984).

[13] For more on the distinction between productive and reproductive societal processes, see Lorenne Clark, "The Rights of Women: The Theory and Practice of the Ideology of Male Supremacy," in *Contemporary Issues in Political Philosophy*, ed. William R. Shea and John King-Farlow (New York: Science History Publications, 1976), pp. 49–65.

[14] For a thorough discussion of these topics, see Wini Breines and Linda Gordon, "The New Scholarship on Family Violence," *Signs* 8 (1983):493–507.

[15] Jonathan Schell, *The Fate of the Earth* (New York: Avon, 1982), p. 175.

about the ideals governing the education of both sexes. Only then will we understand that the education most of us receive today is too narrow. Only then can we begin to construct theories of education that give the reproductive as well as the productive processes of society their due, and only then can we press our questions of "value, virtue, veracity, and validity" in relation to the whole range of educational concerns. Is education for rearing children and caring for home and family desirable? If so, for whom? Should this education be placed on a par with citizenship education and become a universal requirement or should it be considered a specialty? If it is a specialty, does it properly belong to vocational or professional education? These are a few of the submerged questions that rise to the surface when conversation about women's education is incorporated into public learning. . . .

Redefining the Educational Realm

The larger effort of reclamation—even the conversation reclaimed here—has important implications for the content, methodology, and structure of the history of educational thought. Earlier I raised the question of why this discipline has censored conversation about the education of half the world's population. Now that we know the subject matter of that conversation, we are in a position to answer the question. We have heard Plato, Rousseau, Wollstonecraft, Beecher, and Gilman repeatedly discuss marriage, home, family, child rearing, and domestic management. Of course, they also addressed political and economic issues, but no matter what sort of education our five philosophers were claiming for women, they could not ignore the reproductive processes of society and their associated traits, tasks, functions, and institutions. Historians of educational thought consider these topics to be none of their concern, however.

Lorenne Clark has shown that from the standpoint of political theory the consignment of women, children, and the family to the ontological basement—that is, their apolitical status—is due not to historical accident or necessity but to arbitrary definition.[16] The reproductive processes of society, broadly interpreted to include the rearing of children to more or less independence, are excluded by fiat from the political domain, which is defined in relation to the world of productive processes—political, social, and cultural as well as economic. Since the subject matter of political theory is politics, and since the reproductive processes have traditionally been assigned to women and have taken place within the family, it follows that women and the family are excluded from the subject matter of the discipline.

The analogy between political theory and educational thought is striking. Despite the fact that the reproductive processes of society, broadly understood, are largely devoted to child rearing and include the transmission of skills, beliefs, feelings, emotions, values, and even world views, they are not considered to belong to

---

[16] Lorenne M. G. Clark, "The Rights of Women: The Theory and Practice of the Ideology of Male Supremacy," in *Contemporary Issues an Political Philosophy* ed. William R. Shea and John King-Farlow (New York: Science History Publications, 1976), pp. 49–65.

the educational realm. Thus education, like politics, is defined in relation to the productive processes of society, and the status of women and the family is every bit as "a-educational" as it is apolitical. No wonder Sophie is overlooked by historians of educational thought. Unless the borders of the educational realm are altered, Emily, Sarah, and Ellador will be, too.

To be sure, the education Plato prescribes for his female guardians is designed to equip them to carry on that most important productive process, ruling. If my explanation of the way the history of educational thought defines its subject matter is correct, why is the education of these women neglected by the field? Two reasons come to mind. In the first place, Plato's female guardians constitute an anomaly for the field's definition of itself: productive processes fall within the educational realm; women fall outside it. One way to resolve the problem posed by Plato's women is to ignore them; another is to discuss their education but treat as irrelevant the fact that they are women. Furthermore, to understand and evaluate Plato's theory of female education, one must take into account his views on the institutions of private marriage, home, family, and child rearing. Since these fall outside the educational realm, it is easy enough to perceive the education of his female guardians as falling there, also.

If conversation about women's education is to be incorporated in the history of educational thought, the definition of that discipline's subject matter must be expanded to include the processes of society with which women's lives have historically been intertwined. If the conversational circle is to be enlarged and the discussion enriched, the methods of this field will also have to become more inclusive.

The five theories of female education reclaimed here were reconstructed from the pages of books. Although the last three of the works I have drawn on—*A Vindication, A Treatise, Herland*—are not part of the established canon of educational theory and philosophy, my approach has nonetheless been one of looking to books for data. Recall, however, that one of the books—*Herland*—was originally published in serialized form in a popular magazine. Had it not been for Ann Lane's retrieval, *Herland,* independent of its subject matter, might have been considered a suspect source to use in the reconstruction of the history of educational thought. Thus if we are finally to be able to listen to the full range of our conversation, we will have to change our notion not only of what counts as a bona fide topic of study but also of what counts as a bona fide source of data.

The general expectation that any educational theory worth recording is readily accessible in books or academic journals becomes unreasonable when the objects or the subjects of educational thought are considered marginal. Marginal people do not normally have access to established channels of communication, and those channels rarely give equal time to topics concerning marginal people. Yet marginal is precisely what society has considered women to be. Thus, as the larger effort of reclamation proceeds, we will have to look to sources of data that the history of educational thought regards as far from standard: to personal letters, diaries, pamphlets, newsletters, pieces of fiction, and to oral sources as well.

As our conception of sources is affected by the entrance of women into the educational realm, so too will be our conception of the discipline's techniques.

Historians of educational thought are accustomed to having their philosophers and their sources handed to them ready-made—Dewey's *Democracy and Education*, Whitehead's *The Aims of Education*—so that the investigator's task is the relatively straightforward one of interpretation and evaluation. Occasionally a new work or a new thinker will be discovered and made a part of the canon. Occasionally a person's philosophical thought will be reconstructed from lecture notes rather than polished essays. It is rare, however, for a historian of educational thought to become a historian in the more primary sense of digging up the sources and, in the process, determining whether the author is indeed to be considered an educational philosopher. Yet this is precisely what will be required of those engaged in the larger reclamation effort concerning the education of women—on the one hand, if letters, pamphlets, and the like are even to serve as sources for a reconstructed conversation and, on the other, if we are to discover which individuals in our past have actually constructed theories of female education.

Even this way of putting the problem, however, is a function of present conceptions of methodology, in particular of what counts as an author or creator of an educational philosophy. It is normally assumed that the educational thought of the past worth preserving has been created by individuals. When the topic of study is women's education, this assumption too must be questioned.

Wollstonecraft, Beecher, Gilman: we must not be misled by the fact that these women wrote philosophical works into supposing that women in general have had access to the social, economic, and educational resources philosophy requires. The life stories of the three female participants in our conversation testify to the enormous difficulties even the most successful women have had to overcome in order to do the sort of intellectual labor reclaimed here. Although our three are by no means the only women in history to have attained philosophical authorship in the field of education, we need to follow Wollstonecraft's lead. Just as she refused to ground her case for women's rationality on the existence of the extraordinary women of her time, so we should refuse to ground our larger effort of reclamation on the existence of the relatively few extraordinary women—and those men—who have written extensively on female education. Rather, we must understand that some of the most interesting and significant theories of female education may have been authored not by single individuals but by groups of individuals—for instance, those founding and running schools—and others may have simply emerged out of social movements.

When our conception of authorship changes, historians of educational thought will have to take on the role of anthropologist. Just as the reconstruction of Hopi ethics required the skills of both philosopher and anthropologist,[17] so the reconstruction of the philosophy of education of a school or social movement may require the skills of these two professions and of the primary historian besides. The standard philosophical processes of analysis, criticism, interpretation, and evaluation will continue to be essential activities. Otherwise the very policies and practices whose "value, virtue, veracity, and validity"

---

[17] Richard Brandt, *Hopi Ethics* (Chicago: University of Chicago Press, 1954).

have never been enlightened by philosophy will continue to be denied this needed source of illumination. Nevertheless, when half of the world's population and with it the reproductive processes of society are admitted into the subject matter of a discipline, some very real methodological and substantive changes will occur. The extent of these changes cannot be predicted, but the shape and structure of the narrative of educational thought will undoubtedly be affected.

Once the absence of women from the standard texts and anthologies has been recognized, can we not simply add sections about female education to existing chapters on Plato and Rousseau and introduce new chapters on Wollstonecraft, Beecher, and Gilman? Whatever methodological adjustments may be required, are not revised editions all that we need?

The history of educational thought is no exception to the rule discovered by scholars in a wide range of fields that a simple additive solution to the problem of the inclusion of women will not work. Consider Sophie. As we have seen, it is not just that the accepted interpretation of Rousseau's thought does not mention her education. Sophie's education constitutes an anomaly for that interpretation since what Rousseau says about her stands in contradiction to it. Of course, it is possible to add a section about Sophie to a chapter on Rousseau, but the result will be unsatisfactory: Rousseau will be made to look the fool who spent the last hundred pages of *Emile* contradicting the first three hundred. And Rousseau was no fool. Moreover, the additive approach obscures the important fact that when book 5 of *Emile* is taken seriously, our reading of books 1–4 changes.

How tempting it is to think of women's entry into the educational realm as requiring, if not simply brief addenda to the history of educational thought, then at most the introduction of a second and separate narrative strand. Taking female education as its object of study, would not a second strand complement the already existing one, now acknowledged to constitute a narrative only of the education of males? The suggestion may sound promising, but the separate-strand approach to the history of educational thought is self-defeating: once the female narrative is constructed, the inadequacy of the original strand for even the limited task of tracing theories about the education of boys and men becomes apparent.

Again Sophie is a case in point. Since Rousseau ties her education so closely to her societal role, it is all but impossible to understand *Emile,* book 5, unless concepts like the ones employed in reclaiming the present conversation are introduced. Whether or not the interpretive framework ultimately adopted for Sophie's education is the one used here, it is necessary in capturing Rousseau's intent to introduce such notions as the wife-mother role, domesticity, the patriarchal family, and the reproductive processes of society, which have no place at all in the interpretations that currently constitute the history of educational thought. Home, family, marriage, children: the original narrative strand has nothing to say about such phenomena. Given a second narrative strand in which they figure prominently, the silences of the original narrative will become intolerable. If Sophie is educated for marriage to Emile, the question of his education for marriage to her inevitably arises. If she is educated to be his "other half," questions about the extent and nature of his self-sufficiency can no longer go unasked.

Sophie's case is instructive. Since we have seen in the conversation reclaimed here the standard interpretation of both Rousseau's and Plato's philosophies of education brought into question, the hypothesis that the inclusion of women in the educational realm will have little if any effect on the accepted narrative of the field lacks credibility. When it is understood that females can carry out the guardian duties to Plato's satisfaction only because he has stripped his guardian class of private home, marriage, and family and of all responsibility for the reproductive processes of society, the one-sidedness of the education he prescribes for the guardians is revealed. When his educational ideal of self-disciplined, self-contained individuals is juxtaposed with Gilman's ideal for mother love, the inadequacy of the Platonic scheme for achieving the communal feelings he believes to be essential for unity is exposed. From the examples of Plato and Rousseau one must conclude that those who listen to and engage in conversation about women's education can expect to find enlightenment not only about the education of females but also about that of males.

In a two-sex society it is to be expected that theories of male and female education are mutually illuminating. But the major reason for rejecting the two-strand approach is not that the theoretical separation of females and males keeps out badly needed light, although it does. The more important fault is its failure to recognize that in our two-sex society, educational theory and philosophy must place males and females in one world—a world in which the sexes live together interdependently. Only when Sophie and Emile are seen to be interdependent individuals and their education is interpreted in light of their relationship to each other is an adequate understanding of Rousseau's educational thought possible. Only when the reproductive processes of society are seen to stand in relation to the productive ones is an adequate understanding of Plato's educational thought possible.

Of the parties to our conversation, both Plato and Rousseau understand that so long as the societies they envision contain males and females, the theories of education they construct will have to take both sexes into account. Rousseau, in particular, understands the importance of developing an educational theory that recognizes the ways in which the sexes interact. It is no accident that Sophie is educated for dependence: that is the relation in which she is supposed to stand to Emile. It is no accident that he is educated to be his own legislator: that is the relation in which he, as citizen, is supposed to stand to the state and he, as husband, is supposed to stand to Sophie. To be sure, if Emile is educated according to plan, he may not in fact acquire the loving qualities he must possess if his union with Sophie is to flourish. But this is because Rousseau is mistaken about what a harmonious marriage involves, not because he does not realize that males and females must be educated to live in the same world.

As a woman who had founded a highly successful female seminary, Beecher had ample justification for directing her attention specifically to the education of females. Yet it must not be forgotten that in Beecher's philosophy Sarah requires a husband who acknowledges her competence. Beecher's ideal society could perhaps incorporate legal sanctions to force men to give way to their wives in domestic affairs, but it certainly would run more smoothly and happily if, instead, the early education of males instilled in them a willingness to accept the judgment of professionals of both sexes.

Given her desire to extend the rights of men to women, Wollstonecraft also had good reason to develop a theory of female, not male, education. Yet her daughters require husbands who will treat them as equals in marriage and politics, and there is no reason to suppose that without reeducation the men they marry will do so. Of course, by extending to women the education she takes to be suitable for men, in *A Vindication* Wollstonecraft indirectly takes a stand on the education of males. But if she really wants to educate a new woman, she cannot realistically advocate the same old education for men. Just as Plato must reeducate his male guardians to respect and treat as equals the females he would educate to be rulers, so to transform the marriage relation and to add to women's traditional wife-mother role that of citizen, Wollstonecraft must reeducate her sons as well as her daughters.

Wollstonecraft is correct that Sophie is an artifact of society. What she fails to note is that Emile is socialized, too, and that so long as his socialization and formal education remain unchanged, the new educational program she constructs for Emily will be insufficient. Will men treat Emily as an equal citizen—will they, indeed, allow her to be a citizen—if they continue to believe that Sophie represents every woman? Will Emily be willing or able to reject Sophie if the man in her life continues to desire a toy rather than a friend and colleague? Will she derive the anticipated benefits from the male education extended to her if Sophie remains the norm in male eyes?

So long as Sophie represents the norm for femininity, Emily will be evaluated negatively for her rationality and independence.[18] Thus even as Wollstonecraft educates her daughters to be citizens and rational wives-mothers, she must educate her sons to see Sophie as she does. She can hope that, because of their own rationality, without her intervention her Emiles will appreciate her Emilys once they get to know them, but she had best not count on their relinquishing voluntarily their monopoly in political affairs and their ultimate authority in marriage. For this end to be realized, Wollstonecraft's sons must come to see the world—and women in particular—differently. Even as Wollstonecraft extends men's formal education to women, she must change men's informal education so as to transform their consciousness.

Moreover, if men's *formal* education remains unchanged, Wollstonecraft's social and political program for women will not succeed. In extending to females the liberal education traditionally limited to males, Wollstonecraft

---

[18] Consider the following excerpts from interviews conducted in 1969–70 with members of the senior class of an Ivy League male college: "I enjoy talking to more intelligent girls, but I have no desire for a deep relationship with them. I guess I still believe that the man should be more intelligent." "I may be frightened of a man who is superior to me in some field of knowledge, but if a girl knows more than I do, I resent her" (Mirra Komarovsky, "Cultural Contradictions and Sex Roles: The Masculine Case," in *Changing Women in a Changing Society,* ed. Joan Huber (Chicago: University of Chicago Press, 1973), p. 112.

makes the mistake Plato makes of initiating both sexes into cognitive perspectives according to which women are viewed as the Other, as beings defined and differentiated by reference to men.[19] Surely the exclusion or distortion of the lives, works, and experiences of women from the subject matter of the theoretical disciplines is not a modern phenomenon. Philosophers did not begin portraying women as less rational than men in the nineteenth and twentieth centuries. With few exceptions, Greek, medieval, Renaissance, and Enlightenment philosophies all contain a vision of women as creatures both alien and inferior. And until the past two decades historians have tended to overlook the accomplishments of individual women and to ignore entirely topics having to do specifically with female experience. Thus, unless Wollstonecraft takes measures to transform the content of the liberal education she extends to both males and females, there is little reason to expect the males to view the females as their equals in the state or in the home, or for that matter for the females to consider themselves their husbands' equals.

Beecher is guilty also of prescribing a liberal education for women in which they are either seen through male eyes or not seen at all. Gilman, as we know, gets around this problem by constructing a one-sex society in which women have created their own forms of knowledge. That she does not endow Herland with the ready-made disciplines of her own society suggests that she perceived their male biases. Furthermore, Gilman's treatment of the intrusion of the three American males, and especially her differentiation of the views of women held by Terry, Jeff, and Van, indicate that she was well aware of both male socialization and the need for male reeducation. Still, Gilman does not provide us with a two-sex philosophy of education in which these insights are fully incorporated.

Educating Our Sons

"What do we want for our sons?" asks Adrienne Rich in *Of Woman Born*. "We want them to remain, in the deepest sense, sons of the mother, yet also to grow into themselves, to discover new ways of being men even as we are discovering new ways of being women."[20] If she could have one wish for her own sons, Rich continues, it is that they should have the courage of women: "I mean by this something very concrete and precise: the courage I have seen in women who, in their private and public lives, both in the interior world of their dreaming, thinking, and creating, and the outer world of patriarchy, are taking greater and greater risks, both psychic and physical, in the evolution of a new vision" (p. 215).

Rich's new vision includes the assimilation of males into a full-time, universal system of child care that would change not only the expectations of both sexes about gender roles but "the entire community's relationship to children." A latter-day Charlotte Perkins Gilman in her insistence that "the mother-child

---

[19] Simone de Beauvoir, in *The Second Sex* (New York: Bantam, 1961), provides an extended discussion of woman as the Other.

[20] Adrienne Rich, *Of Woman Born* (New York: Bantam, 1977), p. 210.

relationship is the essential human relationship" and simultaneously that "the myth that motherhood is 'private and personal' is the deadliest myth we have to destroy,"[21] Rich makes clear the need men will have for "a kind of compensatory education in the things about which their education as males has left them illiterate."[22]

The realm of illiteracy Rich has in mind is populated by the virtues of Sophie and Sarah: a well-developed capacity for sympathetic identification, a denial of the separation between love and work, a desire and an ability to nurture children. One need not adopt Rich's social vision—in which children are no longer "mine" and "thine," the mother-child relationship is placed at the very center of society, and child rearing is a universal responsibility—to agree that in the late twentieth century men should be claiming for themselves an education in Sophie's and Sarah's virtues as well as Emile's. Family living and child rearing are not today, if they ever were, solely in the hands of women. Males and females alike have responsibility for making the reproductive processes of society work well. Thus, men must claim an education that does justice to those processes even as they claim one that gives the productive processes their due.

The reproductive processes are of central importance to any society. It is no small matter, then, to insist that men as well as women be educated to carry them on. It would be a terrible mistake, however, to suppose that in our own society the virtues of Sophie and Sarah have no relevance beyond marriage, home, family, and child rearing. Ours is a country in which one out of four women is raped at some time in her life, one out of four girls and one out of ten boys is sexually abused before the age of eighteen, and some $4–6 billion per year are grossed by the pornography industry.[23] Our country belongs to a world on the brink of nuclear and/or ecological disaster. Efforts to overcome these problems, as well as the related ones of poverty, economic scarcity, and racial injustice, flounder today under the direction of people who do not know how to sustain human relationships or respond directly to human needs, indeed, do not even see the value of trying to do so. We should not suppose that education can solve the world's problems. Yet if there is to be any hope of the continuation of life on earth, let alone of a good life for all, those who carry on society's productive processes must acquire the nurturing capacities and ethics of care Rousseau attributes to Sophie's nature.

Unfortunately, easy as it is to say that men's education must take Sophie and Sarah into account, and convincing as it may sound, our Platonic heritage stands between us and this goal. A case study of what almost everyone today would consider American education at its best reveals the extent to which Plato's educational vision persists in our own time and the damage it does.

[21] Adrienne Rich, "The Contemporary Emergency and the Quantum Leap," in *On Lies, Secrets, and Silence* (New York: Norton, 1979), p. 271.

[22] Rich, *Of Woman Born*, p. 216.

[23] Allen Griswold Johnson, "On the Prevalence of Rape in the United States," *Signs* 6 (1980):136–46; Bernice Lott, Mary Ellen Reilly, and Dale R. Howard, "Sexual Assault and Harassment: A Campus Community Case Study," *Signs* 8 (1982):296–319; Jack Thomas, "Subject: Child Abuse," *Boston Globe*, September 15, 1984, p. 18; "The Pornographic Industry," *Boston Globe*, February 13–18, 1983.

In his educational autobiography *Hunger of Memory,* Richard Rodriguez tells of growing up in Sacramento, California, the third of four children in a Spanish speaking family.[24] Upon entering first grade he could understand perhaps fifty English words. For half a year he resisted his teachers' demands that he speak English. When asked questions, he mumbled; otherwise he sat waiting for the bell to ring. One Saturday morning three nuns descended upon his house: "Do your children speak only Spanish at home?" they asked his mother. "Is it possible for you and your husband to encourage your children to practice their English when they are at home?" In an instant, Rodriguez's parents agreed, in his words, "to give up the language (the sounds) that had revealed and accentuated our family's closeness." An astounding resolve, but it bore fruit. Within a year Rodriguez was a fluent speaker of English; a short while later he graduated from elementary school with citations galore and entered high school having read hundreds of books; he next attended Stanford University; and, twenty years after the nuns' visit, he sat in the British Museum working on a Ph.D. dissertation in English literature.

Rodriguez, having learned to speak English, went on to acquire a liberal education in history, literature, science, mathematics, philosophy. His is a story of the cultural assimilation of a Mexican-American, but it is more than this, for by no means do all assimilated Americans conform to our image of a well-educated person. Rodriguez does because, to use the terms philosopher R. S. Peters employs in his analysis of the concept of the educated man, he did not simply acquire knowledge and skill.[25] He acquired conceptual schemes to raise his knowledge beyond the level of a collection of disjointed facts and to enable him to understand the reason for things; moreover, the knowledge he acquired is not inert, but characterizes the way he looks at the world and involves the kind of commitment to the standards of evidence and canons of proof of the various disciplines that comes from "getting on the inside of a form of thought and awareness."

Quite a success story; yet *Hunger of Memory* is notable primarily for being a narrative of loss. In the process of becoming an educated man Rodriguez loses his fluency in Spanish, but that is the least of it. As soon as English becomes the language of the Rodriguez family, the special feeling of closeness at home is diminished. As his days are devoted more and more to understanding the meaning of words, it becomes increasingly difficult for Rodriguez to hear intimate family voices. When it is Spanish-speaking, his home is a noisy, playful, warm, emotionally charged environment; with the advent of English the atmosphere becomes quiet and restrained. There is no acrimony. The family remains loving. But the experience of "feeling individualized" by family members is now rare, and occasions for intimacy are infrequent.

---

[24] Richard Rodriguez, *Hunger of Memory: The Education of Richard Rodriguez* (Boston: David B. Godine, 1982).

[25] R. S. Peters, *Ethics and Education* (London: Allen & Unwin, 1966); "Education and the Educated Man" in *A Critique of Current Educational Aims,* ed. R. F. Dearden, P. H. Hirst, and R. S. Peters (London: Routledge & Kegan Paul, 1972).

Thus, Rodriguez tells a story of alienation: from his parents, for whom he soon has no names; from the Spanish language, in which he loses his childhood fluency; from his Mexican roots, in which he loses interest; from his own feelings and emotions, which all but disappear in the process of his learning to control them; from his body itself, as he discovers when, after his senior year in college, he takes a construction job.

John Dewey spent his life trying to combat the tendency of educators to divorce mind from body and reason from emotion. Rodriguez's educational autobiography documents these divorces and another that Dewey deplored, that of self from other. *Hunger of Memory,* above all, depicts a journey from intimacy to isolation. Close ties with family members are dissolved as public anonymity replaces private attention. Rodriguez becomes a spectator in his own home as noise gives way to silence and connection to distance. School, says Rodriguez, bade him trust "lonely" reason primarily. And there is enough time and "silence," he adds, "to think about ideas (big ideas)."

What is the significance of this narrative of loss for those who want to claim the best possible education for their sons? Not every American has Rodriguez's good fortune of being born into a loving home filled with the warm sounds of intimacy; yet the separation and distance he ultimately experienced are by no means unique to him. On the contrary, they represent the natural end point of the educational journey Rodriguez took.

Dewey repeatedly pointed out that the distinction educators draw between liberal and vocational education represents a separation of mind from body, head from hand, thought from action. Since we define an educated person as one who has profited from a liberal education, these splits are built into our ideal of the educated person. Since most definitions of excellence in education derive from that ideal, these splits are built into them as well. A split between reason and emotion is built into our definitions of excellence, too, for we take the aim of a liberal education to be the development not of mind as a whole but of rational mind. We define this in terms of the acquisition of knowledge and understanding, construed very narrowly. It is not surprising that Rodriguez acquires habits of quiet reflection rather than noisy activity, reasoned deliberation rather than spontaneous reaction, dispassionate inquiry rather than emotional response, abstract analytic theorizing rather than concrete storytelling. These are integral to our ideal of the educated person, an ideal familiar to readers of the *Republic.*

Upon completion of his educational journey Rodriguez bears an uncanny resemblance to the guardians of the Just State. Granted, not one of Plato's guardians will be the "disembodied mind" Rodriguez says he became. Yet Plato designs for his guardians an education of heads, not hands. (Presumably the artisans of the Just State will serve as their hands.) Furthermore, holding up for the guardians an ideal of self-discipline and self-government he emphasizes inner harmony at the expense of outward connection. If his guardians do not begin their lives in intimacy, as Rodriguez did, their education, like his, is intended to confirm in them a sense of self in isolation from others.

Do the separations bequeathed to us by Plato matter? The great irony of the liberal education that comes down to us from Plato and still today is the mark of an educated man or woman is that it is neither tolerant nor generous. As Richard Rodriguez discovered, there is no place in it for education of the body, and since most action involves bodily movement, this means there is little room in it for education of action. Nor is there room for education of other-regarding feelings and emotions. The liberally educated man or woman will be provided with knowledge about others but will not be taught to care about their welfare or to act kindly toward them. That person will be given some understanding of society, but will not be taught to feel its injustices or even to be concerned over its fate. The liberally educated person will be an ivory-tower person—one who can reason but has no desire to solve real problems in the real world—or a technical person—one who likes to solve real problems but does not care about the solutions' consequences for real people and for the earth itself.

The case of Rodriguez illuminates several unhappy aspects of our Platonic heritage while concealing another. No one who has seen Fred Wiseman's film *High School* can forget the woman who reads to the assembled students a letter she has received from a pupil in Vietnam. But for a few teachers who cared, she tells her audience, Bob Walters, a subaverage student academically, "might have been a nobody." Instead, while awaiting a plane that is to drop him behind the DMZ, he has written her to say that he has made the school the beneficiary of his life insurance policy. "I am a little jittery right now," she reads. She is not to worry about him, however, because "I am only a body doing a job." Measuring his worth as a human being by his monetary provision for the school, she over-looks the fact that Bob Walters was not merely participating in a war of dubious morality but was taking pride in being an automaton.

High School was made in 1968, but Bob Walters's words were echoed many times over by eighteen- and nineteen-year-old Marine recruits in the days imme-diately following the Grenada invasion. Readers of *Hunger of Memory* will not be surprised. The underside of a liberal education devoted to the development of "disembodied minds" is a vocational education whose business is the produc-tion of "mindless bodies." In Plato's Just State, where, because of their rational powers, the specially educated few will rule the many, a young man's image of himself as "only a body doing a job" is desirable. That the educational theory and practice of a democracy derives from Plato's explicitly undemocratic philo-sophical vision is disturbing. We are not supposed to have two classes of people, those who think and those who do not. We are not supposed to have two kinds of people, those who rule and those who obey.

The Council for Basic Education has long recommended and some people concerned with excellence in education now suggest that a liberal education at least through high school be extended to all.[26] For the sake of argument, let us suppose that this program can be carried out without making more acute the inequities it is meant to erase. We would then presumably have a world in which no one thinks of him- or herself as simply a body doing a job. We would,

---

[26] See, for example, Mortimer J. Adler, *The Paideia Proposal* (New York: Macmillan Co., 1982); Ernest J. Boyer, *High School* (New York: Harper & Row, 1983).

however, have a world filled with unconnected, uncaring, emotionally impoverished people. Even if it were egalitarian, it would be a sorry place in which to live. Nor would the world be better if somehow we combined Rodriguez's liberal education with a vocational one. For assuming our world were then peopled by individuals who joined "head" and "hand," reason would still be divorced from feeling and emotion, and each individual cut off from others.

The Platonic divorce of reason from feeling and emotion and of self from other is built into our prevailing theories of liberal and vocational education as well as into our very definition of the function of education. For Rodriguez, the English language was a metaphor. In the literal sense of the term he had to learn English to become an educated *American,* yet in his narrative the learning of English represents the acquisition not so much of a new natural language as of new ways of thinking, acting, and being, which he associates with the public world. Rodriguez makes it clear that the transition from Spanish to English for him represented the transition almost every child in our society makes from the "private world" of home to the "public world" of business, politics, and culture. He realizes that Spanish is not intrinsically a private language and English a public one, although his own experience made it seem this way. He knows that the larger significance of his story lies in the fact that whether English is one's first or second language, education inducts one into new activities and processes. His autobiography thus reveals that it is not just historians of educational thought and philosophers who define education as preparation solely for carrying on the productive processes of society.

Needless to say, the liberal education Rodriguez received did not fit him to carry on *all* productive processes of society. Aiming as it did at the development of a rational mind, his liberal education prepared him to be a consumer and creator of ideas, not an auto mechanic or factory worker. A vocational education— had he received one—would have prepared him to work with his hands and use procedures designed by others. Very different kinds of education, yet both kinds are designed to fit students to carry on productive, not reproductive, societal processes.[27]

Rodriguez's perception that the function of education is to induct us into the public world and its productive processes is of great consequence. Yet although this function harks back to Plato and constitutes an implicit presupposition of almost all educational thought in our own time, it has never been explicitly acknowledged and so its implications have not been traced. *Hunger of Memory* contains a wonderful account of Rodriguez's grandmother taking him to her room and telling him stories of her life. He is moved by the sounds she makes and by the message of intimacy her person transmits. The words themselves are not important to him, for, as he makes clear, he perceives the private world in which she moves—the world of child rearing and homemaking—to be one of feeling and emotion, intimacy and connection, and hence a realm of the nonrational. In contrast, he sees the public world—the world of productive processes

---

[27] Home economics is the exception to this generalization. However, the chances that Rodriguez would have studied this subject are slight.

for which his education fit him—as the realm of the rational. Feeling and emotion have no place in it, and neither do intimacy and connection. Instead, analysis, critical thinking, and self-sufficiency are the dominant values.

Rodriguez's assumption that feeling and emotion, intimacy and connection are naturally related to the home and society's reproductive processes and that these qualities are irrelevant to carrying on the productive processes is commonly accepted. But then, it is to be expected that their development is ignored by education in general and by liberal education in particular. Since education is supposed to equip people for carrying on productive societal processes, from a practical standpoint would it not be foolhardy for liberal *or* vocational studies to foster these traits?

Only in light of the fact that education turns its back on the reproductive processes of society and the private world of the home can Rodriguez's story of alienation be properly understood. His alienation from his body will reoccur as long as we equate being an educated person with having a liberal education. His journey of isolation and divorce from his emotions will be repeated as long as we define education exclusively in relation to the productive processes of society. But the assumption of inevitability underlying *Hunger of Memory* is mistaken. Education need not separate mind from body and thought from action, for it need not draw a sharp line between liberal and vocational education. More to the point, it need not separate reason from emotion and self from other. The reproductive processes *can* be brought into the educational realm, thereby overriding the theoretical and practical grounds for ignoring feeling and emotion, intimacy and connection.

If we define education in relation to *both* kinds of societal processes and then act upon our redefinition, future generations will not have to experience Rodriguez's pain. The dichotomies upon which his education rested—and which he never questions—must be questioned if we want our sons to be educated well. We must recognize, however, that to challenge the productive/reproductive dichotomy is to call for a basic rethinking of education.

Toward a Gender-Sensitive Ideal

It is no accident that in *Hunger of Memory* the person who is the embodiment of nurturing capacities and an ethics of care is a woman—Rodriguez's grandmother. The two kinds of societal processes, productive and reproductive, are gender-related, and so are the traits our culture associates with them. According to our cultural stereotypes, males are objective, analytical, rational, interested in ideas and things; they have no interpersonal orientation; they are not nurturant or supportive, empathetic or sensitive. Women, on the other hand, possess the traits men lack.[28] Education is also gender-related. Our definition of the function of education makes it so. For if education is viewed as preparation for carrying

---

[28] For discussions of our male and female stereotypes, see, for example, Alexandra G. Kaplan and Joan P Bean, eds., *Beyond Sex-role Stereotypes* (Boston: Little, Brown & Co., 1976); Alexandra G. Kaplan and Mary Anne Sedney, *Psychology and Sex Roles* (Boston: Little, Brown & Co., 1980).

on processes historically associated with males, it will inculcate traits the culture considers masculine. If the concept of education is tied by definition to the productive processes of society, our ideal of the educated person will coincide with the cultural stereotype of a male human being, and our definitions of excellence in education will embody "masculine" traits.

The conversation reclaimed here has shown that it is possible for members of one sex to possess personal traits our cultural stereotypes attribute to the other. Thus, the fact that the traits incorporated in our educational ideal are genderized in favor of males does not mean that girls and women cannot or do not acquire them. It does mean, however, that when females today embark on Rodriguez's journey of becoming educated, they experience hardships that Rodriguez did not. That our daughters do regularly travel the route taken by Rodriguez cannot be doubted. It may have been premature for Virginia Woolf to call Wollstonecraft's philosophy her "commonplace,"[29] but in late-twentieth-century America, Wollstonecraft's proposal to extend Emile's education to Emily has been accomplished.

Having pondered the fate of both Emily and the female guardians of the Just State, we have some idea of the difficulties girls and women encounter when their education is guided by ideals developed for boys and men. Because women today participate in the productive processes of society, they must acquire the traits that are functional for carrying them on. Because they are responsible also for performing at least some of the reproductive processes, they must, as Beecher argued, apply those "masculine" traits of rationality and self-government in this area, too, if these processes are to be performed well.

In claiming their education women would be well advised to reject the Platonic mold placed on Rodriguez, but in doing so they should not deny themselves access to all the traits our culture associates with males. While opting for a new ideal that joins reason to feeling and emotion and self to other, women must make such qualities as critical thinking, abstract reasoning, and self-government their own as they claim both Sophie's and Sarah's virtues for themselves.

Do girls and women today really need to claim an education in Sophie's virtues? Doesn't Nancy Chodorow's thesis that women develop nurturing capacities just because they are mothered by women imply that no education for females in an ethics of care is required? And is Carol Gilligan's finding of "a different voice" proof that at least this kind of education need not be claimed for females? The answer to these questions must be no: Chodorow's theory does not rule out education in nurturance, nor has Gilligan suggested that all females possess Sophie's virtues. The moral to be drawn from the new scholarship on women is not that females have no need for an education in nurturance but rather that an education in Sophie's virtues for females may have to proceed differently from one designed for males. Where the different voice exists it may simply need to be fostered; where it does not exist it must be constructed.

---

[29] Virginia Woolf, "Mary Wollstonecraft," reprinted in Mary Wollstonecraft, *A Vindication of the Rights of Women*, ed. Carol H. Poston (New York: Norton, 1975), p. 221.

Insofar as we contemplate, as Plato did, an education for both sexes in traits and tasks associated with the productive processes of society, and insofar as we contemplate, as Gilman did, an education for both sexes in traits and tasks associated with the reproductive processes—we should not make the mistake of uncritically accepting the Identity Postulate. The educational treatment given males and females may have to be different if equivalent results are to be achieved. Before I became a participant in the conversation reclaimed here I assumed, as many people do, that the sole alternative to separate gender-bound ideals of education such as Rousseau's was one that, like Plato's, remained gender-blind. Once I entered into this conversation, however, I began to see that there is another alternative—namely, a *gender-sensitive* educational ideal.

In a society in which traits are genderized and socialization according to sex is commonplace, an educational philosophy that tries to ignore gender in the name of equality is self-defeating. Implicitly reinforcing the very stereotypes and unequal practices it claims to abhor, it makes invisible the very problems it should be addressing. So long as sex and gender are fundamental aspects of our personal experience, so long as they are deeply rooted features of our society, educational theory—and educational practice, too—must be gender-sensitive. This does not mean that we must, in the manner of Rousseau, hold up different ideals for the two sexes. It does not mean that we should agree with him that sex is the difference that makes all the difference. What it does mean is that we must constantly be aware of the workings of sex and gender because in this historical and cultural moment, paradoxically they sometimes make a big difference even if they sometimes make no difference at all.

When education is defined solely in relation to the productive processes of society, trait genderization is seen as "a woman's problem." Once we redefine education so as to give the reproductive processes of society their due, once the virtues of nurturance and care associated with those processes are fostered in both males and females, educated men can expect to suffer for possessing traits genderized in favor of females, as educated women do now for possessing traits genderized in favor of males. This is not to say that males would be placed in the double bind educated females find themselves in now, for males would continue also to acquire traits genderized in their own favor, whereas the traits educated females must acquire today are *all* genderized in favor of males. On the other hand, since traits genderized in favor of females are considered by our culture to be lesser virtues, if virtues at all, and the societal processes with which they are associated are judged relatively unimportant, males would be placed in the position of having to acquire traits both they and their society consider inferior. Because his hands were soft Rodriguez worried that his education was making him effeminate. Imagine his anxieties if he had been educated in those supposedly feminine virtues of caring and concern and had been taught to sustain intimate relationships and to value connection.

When we claim Sophie's and Emile's virtues for both sexes, trait genderization becomes everyone's problem. Yet despite the fact that males as well as females can be made to feel abnormal if they acquire traits genderized in favor of their "opposites"—and that, as Elizabeth Janeway has pointed out, "natural" and "abnormal" are our equivalents of what being "damned" meant to our ancestors[30] —the issues genderized traits raise for males and females differ. Educate our daughters according to an ideal incorporating "masculine" traits and, whatever damage done them, they can at least console themselves that the qualities they acquire are considered valuable and the societal processes to which these traits are attached are considered worthwhile. Educate our sons in Sophie's and Sarah's virtues and they will have no such consolation.

The existence of genderized traits makes sensitivity to gender a prerequisite of sound educational policy and so does the persistence into our own time of the value hierarchy Beecher tried to overturn. Assigning greater importance to its productive than its reproductive processes, our society places a higher value on the masculine than the feminine gender. Those who remain blind to gender will not see this disparity and consequently will not address it explicitly. Yet our policymakers must address it or the prospects of extending to our sons the education they deserve will remain slight.

What is to be done by those who believe that humanity's fate and that of the earth itself require that boys and girls, women and men, should all possess Sophie's and Sarah's virtues as well as Emile's? One essential first step is to raise to consciousness the hidden curriculum of schooling: its denigration of women and the tasks, traits, and functions our culture associates with them.[31] The subject matter of the liberal curriculum is drawn from disciplines of knowledge—history, literature, science—that give pride of place to male experience and achievement and to the societal processes associated with men. Implicitly, then, this curriculum is the bearer of bad news about women and the reproductive processes of society.

At college and university campuses across the country programs in women's studies thrive and projects incorporating the ever increasing body of scholarship on women into the liberal curriculum as a whole are underway. Such efforts must be undertaken at all levels of schooling, for it is too little, too late, and too elitist to postpone until the college years the revelations of the new research. Taking our cue from Plato, moreover, we must acknowledge that our schools and colleges are not our only educative—or in this instance miseducative—institutions, and we must expand our sights accordingly. Even as we work directly to change the negative messages about women and the reproductive processes of society transmitted by religious and secular, popular and high culture, we should raise to a conscious level in all students the hidden value hierarchy of society itself.

Another essential step is to build nurturing capacities and an ethics of care into the curriculum itself. I do not mean by this that we should fill up school time with courses in the 3 Cs of caring, concern, and connection. In an education that gives Sophie, Sarah, and the reproductive processes of society their due, Compassion 101a need no more be listed in a school's course offering

---

[30] Elizabeth Janeway, *Man's World, Woman's Place* (New York: Morrow, 1971), p. 96.

[31] Jane Roland Martin, "What Should We Do with a Hidden Curriculum When We Find One?" *Curriculum Inquiry* 6 (1976):135–51.

than Objectivity 101a is now. Just as the general curricular goals of rationality and individual autonomy derive from the productive processes of society, so too the reproductive processes yield general goals. And just as rationality and autonomy are posited as goals of particular subjects, such as science, as well as of the curriculum as a whole, so nurturance and connection can become over-arching educational goals as well as the goals of particular subjects.

In making nurturance, caring, concern, and connection goals of education, we must beware of replicating within the curriculum the split between the productive and reproductive processes of society. If education links nurturing capacities and the 3 Cs only to subjects such as home economics that arise out of the reproductive processes, we will lose sight of the *general* moral, social, and political significance of these traits. So long as rationality and autonomous judgment are linked exclusively with the productive processes of society, the reproductive ones will continue to be devalued. Thus, we must find ways of incorporating Sophie's and Sarah's virtues into our science, math, history, literature, and auto mechanics courses, even as we emphasize theoretical knowledge and the development of reason in the teaching of nutrition or family living.

Essential as these measures are, however, consciousness raising, the setting of new goals, and the integration of the new scholarship on women into the curriculum are only the first steps in the transformation of the journey of becoming educated. We should not underestimate the changes to be wrought by redefining the function of education and restructuring the ideal of an educated man or woman. When the productive/reproductive dichotomy and its accompanying hierarchy of values is rejected, teaching methods, learning activities, classroom atmospheres, teacher-pupil relationships, school structures, attitudes toward education may all be affected. As a matter of fact, we cannot even assume that our definitions of the virtues of Sophie and Emile will remain the same. Combine his rationality and objectivity with her nurturance and caring and who knows—his "masculine" qualities and her "feminine" ones may both be transformed.

The details of these changes must be worked out, but I can think of few tasks as important or exciting. Too seldom do we perceive education to be the creative endeavor it really is. The subjects taught in our schools are not God-given; the way our schools are organized and children learn is by no means writ in stone; our educational ideals and our view of the function of education are not immutable truths.[32] We should not delude ourselves that education can be created anew: as a social institution it has a history and traditions, and it is bound by economic and cultural constraints. Nevertheless, old habits of educational thinking can change, long-standing assumptions can be discarded, and fresh vision can improve practice. One of the unanticipated rewards of bringing women into the educational realm is that the study of the education of the "other" half of the population enables us to see all of education differently. The changed vision resulting from acquaintance with the conversation reclaimed here makes our own journey of transforming the education of our sons and

---

[32] Jane Roland Martin, "Two Dogmas of Curriculum," *Synthese* 51 (1982):5–20.

daughters possible. If we let it, it will also enable us to discern ways to bring educational practice into tune with the full range of people's lives and with the present perils to life on earth.

Questions

1. What does Jane Roland Martin mean by suggesting that education should be viewed as a sort of "conversation"?
2. Do you think the kinds of conversation Socrates engaged his students in would have been different if the students were girls? if they had included girls? if Socrates had been a woman?
3. What do Lorenne Clark and Martin mean by the claim that political theorists have relegated women, children, and the family to the "ontological basement"?
4. What is a separate-strand approach to the history of educational thought, and why, according to Martin, is it self-defeating?
5. What does Martin mean by a gender-sensitive ideal of education?
6. How is *gender-sensitive* different from *gender-biased*?
7. What does it mean, in terms of education, for a person or a group to be marginal?

chapter **12**

Cornel West

TIME LINE FOR WEST

1953	Is born June 2 in Tulsa, Oklahoma. His father, a civilian air force administrator, his mother, an elementary school teacher, and his older brother and younger sisters moved frequently, finally settling down in Sacramento, California.
1970	Enrolls at Harvard University.
1973	Receives an A.B. degree.
1975	Receives an M.A. from Princeton University.
1975/6	Returns to Harvard as a Du Bois Fellow.
1980	Receives a Ph.D. from Princeton University.
1977–1984	Is assistant professor of philosophy and religion at Union Theological Seminary.
1979–1980	Serves as visiting professor at Yale University Divinity School.
1981	Serves as visiting professor at Barnard College, New York.
1982	Serves as visiting professor at Williams College, Williamstown, Massachusetts.
	Publishes *Prophecy Deliverance! An Afro-American Revolutionary Christianity.*
1983	Serves as visiting professor at Haverford College, Pennsylvania.
1984	Is appointed associate professor at Union Theological Seminary.

1984–1987	Is associate professor of philosophy and religion at Yale University.
1985	Publishes, with John Rajchman, an edited work, *Post-Analytic Philosophy*.
1987	Serves as visiting professor at University of Paris.
1988	Is named director of Afro-American studies at Princeton University.
	Publishes *Prophetic Fragments*.
1989	Publishes *The American Evasion of Philosophy: A Genealogy of Pragmatism*.
1991	Publishes *The Ethical Dimensions of Marxist Thought* and *Breaking Bread: Insurgent Black Intellectual Life*.
1993	Publishes *Race Matters; Keeping Faith; Prophetic Thought in Postmodern Times;* and *Prophetic Reflections: Notes on Race and Power in America*.
1995	Publishes, with Henry Louis Gates, *Colored People: A Memoir*.
1996	Publishes, with Henry Louis Gates, *The Future of the Race*.
1996	Publishes, with Michael A Lerner, *Jews and Blacks: A Dialogue on Race, Religion and Culture in America*.
1996	Publishes, with George E. Curry, *The Affirmative Action Debate*.
1998	Publishes, with Sylvia Ann Hewlett, *The War Against Parents: What We Can Do for America's Beleaguered Moms and Dads*.

Introduction

Cornel West is an enigma in a three-piece suit. Characterized by the *New York Times* as "a young, hip black man in an old, white academy; a believing Christian in a secular society; a progressive socialist in the age of triumphant capitalism; a cosmopolitan public intellectual among academic specialists," West defies easy classification.[1] Much like his characterization of Emerson, West refuses to "swim in a regulated pool nor allow others to imitate his stroke."[2] A professor of philosophy at Princeton, West has, in recent years, become more than just an academic celebrity. With his recent work *Race Matters* hovering on or near the best-seller list, West has become a public phenomenon.

Born in Tulsa, Oklahoma, West grew up in a working-class black area of Sacramento, California. According to his parents, young Cornel West set high standards for himself "academically, athletically, socially, and spiritually."[3] Very early in life he exhibited the ability to inspire others to focus on their best qualities and to overcome their weaknesses. While his personal accomplishments have been many—including acceptance at Harvard at age 16—West has remained a teacher (some might say a preacher), always using his intellectual prowess to assist others in making the most of themselves. Perhaps his greatest gift is his ability to live both in the "rarefied world of the mind"[4] and in the world of the oppressed African American, contributing to the transformation of both.

In short, West embodies his vision of the ideally educated individual. His ideally educated person, his prophetic thinker, is one who lives in and understands multiple realities and uses such understanding in building bridges between and among these varied worlds. Such an individual is fallible: No one has unmediated access to God, and progress toward creating a better world for humankind is in no way preordained or guaranteed. Though painfully aware of the bigotry and hatred that characterize much of our contemporary world, West refuses to abandon hope. It is at this point that West's spirituality emerges, manifesting itself in his faith that prophetic thinkers can make positive differences in our own and others' lives.

Long recognized as an outstanding scholar known for his critique of American religious and philosophic thought, West has more recently entered the public arena. In a recent work, published almost verbatim from his public lectures, West is clearly attempting to achieve a "public" voice. In this little book, *Prophetic Thought in Postmodern Times,* West explains for a general audience what he means by "prophetic thought." "There are," he suggests, "four basic components, four fundamental features, four constitutive elements."[5] These include discernment, connection, tracking hypocrisy, and hope.

Regarding discernment, West suggests that "prophetic thought must have the capacity to provide a deep and broad analytical grasp of the present in light of the past."[6] Such a deep understanding is necessary for grasping the complexities of the present and for conceptualizing possible visions of the future that build upon and extend the best that the past and present have to offer. In short, a prophetic thinker must be a bit of a historian, developing a vision of what should be out of a sophisticated understanding of what has been and is.

The second component of prophetic thought concerns the necessity of human connection. Here West suggests that a prophetic thinker must relate to or connect with others. Rather than just considering humankind in the abstract, prophetic thinkers must value and have empathy for fellow human beings. To West "empathy is the capacity to get in contact with the anxieties and frustrations of others."[7] Such empathy is in short supply in our modern world. Like William James before him, West agonizes over the all too common tendency of individuals today to treat others as stereotypical objects rather than as fellow beings worthy of respect.

To students, this failure to connect means that teachers just don't care. But many teachers do care and work very hard to help students. They are often "unable to make the connection that would complete caring relations with their students."[8] Their willingness to empathize with students is often thwarted by the dominant culture's desire to establish teaching "onto a firm scientific footing." As Noddings explains, both teachers and students have become victims in the search for the one best method of instruction. Both teachers and students have become "treatments" and "subjects" in the most recent manifestation of the science of pedagogy.

While the relationship between the need for empathy with others and pedagogy is fairly obvious, equally important for the prophetic thinker is the ability to identify and make known "the gap between principles and practice, between promise and performance, between rhetoric and reality." West identifies this third component of prophetic thought as a tracking of hypocrisy and suggests that it ought to be done in a self-critical rather than a self-righteous manner. It takes courage to boldly and defiantly point out human hypocrisy, but we must retain our humility by "remaining open to having others point out that of [our] own."[9]

West explains that a prophetic thinker cannot be one who has unmediated access to God. Such a view does not deny the necessity of faith for the prophetic thinker, but suggests that faith rests in humankind's ability to create better, more meaningful lives by learning from our mistakes. To participate in this component of prophetic thought is to be open to opinions different from our own. By considering other points of view, new evidence may emerge that refutes part or all of the original stance. In scrutinizing this new evidence it may prove to be inadequate or incorrect, thus enhancing the original position. In either case, knowledge has been expanded and progress made.

The fourth and perhaps most important component of prophetic thought is, simply, hope. West admits that, given the numerous and horrific examples of humankind's inhumanity to each other, it is hard to take hope seriously. Still, without it, all thought—including prophetic thought—is meaningless. As West explains,

> To talk about human hope is to engage in an audacious attempt to galvanize and energize, to inspire and to invigorate world-weary people. Because that is what we are. We are world-weary; we are tired. For some of us there are misanthropic skeletons hanging in our closet. And by misanthropic I mean the notion that we have given up on the capacity to do *anything* right. The capacity of human communities to solve any problem.[10]

West suggests that "we must face that skeleton as a challenge, not a conclusion." Even when confronted with numerous atrocities and multiple failures at creating community, the prophetic thinker must keep foremost in mind "the notion that history is incomplete, that the world is unfinished, that the future is open-ended and that what we think and what we do can make a difference."[11] Without hope, in this sense, all that is left is sophisticated analysis resulting in a rather limited and largely meaningless life of the mind.

In the selection included here, taken from a public lecture titled "Beyond Multiculturalism and Eurocentrism," West illustrates the significance of each of these four components for confronting the crucial issues of our postmodern world. In a recent scholarly work, *Keeping Faith: Philosophy and Race in America*, West suggests that it takes all that is within him to remain hopeful about the "struggle for human dignity and existential democracy." Noting "that not since the 1920s have so many black folk been disappointed and disillusioned with America," West admits that he shares these sentiments.[12] Still, in remaining true to the fourth component of prophetic thought, West refuses to abandon hope. West suggests that his branch of "prophetic pragmatism" offers a better way of illuminating and responding to contemporary crises. In short, West believes that the choice is clear for educators. As prophetic thinkers, and for our lives to have meaning, we must believe that what we think and do makes a difference.

Notes

1. An interview with Cornel West by Lucy Hodges, "Read, Hot and Black," *The Times Higher Education Supplement* vol. 1096 (November, 1993), p. 15.
2. Cornel West, *The American Evasion of Philosophy: A Genealogy of Pragmatism* (Madison: University of Wisconsin Press, 1989), p. 37.
3. Irene West and Clifton West, Foreword to Cornel West, *Prophetic Thought in Postmodern Times* (Monroe, ME: Common Courage Press, 1993), p. vii.
4. "Read, Hot and Black," p. 15.
5. West, *Prophetic Thought*, p. 3.
6. Ibid.
7. Ibid., p. 5.
8. Nel Noddings, *The Challenge to Care in Schools* (New York: Teachers College Press, 1993), p. 2.
9. West, *Prophetic Thought*, p. 5.
10. Ibid., p. 6.
11. Ibid.
12. Cornel West, *Keeping Faith: Philosophy and Race in America* (New York: Routledge, 1993), p. xvii.

From *Prophetic Thought in Postmodern Times* (1993)

. . . I am sure that most of you know that there has been a lot of talk about multiculturalism these days. It is a buzzword. It is often undefined. It tends to function in a rather promiscuous manner, to lie down with any perspective, any orientation. So we need to handle it. It is a rather elusive and amorphous term.

The same is true with Eurocentrism. What do we mean by Eurocentrism? Which particular European nation do you have in mind? Which classes of Europeans do you have in mind? Certainly, Sicilian peasants don't have the same status as Oxbridge elites. What Europe do you have in mind?

From *Prophetic Thought in Postmodern Times* by Cornel West (Monroe, ME: Common Courage Press ©. 1993 by Cornel West), pp. 7–21. Reprinted by permission of Common Courage Press, Box 702, Monroe, Maine, 04951.

We begin with the first moment of this lecture. There are three historical coordinates that will help us "situate and contextualize" this debate that is going on, as Brother John [Bolin who introduced this lecture series] puts it.

The Value of the Age of Europe

The first historical coordinate is the fact that we have yet to fully come to terms with the recognition that we live 48 years after the end of the Age of Europe. Between 1492 and 1945, powerful nations between the Ural mountains and the Atlantic Ocean began to shape the world in their own image. Breakthroughs in oceanic transportation, breakthroughs in agricultural production, breakthroughs in the consolidation of nation status, breakthroughs in urbanization, led toward a take-off.

1492, the problem of degrading other people and the expulsion of Jews and Muslims and wars in Spain. 1492, Christopher Columbus shows up in what to him is a New World. It is not new to indigenous peoples; they have been there for thousands of years, two hundred nations, as those of you who are here tonight in Tulsa know quite intimately.

But the New World concept was part of an expansionism, keeping in mind our ambiguous legacies. We don't want to romanticize and we don't want to trivialize. There were structures of domination already here before the Europeans got here. The plight of indigenous women, for example. It doesn't mean that the wiping out of indigenous peoples by disease and conquest some-how gets European conquistadors off the hook. But it means that there was always, already, oppression. In new forms it was brought.

1492, publication of the first grammar book in Indo-European languages by Antonio de Nebrija in Spanish. Language, of course, being the benchmark in the foundation of a culture. This is what is so interesting about multiculturalism these days. The fact that the dialogue takes place in English already says some-thing. For me, English is an imperial language. My wife is Ethiopian and she dreams in Amharic. I dream in English. That says something about us culturally. We still love each other, but it says something about us culturally. Namely, that I am part of a profoundly hybrid culture. I happen to speak the very language of the elite who tell me that I am not part of the human family, as David Walker said in his Appeal of September 1829. And she speaks Amharic, a different elite, in a different empire, an Ethiopian empire. Different hybridity. Different notions about what it means to be multicultural in this regard.

1492, a crucial year. Between 1492 and 1945, we see unprecedented levels of productivity. We see what, in my view, is the grand achievement of the Age of Europe. Because it was in some way marvelous, and it was in some other ways quite ugly. What was marvelous about it was the attempt to institutionalize cri-tiques of illegitimate forms of authority. Let me say that slowly: The attempt to hammer out not just critical gestures but critiques that could be sustained of arbitrary forms of power. That's what the Reformation was about in its critique of the Catholic Church.

Think what you will about Martin Luther. He was bringing critique to bear on what he perceived to be arbitrary forms of power. That is what the Enlightenment was about, fighting against national churches that had too much unaccountable power leading to too many lives crushed. That's what liberalism was about against absolute monarchy. That is what women's movements are about against male authority. That's what anti-racist movements are about against white supremacist authority.

They are building on traditions of critique and resistance. And, during the Age of Europe, given levels of productivity, there were grand experiments. Each and every one of them flawed, but grand experiments to try to live in large communities while institutionalizing critiques of illegitimate forms of authority. This was the makings of the democratic ideal, to which accountability to ordinary people became not just an abstract possibility, but realizable. As I say, it was deeply flawed.

The greatest experiment, as we know, began in 1776. But they were institutionalizing these critiques. It didn't apply to white men who had no property. It didn't apply to women. It didn't apply to slaves, people of African descent in the United States who were 21 percent of the population at that time. But that is not solely the point. It is in part the point. But it is not fully the point. The courageous attempt to build a democratic experiment in which the uniqueness of each and every one of us, the sanctity of each and every one of us who has been made equal in the eyes of God becomes at least possible.

That democratic idea is one of the grand contributions of the Age of Europe even given the imperial expansion, the colonial subjugation of Africa and Asia, the pernicious and vicious crimes against working people and people of color and so forth. So ambiguous legacy means, in talking about multiculturalism, we have got to keep two ideas in our minds at the same time. The achievements as well as the downfalls. The grand contributions and the vicious crimes.

The End of the Age of Europe and the Rise of the United States

1945. The Age of Europe is over. Europe is a devastated and divided continent. Mushroom clouds over Nagasaki and Hiroshima. Indescribable concentration camps in Germany. Again, Europe's inability to come to terms with the degradation of others. Now upon the hills of a divided continent emerges the first new nation. The U.S.A. Henry James called it a "hotel civilization." A hotel is a fusion between the market and the home. The home, a symbol of warmth and security, hearth. The market, dynamic, mobile, the quest for comfort and convenience. Both home and market. Deeply privatistic phenomenon. By privatistic, I mean being distant from, even distrustful of, the public interest and the common good.

In the first new nation, American civilization with tremendous difficulty was trying to define its national identity. What ought to be the common interest. What ought to be the common good. It is quite striking in fact that this first new nation doesn't even raise the question of what it means to be a citizen until after the Civil War, when they have to decide what is the status of the freed men and women, the ex-enslaved persons. The first new nation, a heterogenous population. People come from all around the world. In quest for what? Opportunity. In quest for what? A decent life. The quest for what? More comfort and convenience.

In 1945, we thought it would be—not "we," but Henry Luce did at least—the American Century. It only lasted 28 years. For the first time in human history, Americans created a modern social structure that looks like a diamond rather than a pyramid. Mass middle class, owing to the GI Bill, Federal Housing Administration programs, Workers' Compensation, Unemployment Compensation. The Great Society that played such a fundamental role in moving persons from working class to middle class in the United States. And yet, the distinctive feature of American civilization in its negative mode would be the institutionalizing of a discourse of whiteness and blackness.

The issue of race. Race is not a moral mistake of individuals, solely. It is a feature of institutions and structures that insures that one group of people have less access to resources, both material and intangible. By material, I mean money, housing, food, health care. By intangible, I mean things like self-confidence. I mean things like self-respect and self-regard and self-esteem. The discourse of whiteness and blackness would result in the incessant bombardment of people of color. Attacks on black beauty. Attacks on black intelligence. You can still get tenure in some universities for arguing that black people are not as intelligent as others. Where did that come from?

We are not concerned about eye color, not concerned about the shape of ears. But we are still concerned about pigmentation. It has a history. Of attacks on black intelligence. Attacks on black possibility. What is fascinating about this discourse, that in many ways is distinctive to the U.S.A., though South Africa shares it as well, is that those who came to the United States didn't realize they were white until they got here. They were told they were white. They had to learn they were white. An Irish peasant coming from British imperial abuse in Ireland during the potato famine in the 1840s arrives in the States. You ask him or her what they are. They say "I am Irish." No, you're white. "What do you mean I am white?" And they point me out. Oh, I see what you mean. This is a strange land.

Jews from Ukraine and Poland and Russia undergoing ugly pogroms, assaults and attacks, arrive in Ellis Island. They are told they have to choose, either white or black. They say neither, but they are perceived as white. They say I will not go with the goyim, the goyim have treated me like whites treat black people here. But, I am certainly not black either.

This is the 1880s. This is a time in which that peculiar American institution in which a black woman, a man, a child was swinging from a tree every two and a half days for thirty years. An institution unique to the United States called lynching, that "strange fruit that Southern trees bear" which Billy Holiday sang so powerfully about. It's happening every other day. And many Jews would say, no baby, I'm sure not identifying with these folk.

Arbitrary use of power. Unaccountable. Segregated laws, Jim and Jane Crow unaccountable. But yet, this new nation, after 1945, would emerge to the center of the historical stage. We now come to the third historical coordinate; the first was the end of the Age of Europe, the second was the emergence of the United States as a world power, and the third is the decolonization of the Third World.

The Decolonization of the Third World

By decolonization, I mean the quest of colonized people around the world, between 1945 and 1974, to break the back of European maritime empires. 1947, India. Exemplary anti-colonial struggle. Young preacher, 26 years old, Dexter Avenue Baptist Church, Montgomery, Alabama. He and courageous others look to India for anti-colonial strategy. Nonviolent struggle. Applies the same techniques and strategies to try to break the back of an apartheid-like rule of law in the United States.

The civil rights movement was part of a larger international attempt to bring critiques to bear on the empire building that had taken place during the heyday of the Age of Europe, namely the nineteenth century. '47 India, '49 China, '57 Ghana, '59 Cuba, '60 Guinea. We go on and on and on. '74 Angola. South Africa as yet to come. There is no way, of course, of looking past some of the colossal failures of the post-colonial regimes in some of those places, or the greed and corruption of the post-colonial elites, like Moi in Kenya, or Mengistu in Ethiopia, or Mobutu. The list is long.

But the decolonization points out the degree to which we are living in a fundamentally different world. In 1945, the U.N. had 45 nations; there are now 172 and there will be more soon given the disintegration of the Soviet Empire. It is a different world.

This is a way of situating broadly what the debate between multiculturalism and Eurocentrism is about. But it forces us to call into question anyone who would criticize Eurocentrism, as if, as I said before, it is monolithic. Because there are struggles going on in Europe between a whole host of different peoples with different cultures and different nations. And one has to begin with a nuanced historical sense in laying bare a genealogy or a history of the very term Europe itself.

Before the debate begins, when was Europe used for the first time as a noun? Christmas, 800, Charles the Great. Pope Leo III puts the crown upon his head. There's only Lombards and the Franks. Two out of eight clans. No Alamans. No Bavarians. An attempt to impose a unity from above. Arab caliphs threatening, Empress Irene in Greek Christendom. Unstable. Historians tell us that without Mohammed, Charlemagne would have been inconceivable. That is what Henri Pirenne says in his magisterial reading of this moment. And yet, at the same time, the attempt to conceive of Europe as some kind of homogenous entity collapses. 843. Partition. At Verdun. Territorial principalities. Their particularisms. Their multiplicities expand and surface. Europe as an entity is not taken seriously.

Second attempt, 1458. Pope Pius II, five years after the Turkish invasion of Constantinople. Responding to the Turkish menace, Europe is attempting to forge some collective identity. Reformation. Churches under national government, particularism again. Multiplicity again.

Last attempt made, 1804. Napoleon puts crown on his own head. And he calls himself not Emperor of Europe, but Emperor of France.

Francis II withdrew himself as Emperor, and said I am simply part of Austria now. After May, 1804, the collapse of Napoleon and we see the emergence of nationalism. A new tribalism in the human adventure. A nationalism that would strain the moral imagination. Populations around the world remain to this day in this central tribal division of humankind.

That is what is going on in Yugoslavia, that is what is going on in Russia. That is what is going on in Ethiopia between the Tigrans and the Amhara, and the Oromo. Nationalism. And this nationalism would dictate the rules of power during the heyday of the Age of Europe. So strong that people would be willing to die for it. That is pretty deep. That is pretty deep, that we all have to impose or endow some sense of meaning to our lives and one test is what we are willing to die for. And citizens around the world are willing to die for their nation-state. That's how deep the thread of nationalism is. That particular form of tribalism. And by calling it tribalism, I am not using that in a degrading sense. Because all of us are born under circumstances not of our own choosing, in particular families, clans, tribes and what-have-you. We all need protection. Tribes protect. Nation-states protect.

We all need identity. Tribes provide identity. But, of course, prophetic critique, and of course, in my view the Christian version of the prophetic critique, is that when any form of tribalism becomes a form of idolatry, then a critique and resistance must be brought to bear. When any form of tribalism becomes a justification for hiding and concealing social misery, critique and resistance must be brought to bear.

Economic & Social Decline

Let's come closer in our first moment of discernment. In our present moment here, and I will be saying more about this in the last lecture, but I want to touch on this now. From 1973 to 1989 was a period of national decline. For the first time since the '30s. Levels of productivity nearly freeze. A 0.4 percent increase in 1973–4.

There are reasons that we need not go into as to fragility of the debt structure linked to Third World nations. It has much to do, of course, with the rise of OPEC and the Third World monopoly of one of the crucial resources of the modern world, oil. We saw that in January [1991, during the Gulf War]. I think most of us are convinced that if the major resource of Kuwait was artichokes we would not have responded so quickly.

Which doesn't take away from the rhetoric of the liberation of Kuwait. Kuwaitis were, in fact, living under vicious and repressive regime under Sadaam Hussein. But there are a whole lot of regimes where people are living that we don't respond to. The rise of OPEC in '74 made a fundamental difference. The slowdown of the U.S. economy. No longer expanding. The unprecedented economic boom no longer in place. And since 1974, the real wages—by real wages I mean inflation-adjusted wages of non-supervisory workers in

America—have declined. Which means social slippage, which means downward mobility that produces fear.

Material uncertainty becomes real. As you can imagine, it serves as a raw ingredient for scapegoating. And from '73 to '89, we have seen much scapegoating. The major scapegoats have been women and black people, especially at the behest of certain wings of the Republican Party. We don't want to tar the Republican Party as a whole, but yes indeed, in '68 Nixon was talking about busing as a racially coded term. Harry Dent, the same architect of the strategy that led to the walkout of Strom Thurmond in 1948, due to the civil rights plank in the party, and the formation of the Dixiecrats. The same Harry Dent who served as the principal architect in '48 and lingered in '68.

Kevin Phillips wrote a book in '69 called *The New Republican Majority* which is an appeal to race to convince white working class ethnic workers that black people were receiving too much and were unjustified in what they were receiving and that whites were getting a raw deal and ought to come to the Republican Party.

Thomas and Mary Edsall tell the story in their recent *Chain Reaction*. The impact of rights and race and taxes on American politics. '76 the Democrats ride on the coattails of Watergate, but they have very little substance. In '80, Ronald Reagan consolidates it all and begins his campaign in Philadelphia, Mississippi and says state rights forever. Racially coded language. Political realignment. The Republican Party becomes essentially a lily-white party. Which is not to say that all Republicans are racist. It is a lily-white party.

Another feature is inadequate education for workers so that the products that they produce cannot compete. Japan, Taiwan and South Korea surge. Even Brazil. Stubborn incapacity to generate resources for the public square. No New Taxes, read my lips. Inability to generate resources means public squalor alongside private opulence.

The Ravages of the Culture of Consumption

Added to these problems is the undeniable cultural decay, which is in fact quite unprecedented in American history. This is what frightens me more than anything else. By unprecedented cultural decay I mean the social breakdown of the nurturing system for children. The inability to transmit meaning, value, purpose, dignity, decency to children.

I am not just talking about the one out of five children who live in poverty. I am not just talking about the one out of two black and two out of five brown children who live in poverty. I am talking about the state of their souls. The deracinated state of their souls. By deracinated I mean rootless. The denuded state of their souls. By denuded, I mean culturally naked. Not to have what is requisite in order to make it through life. Missing what's needed to navigate through the terrors and traumas of death and disease and despair and dread and disappointment. And thereby falling prey to a culture of consumption. A culture that promotes addiction to stimulation. A culture obsessed with bodily stimulation. A culture obsessed with consuming as the only way of preserving some vitality of a self.

You are feeling down, go to the mall. Feeling down, turn on the TV. The TV with its spectator passivity. You are receiving as a spectator, with no sense of agency, no sense of making a difference. You are observing the collapse of an empire and feeling unable to do anything about it, restricted to just listening to Dan Rather talk about it. A market culture that promotes a market morality.

A market morality has much to do with the unprecedented violence of our social fabric. The sense of being haunted every minute of our lives in our homes and on the street. Because a market morality puts money-making, buying and selling, or hedonistic self-indulgence at the center of one's behavior. Human life has little value. I want it, I want it now. Quick fix, I've got the gun, give it to me. It affects us all. I know some people try to run and move out to the suburbs and the technoburbs and so forth, but it affects us all. Market morality.

We should keep in mind that one of the great theorists of market society, namely Adam Smith, wrote a book in 1776, *The Wealth of Nations*. It is a powerful book in many ways. He talked about ways in which you generate wealth, but he also wrote a book in 1759 called *The Theory of Moral Sentiments*. And in that book Adam Smith argues that a market culture cannot sustain a market economy.

You need market forces as necessary conditions for the preservation of liberties in the economy. But when the market begins to hold sway in every sphere of a person's life, market conceptions of the self, market conceptions of time, you put a premium on distraction over attention, stimulation over concentration, then disintegration sets in. Also in this book, Adam Smith talks about the values of virtue and propriety, and especially the value of sympathy that he shared with his fellow Scot, David Hume. And when these nonmarket values lose influence or when their influence wanes, then you have got a situation of Hobbes' war of all against all, of cultural anarchy and social chaos.

Emile Durkheim put it another way, put it well when he said that a market culture evolves around a notion of contract, but every contractual relation presupposes precontractual commitments. So, a contract means nothing if there is no notion of truth telling and promise keeping. It has no status. It collapses. Now all we have is manipulative relations. I don't know how many of you have been reading Michael Levine's book, *The Money Culture*. I don't want to make an advertisement for it, but the book looks at what happens when a market culture begins to take over the center of a person's life. It tells stories about a Wall Street speculator who is upset because he only made 550 million dollars in a year. He has to make 555, and he is willing to take a risk and break the law to do it.

You say, what is going on? It cannot be solely a question of pointing fingers at individuals. We are talking about larger cultural tendencies that affect each and every one of us. It takes the form of self-destructive nihilism in poor communities, in very poor communities. The lived experience of meaninglessness and hopelessness and lovelessness. Of self-paralyzing pessimism among stable working-class and lower working-class people in which they feel as if their life, their standard of living is declining, they are convinced that the quality of life is declining. And yet, they are looking for quick solutions. I think in part that is what David Duke is all about. It is not just that the people who support him are racist, though, of course, many are. It's that they are looking for a quick solution to a downward slide they experience in their lives. He speaks to it in his own xenophobically coded language. The racist coded language. He is gaining ground.

There is a self-indulgent hedonism and self-serving cynicism for those at the top. To simply let it collapse and pull back. Public school, nothing to do with it. Public transportation, nothing to do with it. Public health, nothing to do with it. Privatize them because I have access to resources that allow me to privatize in such a way that I can have quality. The rest, do what you will, make it on your own.

In such a context, is it a surprise then, that we see tribal frenzy and xenophobic strife? Multiculturalism and Eurocentrism; two notions that go hand in hand. Our attempts on the one hand to respond to the tribal frenzy and xenophobic strife, and yet in their vulgar versions they contribute to it. These are highly unfortunate times which prepackage a debate resulting in even more polarization because it obscures and obfuscates what is fundamentally at stake in our moment. Intellectually, as I noted before, this means preserving the nuanced historical sense. But how do you preserve a historical sense in a market culture that effaces the past? A past that comes back to us through televisual means solely in the form of icons.

You go into any school today, who are the great figures? Martin Luther King, Jr. That is fine. Can you tell me something about the context that produced him. There is no King without a movement, there is movement without King. King is part of a tradition. But all we have is icons. George Washington. Icon. He was part of an armed revolutionary movement. He picked up guns and threw out the British imperialists. And he tried to institutionalize his conception of democracy. Grand but flawed, as I said before.

How do we preserve a sense of history in such a moment? What a challenge. But this is what is intellectually at stake. It makes no sense. Students read Toni Morrison and simply look in her text and see themselves rather than the challenge of a great artist who is dealing with collective memory and community breakdown in *Beloved,* for example. Challenge. If you look in a text and see yourself, that is market education, done in the name of education. But education must not be about a cathartic quest for identity. It must foster credible sensibilities for an active critical citizenry.

How do we preserve critical sensibility in a market culture? In our churches, in our synagogues, in our mosques, they are often simply marketing identity. It must be a rather thin identity, this market. It won't last long. Fashion, fad. Someone benefitting, usually the elites who do the marketing and benefitting. How deep does one's identity cut? Most importantly, what is the moral content of one's identity? What are the political consequences of one's identity? These are the kinds of questions that one must ask in talking about multiculturalism and Eurocentrism.

If one is talking about critiques of racism, critiques of patriarchy, critiques of homophobia, then simply call it that. Eurocentrism is not identical with racism. So, you deny the John Browns of the world. You deny the anti-racist movement in the heart of Europe. Eurocentrism is not the same as male supremacists. Why? Because every culture we know has been patriarchal in such an ugly way and that you deny the anti-patriarchal movements within the heart of Europe. And the same is so with homophobia. Demystify the categories in order to stay tuned to the complexity of the realities. That is what I am calling for. That is the role of prophetic thinkers and prophetic activists who are willing to build on discernment, human connection. Who are willing to hold up human hypocrisy, including their own, and also willing to hold up the possibility of human hope.

What I shall attempt to do tomorrow [in the second lecture] is to look at a distinctive American tradition that makes democracy its object of focus, its object of investigation, namely, American pragmatism. And pragmatism has nothing to do with practicalism or opportunism, which is the usual meaning of that term which you see in your newspapers. So and so was pragmatic. No principles, just did what had to be done. No, no. That is not what we will be talking about. American pragmatism is a distinct philosophical tradition begins with Charles Sanders Peirce, through William James Dewey, and Sidney Hook and W. E. B. Du Bois, all the And, it makes democracy a basic focus.

Its fundamental focus and question is, what are How do you promote individuality and allow it to linking this tradition with the deep sense of the tragic, matic tradition lacks. I will try to show ways in which Christian resou brought to bear to keep track of the sense of the tragic without curtailing agency. Without curtailing possibilities for action and then I will end [in the third lecture] with what the future of prophetic thought looks like. And I will try to answer some of those questions about whether indeed we can even talk about preserving a historical sense and subtle analysis in a culture that is so saturated by market sensibilities. Thank you so very much.

Questions

1. What are the four basic components of "prophetic thought"?
2. How does West apply each of these components in his discussion of Eurocentrism and multiculturalism?
3. According to West, what was marvelous about the Age of Europe?
4. In terms of multiculturalism, why is the legacy of the Age of Europe ambiguous?
5. According to West, what are the pros and cons of tribalism?
6. Why does race matter so much in the cultures of the United States?
7. What are the chief characteristics of the cultural decay we are experiencing?
8. Why does this cultural decay frighten West more than anything else?
9. What does West mean by the phrase "public squalor alongside private opulence"?
10. In a society ravaged by a culture of consumption, how do we foster the development of prophetic thinkers?
11. In your own words, describe West's vision of the ideally educated individual.

chapter 13

Paulo Freire

TIME LINE FOR FREIRE

1921	Is born in Recife, Brazil.
1959	Receives Ph.D. from University of Recife.
	Is named professor of philosophy and education.
1962	Is named director of the university's Cultural Extension Service.
	Begins a literacy program for peasants and workers.
1964	Is arrested and imprisoned (for seventy days). He is then forced into exile with his wife, Elza, and their five children.
	Travels from Brazil to Bolivia to Chile to Massachusetts and then to Switzerland.
1970	Works for the World Council of Churches in Geneva.
1972	Publishes *Pedagogy of the Oppressed.*
1974	Publishes *Education for Critical Consciousness.*
1976	Publishes *Educational Practice of Freedom.*
1980	Returns with his family to Brazil.
1985	Is appointed minister of education, Rio de Janeiro.
1986	Receives the UNESCO Prize for Education award.
1994	Publishes *Pedagogy of Hope.*
1996	Publishes *Letters to Cristina.*
1997	Publishes *Pedagogy of the Heart.*

| **1997** | Publishes *Teachers as Cultural Workers.* |
| **1997** | Dies. |

◅◦▻

Introduction

It can be said of Paulo Freire that he practices what he preaches. Freire offers us a utopian vision of what life should be and articulates a progressive pedagogy for attaining this desired goal. Though utopian, his democratic vision is grounded in the poverty and oppression that characterized his native area of Recife, Brazil. As Richard Shaull suggests in his foreword to *Pedagogy of the Oppressed,* "Freire's thought represents the response of a creative mind and sensitive conscience to the extraordinary misery and suffering of the oppressed around him."[1] Living in abject poverty as a child, Freire experienced and understood what he later named the "culture of silence" that characterizes the dispossessed. Victimized by the economic, social, and political paternalism of the dominant classes, the poor and dispossessed are not equipped, suggests Freire, to respond to the world's realities in a critical fashion. According to Freire, the dominant classes devised an educational system for the purpose of keeping the masses "submerged" and contained in a "culture of silence."

Perhaps because he shared the plight of the "wretched of the earth",—his family lost its middle-class status during the worldwide depression of the 1930s—Freire realized that the "culture of silence" could and should be overcome. Aware that the extant educational system fostered and sustained this culture of silence, Freire retained his faith in the power of a genuine education to enable and empower even the most wretched to first recognize their oppressed condition and then participate in its transformation. To assist those submerged in this culture of silence, Freire combined theory and practice into what is best known as a "pedagogy of the oppressed." It is important to note that this pedagogy did not emerge full-blown out of the mind of Freire but evolved as he worked with the dispossessed of his own country. In developing a pedagogy that centers on dialogue, that is, "the encounter between men, mediated by the world, in order to name the world," Freire remained true to his basic beliefs that all human beings merit our respect and are capable of understanding and transforming the world of which they are a part.

Experiencing firsthand the hunger and poverty that characterized Recife during the 1930s, Freire fell behind in school and was thought by some to be mentally retarded. Though he suffered no serious or permanent damage from his malnourishment, the experience affected him greatly. While still an adolescent, Freire devoted himself to working among the poor to assist them in improving their lot in life. This led to the study of law and to working as a labor union lawyer "among the people of the slums." In trying to help the poor understand their legal rights, Freire became involved in adult literacy programs during the late 1940s. Working with such programs for more than a decade, Freire rejected traditional methods of instruction, finding them much too authoritarian to be effective in teaching adults to read.

As he began doctoral study at the University of Recife, Freire read and made use of the insights of such great minds as "Sartre and Mounier, Eric Fromm and Lois Althusser, Ortega y Gassett and Mao, Martin Luther King and Che Guevara, Unamuno and Marcuse,"[2] but his educational philosophy remained grounded in these experiences of working with the dispossessed of Brazil. Though he first articulated his philosophy of education in his doctoral dissertation, Freire continued to advocate for a "problem-posing" approach to teaching as a member of the faculty of the University of Recife and of Harvard University.

In contrast to the "banking" method of education—where one privileged to know the truth deposits it in the appropriate amount and form into the empty and limited minds of the unwashed or dispossessed—Freire advocates an education or pedagogy that enhances and expands every human being's ability to understand and transform the world of which she or he is a part. For example, in teaching Brazilian peasants to read, Freire did not lecture to them. Instead, by beginning with a concept or concepts with which they were already familiar, Freire helped the peasants understand that they too were makers of culture and that they could contribute to the transformation of their own reality.

Beginning with a series of pictures "designed to demonstrate the fundamental differences between *nature* (the natural world) and *culture* (all that is created or transformed by men and women),"[3] Freire was able to assist illiterates in developing rudimentary literacy skills within thirty hours. As the peasants begin to learn the symbols for the words that name concepts familiar to them, their view of their world gradually expands. Through this process they begin to understand that "their world is not fixed and immutable," but is a reality in process that can be transformed.

Clearly, Freire's "pedagogy of the oppressed" is more than just literacy training. It is nothing less than a liberating process that enables and empowers each human being to achieve humankind's ontological vocation, that is, "to be a Subject who acts upon and transforms his world. . . ."[4] As human beings regain the right to rename their worlds, individually and collectively they consciously engage in the uniquely human activity of constructing and reconstructing their own worlds.

Though Freire's ideas are grounded in the poverty and oppression of his earlier years, the utility of his approach transcends national, class, and ethnic boundaries. According to Freire, the transforming power of words enables all of us to live fuller, more humane lives. As Peter J. Caulfield explains, "words," for Freire, "have meaning only in relation to their effect on human beings and the world in which we live." For example, the word *Chernobyl* connotes much more than merely a geographic location in what was once the Soviet Union. Many of us probably correctly associate the word with the worst nuclear accident in human history, but to appreciate the richness of such a statement, its many layers of meaning need to be connected to each person's personal reality. In short, for those who relate it to the dropping of atomic bombs during World War II and to the effects of radiation exposure produced by continued testing of nuclear weapons during the 1950s and 1960s, *Chernobyl* connotes more than it does for someone whose knowledge is limited to the accounts of the disaster provided by the news media. From Freire's point of view, it is the educator's task to assist individuals in expanding the connection between concepts or issues of importance to them to a larger evolving reality. As Caulfield suggests:

> In order for students to comprehend truly the meaning of Chernobyl, they would probably need to discuss among themselves (with the teacher's help) the effects of radiation on neighboring grasses, vegetables, animals, and people, perhaps through generations. Indeed, how could they grasp the threat suggested by Chernobyl unless they researched Hiroshima and Nagasaki; they might also inquire into the long-term effects of radiation exposure to Americans living near atomic testing sites in Nevada in the 1950s. Only then would students begin to comprehend the significance of a statement like "Chernobyl was the site of the first serious nuclear accident."[5]

Such a progressive approach to pedagogy is a far cry from the "banking" education so prevalent in educational institutions throughout the world. In the selections that follow, Freire, in addition to critiquing such traditional pedagogies, explains his "problem-posing" approach to education.

Notes

1. Paulo Freire, *Pedagogy of the Oppressed* (New York: The Seabury Press, 1972), p. 10.
2. Ibid., p. 11.
3. Peter J. Caulfield, "From Brazil to Buncombe County: Freire and Posing Problems," *Educational Forum* 55:4 (Summer 1991), p. 312.
4. Freire, *Pedagogy of the Oppressed*, p. 12.
5. Caulfield, "From Brazil to Buncombe County," pp. 309–310.

From *Pedagogy of the Oppressed* (1972)

A careful analysis of the teacher-student relationship at any level, inside or outside the school, reveals its fundamentally *narrative* character. This relationship involves a narrating Subject (the teacher) and patient, listening objects (the students). The contents, whether values or empirical dimensions of reality, tend in the process of being narrated to become lifeless and petrified. Education is suffering from narration sickness.

The teacher talks about reality as if it were motionless, static, compartmentalized, and predictable. Or else he expounds on a topic completely alien to the existential experience of the students. His task is to "fill" the students with the contents of his narration—contents which are detached from reality, disconnected

---

from the totality that engendered them and could give them significance. Words are emptied of their concreteness and become a hollow, alienated, and alienating verbosity.

The outstanding characteristic of this narrative education, then, is the sonority of words, not their transforming power. "Four times four is sixteen; the capital of Pará is Belém." The student records, memorizes, and repeats these phrases without perceiving what four times four really means, or realizing the true significance of "capital" in the affirmation "the capital of Pará is Belém," that is, what Belém means for Pará and what Pará means for Brazil.

Narration (with the teacher as narrator) leads the students to memorize mechanically the narrated content. Worse yet, it turns them into "containers," into "receptacles" to be "filled" by the teacher. The more completely he fills the receptacles, the better a teacher he is. The more meekly the receptacles permit themselves to be filled, the better students they are.

Education thus becomes an act of depositing, in which the students are the depositories and the teacher is the depositor. Instead of communicating, the teacher issues communiqués and makes deposits which the students patiently receive, memorize, and repeat. This is the "banking" concept of education, in which the scope of action allowed to the students extends only as far as receiving, filing, and storing the deposits. They do, it is true, have the opportunity to become collectors or cataloguers of the things they store. But in the last analysis, it is men themselves who are filed away through the lack of creativity, transformation, and knowledge in this (at best) misguided system. For apart from inquiry, apart from the praxis, men cannot be truly human. Knowledge emerges only through invention and re-invention, through the restless, impatient, continuing, hopeful inquiry men pursue in the world, with the world, and with each other.

In the banking concept of education, knowledge is a gift bestowed by those who consider themselves knowledgeable upon those whom they consider to know nothing. Projecting an absolute ignorance onto others, a characteristic of the ideology of oppression, negates education and knowledge as processes of inquiry. The teacher presents himself to his students as their necessary opposite; by considering their ignorance absolute, he justifies his own existence. The students, alienated like the slave in the Hegelian dialectic, accept their ignorance as justifying the teacher's existence—but, unlike the slave, they never discover that they educate the teacher.

The *raison d'être* of libertarian education, on the other hand, lies in its drive towards reconciliation. Education must begin with the solution of the teacher-student contradiction, by reconciling the poles of the contradiction so that both are simultaneously teachers *and* students.

This solution is not (nor can it be) found in the banking concept. On the contrary, banking education maintains and even stimulates the contradiction through the following attitudes and practices, which mirror oppressive society as a whole:

   a. the teacher teaches and the students are taught;
   b. the teacher knows everything and the students know nothing;

c. the teacher thinks and the students are thought about;

d. the teacher talks and the students listen—meekly;

e. the teacher disciplines and the students are disciplined;

f. the teacher chooses and enforces his choice, and the students comply;

g. the teacher acts and the students have the illusion of acting through the action of the teacher;

h. the teacher chooses the program content, and the students (who were not consulted) adapt to it;

i. the teacher confuses the authority of knowledge with his own professional authority, which he sets in opposition to the freedom of the students;

j. the teacher is the Subject of the learning process, while the pupils are mere objects.

It is not surprising that the banking concept of education regards men as adaptable, manageable beings. The more students work at storing the deposits entrusted to them, the less they develop the critical consciousness which would result from their intervention in the world as transformers of that world. The more completely they accept the passive role imposed on them, the more they tend simply to adapt to the world as it is and to the fragmented view of reality deposited in them.

The capability of banking education to minimize or annul the students' creative power and to stimulate their credulity serves the interests of the oppressors, who care neither to have the world revealed nor to see it transformed. The oppressors use their "humanitarianism" to preserve a profitable situation. Thus they react almost instinctively against any experiment in education which stimulates the critical faculties and is not content with a partial view of reality but always seeks out the ties which link one point to another and one problem to another.

Indeed, the interests of the oppressors lie in "changing the consciousness of the oppressed, not the situation which oppresses them";[1] for the more the oppressed can be led to adapt to that situation, the more easily they can be dominated. To achieve this end, the oppressors use the banking concept of education in conjunction with a paternalistic social action apparatus, within which the oppressed receive the euphemistic title of "welfare recipients." They are treated as individual cases, as marginal men who deviate from the general configuration of a "good, organized, and just" society. The oppressed are regarded as the pathology of the healthy society, which must therefore adjust these "incompetent and lazy" folk to its own patterns by changing their mentality. These marginals need to be "integrated," "incorporated" into the healthy society that they have "forsaken."

The truth is, however, that the oppressed are not "marginals," are not men living "outside" society. They have always been "inside"—inside the structure which made them "beings for others." The solution is not to "integrate" them into the structure of oppression, but to transform that structure so that they can

---

[1] Simone de Beauvoir, *La Pensée de Droite, Aujord'hui* (Paris); ST, *El Pensamiento político de la Derecha* (Buenos Aires, 1963), p. 34.

become "beings for themselves." Such transformation, of course, would undermine the oppressors' purposes; hence their utilization of the banking concept of education to avoid the threat of student *conscientização*.

The banking approach to adult education, for example, will never propose to students that they critically consider reality. It will deal instead with such vital questions as whether Roger gave green grass to the goat, and insist upon the importance of learning that, on the contrary, Roger gave green grass to the rabbit. The "humanism" of the banking approach masks the effort to turn men into automatons—the very negation of their ontological vocation to be more fully human.

Those who use the banking approach, knowingly or unknowingly (for there are innumerable well-intentioned bank-clerk teachers who do not realize that they are serving only to dehumanize), fail to perceive that the deposits themselves contain contradictions about reality. But, sooner or later, these contradictions may lead formerly passive students to turn against their domestication and the attempt to domesticate reality. They may discover through existential experience that their present way of life is irreconcilable with their vocation to become fully human. They may perceive through their relations with reality that reality is really a *process,* undergoing constant transformation. If men are searchers and their ontological vocation is humanization, sooner or later they may perceive the contradiction in which banking education seeks to maintain them, and then engage themselves in the struggle for their liberation.

But the humanist, revolutionary educator cannot wait for this possibility to materialize. From the outset, his efforts must coincide with those of the students to engage in critical thinking and the quest for mutual humanization. His efforts must be imbued with a profound trust in men and their creative power. To achieve this, he must be a partner of the students in his relations with them.

The banking concept does not admit to such partnership—and necessarily so. To resolve the teacher-student contradiction, to exchange the role of depositor, prescriber, domesticator, for the role of student among students would be to undermine the power of oppression and serve the cause of liberation.

Implicit in the banking concept is the assumption of a dichotomy between man and the world: man is merely *in* the world, not *with* the world or with others; man is spectator, not re-creator. In this view, man is not a conscious being *(corpo consciente)*; he is rather the possessor of *a* consciousness: an empty "mind" passively open to the reception of deposits of reality from the world outside. For example, my desk, my books, my coffee cup, all the objects before me—as bits of the world which surrounds me—would be "inside" me, exactly as I am inside my study right now. This view makes no distinction between being accessible to consciousness and entering consciousness. The distinction, however, is essential: the objects which surround me are simply accessible to my consciousness, not located within it. I am aware of them, but they are not inside me.

It follows logically from the banking notion of consciousness that the educator's role is to regulate the way the world "enters into" the students. His task is to organize a process which already occurs spontaneously, to "fill" the students by making deposits of information which he considers to constitute true knowledge.[2] And since men "receive" the world as passive entities, education should make them more passive still, and adapt them to the world. The educated man is the adapted man, because he is better "fit" for the world. Translated into practice, this concept is well suited to the purposes of the oppressors, whose tranquility rests on how well men fit the world the oppressors have created, and how little they question it.

The more completely the majority adapt to the purposes which the dominant minority prescribe for them (thereby depriving them of the right to their own purposes), the more easily the minority can continue to prescribe. The theory and practice of banking education serve this end quite efficiently. Verbalistic lessons, reading requirements,[3] the methods for evaluating "knowledge," the distance between the teacher and the taught, the criteria for promotion: everything in this ready-to-wear approach serves to obviate thinking.

The bank-clerk educator does not realize that there is no true security in his hypertrophied role, that one must seek to live *with* others in solidarity. One cannot impose oneself, nor even merely co-exist with one's students. Solidarity requires true communication, and the concept by which such an educator is guided fears and proscribes communication.

Yet only through communication can human life hold meaning. The teacher's thinking is authenticated only by the authenticity of the students' thinking. The teacher cannot think for his students, nor can he impose his thought on them. Authentic thinking, thinking that is concerned about *reality*, does not take place in ivory tower isolation, but only in communication. If it is true that thought has meaning only when generated by action upon the world, the subordination of students to teachers becomes impossible.

Because banking education begins with a false understanding of men as objects, it cannot promote the development of what Fromm calls "biophily," but instead produces its opposite: "necrophily."

> While life is characterized by growth in a structured, functional manner, the necrophilous person loves all that does not grow, all that is mechanical. The necrophilous person is driven by the desire to transform the organic into the inorganic, to approach life mechanically, as if all living persons were things. . . . Memory, rather than experience; having, rather than being, is what counts. The necrophilous person can relate to an object—a flower or a person—only if he possesses it; hence a threat to his possession is a threat to himself; if he loses possession he loses contact with the world. . . . He loves control, and in the act of controlling he kills life.[4]

---

[2] This concept corresponds to what Sartre calls the "digestive" or "nutritive" concept of education, in which knowledge is "fed" by the teacher to the students to "fill them out." See Jean-Paul Sartre, "Une idée fondamentale de la phénoménologie de Husserl: L'intentionalité," *Situations I* (Paris, 1947).

[3] For example, some professors specify in their reading lists that a book should be read from pages 10 to 15—and do this to "help" their students!

[4] Eric Fromm, *The Heart of Man* (New York 1966), p. 41.

Oppression—overwhelming control—is necrophilic; it is nourished by love of death, not life. The banking concept of education, which serves the interests of oppression, is also necrophilic. Based on a mechanistic, static, naturalistic, spatialized view of consciousness, it transforms students into receiving objects. It attempts to control thinking and action, leads men to adjust to the world, and inhibits their creative power.

When their efforts to act responsibly are frustrated, when they find themselves unable to use their faculties, men suffer. "This suffering due to impotence is rooted in the very fact that the human equilibrium has been disturbed."[5] But the inability to act which causes men's anguish also causes them to reject their impotence, by attempting

> . . . to restore [their] capacity to act. But can [they], and how? One way is to submit to and identify with a person or group having power. By this symbolic participation in another person's life, [men have] the illusion of acting, when in reality [they] only submit to and become a part of those who act.[6]

Populist manifestations perhaps best exemplify this type of behavior by the oppressed, who, by identifying with charismatic leaders, come to feel that they themselves are active and effective. The rebellion they express as they emerge in the historical process is motivated by that desire to act effectively. The dominant elites consider the remedy to be more domination and repression, carried out in the name of freedom, order, and social peace (that is, the peace of the elites). Thus they can condemn—logically, from their point of view—"the violence of a strike by workers and [can] call upon the state in the same breath to use violence in putting down the strike."[7]

Education as the exercise of domination stimulates the credulity of students, with the ideological intent (often not perceived by educators) of indoctrinating them to adapt to the world of oppression. This accusation is not made in the naïve hope that the dominant elites will thereby simply abandon the practice. Its objective is to call the attention of true humanists to the fact that they cannot use banking educational methods in the pursuit of liberation, for they would only negate that very pursuit. Nor may a revolutionary society inherit these methods from an oppressor society. The revolutionary society which practices banking education is either misguided or mistrusting of men. In either event, it is threatened by the specter of reaction.

Unfortunately, those who espouse the cause of liberation are themselves surrounded and influenced by the climate which generates the banking concept, and often do not perceive its true significance or its dehumanizing power. Paradoxically, then, they utilize this same instrument of alienation in what they consider an effort to liberate. Indeed, some "revolutionaries" brand as "innocents," "dreamers," or even "reactionaries" those who would challenge this

---

[5] Ibid., p. 31.
[6] Ibid.
[7] Reinhold Niebuhr, *Moral Man and Immoral Society* (New York, 1960), p. 130.

educational practice. But one does not liberate men by alienating them. Authentic liberation—the process of humanization—is not another deposit to be made in men. Liberation is a praxis: the action and reflection of men upon their world in order to transform it. Those truly committed to the cause of liberation can accept neither the mechanistic concept of consciousness as an empty vessel to be filled, nor the use of banking methods of domination (propaganda, slogans—deposits) in the name of liberation.

Those truly committed to liberation must reject the banking concept in its entirety, adopting instead a concept of men as conscious beings, and consciousness as consciousness intent upon the world. They must abandon the educational goal of deposit-making and replace it with the posing of the problems of men in their relations with the world. "Problem-posing" education, responding to the essence of consciousness—*intentionality*—rejects communiqués and embodies communication. It epitomizes the special characteristic of consciousness: being *conscious of*, not only as intent on objects but as turned in upon itself in a Jasperian "split"—consciousness as consciousness *of* consciousness.

Liberating education consists in acts of cognition, not transferrals of information. It is a learning situation in which the cognizable object (far from being the end of the cognitive act) intermediates the cognitive actors—teacher on the one hand and students on the other. Accordingly, the practice of problem-posing education entails at the outset that the teacher-student contradiction be resolved. Dialogical relations—indispensable to the capacity of cognitive actors to cooperate in perceiving the same cognizable object—are otherwise impossible.

Indeed, problem-posing education, which breaks with the vertical patterns characteristic of banking education, can fulfill its function as the practice of freedom only if it can overcome the above contradiction. Through dialogue, the teacher-of-the-students and the students-of-the-teacher cease to exist and a new term emerges: teacher-student with students-teachers. The teacher is no longer merely the-one-who-teaches, but one who is himself taught in dialogue with the students, who in turn while being taught also teach. They become jointly responsible for a process in which all grow. In this process, arguments based on "authority" are no longer valid; in order to function, authority must be *on the side of* freedom, not *against* it. Here, no one teaches another, nor is anyone self-taught. Men teach each other, mediated by the world, by the cognizable objects which in banking education are "owned" by the teacher.

The banking concept (with its tendency to dichotomize everything) distinguishes two stages in the action of the educator. During the first, he cognizes a cognizable object while he prepares his lessons in his study or his laboratory; during the second, he expounds to his students about that object. The students are not called upon to know, but to memorize the contents narrated by the teacher. Nor do the students practice any act of cognition, since the object towards which that act should be directed is the property of the teacher rather than a medium evoking the critical reflection of both teacher and students. Hence in the name of the "preservation of culture and knowledge" we have a system which achieves neither true knowledge nor true culture.

The problem-posing method does not dichotomize the activity of the teacher-student: he is not "cognitive" at one point and "narrative" at another. He is always "cognitive," whether preparing a project or engaging in dialogue with the students. He does not regard cognizable objects as his private property, but as the object of reflection by himself and the students. In this way, the problem-posing educator constantly re-forms his reflections in the reflection of the students. The students—no longer docile listeners—are now critical co-investigators in dialogue with the teacher. The teacher presents the material to the students for their consideration, and reconsiders his earlier considerations as the students express their own. The role of the problem-posing educator is to create, together with the students, the conditions under which knowledge at the level of the *doxa* is superseded by the true knowledge, at the level of the *logos*.

Whereas banking education anesthetizes and inhibits creative power, problem-posing education involves a constant unveiling of reality. The former attempts to maintain the *submersion* of consciousness; the latter strives for the *emergence* of consciousness and *critical intervention* in reality.

Students, as they are increasingly posed with problems relating to themselves in the world and with the world, will feel increasingly challenged and obliged to respond to that challenge. Because they apprehend the challenge as interrelated to other problems within a total context, not as a theoretical question, the resulting comprehension tends to be increasingly critical and thus constantly less alienated. Their response to the challenge evokes new challenges, followed by new understandings; and gradually the students come to regard themselves as committed.

Education as the practice of freedom—as opposed to education as the practice of domination—denies that man is abstract, isolated, independent, and unattached to the world; it also denies that the world exists as a reality apart from men. Authentic reflection considers neither abstract man nor the world without men, but men in their relations with the world. In these relations consciousness and world are simultaneous; consciousness neither precedes the world nor follows it.

> La conscience et le monde sont dormés d'un même coup: extérieur par essence à la conscience, le monde est, par essence relatif à elle.[8]

In one of our culture circles in Chile, the group was discussing . . . the anthropological concept of culture. In the midst of the discussion, a peasant who by banking standards was completely ignorant said: "Now I see that without man there is no world." When the educator responded: "Let's say, for the sake of argument, that all the men on earth were to die, but that the earth itself remained, together with trees, birds, animals, rivers, seas, the stars . . . wouldn't all this be a world?" "Oh no," the peasant replied emphatically. "There would be no one to say: 'This is a world.'"

The peasant wished to express the idea that there would be lacking the consciousness of the world which necessarily implies the world of consciousness. *I* cannot exist without a *not-I*. In turn, the *not-I* depends on that existence. The

---

[8] Sartre, *Une idée fundamentale*, p. 32.

world which brings consciousness into existence becomes the world *of* that consciousness. Hence, the previously cited affirmation of Sartre: *"La conscience et le monde sont dormés d'un même coup."*

As men, simultaneously reflecting on themselves and on the world, increase the scope of their perception, they begin to direct their observations towards previously inconspicuous phenomena:

> In perception properly so-called, as an explicit awareness [*Gewahren*], I am turned towards the object, to the paper, for instance. I apprehend it as being this here and now. The apprehension is a singling out, every object having a background in experience. Around and about the paper lie books, pencils, ink-well, and so forth, and these in a certain sense are also "perceived," perceptually there, in the "field of intuition"; but whilst I was turned towards the paper there was no turning in their direction, nor any apprehending of them, not even in a secondary sense. They appeared and yet were not singled out, were not posited on their own account. Every perception of a thing has such a zone of background intuitions or background awareness, if "intuiting" already includes the state of being turned towards, and this also is "conscious experience," or more briefly a "consciousness of" all indeed that in point of fact lies in the co-perceived objective background.[9]

That which had existed objectively but had not been perceived in its deeper implications (if indeed it was perceived at all) begins to "stand out," assuming the character of a problem and therefore of challenge. Thus, men begin to single out elements from their "background awarenesses" and to reflect upon them. These elements are now objects of men's consideration, and, as such, objects of their action and cognition.

In problem-posing education, men develop their power to perceive critically *the way they exist* in the world *with which* and *in which* they find themselves; they come to see the world not as a static reality, but as a reality in process, in transformation. Although the dialectical relations of men with the world exist independently of how these relations are perceived (or whether or not they are perceived at all), it is also true that the form of action men adopt is to a large extent a function of how they perceive themselves in the world. Hence, the teacher-student and the students-teachers reflect simultaneously on themselves and the world without dichotomizing this reflection from action, and thus establish an authentic form of thought and action.

Once again, the two educational concepts and practices under analysis come into conflict. Banking education (for obvious reasons) attempts, by mythicizing reality, to conceal certain facts which explain the way men exist in the world; problem-posing education sets itself the task of demythologizing. Banking education resists dialogue; problem-posing education regards dialogue as indispensable to the act of cognition which unveils reality. Banking education

---

[9] Edmund Husserl, *Ideas—General Introduction to Pure Phenomenology* (London, 1969), pp. 105–106.

treats students as objects of assistance; problem-posing education makes them critical thinkers. Banking education inhibits creativity and domesticates (although it cannot completely destroy) the *intentionality* of consciousness by isolating consciousness from the world, thereby denying men their ontological and historical vocation of becoming more fully human. Problem-posing education bases itself on creativity and stimulates true reflection and action upon reality, thereby responding to the vocation of men as beings who are authentic only when engaged in inquiry and creative transformation. In sum: banking theory and practice, as immobilizing and fixating forces, fail to acknowledge men as historical beings; problem-posing theory and practice take man's historicity as their starting point.

Problem-posing education affirms men as beings in the process of *becoming*—as unfinished, uncompleted beings in and with a likewise unfinished reality. Indeed, in contrast to other animals who are unfinished, but not historical, men know themselves to be unfinished; they are aware of their incompletion. In this incompletion and this awareness lie the very roots of education as an exclusively human manifestation. The unfinished character of men and the transformational character of reality necessitate that education be an ongoing activity.

Education is thus constantly remade in the praxis. In order to *be*, it must *become*. Its "duration" (in the Bergsonian meaning of the word) is found in the interplay of the opposites *permanence* and *change*. The banking method emphasizes permanence and becomes reactionary; problem-posing education—which accepts neither a "well-behaved" present nor a predetermined future—roots itself in the dynamic present and becomes revolutionary.

Problem-posing education is revolutionary futurity. Hence, it is prophetic (and, as such, hopeful). Hence, it corresponds to the historical nature of man. Hence, it affirms men as beings who transcend themselves, who move forward and look ahead, for whom immobility represents a fatal threat, for whom looking at the past must only be a means of understanding more clearly what and who they are so that they can more wisely build the future. Hence, it identifies with the movement which engages men as beings aware of their incompletion—an historical movement which has its point of departure, its Subjects and its objective.

The point of departure of the movement lies in men themselves. But since men do not exist apart from the world, apart from reality, the movement must begin with the men-world relationship. Accordingly, the point of departure must always be with men in the "here and now," which constitutes the situation within which they are submerged, from which they emerge, and in which they intervene. Only by starting from this situation—which determines their perception of it—can they begin to move. To do this authentically they must perceive their state not as fated and unalterable, but merely as limiting—and therefore challenging.

Whereas the banking method directly or indirectly reinforces men's fatalistic perception of their situation, the problem-posing method presents this very situation to them as a problem. As the situation becomes the object of their cognition, the naïve or magical perception which produced their fatalism gives way to perception which is able to perceive itself even as it perceives reality, and can thus be critically objective about that reality.

A deepened consciousness of their situation leads men to apprehend that situation as an historical reality susceptible of transformation. Resignation gives way to the drive for transformation and inquiry, over which men feel themselves to be in control. If men, as historical beings necessarily engaged with other men in a movement of inquiry, did not control that movement, it would be (and is) a violation of men's humanity. Any situation in which some men prevent others from engaging in the process of inquiry is one of violence. The means used are not important; to alienate men from their own decision-making is to change them into objects.

This movement of inquiry must be directed towards humanization—man's historical vocation. The pursuit of full humanity, however, cannot be carried out in isolation or individualism, but only in fellowship and solidarity; therefore it cannot unfold in the antagonistic relations between oppressors and oppressed. No one can be authentically human while he prevents others from being so. Attempting *to be more* human, individualistically, leads to *having more*, egotistically: a form of dehumanization. Not that it is not fundamental *to have* in order *to be* human. Precisely because it *is* necessary, some men's *having* must not be allowed to constitute an obstacle to others' *having*, must not consolidate the power of the former to crush the latter.

Problem-posing education, as a humanist and liberating praxis, posits as fundamental that men subjected to domination must fight for their emancipation. To that end, it enables teachers and students to become Subjects of the educational process by overcoming authoritarianism and an alienating intellectualism; it also enables men to overcome their false perception of reality. The world—no longer something to be described with deceptive words—becomes the object of that transforming action by men which results in their humanization.

Problem-posing education does not and cannot serve the interests of the oppressor. No oppressive order could permit the oppressed to begin to question: Why? While only a revolutionary society can carry out this education in systematic terms, the revolutionary leaders need not take full power before they can employ the method. In the revolutionary process, the leaders cannot utilize the banking method as an interim measure, justified on grounds of expediency, with the intention of *later* behaving in a genuinely revolutionary fashion. They must be revolutionary—that is to say, dialogical—from the outset.

From *Letters to Cristina* (1996)

Second Letter

> The piano in our house was like the tie around my father's neck. In spite of all our difficulties, we did not get rid of the piano, nor did my father do away with his necktie.

From *Letters to Cristina* by Paulo Freire (N.Y.: Routledge, 1996), pp. 21–24. Reprinted by permission of Routledge.

Born into a middle-class family that suffered the impact of the economic crisis of 1929, we became "connective kids." We participated in the world of those who ate well, even though we had very little to eat ourselves, and in the world of kids from very poor neighborhoods on the outskirts of town.[1]

We were linked to the former by our middle-class position; we were connected to the latter by our hunger, even though our hardships were less than theirs.

In my constant attempt to recollect my childhood, I remember that—in spite of the hunger that gave us solidarity with the children from the poor outskirts of town, in spite of the bond that united us in our search for ways to survive—our playtime, as far as the poor children were concerned, marked us as people from another world who happened to fall accidentally into their world.

Such class borders, which the man of today so clearly understands when he revisits his past, were not understood by the child of yesterday. Those borders were expressed more clearly by some of our friends' parents. Immersed in the alienating day-to-day routine, not understanding the causes behind the circumstances in which they were involved, the parents of these children were, by and large, existentially tired men and women who were historically anesthetized.

I cannot resist the temptation of making a parenthetical comment in this letter, calling attention to the relationship between class violence, class exploitation, existential tiredness, and historical anesthesia; that is, the fatalism among dominated and violated people before a world that is considered immutable. For this reason, the moment such people commit themselves to their political struggle, they begin to assert their position as a class. They transcend the fatalism that had anesthetized them historically. Such fatalism caused the parents of our poor friends to look at us as if they were thanking us for being friends with their sons and daughters. As if we and our parents were doing them a favor. To them, we were the sons of Captain Temístocles, we lived in a house in another section of the city; and our house was not like their huts in the woods.

---

[1] At the end of the past century and the beginning of this one, when the newly liberated slaves were settling themselves in the biggest and most important Brazilian cities, they evidently occupied the areas despised by the middle class and local elites. The narrow paths between the mountains and hills have been their leftovers ever since.

The narrow paths were no more than what many continue to be: gutters in which filthy, polluted, green water passed through. In them, even clean rain water turned to sludge due to trash, including that from the sewers. The imprudent children spent their leisure time swimming these waters before they reached the ocean and rivers. On its fetid banks, in areas prone to floods, the very poor built and continue to build their houses.

The residences in the hills do not present more comfort than those located on the banks of the narrow paths. The inhabitants have to descend and climb the slopes on foot, and if their houses are spared floods, the strong winds and torrential rains of the tropical zone can easily destroy them.

The mocambos endure the damage of inclemency better than the residences built with urban debris. The houses of the hills and narrow paths are without running water, electricity, sewage, or garbage collection.

In this manner, when Freire speaks of the "world of the kids who were from very poor neighborhoods on the outskirts of town" he is speaking about the excluded children, the children of the mocambos and of the hills. They are excluded from eating, attending school, being clothed properly, sleeping well, taking baths in clean water, and waiting for better days.

In our house, we had a German piano on which Lourdes, one of our aunts, played Chopin, Beethoven, and Mozart. The piano alone was enough to distinguish our class from that of Dourado, Reginaldo, Baixa, Toinho Morango, and Gerson Macaco, who were our friends in those days. The piano in our house was like the tie around my father's neck. In spite of all our difficulties, we did not get rid of the piano, nor did my father do away with his necktie. Both the piano and the necktie were, in the end, symbols that helped us remain in the class to which we belonged. They implied a certain lifestyle, a certain way of being, a certain way of speaking, a certain way of walking, a special way of greeting people that involved bowing slightly and tipping your hat, as I had often seen my father do. All of these things were an expression of class. All of these things were defended by our family as an indispensable condition of survival.

The piano was not a mere instrument for Lourdes's artistic enjoyment, nor were my father's neckties just a clothing style. They both marked our class position. To lose those class markers would have meant losing our solidarity with members of the middle class in a step-by-step march toward the poor people on the outskirts of town. From there it would have been very difficult to return to our middle-class milieu. It therefore became necessary to preserve those class markers in order psychologically to enable our family to deal with our financial crisis and maintain our class position.

Lourdes's piano and my father's neckties made our hunger appear accidental. With those markers, we were able to borrow money. Even though it was not easy, without them, it would have been almost impossible. With those markers, our childhood fruit thefts, if discovered, would have been treated as mere pranks. At most, they would have been a minor embarrassment for our parents. Without them, they would certainly have been characterized as child delinquency.

Lourdes's piano and my father's neckties played the same class role that the tropical jacaranda trees and fine china play today among Northeast Brazil's aristocracy, who are in decline. Perhaps aristocratic class markers are less effective today than Lourdes's piano and my father's neckties were during the 1930s.

I highlight the issue of social class because the dominant class insists, in eloquent discourses full of deceit, that what is important is not class, but the courage to work and be disciplined, and the desire to climb and grow. Therefore, those who triumph are those who work hard without complaining and are disciplined; that is, those who do not create problems for their masters.

It is for this reason that I have emphasized our origin and class position, explaining the gimmicks that our family developed in order to transcend our economic crisis.

I will never forget one of our gimmicks. It was a Sunday morning. Perhaps it was ten or eleven o'clock. It doesn't matter. We had just teased our stomachs with a cup of coffee and a thin slice of bread without butter. This would not have been enough food to keep us going, even if we had eaten plenty the day before, which we hadn't.

I don't remember what we were doing, if we were conversing or playing. I just remember that my two older brothers and I were sitting on the ledge of the cement patio at the edge of the yard where we lived. The yard contained some flower beds—roses, violets, and daisies—and some lettuce, tomatoes, and kale plants that my mother had pragmatically planted. The lettuce, tomatoes, and kale improved our diet. The roses, violets, and daisies decorated the living room in a vase that was a family relic from the last century. (Of these relics, my sister Stela still has the porcelain sink that was used to give us our first baths upon arriving in the world. Our sons and daughters were also bathed in the same porcelain sink. Regretfully, our grandchildren have broken with this family tradition.)

It was then that our attention was attracted by the presence of a chicken that probably belonged to our next-door neighbors. While looking for grasshoppers in the grass, the chicken ran back and forth, left to right, following the movements of the grasshoppers as they tried to survive. In one of those runs, the chicken came too close to us. In a split second, as if we had rehearsed it, premeditated it, we had the kicking chicken in our hands.

My mother arrived shortly after. She did not ask any questions. The four of us looked at each other and at the dead chicken in one of our hands.

Today, many years after that morning, I can appreciate the conflict that my mother, who was a Christian Catholic, must have felt as she looked at us in perplexity and silence. Her alternatives were either to reproach us severely and make us return the still warm chicken to our neighbors or to prepare the fowl as a special dinner. Her common sense won. Still silent, she took the chicken, walked across the patio, entered the kitchen, and lost herself in doing a job she had not done in a long time.

Our dinner that Sunday took place some hours later without any exchange of words. It is possible that we were tasting some remorse among the spices that seasoned our neighbor's chicken. The dish killed our hunger, yet the chicken was an accusatory "presence" that reminded us of the sin, the crime against private property, that we had committed.

The next day, our neighbor, upon noticing the loss of his chicken from the pen, must have cursed the thieves who could only have been the "little people," poor lower-class people, the kind who steal chickens.[2] He would never have imagined that the authors of the theft were close, very close to him indeed. Lourdes's piano and my father's neckties made any other conjecture impossible.

---

[2] Chicken thief was the name used in Northeast Brazil, before the violence of burglars had reached its cities, for those who committed small thefts to survive, having no job due to a sluggish economy.

The term indicated a thief who stole, almost accidentally, things he found in the backyards of the well-to-do—clothes, fruit, or even chickens.

"Little people" is the Brazilian term that arrogant middle-class and upper-class people call, even today, people deprived of material goods. Besides being discriminatory, the term is intended to hurt the individual, and rob him or her of the dignity of belonging.

It is as if being poor or miserable was disgraceful and worked against possessing moral or ethical qualities because of a nonprivileged social status. Therefore, "little people," men or women, were considered inferior individuals to whom we ought not give any respect or esteem. This term is highly pejorative, [and] therefore, Freire uses it in quotes.

Questions

1. What is a "culture of silence"?
2. How has our traditional education system submerged the masses in a "culture of silence"?
3. How did Freire develop a pedagogy of the oppressed?
4. Explain Freire's assertion that "education is suffering from narration sickness."
5. What is the "banking" concept of education?
6. What does Freire mean by the phrase "humankind's ontological vocation"?
7. How does this view of humankind differ from the perspective of humankind associated with "banking" education?
8. How do "bank-clerk" teachers dehumanize themselves and their students?
9. What is the difference between being *in* the world rather than *with* the world?
10. What does Freire mean by praxis?
11. Describe in your own words the problem-posing education advocated by Freire.
12. What role does dialogue play in problem-posing education?
13. If one embraces teaching as a problem-posing activity, what does one teach? What is the curriculum? Where does one begin?
14. What is humanization and why is this a goal worthy of Freire's pedagogy?
15. How might economic class determine classroom practice?
16. In your own words, describe the ideally educated individual from Freire's point of view.

chapter 14

Matthew Lipman

TIME LINE FOR LIPMAN

1923	Is born August 24 in Vinelend, New Jersey.
1948	Receives B.S. from Columbia University.
1950–1951	Is Fulbright Scholar to Sorbonne University, Paris.
1953	Receives Ph.D. from Columbia University.
1954–1957	Is assistant professor of philosophy at Columbia.
1957–1961	Is associate professor at Columbia.
1961–1967	Is professor of philosophy at Columbia.
1967	Publishes *What Happens in Art*.
1972	Is named professor of philosophy at Montclair State College.
1973	Publishes *Contemporary Aesthetics*.
1974	Establishes the Institute for the Advancement of Philosophy for Children at Montclair State.
	Publishes *Harry Stottlemeier's Discovery* and the accompanying manual, *Philosophical Inquiry*.
1976	Publishes *Lisa*.
1977	Publishes *Philosophy in the Classroom*.
1978	Publishes *Growing Up with Philosophy* and *Suki*.
	Initiates publication of *Thinking: The Journal of Philosophy for Children*.
1980	Publishes *Mark*.

1981	Publishes *Pixie.*
1982	Publishes *Kio and Gus.*
1987	Publishes *Elfie.*
1988	Publishes *Philosophy Goes to School.*
1993	Publishes *Thinking in Education.*
1994	Publishes *Thinking Children and Education.*
1996	Publishes *Natasha.*

Introduction

Philosophy for children began in the late 1960s when Matthew Lipman, who at the time was a professor of philosophy at Columbia University, became upset with some fundamental problems. Put into the contemporary language of education, Lipman was upset with a cognitive and an affective problem. The cognitive problem related to a perceived diminution of American children's ability to reason and to solve problems. The perception was supported by declining scores on standardized tests. The affective problem, a more diffuse but equally upsetting one, was concerned with how children felt about schooling and about the academic endeavor. Stated simply, the longer children were in school, the less they seemed to like and to value it.

At first, Lipman toyed with the idea of writing a story that individual children might chance upon in a library or bookstore and that would model a cooperative community of inquiry with children (almost like an intellectual version of the *Peanuts* comic strip) and would, in effect, invite children into the fictional world, giving them a place where they would practice and hone the art and craft of thinking.[1]

Over the course of the next few years (1970–1974) as Lipman field-tested his novel, now known as *Harry Stottlemeier's Discovery*, in schools around the Columbia campus, that idea was modified and expanded. The quality of happenstance—the individual child stumbling over the volume on a library shelf—was jettisoned. In its place, especially as Lipman left Columbia in 1972 and moved to Montclair State College and, with Dr Ann Margaret Sharp, formed the Institute for the Advancement of Philosophy for Children (I.A.P.C.), came the notion that *Harry Stottlemeier's Discovery* would be the first element in a conscious process of reforming and reconstructing the educational enterprise.

Between 1973 and 1988, six more programs were constructed by Lipman and his associates at I.A.P.C. *Elfie,* for grades K-2, concentrates on the making of distinctions, connections, and comparisons within the context of a variety of broad philosophical issues. Two programs were constructed for grades 3 and 4: *Pixie* concentrates on analogical reasoning skills and philosophy of language, and *Kio and Gus* emphasizes practice in a variety of reasoning skills that prepare children to investigate nature. *Lisa,* for grades 7 and 8, focuses on ethical inquiry; *Suki,* for grades 9 and

10, on aesthetics inquiry; and *Mark,* for grades 11 and 12, on social and political inquiry.

At this point, philosophy for children is being taught in some five thousand schools in the United States. The program has been translated into 18 languages, and there are philosophy for children centers throughout the United States and in Chile, Costa Rica, Brazil, Mexico, Nigeria, Spain, Portugal, Guatemala, Iceland, Denmark, Canada, Austria, Australia, and Taiwan. Experimental research in the United States and in many of the countries cited above has demonstrated that children exposed to philosophy by well-prepared teachers gain significantly in reasoning, reading comprehension, and mathematical performance.

There has been, then, a quiet—if explosions can be quiet—explosion in philosophy for children over the course of two decades. Philosophy for children is no longer the creation of one person. It has been changed, expanded, restructured, and transformed as it has passed through different hands and different cultures. Especially when philosophy for children went overseas it changed and, in many ways, the change has been dramatic. Philosophy for children today may be a family of practices and practitioners, but as is the case with many large families, individual members may not even be recognizable to others. Still, there are two things that hold these philosophy for children programs together: the notion of the educated person as one who can think for herself or himself and a general methodology for helping nurture the educated person.

Philosophy for children is one of the oldest and most respected of the family of critical thinking programs, known generally as the critical thinking movement, that have emerged in the United States since the 1970s. Virtually all of those programs would accept in theory some variant of the claims that a critical thinker is a person who is self-reflective and self-corrective, that is, is a person who monitors her or his own thinking, is sensitive to the nuances and subtleties of the context in which thinking takes place, is governed by appropriate criteria and standards, is disposed to or has the habit of thinking critically, and values the act of thinking critically.

As one can see, the definition of critical thinking is quite complex, but what has happened in practice is that many of the critical thinking programs have focused on a truncated notion of critical thinking, reducing it to a series of skills, analogous to bicycle riding or needlepoint, that can be improved by drill and repetition. A quick glance at *Harry Stottlemeier's Discovery* and at the manual *(Philosophical Inquiry)* that accompanies *Harry* should be sufficient to show that that assumption is not justified regarding philosophy for children. In *Harry,* every time a logical rule is learned it comes with a caveat attached, almost like the warning on a package of cigarettes. Consider, for example, this exchange that occurs early on in *Harry:*

> "I mean," said Harry, "your father said, 'All engineers are good in math,' right? but that's one of those sentences which can't be turned around. So it doesn't follow that all people who're good in math are engineers. And I'm sure that's so. I'm sure that there are lots of doctors who're good in math, and airplane pilots who're good in math, and all sorts of other people

who aren't engineers who're good in math. So it doesn't follow that just because you're good in math, you have to be an engineer!"

Tony said, "That's right! Even if it's true that all engineers are good in math, it doesn't follow that only engineers are good in math." He stood up, gave Harry a snappy salute, and raced off home.

Harry decided to try the monkey bars awhile before going home. He had a feeling that Tony's father wouldn't be too much impressed with Tony's new argument. But at least he'd gotten Tony to see that the idea had some use. With that thought Harry put the matter out of his mind, and tried a new trick on the jungle gym.[2]

Consider also that Lisa, the character who may be most directly responsible for the development of the formal logic in *Harry,* is perhaps the least analytical, the least methodological, the most intuitive character in the book. Indeed, by the end of the book, Lisa has serious doubts about any attempt to reduce thinking to a set of mechanical skills.

When one looks at the traditional corpus (Lipman's novels) along with the manuals that accompany them, and when one recalls the style and the extent of education in philosophy for children, it becomes clear that thinking itself is complex. Anticipating the current fascination with multiple intelligences, Lipman recognized the fact that there was no such thing as intelligence defined as a single quality of mind that could be enhanced by a single methodology. From the inception of philosophy for children thinking was conceived of as having cognitive, affective, visual, mechanical, intuitive, aesthetic, ethical, and logical characteristics. To enhance thinking, in effect, was to attempt to deal with *all* of those qualities.

In regard to the general methodology of philosophy for children, it is deceptively simple. One starts from a well-chosen text—some novel or short story, some poem or play, a scientific discovery, a piece of music, a painting—that is philosophically rich and interesting. One reads (or views or listens to) the text with a group of children and then one asks them what they find interesting in the text. Their interests are typically phrased in the form of a problem or question, recorded by the teacher, which forms the agenda for inquiry into the text. Even more loosely formulated, philosophy for children is about reading a text and talking about it.

In the traditional classroom, talk mainly is dyadic, going from teacher to student and student to teacher. The teacher asks a question and the student, if she or he is astute, answers it; the teacher gives information and the student records it; the teacher commands and the students obey. In a philosophy for children classroom, the talk is more diffuse precisely because philosophy for children puts such a premium on talk as a way of enhancing thought. The assumption behind philosophy for children is that if you can get children to talk well—to listen to each other, correct others and themselves, be sensitive to the nuances of the conversation, search for appropriate rules and standards for deciding what to say—you are well on your way to achieving the goal of creating a person who can think well for herself or himself.

Notes

1. Matthew Lipman, "On Writing a Philosophical Novel," in *Studies in Philosophy for Children*, ed. Ann Margaret Sharp and Ronald F. Reed. (Philadelphia: Temple University Press, 1992), pp. 3–7.
2. Matthew Lipman, *Harry Stottlemeier's Discovery* (Upper Montclair, NJ: First Mountain Foundation, 1982), p. 8.

Do Elementary School Children Need Philosophy? (1994)

Educators are beginning to take a second look at philosophy, and are asking whether this subject, so long a part of higher education, might be adapted for use in primary education. Is it possible that philosophy could be redesigned so as to be accessible to elementary school children, with the consequence that the result would be a redesign, for the better, of the educational process itself?

I. There have been many attempts to introduce thinking into education. Why do they often fail? Here are a few of the reasons:

1.   Failure to distinguish between more thinking and better thinking. Many approaches introduce more stimuli to thinking in the curriculum, but fail to provide strategies for improving the *quality* of that thinking.

2.   Confusion between thinking skills and study strategies. Some programs which purport to sharpen thinking skills in fact do nothing more than coach students on how to do better on tests, such as by distinguishing between test items favoring and not favoring answering by guessing.

3.   Concentration on problem-solving rather than problem-finding. It is essential that students become sensitized to whatever is problematic in their environment, so that they can formulate it as a problem and deal with it rationally. It is not enough for them to attempt to solve only those problems posed to them by others.

4.   Concentration on paper-and-pencil problems. Many students are not prepared to insert an interface of writing between themselves and the problems they encounter in their environment. Requiring that these problems be dealt with exclusively by writing or computation puts these more verbal students at a further disadvantage.

5.   Isolation of students from one another. Many students are inclined to engage first in cognitive collaboration with their peers and then move on to more individualized performances. Requiring them to "do their own work" puts them at a disadvantage contrasted with those more introverted students who are inclined from the start to work by themselves.

6.   Lack of standards for cognitive work. Some approaches to the teaching of thinking are candidly relativistic, taking the position that, since each point of view is unique, the claims made for one perspective can be no better than the claims made for any other. This denies the role of logical standards in reasoning,

Matthew Lipman, "Do Elementary School Children Need Philosophy?", *The Finnish Journal of Education*, March, 1994, pp. 281–86. Used by permission of Matthew Lipman.

the importance of grounding truth-claims in evidence, and the need to base judgments on good reasons.

7. **The absence of conceptual components.** Many approaches to the teaching of thinking place a low value on thinking, equating it with a kind of cognitive trouble-shooting or problem-solving. They fail to recognize that students often have trouble thinking because they only dimly understand such central concepts as truth, fairness, reasons, etc. Without access to the philosophical repertoire of concepts, students can be at a loss when it comes to dealing with questions of value as well as with questions of fact.

8. **Failure to make provision for language.** On the one hand, many students require preliminary discussion and deliberation in order to orient themselves regarding the assumptions to be taken into account in the ensuing inquiry. On the other hand, the use of language exposes students to many pitfalls which they can avoid only by learning some elementary techniques of linguistic analysis. Most "thinking" programs fail to provide these safeguards.

9. **Lack of cognitive modeling.** Learners need models, but models of thinking are admittedly hard to provide. It is too much to ask the teacher to provide the exclusive model. The curriculum needs to accept responsibility here, but few curricula do so.

10. **Misunderstanding of the role of cognitive skills in thinking.** Many approaches to thinking instruction operate on the assumption that one first perfects the students' discrete cognitive skills and then gets them to coordinate those skills in a systematic way. This assumption contradicts practical experience, which is that students taught cognitive skills first, and in isolation from a context of inquiry, have great difficulty combining them and using them appropriately.

II. What are the criteria which an enlightened educator, at the tailend of the 20th century, would expect an educational approach to satisfy? The following list surely contains a good number of such requirements:

1. **Thinking in the disciplines.** Students of history must learn to think not merely *about* history: they should learn to think *historically*, as students of logic should learn to think logically and students of psychology should learn to think psychologically.

2. **Thinking among the disciplines.** Just as people who speak many languages should be able to translate from one to the other, so the educated person needs the fluency and flexibility to discover the connections that link each discipline to the others.

3. **Thinking about the disciplines.** The educated person is not merely knowledgeable about one or more disciplines, but is *critical* as well. He or she is able to question the assumptions of the disciplines, much as a philosopher of, say, education can question the fundamental assumptions of education.

4. **Thinking about thinking.** Just as artists think much about art and scientists think much about science, so those who are concerned to think well must be prepared to think extensively about thinking. This can be called "metacognition" or it may be thought of as systematic self-correction.

5. **Fostering of concept-formation.** Every discipline contains a conceptual network whose understanding is essential for the grasp of that discipline.

Education therefore necessarily involves concept-formation techniques such as definition and classification as well as meaning-clarification techniques such as the identification of relationships and the use of criteria.

6.   **Fostering of reasoning.** Educated persons can coordinate their understandings, can extend their knowledge by seeing what follows validly from it, and can defend their knowledge by means of appropriate arguments. They are able to distinguish the circumstances that make for valid inference from the circumstances that are likely to result in invalid inference. Reasonableness has become a major goal of education.

7.   **Strengthening of judgment.** Judgments are pronouncements by means of which we distinguish the true from the false, the correct from the incorrect, the good from the bad, etc. Judgments are of two kinds: rule-guided and non-rule-guided. Judgments are applications of general understandings to specific circumstances: the rule to the case, the universal to the particular. One who lacks judgment can hardly be educated.

8.   **Facilitation of transfer.** One who drives an automobile may transfer that *knowledge how* more readily to a truck than to a motorboat or airplane. What governs transfer? Among other things, surely, would be the ability to make judgments of similarity, difference and identity, as well as extreme sensitivity to context, and facility in analogical reasoning.

9.   **Provision of conditions for deliberative discussion.** If thinking is the internalization of utterance, then logically disciplined, inquisitive thinking results from the internalization of logically disciplined, inquisitive utterance. Ill-defined concepts exemplify the sorts of problems that provoke classroom dialogue consisting of diversified mental acts and distributed thinking, subsequently internalized by participants.

10.   **Relevance.** Students find it difficult to take education seriously if the knowledge they acquire seems inapplicable to their lives as well as being theoretically meaningless. The use of examples and illustrations, like the use of stories, represents a way of connecting the experience and values of the culture with those of the student.

III. What are these virtues (i.e., powers or strengths) of philosophy that carry over from the academic, higher-education version to the elementary school version?

1.   **Ethical inquiry.** Engaging students in investigation of problems dealing with the role of moral values and norms in human conduct.

2.   **Aesthetic inquiry.** Getting students to explore problematic issues that involve the relationships between artistic creation, aesthetic appreciation and aesthetic criticism.

3.   **Metaphysical inquiry.** Encouraging students to reach for greater and greater generality in their understanding of the world and its ways of working.

4.   **Logical inquiry.** Inquiry into the rules of inquiry, and into whatever principles are appealed to when thinking about thinking.

5.   **Epistemological inquiry.** Having students seek to answer such questions as "What counts for true?" and "What is the relationship between truth and meaning?"

Additionally, philosophy provides a methodology of linguistic and logical analysis; a repertoire of distinctively philosophical concepts that are important to students but not dealt with specifically by other disciplines, examples of such concepts being *friendship, justice, personhood, individuality* and so on; and a methodology for dialogical inquiry through impartial but collaborative deliberation.

IV. When one first hears of Philosophy for Children, one may well be inclined to wonder why so circuitous an enterprise would be needed to achieve a result as simple and straightforward as improving students' thinking. But when one examines the list just provided of criteria for a successful approach, together with the list of common obstacles to success, and when one adds to these the many minor difficulties that attend any effort to improve students' cognitive performance, one begins to see that only a fairly complex intervention can accomplish all that has to be accomplished while avoiding the countless pitfalls that attend every educational intervention. This is not an area in which success is easily attained.

On the face of it, philosophy would seem to be an unlikely candidate for use in strengthening children's thinking at the elementary school level. But this may be due to a failure on our part to be able to conceive of a way of redesigning a traditional university-level subject into one accessible to school children. Moreover, the cases we have seen of other disciplines (such as history and economics) being brought into the elementary school classroom do not inspire that much confidence, for they are often accomplished by reduction of the subject-matter to a series of oversimplifications. In the case of philosophy, it would be absolutely essential that the integrity of the discipline be retained whatever the redesign.

This is what has been attempted in the case of Philosophy for Children. It does not seek to oversimplify or vulgarize philosophy, but to keep its virtues intact while making sure that they are within the range of children's capacities and dispositions.

V. Philosophy for Children embodies all of the above virtues, aligning them with a fresh approach to curriculum development and pedagogy. The Philosophy for Children version of philosophy possesses these unique characteristics:

1.   Novelistic texts. The textual materials read by the children using the Philosophy for Children curriculum are neither primary texts derived from the writings of the major philosophers of the academic tradition nor secondary texts representing warmed-over accounts of that tradition. Instead, the students read novels sprinkled with philosophical ideas that are just vague and ill-defined enough as to beg for philosophical discussion. Even badly-educated children find these lures irresistible.

2.   Fictional children as models. Philosophy for Children does not attempt to invent a narrative version of the history of philosophy: it is not *The Story of Philosophy* on the analogy of *The Story of Fire* or *The Story of Stamp Collecting.* Instead, it depicts fictional children together engaged in dialogical inquiry with regard to the philosophical puzzlements they find themselves experiencing. In this sense, the novels provide the live children in the classroom with models of thinking children who readily lend themselves to emulation.

3.   **The incorporation of traditional philosophy in the instructional manuals.** If identifying conceptual puzzles represents one of the first steps involved in *doing* philosophy (for these students are *doing* philosophy, not *learning* it), propounding philosophical questions is one of the next steps. Here, teachers need help, and the huge instructional manual that accompanies every Philosophy for Children program contains a wealth of questions of the kind philosophers have asked or might ask. These questions are organized into discussion plans, exercises, games and activities so as to make them easily available for classroom usage.

4.   **The lack of answers to the philosophical questions in the manuals.** Philosophical questions (excepting those having to do with logic) are not thought of by philosophers as having "right answers." Indeed, philosophers are generally content if they can merely improve a question's formulation. This lack of accepted answers emboldens students to presume to tread where no one has authoritative knowledge, and where their own opinions count as *judgments of practice.*

5.   **The conversion of the classroom into a community of inquiry.** The pedagogy of Philosophy for Children conceives of the teacher as a fosterer of inquiry, a facilitator of dialogue, a guarantor of impartiality and an instigator of thinking for oneself. Teachers are expected to be pedagogically strong (so as to safeguard the relevance of the discussion and the civility of the participants) while at the same time being philosophically self-effacing (so as not to indoctrinate the students). Students in a community of inquiry engage in distributed mental acts that occur dispersed among the participants but are then internalized by each student in the form of that student's own thinking.

VI. There is a sense in which philosophers are critics of thinking in much the way drama critics are critics of plays and political commentators are critics of politics. If this is correct, then philosophy brings to education a dimension that has been glaringly lacking for a long time. This omission is not to be overcome by tacking critical thinking questions on to existing lesson plans and claiming that one is now teaching "thinking across the disciplines." If *transfer* is acknowledged to be an important educational goal, then transfer is precisely what one can reasonably expect from doing philosophy in the elementary school and what one cannot expect from introducing a smattering of thinking skills into each separate subject-matter. What is transferable is, in the case of philosophy, the careful attention to meanings (through analysis of implications and inferences), the awareness of informal fallacies (as well as awareness of the limits of their fallaciousness), the rigor with which one discerns relationships and makes distinctions, the increased sensitivity one displays towards differences of context, and the awareness one has that one often has to make appropriate judgments even though one cannot locate the rules by which the making of such judgments can be guided.

Thus, the doing of philosophy cultivates both reasoning and judgment, and thereby cultivates higher-order thinking. (In the sense that philosophy encourages independence of thought, it certainly encourages intellectual creativity.)

And since it insists upon the priority of classroom dialogue, it most certainly does not make the mistake of developing isolated cognitive skills before students have gained an understanding of how such skills are to work together as parts of a larger whole.

Needless to say, the success of Philosophy for Children is contingent upon the preparation of teachers who have a love of ideas and a concern to establish a community of inquiry in the classroom. Such teachers are to be prepared by virtually the same method as that by which they are expected to educate their own students. (Thus it is unrealistic and unjust to train teachers by the lecture method and then expect them to teach their students by means of collaborative inquiry.) Ultimately, this means that, for philosophy to reach the elementary school classroom, it must first be installed in the School of Education classroom. If it is barred from the schools of teacher preparation, one can be sure that it will not significantly modify education at the primary school level.

From *Philosophy Goes to School* (1988)

Did Plato Condemn Philosophy for the Young?

We all know that philosophy emerged in Greece about a hundred generations ago, and for this achievement we honor such figures as Thales, Anaximander, Anaxagoras, and Anaximines. Apparently philosophy was first embodied in aphorisms, poetry, dialogue, and drama. But this variety of philosophical vehicles was short-lived, and philosophy became that which, by and large, it has remained—an academic discipline, access to which was limited to college and university students.

For the most part, these students in the upper echelons of education have been expected to *learn* philosophy rather than to *do* it. Often they study the history of systems of philosophy (perhaps from the pre-Socratics to Hegel, or from Aristotle to St. Thomas, or from Russell to Quine) in preparation for final examinations, or they prepare extended philosophical arguments on obscure but respected topics to qualify for academic degrees.

Yet philosophy is a survivor. In an era in which most of the humanities have been driven to the wall, philosophy has somehow managed to stay afloat—if only barely—largely by converting itself into a knowledge industry: *pace* Socrates! But the price of survival has been high: philosophy has had to abdicate virtually all claims to exercising a socially significant role. Even the most celebrated professors of philosophy nowadays would be likely to admit that, on the vast stage of world affairs, they appear only as bit players or members of the crowd.

Oddly enough, despite the continued social impotence of philosophy, it has remained internally a discipline of incredible richness and diversity. Only in

From *Philosophy Goes to School* by Matthew Lipman (Philadelphia, PA: Temple University Press, 1988), pp. 11–21. Reprinted by permission of Temple University Press.

the past few centuries has a new note sounded, suggesting that philosophy has practical applications undreamt of by academicians, and here and there are those who marvel (like Descartes amazed that mathematics offered such powerful foundations but was unused) at the great, sweeping panorama of its applicability.

Nevertheless, *applying* philosophy and *doing* it are not identical. The paradigm of doing philosophy is the towering, solitary figure of Socrates, for whom philosophy was neither an acquisition nor a profession but a way of life. What Socrates models for us is not philosophy known or philosophy applied but philosophy *practiced*. He challenges us to acknowledge that philosophy as deed, as form of life, is something that any of us can emulate.

Any of us? Or just the males? Or just the adults? To many philosophers, reasonableness is found only in grown-ups. Children (like women) may be charming, beautiful, delightful, but they are seldom considered capable of being reasoned with, logical, or rational. Descartes, for example, and the young Piaget seem to have thought of childhood as a period of epistemological error that is fortunately sloughed off as one matures. The adult/child dichotomy has an obvious parallel in the dichotomy between ideal industrial management ("rational") and ideal workers ("cheerful"). Nevertheless, it is likely that the dichotomy between adults and children, insofar as the capacity to pursue the philosophical form of life was concerned, would have seemed absurd to Socrates.

Generally, when a discipline is available only on the college level or above, it is because it is considered a discipline inappropriate for children or inessential to their education. However, this has not consistently been the case with philosophy, and Jacques Derrida has shrewdly noted that, until the Reformation, philosophy had been part and parcel of the education of adolescent princes and princesses.[1] But the Reformation put an end to all that: philosophy appeared utterly superfluous when it came to the preparation of future businessmen and scientists. With the ascendency of the business ideology, philosophy was banished from the scene as far as the education of children was concerned. Not even Dewey, easily the most insightful of all philosophers of education, could bring himself to advocate philosophy as an elementary school subject, but that was because he had already committed himself to rebuilding education along the lines of scientific inquiry. For others, philosophy appeared too difficult for children or too frivolous or too arid; some even thought it too dangerous. What was it about philosophy that gave rise to these misgivings?

Let us turn back to Plato and re-examine his attitude toward teaching philosophy to the young. In the earlier dialogues, it will be recalled, Socrates talks to young and old alike, although just how young they are is not clear. (Robert Brumbaugh, for example, places the ages of the two children in the *Lysis* at eleven.) There is no indication that Socrates has any misgivings about these conversations with children (although on other occasions he is certainly capable of expressing the unease he feels about what he is doing: we have only to recall

---

[1] Jacques Derrida, *Qui a peur de la philosophie?*

here his bizarre conduct in the *Phaedrus*). But then comes a seemingly dramatic reversal: in Book 7 of the *Republic,* after genially admonishing us to keep children to their studies by play and not by compulsion and after having perhaps overgenerously praised dialectic ("he who can view things in their connection is a dialectician; he who cannot, is not"), he urges that children not be exposed to dialectic, for "its practitioners are infected with lawlessness" [537]. Young people, he says,

> when they get their first taste of it, treat argument as a form of sport solely for purposes of contradiction. When someone has proved them wrong, they copy his methods to confute others, delighting like puppies in tugging and tearing at anyone who comes near them. And so, after a long course of proving others wrong and being proved wrong themselves, they rush to the conclusion that all they once believed is false; and the result is that in the eyes of the world they discredit, not themselves only, but the whole business of philosophy. [539][2]

Certainly this latter remark is not to be taken too lightly. The situation of philosophy in those turbulent times was precarious enough, without incurring additional risks by encouraging logic-chopping and speculation by Athenian urchins. Nor can we forget that even Aristotle had to make a hurried exit from Athens so as not to afford Athenians an opportunity to do to him what they had done to Socrates and thus "sin twice against philosophy."

This, then, is one reason for sequestering children and philosophy from one another: doing so is for the protection of philosophy, for if children are allowed to do it, philosophy will appear unworthy of adults. The other reason is for the protection of children: dialectic will subvert them, corrupt them, infect them with lawlessness. These reasons, it must be presumed, have been taken as conclusive ever since Plato wrote, and his authority has been invoked to deter educational initiatives that might have given children access to philosophy earlier on. What are we to say about this? Was Plato wrong to have opposed dialectical training for children so vigorously in Book 7? Here it may be helpful to consider the picture of intellectual Athens painted by Gilbert Ryle. Ryle offers us a highly speculative portrayal of the manner in which the procedures and techniques of eristic or dialectic were taught to students. Intellectual contest was paramount: debaters were assigned theses to defend or attack, regardless of their personal beliefs, and it was through these "moot court" procedures, Ryle contends, that cogency in argumentation was fostered and achieved. These moot conditions "proved to be the beginning of methodical philosophical reasoning." Nothing in Ryle's account indicates that he found these forensic or sophistic techniques of instruction objectionable in any way.

Elsewhere, indeed, Ryle seems to feel that Socrates likewise was not inclined to distinguish between philosophical reasoning and philosophy. Thus he argues that in the *Apology* Socrates provides "only a perfunctory answer to the charge of impiety but a protracted defense of the practice of elenctic questioning." Ryle

---

[2] Plato, *Republic*, Book 7, trans. Francis Cornford. New York: Oxford University Press, 1945, p. 261.

identifies such questioning as "the Socratic method" and tells us that it was the right to engage in such questioning that Socrates was most concerned to justify.[3]

Here we must tread with great care. It is one thing to say that debate and argument can be useful disciplinary devices in the preparation of those who are to engage in philosophical reasoning; it is quite something else to assume that philosophy is reducible to argument. The eristic method of teaching, probably introduced into Athens by the sophist Protagoras, may have been suitable for preparing future lawyers and politicians, but was it really serviceable for the preparation of everyone else (including would-be philosophers) who sought a more reasonable view of life? It would be strange indeed if Socrates, for whom the shared examination of the concepts essential to the conduct of life was of the greatest urgency, would have been content to equate that all-important pursuit with the dry, technical procedures of dialectical argumentation. What Socrates stresses is the continued prosecution of philosophical inquiry by following the reasoning wherever it leads (confident that, wherever it leads, wisdom lies in that direction), not the heavy breathing and clanging of armor in dialectical battles, where the premium is not on insight but on victory.

What made classical rhetoric and dialectic dangerous, for young people at any rate, was their separation of technique from conviction. Children should be given practice in discussing the concepts they take seriously. To give them practice in discussing matters they are indifferent to deprives them of the intrinsic pleasures of becoming educated and provides society with future citizens who neither discuss what they care about nor care about what they discuss.

Forensic education, the preparation of lawyers who can argue for any side regardless of their own convictions (if they have any), should be considered a very special case, in no way a model for the rest of education. The breeding ground of amoralism is the training of technicians who assume that ends are given (or do not matter), so that their concern is merely with means, with tactics, with technique. If children are not given the opportunity to weigh and discuss both ends and means, and their interrelationship, they are likely to become cynical about everything except their own well-being, and adults will not be slow to condemn them as "mindless little relativists."

One may readily conjecture, therefore, that what Plato was condemning in the seventh book of the *Republic* was not the practice of philosophy by children as such but the reduction of philosophy to sophistical exercises in dialectic or rhetoric, the effects of which on children would be particularly devastating and demoralizing. How better to guarantee the amoralism of the adult than by teaching the child that any belief is as defensible as any other and that what right there is must be the product of argumentative might? If this is how philosophy is to be made available to children, Plato may be supposed to have been saying, then it is far better that they have none at all.

Plato's condemnation of eristic argumentation by children is consistent with his general suspicions regarding whatever it was that the sophists were up to in Greece. Evidently he saw them as his rivals in subversiveness: they seemed to

---

[3] Gilbert Ryle, "Plato," in *The Encyclopedia of Philosophy*, ed. Paul Edwards. New York: Macmillan, 1967.

him to be undermining the foundations of Greek morality, while he was trying to undermine the foundations of Greek *immorality*. When they glibly equated dialectic with philosophy—equated, in short, the part with the whole—he and Socrates were not taken in. Nowhere does Socrates ever draw the line when it comes to doing philosophy with people of different ages, for doing philosophy is not a matter of age but of ability to reflect scrupulously and courageously on what one finds important. Indeed, when Callicles suggests to Socrates that philosophy is unworthy of grown men, we may imagine Plato's amusement at being able to implant so seditious an idea into the conversation.[4]

It can hardly be doubted that the traditional prohibition of philosophy for children is much indebted to citations from Plato's *Republic*. Nevertheless, it must be concluded that, insofar as that prohibition has rested on an appeal to Plato, it has rested on a mistake.

Philosophical Inquiry as the Model of Education

The contemporary educational system is frequently depicted as monolithic, inflexible, and impenetrable. However, it is considerably more pluralistic than these accounts suggest—more loose woven, open-textured, and diversified. Within its many crevices and interstices are school administrators to whom philosophy for children, for whatever reason, seems irresistible. Some prize it for its promise of improving reasoning skills; others admire it because students seem to enjoy it for its own sake rather than for the sake of grades or because it is relevant to their vocational aspirations. Some see it as the central stem of the elementary and secondary school, out of which the specialized disciplines can emerge; others see it as a wholesome preventive to drug and alcohol abuse. These educators may be familiar with the traditional rejection of philosophy for children, but they are pragmatic enough to reject it in turn. They like what philosophy does when children do it. They may be quite unaware that philosophy for children happens to fulfill Plato's pedagogical admonition that education be conducted "not by compulsion but by play." Although it may not be easy to put philosophy in place, it is enough for them that it works when it is put in place correctly.

Under these circumstances, philosophy for children will continue to find its way into the elementary schools. After all, word of a good thing gets around; already, children who take philosophy are boasting of it to those who do not, and far from being viewed with odium and contempt, philosophy has become a status symbol of elementary school. But all of these changes may be merely symptoms of a shift in fashion. How can philosophy as a required elementary school discipline—perhaps even as the core or armature of the curriculum—be justified?

This will not be easy, because it relentlessly demands of us the kind of self-knowledge that we, as educators, know to be highly elusive but that Socrates was wont to insist is indispensable to the worthwhile life. We must put aside any illusions we may have about the benign influence we exercise as educators

---

[4] Plato, *Gorgias* (p. 485), in *The Collected Dialogues of Plato,* ed. Edith Hamilton and Huntington Cairns. Princeton, N.J.: Princeton University Press, 1961.

and speak frankly to one another as Santayana speaks of the "magnificent example" Spinoza offers us

> of philosophic liberty, the courage, firmness, and sincerity with which he reconciled his heart to the truth. . . . Many a man before Spinoza and since has found the secret of peace: but the singularity of Spinoza, at least in the modern world, was that he facilitated this moral victory by no dubious postulates. He did not ask God to meet him half way: he did not whitewash the facts, as the facts appear to clear reason, or as they appeared to the science of his day. He solved the problem of the spiritual life after stating it in the hardest, sharpest, most cruel terms. Let us nerve ourselves today to imitate his example, not by simply accepting his solution, which for some of us would be easy, but by exercising his courage in the face of a somewhat different world.[5]

If we examine the present educational system with such candor, it is fairly predictable that we will be bound to conclude not simply that our educational system is imperfect but that its imperfections are more responsible than we have cared to admit for the grave circumstances in which the world currently finds itself. If we deplore our leaders and electorates as being self-centered and unenlightened, we must remember that they are the products of our educational system. If we protest, as an extenuating factor, that they are also the products of homes and families, we must remember that the unreasonable parents and grandparents in these families are likewise products of the selfsame process of education. As educators, we have a heavy responsibility for the unreasonableness of the world's population.

Socrates must have known that the tincture of self-knowledge provided by philosophy would in itself hardly suffice to deter an Athenian state hell-bent on its own destruction. Nevertheless he persisted, even to the point of demonstrating that what he was doing was worth more to him than life itself. (Always the teacher, even his final act was intentionally instructive!) Surely Socrates realized that the discussion of philosophical concepts was, by itself, just a fragile reed. What he must have been attempting to show was that the doing of philosophy was emblematic of shared inquiry as a way of life. One does not have to be a philosopher to foster the self-corrective spirit of the community of inquiry; rather, it can and should be fostered in each and every one of our institutions.

There is, then, a narrower and a broader case for philosophy for children. The narrower case is simply that it makes a wholesome contribution to the present curriculum and the classroom. But the broader justification would have to rest on the way in which it paradigmatically represents the education of the future as a form of life that has not yet been realized and as a kind of praxis. The reform of education must take shared philosophical inquiry in the classroom as a heuristic model. Without the guidance of some such paradigm, we will continue to drift and the curriculum will continue to be a hodgepodge.

---

[5] George Santayana, "Ultimate Religion," in *Obiter Scripta*, ed. Justus Buchler and Benjamin Schwartz. New York: Scribner's, 1936.

What Is It To Be Fully Educated?

Some educators today see philosophy for children as prefiguring a thorough going reappraisal of education, and they are eager to recite the characteristics of elementary school philosophy that they think the educational process as a whole should exhibit. This is without a doubt an appealing approach, but it should be accompanied by a comprehensive rationale. One does not usually attempt to redesign something unless one first knows what to expect of it or what to try to accomplish by means of it. The Greeks were probably the first people to insist that institutions (and not only people) needed to be perfected and that only by means of ideals such as justice and freedom could the reform of existing institutions be measured and judged. The notion of perfection is unlikely to stir us in quite the way it did the Greeks. Nevertheless, we may still agree with Dewey that nothing in human society commands our admiration as much as the way human institutions such as science and art, medicine and law seek in their practice to approximate their respective ideals of truth and beauty, health and justice.

What, then, is the ideal that educational practice seeks to approximate? This would seem to be the primary question that the redesign of education must confront. Thus put, the question may be too formidable to answer. Perhaps we should try putting a different question first: in what respect has education most greatly disappointed us? Here our response need not be in the least equivocal, and in answering the second question, we automatically answer the first: the greatest disappointment of traditional education has been its failure to produce people approximating the ideal of reasonableness. (This is not to say that all who are reasonable must have been educated, but rather that whoever is educated ought to be reasonable.) It may well be that in previous centuries unreasonableness was a luxury that human beings could afford, even though the costs were high. It should be evident, however, that the costs of our tolerant attitude toward unreasonableness are now far beyond our reach. We may still smile indulgently as we read of the legendary figures of history who were splendidly capricious and magnificently illogical: they savaged their victims, but they did not endanger everything. This is no longer the case; we will have to reason together or die together.

Traditionally, education has been conceived of as initiation into the culture, and the educated person has been thought to be the "cultivated" person or even the "cultured" person. But a closer look at traditional education might reveal students studying the disciplines, and in fact learning them, while yet failing to think in terms of them or to appropriate them fully. Seldom has traditional education been able to meet Vico's challenge—that the only way really to understand something is to re-enact it in some fashion. (One can understand what it is to be a story-teller only by becoming a story-teller, a painter only by becoming a painter, a dancer or a worker or a slave only by becoming a dancer or a worker or a slave.)

To be fully educated, one must be able to treat every discipline as a language and to think fluently in that language; be cultivated in one's reasoning as well as in everything else, remembering that reasoning is most effectively cultivated in the context of philosophy; and demonstrate educational accomplishments not merely as acquisitions of intellectual properties or as the amassing of spiritual capital but as a genuine appropriation that results in the enlargement of the self. Because philosophy is the discipline that best prepares us to think in terms of the other disciplines, it must be assigned a central role in the early (as well as in the late) stages of the educational process.

Converting Classrooms Into Communities of Inquiry

It would be unrealistic to expect a child brought up among unjust institutions to behave justly. Abusers of the rights of others often turn out themselves to have been abused. Likewise, it is unrealistic to expect a child brought up among irrational institutions to behave rationally. The irrationality of institutions must be considered preventable. There is no excusing them, for to do so permits them in turn to become the excuse offered by children who have been reared in such institutions and who adopt the irrationality of the institutions that fostered them.

The institution with which we as educators have primary concern is education. The irrationalities or "socially patterned defects" that permeate education have to be rooted out because they do not die out on their own: they have a marvelous capacity for self-perpetuation. This involves our bringing a greater degree of rational order than currently exists into the curriculum, into the methodology of teaching, into the process of teacher education, and into the procedures of testing. The adjustments made within each of these must in turn be determined by the interrelationships they have among themselves, as components of education, just as the structure of education depends on what kind of world we want to live in, since it will have much to do with the character of that world.

All too often the components of education have that kind of bizarre interrelationship of which the best analogy is the tail wagging the dog. Testing, which should have only ancillary status at best, tends to be the driving force of the system. The content of the tests structures the curriculum, which in turn controls the nature of teacher education. (This is not to deny that current practice in schools of education is consistent with the ethos of higher education generally, just as that ethos is in general consistent with that of the larger society of which it is a part. Schools of education tend to reflect the values of their societies, rather than the other way around.)

As long as the major goal of education is thought to be learning, as is the case in all tribal societies, the recall model will dominate testing, and teachers will find it difficult not to teach for the tests. Equally sad is that the information-acquisition model that dominates education, rather than encouraging children to think for themselves, is a failure even on its own terms, for we are constantly appalled at how little our children seem to know about the history of the world or about its political and economic organization. The effect of the tribal model is to stifle rather than to initiate thinking in the student. This does not mean we need to begin by producing better tests; we need to ask ourselves what kind of world we want to live in, what kind of education is most likely to contribute to the emergence of such a world, and what kind of curriculum is most likely to produce such an education. We must then set about producing that better curriculum.

There is good reason to think that the model of each and every classroom—that which it seeks to approximate and at times becomes—is the community of inquiry. By inquiry, of course, I mean perseverance in self-corrective exploration of issues that are felt to be both important and problematic. In no way do I mean to imply that inquiry sets a greater premium on discovery than on invention or a greater premium on rule-governed as opposed to improvisational activities. Those who produce works of art are practitioners of inquiry no less than those who produce new epistemological treatises or new discoveries in biology.

If we begin with the practice in the classroom, the practice of converting it into a reflective community that thinks in the disciplines about the world and about its thinking about the world, we soon come to recognize that communities can be nested within larger communities and these within larger communities still, if all hold the same allegiance to the same procedures of inquiry. There is the familiar ripple effect outward, like the stone thrown in the pond: wider and wider, more and more encompassing communities are formed, each community consisting of individuals committed to self-corrective exploration and creativity. It is a picture that owes as much to Charles Peirce as to John Dewey, but I doubt they would quibble over the credits if they thought there was a hope of its realization.

As so often happens when people describe the cloud castles of their dreams, the nitty-gritty realities are all too easily overlooked—realities such as the ladders by means of which the cloud castles are to be reached and the fearsome dragons and lurking trolls that are to be avoided along the way. . . .

Appropriating the Culture

The tribal model of education, in which the child is initiated into the culture, in effect provides for the assimilation of the child by the culture. In contrast, the reflective model of education provides for the appropriation of the culture by the child. A good case in point would be the textbook. As it currently stands, the textbook is a didactic device that stands over against the child as an alien and rigid *other*. It has this obdurate nature because it represents the final end-product of the received or adult view of the discipline. As Dewey would put it, the textbook (a century after *The Child and the Curriculum*) is still organized logically, like a table of contents or a sequence of lectures, rather than psychologically, in terms of the developing interests and motivation of the child. It is not something the child wants to enjoy and possess in the way one enjoys and assimilates a story or a picture; it is instead a formal, dreary, oppressive, and in many ways unintelligible summary of the contents that the child is expected to learn.

All of this is unnecessary, since we know from the work of Bruner and others that the child views material that is contextualized (i.e., presented in the form of a story) as something to be appropriated rather than rejected. If children are to learn to think in the disciplines so as to appropriate their humanistic heritage, they must begin with the raw subject matter of the disciplines and refine it for themselves. Masticating it for them in advance, the way mother birds masticate worms for their fledglings, is hardly the way to provide an education. Children presented with logic as a finished discipline find it repugnant, but they can find it delightful to discover it bit by bit and to see how it all interlocks and applies to language if not the world. This is how logic was probably discovered, and we can surmise that the early Greeks felt the same excitement and sense of power and mastery in discovering the same logic. Indeed, to learn something well is to learn it afresh in the same spirit of discovery as that which prevailed when it was discovered or in the same spirit of invention as that which prevailed when it was invented. When this spirit, which is truly the spirit of inquiry, prevails in the classroom, children will eagerly work through the materials of the arts and sciences and humanities for themselves and will appropriate them to themselves.

From *Philosophy in the Classroom* (1977)

Guiding a Classroom Discussion

A thoughtful discussion is no easy achievement. It takes practice. It requires the development of habits of listening and reflecting. It means that those who express themselves during a discussion must try to organize their thoughts so as not to ramble on pointlessly. Very young children may either wish to talk all at once or not talk at all. It takes time for them to learn sequential procedures that a good discussion requires.

One of the reasons that the process of discussion is so difficult for children to learn is that they are so frequently lacking in models of good discussion with which they can identify. If neither the home nor the school offers them examples of thoughtful discussion—whether of adults with children, or even of adults with adults—then each generation of children must in effect invent the whole process of discussion by itself, because no one ever shows it how. In short, it is useful to have an established tradition of discussion that each child can automatically assimilate and identify with and engage in if dialogue is to enter meaningfully into the educational process.

One of the merits of the novels of the philosophy for children program is that they offer models of dialogue, both of children with one another and of children with adults. They are models that are non-authoritarian and anti-indoctrinational, that respect the values of inquiry and reasoning, encourage the development of alternative modes of thought and imagination, and sketch out what it might be like to live and participate in a small community where children have their own interests yet respect each other as people and are capable at times of engaging in cooperative inquiry for no other reason than that it is satisfying to do so.

Perhaps one of the most distinctive features of the philosophy for children program is that it suggests how children are able to learn from one another. This

From *Philosophy in the Classroom* by Matthew Lipman (Philadelphia, PA: Temple University Press, 1977), pp. 104–109. Reprinted by permission of Temple University Press.

is a problem that is encountered today at every level of education: there are students in colleges, secondary schools, and elementary schools who try to "make it on their own" without really seeking to learn from one another or to assimilate the life experience of their peers even when, through discussion, it might be readily available to them.

While some children speak up readily enough but fail to listen to one another, others listen intently, follow the line of the discussion, and may then respond to it by making a contribution that goes beyond, rather than merely repeats, what has been said. The teacher should, of course, be aware of the possibility that the child who does not always listen may be developing a very unusual set of ideas, and needs to disregard the conversation for a while in order to do so. (The harm some children do to themselves by not listening is therefore likely to be considerably less than the harm other children do to themselves when, having failed to listen, they are constantly forced to cover the same ground that others have already gone over.) On the other hand, there are children who seldom speak up, but who listen intently and constructively to the class discussion. They are alert and involved, even though they fail to join in the discussion.

A discussion should build by way of its own dynamics. Like children in a playground building a pyramid by standing on one another, a discussion builds upon the contributions of each of its members. In asking questions, the teacher is not merely trying to elicit answers already known. Encouraging philosophical thinking is a matter of getting children to reflect in fresh ways, to consider alternative methods of thinking and acting, to deliberate creatively and imaginatively. The teacher cannot possibly know in advance the answers that children are going to come up with. In fact, it is just this element of surprise that has always been so refreshing about teaching philosophical thinking: one never is quite sure what thought will surface next.

It is, of course, important to keep the discussion going. As the children hear about each other's experiences and begin to learn from each other, they begin to appreciate one another's points of view and to respect one another's values. But when it appears that the discussion of one of the leading ideas of the episodes has ceased to be productive, the teacher must be prepared to direct the discussion tactfully to another topic.

The Role of Ideas in a Philosophical Dialogue

You may well be wondering what is distinctive about a philosophical discussion. In what ways may a philosophical discussion be contrasted with other kinds of discussions? Here we may distinguish philosophical discussion from discussions of two other types: scientific and religious.

Scientific Discussions

A scientific discussion is generally concerned with matters of fact, and with theories about matters of fact. The questions raised in a scientific discussion are in principle answerable questions. They can be answered by discovering relevant evidence, or by consulting acknowledged scientific authorities, or by making appropriate observations, or by citing pertinent laws of nature, or by conducting relevant experiments. Discussions in a science class can be very intense and very lively, especially if there is some disagreement as to how certain evidence is to be interpreted, or as to whether a given theory explains all the relevant factual data.

By and large, the scientist is dealing with how some portion of the world is to be described and explained. Therefore, a science class may involve discussion of such questions as what are the causes of sun spots, what is the temperature of dry ice, how does the heart work, how does the blood circulate, what was the Stone Age, what causes earthquakes, and so on. In general, the issues raised by these questions can be clarified and grasped by adequate discussion and analysis of elementary scientific theories and available scientific evidence. So a scientific discussion is subject to the authority of empirical evidence, as such evidence is interpreted within the accepted framework of scientific understanding. In principle, therefore, the resolution of scientific disputes is always possible.

Discussion about Religious Beliefs

Many children in your class are already in possession of a set of religious beliefs acquired from their parents, from their religious schools, from discussion with their peers, and sometimes from their own observations. These beliefs may relate to the purpose of destiny of the world, the question of personal immortality, the existence of a God, the expectation of divine reward or punishment, and so on. These are not generally the sorts of questions that can be decided by factual evidence one way or another. In no way is it part of the role of a philosophy teacher to criticize a child's religious beliefs, or to seek to undermine them even in an indirect fashion. The teacher simply cannot infringe upon the realm of children's religious beliefs without becoming guilty of indoctrination. On the other hand, there can be no serious objection to affording the child a view of the range of alternatives from which human beings throughout the world select their beliefs. After all, if it is not indoctrination to suggest to children who profess to believe in many gods, or in none at all, that there are conceivable alternatives to their views, why should it not also be possible to suggest to those who believe in a solitary supernatural being that there are many numerical alternatives?

It is always unfortunate when a teacher, out of self-righteousness or ignorance, attempts to modify the religious beliefs of children in the classroom. Such invasion of the child's intellectual integrity represents not only a lack of respect for the child but also a misconception on the teacher's part of the nature of science, the nature of philosophy, and the nature of education. Some individuals think that children's religious beliefs are unsound in light of what we know of science and philosophy, and can be corrected with a healthy dash of scientific or philosophical information. But there are no such facts that can dispel religious beliefs one way or another. To the extent that religious beliefs are matters of faith, it is a question whether they are matters that can be resolved by either science or philosophy.

It is, of course, quite possible for children to have religious discussions, just as they may discuss their families, their friends, their fears, their joys, and other private matters among themselves. An informal religious discussion among children typically involves a comparing and contrasting of their respective feelings and thoughts about religious matters. It does not usually involve the search for *underlying assumptions,* or the analysis of the meaning of concepts, or the search for clear definitions that often characterize philosophical discussions. In other words, religious discussions usually do not explore the assumptions on which religious beliefs rest, while a philosophical discussion cannot rest content unless it does explore its own assumptions.

To repeat, teachers must be very careful that this course in philosophical thinking does not serve as a tool in their hands or in the hands of the students to disparage the religious beliefs of some of the children in the class. The course optimally should serve as a tool by means of which children can clarify and find firmer foundations *for their own beliefs.* The teacher's role is twofold. It is not to change children's beliefs but to help them find better and more sufficient reasons for believing those things *they* choose, upon reflection, to believe in. And further, it is to strengthen their understanding of the issues involved in their holding to the beliefs they do hold.

Philosophical Discussions

We have tried to show that science and religion represent very separate areas of human interest in terms of their relevance to the classroom. In other words, from an educational point of view, scientific discussions and religious discussions are separate things and should not be confused with philosophical discussions.

Philosophical discussions need not just take up where science and religion leave off. Philosophical discussions can frequently become involved in questions of science and questions of religion, as philosophical discussions may lead into any other subject. Philosophy may or may not be a party to the dispute over factual descriptions of the world of religious interpretation of reality. As an objective onlooker, a philosopher is no more party to these disputes than an umpire is one of the contestants in a game that he referees. If anything, the umpire represents the spirit of impartiality that tries to see that the game proceeds in the fairest possible fashion. In a somewhat similar fashion, philosophy is concerned to clarify meanings, uncover assumptions and presuppositions, analyze concepts, consider the validity of reasoning processes, and investigate the implications of ideas and the consequences in human life of holding certain ideas rather than others.

This is not to imply that philosophy is concerned only with the clarification of concepts: it is also a fertile source of new ideas. For wherever there is a threshold of human knowledge, those who think about that particular subject area can only grope and cast about speculatively in an effort to understand what is there. Gradually, as methods of investigation of the new subject area are developed, as methods of observation and measurement and prediction and control are perfected, the period of philosophical speculation is replaced by one of scientific understanding. In this sense, philosophy is the mother of all sciences, for as philosophical speculation becomes more rigorous and substantiated, as measurement and experimentation and verification begin to occur, philosophy turns into science. In this sense, philosophy is a source of ideas that precedes the development of every new scientific enterprise.

Now what does all this mean for the role of the teacher in guiding *philosophical* discussions? First, the teacher has to keep in mind the distinctions just made between scientific, religious, and philosophical discussions and must retain these subtle distinctions as guideposts in encouraging children to think philosophically. The teacher must be aware that what began as a philosophical discussion can easily turn into a dispute over factual information that can be settled only by looking up the empirical evidence that is available. It is the teacher's role, once the discussion has taken this turn, to suggest where the empirical evidence may be found, rather than continue along speculative lines. For example, it is not a philosophical dispute if an argument develops in a classroom over the sum of 252 and 323. It *is,* however, a philosophical question to ask, "What is addition?" or "What is a set?" It is easy enough to look up in a book the exact year when Columbus landed in the Western Hemisphere. However, this in no way settles the question of "who was the first person to discover the Western Hemisphere?" a notion that is rich in ambiguity and in need of clarification. We assume that it takes *time* for light to reach the earth from the sun. But we do not have a science of time itself, and therefore, when children ask, "What is time?" they are asking a philosophical question, and there is no reason why, through dialogue with their peers and teachers, they should not be exposed to some of the alternative views that have been offered by philosophers if these views can be phrased in terms that they can understand.

Philosophical discussions can evolve out of a great many of the demands children make for the *meaning* of an idea. It is up to the teacher to seize upon these opportunities and use them as entries into philosophical exploration. If the child wants to know what the word "authority" means, or what the word "culture" means, or what the word "world" means, or what the word "respect" means, or what the word "rights" means, the teacher can take any of these as a starting point for getting as many views out on the table as there are children in the classroom, exposing the children to additional views that have been thought up by philosophers, examining the consequences of holding one view over another, and clarifying the meaning and the underlying assumptions of each view.

Questions

1. List some reasons why attempts to introduce thinking into education may have failed.
2. What are the unique characteristics of philosophy for children?
3. Why did Plato say that philosophy was only for the mature?
4. For Lipman, what does it mean to be fully educated?
5. Distinguish a "community of inquiry" model from other models of teaching.
6. Do you see any problems with a community of inquiry model? What do you think its strengths might be?

7. When Lipman says that a "discussion should build by ways of its own dynamics," what does he mean?

8. If you were guiding a discussion and one child began to monopolize it, what would you do?

9. If some children never took part in the discussion, what would you do?

10. Distinguish among scientific, religious, and philosophical discussions.

chapter **15**

Gareth Matthews

TIME LINE FOR MATTHEWS

1929	Is born July 8.
1951	Receives A.B. from Franklin College (Indiana).
1952	Receives A.M. from Harvard.
1961	Receives Ph.D. from Harvard.
1980	Runs first National Endowment for the Humanities Summer Seminar on Philosophy and Childhood; similar workshops would be held 1985, 1988, and 1998.
1980	Publishes *Philosophy and the Young Child*.
1984	Publishes *Dialogues with Children*.
1994	Publishes *The Philosophy of Childhood*.

Introduction

Gareth Matthews is an important American philosopher whose work in education is best known outside of the United States. Although Matthews is one of the four leading historical figures in Philosophy for Children, his role has been spectral. Where Matthew Lipman, Ann Sharp, and Frederick Oscanyan pieced together a K through 12 educational curriculum in which children were introduced to philosophy and formal and informal logic, Matthews has never been involved in the day-to-day making and implementation of that curriculum. Instead, he has been content to write a regular column on children's literature for the journal *Thinking*, publish three very well-received books about children and philosophy, and give occasional lectures about the same subjects at national and international conferences. In effect, Matthews has cultivated a freedom and independence from the American educational establishment that has enabled him to see things fresh. Where Lipman, Sharp, and the late Frederick Oscanyan were bound to show how Philosophy for Children could exist in and support the network of standardized tests, the assumptions about child development, and the varied political, social, economic and religious demands that make up American schooling, Matthews has resisted such occupations.

Perhaps that is why Matthews has been exempt from the charges of Americanism, if not American imperialism, that have been leveled at Philosophy for Children when it has been exported to other countries. His explicit agenda has never involved creating conditions in which a certain kind of person—educated, trained, American—could be formed. Rather, he has always been more concerned with understanding what children are like and, in particular, to what extent they can be called "philosophical."

In service to that understanding he has done three things: First, he has looked at some of the books that children read and has discovered that they are philosophically rich, complex, and interesting. They (*Frog and Toad, Lulu and the Flying Babies,* for example) present activities that are interesting and perplexing for mature philosophers and, judging by their sales and popularity, are interesting and perplexing for children.

Second, he has recorded and analyzed scores of children's conversations. Then, in the course of his three books and numerous lectures, he has shown how subtle and intelligent children can be when confronted with philosophical problems. What Matthews has shown is that some children at some times are capable of the same level of philosophical sophistication that adults show at times.

Finally, he has engaged children in dialogue and in his very gentle and caring way has done precisely what Socrates attempted to do in the *Meno* with that famous slave boy—show that children know and are capable of far more than we might ordinarily think. But where Socrates was intent on presenting a theory of remembrance about mathematical things, Matthews is simply curious about what children can do philosophically. The children with whom Matthews speaks exhibit the sort of intellectual aliveness, curiosity, and wonder that characterize the best of philosophers and philosophy. In addition, these children, in consort with Matthews, make philosophical moves parallel to and at times surpassing those shown in many of Plato's dialogues.

It is easy when reading Gareth Matthews' work—the passages from literature, the example of conversations, and Matthews own dialogues with children—to suggest that children are, somehow, natural philosophers and that all that is needed is the creation of an environment where children are left alone to discover and display their philosophical abilities. It is easy to romanticize Matthews' findings and use them to support a Rousseau-like state of nature where the teacher's main responsibility is to keep the innocent child away from the influence of a corrupt social educational system. It is easy to do that, but it misses all of the cautionary advice implicit in Matthews work.

Matthews does show the philosophical richness of some children's literature. It is reasonable to assume, however, that there is a good deal of children's literature—literature with which he does not concern himself—that although children may and do take delight in, is philosophically uninteresting. Simply, some children may be drawn to philosophically interesting material because it is philosophically interesting, but it does not follow that all children find a similar delight. Neither does it follow, that because some children's conversations are philosophically sophisticated, that all are *or* that because Gareth Matthews can lead some children in a meaningful philosophical dialogue that (a) he could lead any group of children in a similar dialogue or (b) that any other adult could do with a group of children what Gareth Matthews can do.

Gareth Matthews then, does not force us to conclude anything. What he does do, however, is to create a context in which we are encouraged to question our assumptions about the nature of childhood. Here are a couple of the questions that Matthews urges upon us:

1. **What are children capable of and at what age does that capability arise?** Up until very recently, most American educators assumed a model of child development based upon the works of Jean Piaget. That work, as presented in the United States, assumed an invariant sequential model of intellectual development which suggested that the younger the child, the less capable is the child of formulating or understanding abstract thought. If Matthews' examples are taken seriously then it would appear that either philosophy is a very concrete subject or (very young) children are capable of abstract thought.

2. **How do children learn most effectively?** At least from the time of John Locke, it has been assumed that children learn by moving from the simple to the complex. If there is an article of faith that might appear in any teacher's lounge, it is that the task of the teacher is to present complex matters in such a way that they are understandable to the simple minds of children. Now if philosophy is a complex activity and if children are adept at it, it might suggest that in some educational context, at least, it might move from the complex to the simple. Interestingly this seems to be the way children learn outside the boundaries of the classroom. Consider the quotidian cases of children learning and manipulating complex linguistic concepts of "Mother" and "Father" prior to coming to know or understand the simple rules of grammar.

Before moving on, it might prove helpful to return to a comment made at the beginning of this introduction. Gareth Matthews' work has far more currency in Europe than it does in the United States. American philosophers are aware of him and some American philosophers of education recognize the importance of his work, but he has not had the sort of impact on American education that he had on, say, German education.

It is dangerous to generalize about national systems of education, but beside the fact that German and other European countries have long histories of taking philosophy seriously as a subject that children might study in high school, the

Germans, at least since the second World War, have avoided much of the mania for standardized testing that has swept the United States, and have encouraged teachers to determine their own curriculum materials and methods.

That which Matthews does best is to speak to the adult who is involved with conversations with children saying, in effect, "Look at how philosophically rich and complex this exchange really is" and "See how this exchange might be developed and nurtured if only we would pay sufficient attention to it." If the adult-teacher has the time and encouragement to do so, as the German teacher might and as the American teacher might not, she or he might find that many of the characteristics of the educated person—the sense of curiosity and the sense of wonder, and the sense of being intellectually alive—are already in place when the child enters school. In a time of shrill voices, Matthews is one of the quietest, but it may be one of the most thought-provoking.

From *The Philosophy of Childhood* (1994)

A Philosopher's View of Childhood

"Do you think there could be any such thing as the beginning of time?" I asked the dozen third and fourth graders in my philosophy discussion group in Newton, Massachusetts. (We had been trying to write a story about time travel.)

"No," several of the kids replied.

Then Nick spoke up. "The universe is everything and everywhere," he announced, and then paused. "But then if there was a big bang or something, what was the big bang *in*?"

Nick's question had long puzzled me, too. In my own case, hearing lectures on the "big bang" theory of the origin of the universe given by learned astrophysicists and cosmogonists had never quelled the conceptual worry that Nick articulated so simply and directly.

At the time of this discussion Nick had just turned nine years old. The others in the group were anywhere from nine to ten and a half.

Not only did Nick have a genuine puzzle about how the universe could have begun, he also had a metaphysical principle that required beginnings for everything, the universe included. Everything there is, he said, has a beginning. As he realized, that principle reintroduces the problem about the universe. "How did the universe start?" he kept asking.

"The universe," said Sam, "is what everything appeared *on*. It's not really anything. It's what other things started *on*."

"So there always has to be a universe?" I asked.

"Yeah," agreed Sam, "there always has to be a universe."

"So if there was always a universe," I went on, "there was no first time, either."

"There was a first time for certain things," explained Sam, "but not for the universe. There was a first time for the earth, there was a first time for the stars, there was a first time for the sun. But there was no first time for the universe."

"Can you convince Nick that the universe has to always be there?" I asked Sam.

Sam replied with a rhetorical question. "What would the universe have appeared *on?*" he asked simply.

"That's what I don't understand," admitted Nick.

Sam's conception of the universe (what everything else appears "on") is reminiscent of Plato's idea of the "receptacle" in his dialogue *Timaeus*: ". . . the mother and receptacle of all created and visible and in any way sensible things is not to be termed earth or air or fire or water, or any of their compounds, or any of the elements from which these are derived, but is an invisible and formless being which receives all things . . ." (*Timaeus* 51A). On this view the universe itself never came to be; it is what other things come to be in, or "on." If, as Ross, another child in the same group, put the point later in our discussion, things "started out on vast blackness, then that's just the universe then; the universe is vast blackness."

I have said that Sam's conception is reminiscent of Plato's. But there is a respect in which Sam's idea may be superior to Plato's. The idea of a receptacle is the idea of a container. A container walls some things in and other things out. To wall things in and out it must have walls. Sam's idea of what other things appear "on" projects three-dimensional reality onto two dimensions, but it allows us to think of the "ground of being" as having indefinite borders. Whether the universe is finite or infinite can be left indeterminate. By contrast, Plato's receptacle must be finite. Moreover, we must wonder what the nature of the receptacle's walls could be, though there is no answer to this question in Plato.

In our discussion Nick never gave up his principle that everything there is has a beginning. But he remained puzzled about how this principle could be applied to the universe itself. Every time he was asked what the universe could have first appeared on, he replied with engaging candor, "That's the part I don't get." Of course it was he who first raised this problem with his principle that everything there is has a beginning.

Many people are familiar with Saul Steinberg's *New Yorker* cover depicting the New Yorker's view of the country. Manhattan Island dominates the scene; the other boroughs of New York City are prominent, though smaller than Manhattan. San Francisco is to be seen in the distance at the other coast. And there is not much in between.

A philosopher's view of childhood is likely to be just as distorted. On the philosopher's view, children sit around conducting virtuoso discussions of mind-bending questions like "Did the universe itself have a beginning, and if so, what did it begin on?" Although I have tried to document in my writings the claim that *some* children *sometimes* do this, even I would have to admit that this sort of activity is not the most obvious feature of childhood.

Still, it is worth pointing out that discussions such as the one I have just recorded can, and sometimes do, occur. There are at least two reasons why it is important to point this out. First, philosophical thinking in children has been left out of the account of childhood that developmental psychologists have given us. Even if philosophical thinking is far from the most prominent feature of childhood, its presence should be duly noted. For one thing, leaving it out encourages undeserved condescension toward children. If the most daunting intellectual challenges that Sam and Nick face are to learn the twelve-times table and the passive form of the verb "to be," condescension toward these children as thinkers has some warrant in fact. But if Sam and Nick can raise for us in vivid and compelling form the puzzles of how the universe could have begun, then there are at least some contexts in which they should be considered our partners in a joint effort to understand it all.

There is a second reason why it is important to take due account of philosophical thinking in young children. Doing so helps us understand philosophy.

Much of philosophy involves giving up adult pretensions to know. The philosopher asks, "What is time, anyway?" when other adults assume, no doubt unthinkingly, that they are well beyond the point of needing to ask that question. They may want to know whether they have enough time to do the week's shopping, or to pick up a newspaper. They may want to know what time it is, but it doesn't occur to them to ask, "What is time?" St. Augustine put the point well: "What, then, is time? Provided that no one asks me, I know. But if I want to explain it to a questioner, I am baffled" (*Confessions* 11.14). Among the annoying questions that children ask are some that are genuinely baffling. In important part, philosophy is an adult attempt to deal with the genuinely baffling questions of childhood.

I can't remember asking myself, as a child, what time is. But I did puzzle over the beginning of the world. My puzzlement as a child of five or six took the form of the following question: "Supposing that God created the world at some particular time, how is it that the world looks as though it had been going on forever?"

I know now that my problem in cosmogony was a bit like that of St. Thomas Aquinas. Like me, Aquinas accepted the Christian doctrine that God created the world, indeed, created it, Aquinas supposed, out of nothing. (I don't know now whether the *ex nihilo* part belonged to my theology as a six-year-old.) But Aquinas was also very respectful of Aristotle's arguments for the eternity of the world. He had, then, somehow, to reconcile the appearance of beginninglessness, as captured in Aristotle's rather impressive reasoning, with the revealed doctrine of creation, which, he thought, was an absolute beginning.

For myself—that childhood self—I came up with an analogy. Having posed my question to my mother and received no helpful response, I returned later to reassure her. "Don't worry, Mom," I said, "I think it's like a perfect circle someone has drawn. If you had been there when it was drawn, you would know where the circle begins. But as you look at it now, there's no way of telling. It's like a perfect circle, where the end connects up with the beginning without showing."

When now, sixty years later, I teach Aristotle or Aquinas to university students, I try to locate the questioning child in me and my students. Unless I do so, the philosophy we do together will lose much of its urgency and much of its point.

Let's return to the point about respecting children as partners in inquiry. Parents and teachers are often so impressed with the burdens they bear in having to nurture, instruct, reassure, and inspire their children that they fail to appreciate what children have to offer adults. One of the exciting things that children have to offer us is a new philosophical perspective.

Consider the case of Kristin, who was four years old. She was teaching herself to use watercolors. As she painted, she began to think about the colors themselves. Sitting on her bed, talking to her father, she announced, "Dad, the world is all made of colors."

Kristin's father, who, as I happen to know, wants to make sense of it all as much as his four-year-old daughter did, liked Kristin's hypothesis, and reacted positively. But, recognizing a difficulty, he asked her, "What about glass?"

Kristin thought for a moment. Then she announced firmly, "Colors *and* glass."

Like any good philosopher, Kristin knew what to do when one's grand hypothesis runs into a counterexample. One simply incorporates the counterexample into the hypothesis!

Kristin's color hypothesis is not only fresh and exciting—at least as uniquely wonderful a gift to her father, I should say, as any one of the watercolor pictures she might have presented to him—it also recalls the thinking of the earliest philosophers we have any record of, the ancient Milesians. Like Kristin, the Milesians wanted to know what everything is made of. Thales said "Water" (presumably he thought that the earth was something like frozen or compacted water, and that air was very rarefied steam); Anaximander said "The infinite" or "The indefinite"; whereas Anaximines said "Air." (I like Kristin's hypothesis better than any of these.)

A later anecdote from Kristin recalls another pre-Socratic philosopher, Parmenides. Kristin was five, and learning how to read. She was learning to recognize syllables and to sound them out so as to be able to recognize words. She was quite proud of her success.

Again, sitting on her bed talking to her father, she commented, "I'm sure glad we have letters."

Kristin's father was somewhat surprised at that particular expression of gratitude. "Why?" he asked.

"'Cause if there was no letters, there would be no sounds," explained Kristin. "If there was no sounds, there would be no words . . . If there was no words, we couldn't think . . . and if we couldn't think, there would be no world."

Kristin's chain reasoning is breathtaking. It is also reminiscent of Parmenides' enigmatic fragment *to gar auto noein estin te kai einai* ("For the same thing is there both to be thought of and to be"). That might be understood to entail 'Only what can be thought, can be.' If, then, we grant Kristin her interesting assumptions that (1) without words nothing could be thought and (2) without letters there would be no words, we get the fascinating conclusion 'Without letters there could be no world.'

Both these anecdotes from Kristin show how the thought of a child may be a priceless gift to a parent or teacher with ears to hear. And both of them also give us reason to think of philosophy as, in part, an adult response to the questions of childhood.

The twentieth century has seen an amazing growth in the study of childhood. Two ideas have been central to the way childhood has been studied in our time. One is the idea that children develop and that their development is a *maturational* process. In part, maturation is, quite obviously, a biological process. Children grow bigger, their legs and arms grow longer, baby faces grow into older-looking faces, baby teeth fall out and are replaced by adult teeth, and so on. But maturation is also a psychological and social process. Baby talk, baby thoughts, and baby behavior are replaced by the talk, thoughts, and behavior of young children, then by that of older children, adolescents, and, finally, adults.

The second idea central to the recent study of childhood is that growth takes place in identifiable *stages*. As school teachers can testify, the stages of biological growth children experience can be correlated only roughly with their actual ages. Thus one child in a given class will tower over the rest, while another has yet to catch up with the class average. But the stages of biological, as well as intellectual and social, growth are at least broadly related to age. Putting the idea of maturation and the idea of a sequence of age-related stages together, we get the conception of child development as a maturational process with identifiable stages that fall into an at least roughly age-related sequence.

Clearly maturation has a goal; its goal is maturity. Early stages are superseded by later stages that are automatically assumed to have been less satisfactory. Thus the "stage/maturational model" of child development, as we can call it, which has found unquestioned acceptance in the study of childhood, has an evaluational bias built into it. Whatever the biological or psychological structures in a standard twelve-year-old turn out to be, the stage/maturational model of development guarantees, before any research is done at all, that these structures will be more nearly satisfactory than the superseded structures of, say, a six-year-old.

In many areas of human development this evaluational bias seems quite appropriate. We don't want grown-ups, or even adolescents, to have to chew their adult-sized steaks with baby teeth. But when it comes to philosophy, the assumption is quite out of place. There are several reasons for this.

First, there is no reason whatsoever to suppose that, simply by virtue of growing up in some standard way, adolescents or adults naturally achieve an appropriate level of maturity in handling philosophical questions—in, for example, being able to discuss whether time might have had a beginning, or whether some super-computer might be said to have a mind.

Second, it should be obvious to anyone who listens to the philosophical comments and questions of young children that these comments and questions have a freshness and inventiveness that is hard for even the most imaginative adult to match. Freshness and inventiveness are not the only criteria for doing philosophy well: discipline and rigor should also count heavily. And children can be expected to be less disciplined and less rigorous than their adult counterparts. Still, in philosophy, as in poetry, freshness and inventiveness are much to be prized.

I recently asked a college class to respond, in writing, to Tim's question from the beginning of *Philosophy and the Young Child*: "Papa, how can we be sure that everything is not a dream?" A mother in my class recalled that her daughter, then three and a half, had once asked, "Mama, are we 'live' or are we on video?" This child's question obviously bears an important resemblance to the traditional dream question. But it is also a delightedly fresh and new question, one that could not have been conceived before TV, indeed before the development of video cameras and VCRs.

Some features of the dream problem carry over into the video problem. Thus just as I might have had the thought, in my dream, that I am awake, so the word "live" might appear on the screen when I am watching a video. But some features are new. Unlike the dream problem, the video problem suggests that our lives are already on tape, just waiting to be shown.

So children are often fresh and inventive thinkers. All too often, maturity brings with it staleness and uninventiveness. This is a second reason for rejecting the evaluational assumption built into the stage/maturational model of child development.

Third, Descartes taught us to do philosophy by "starting over." Instead of assuming the correctness of what my teachers have taught me, or what the society around me seems to accept, I am to make a fresh beginning to see if I can show by some means of my very own that I really do know whatever it is I claim to know. As college students soon learn in their first philosophy course, it isn't easy to rid oneself of adult assumptions, even temporarily, and even for a fairly circumscribed purpose. It isn't easy, that is, for adults. Children have far less of a problem. In a certain way, then, adult philosophers who follow Descartes in trying to "start over" are trying to make themselves as little children again, even if only temporarily. That is hard for adults. It is unnecessary for children.

It isn't that "starting over" is all there is to doing philosophy. That isn't true at all. But learning to be comfortable with "naive" questions is an important part of doing philosophy well. Thus for this reason, as well as for the other two, when it comes to doing philosophy, the evaluational assumption of the stage/maturational model gets things all wrong.

Like the *New Yorker's* view of the United Slates, my view of children as little philosophers is a distortion. But so also is the conventional view of childhood as a development through a sequence of roughly age-related stages that aims at maturity. Sometimes, it seems, the best way to correct one distortion is to pair it with an appealing, but opposed, distortion. I hope that that is true in this case.

From *Philosophy and the Young Child* (1980)

Puzzlement

> Tim (about six years), while busily engaged in licking a pot, asked, "Papa, how can we be sure that everything is not a dream?"

No doubt it seems to Tim that he is busily engaged in licking a pot. If he were dreaming, he would, presumably, be dreaming that he is busily engaged in licking a pot. What is the difference between really licking a pot and only dreaming that one is doing so? Perhaps the difference is only this: if one is dreaming, one may wake up from the dream and then know that the pot-licking episode was only a dream.

Does it, or should it, make any difference to Tim to know whether he is awake or dreaming? If so, what difference? Wouldn't the pot taste just as good?[1]

I have been talking as though Tim's question were "How do I know whether I am now dreaming?" But, of course, it isn't that. Rather, it is this: "How can we be sure that not *everything* is a dream?" That is, how can we be sure that we are ever awake?

Suppose that everything is a dream, my dream. There would be parts of my dream in which I seem to be awake and parts of it in which I seem to be asleep. What could be the difference between life as I now believe it to be, with its waking periods and its dream episodes, and a lifelong dream in which I seem sometimes to be awake and sometimes to have dreamt this or that?

Tim's puzzlement and wonder are closely related. Aristotle says that philosophy begins in wonder (*Metaphysics* 982b12). Bertrand Russell tells us that philosophy, "if it cannot *answer* so many questions as we could wish, has at least the power of *asking* questions which increase the interest of the world, and show the strangeness and wonder lying just below the surface even in the commonest things of daily life."[2]

Aristotle also suggests that the wonder that initiates philosophy is akin to puzzlement (Metaphysics 982b17–18). And Wittgenstein says, "A philosophical problem has the form: 'I don't know my way about.'"[3]

Sometimes philosophical puzzlement is dissolved. One learns to find one's way about; perhaps one reasons one's way out of the difficulty. But sometimes the puzzlement is not dissolved, at least not for a long time.

> Jordan (five years), going to bed at eight one evening, asked, "If I go to bed at eight and get up at seven in the morning, how do I really know

---

[1] Augustine seems to have thought so; see his *Contra academicos* (Against the academicians] 3.11.26.
[2] Bertrand Russell, *The Problems of Philosophy* (New York: Oxford University Press, 1959), p. 16.
[3] Ludwig Wittgenstein, *Philosophical Investigations* (Oxford: Basil Blackwell, 1967), no. 123, p. 49.

that the little hand of the clock has gone around only once? Do I have to stay up all night to watch it? If I look away even for a short time, maybe the small hand will go around twice."

In part, perhaps, Jordan's puzzlement rests on an unease about not having enough evidence, or maybe not enough evidence of the right sort, to draw a common sense conclusion, namely, the conclusion that between a given night and the next morning the little hand of the clock goes around once and only once.

Usually, one's observations of a clock are sporadic. Jordan, for example, may check on his clock from time to time during the day, but not, obviously, when he is out of the room: not when he eats his meals, watches television, goes out to play or off to school. In principle Jordan could surely devote a whole day to watching his clock. He could ask that his meals be brought to his bedroom, or he could take his clock with him to the dinner table. By these means Jordan could keep the clock under constant surveillance.

Jordan's final comment—"If I look away even for a short time, maybe the small hand will go around twice"—suggests that his problem may not be the practical one of, as a philosopher of science might say, enlarging his evidence base. Rather, it suggests that no matter how much constant attention Jordan lavishes on his clock, there may still be a worry about how he can justifiably extrapolate from observed periods to unobserved ones.

Are observed states and actions a reliable guide to unobserved states and actions? Jordan may have a friend at kindergarten who manages to make faces at the teacher whenever her back is turned, and not otherwise. How do we know that clocks are not like that? *Do* we know that they aren't? Maybe induction rests on an assumption as naïve as the belief that what Jordan and his friend do under the watchful eye of the teacher is a reliable guide to what they do when the teacher leaves the room or looks away.

I don't know whether Jordan found a way to deal with his puzzlement. Perhaps he did, or perhaps he eventually lost interest in it. If, someday, he takes a college philosophy course, he may find that it includes discussion of what is called "the problem of induction." Stripped to its essentials, this is a problem of saying whether, and if so, on what basis, we can be justified in taking observed instances as a guide to unobserved instances. Jordan may find in the problem of induction an old friend. Of course, by the time Jordan gets to college, he may have forgotten that he had ever worried about the unobserved behavior of his clock.

> One day John Edgar (four years), who had often seen airplanes take off, rise, and gradually disappear into the distance, took his first plane ride. When the plane stopped ascending and the seat-belt sign went out, John Edgar turned to his father and said in a rather relieved, but still puzzled, tone of voice, "Things don't really get smaller up here."

Philosophers and psychologists have long debated whether an airplane disappearing into the distance seems to be getting smaller and we learn to interpret the appearance of a shrinking object as a case of an object receding into space, or whether, after we have had sufficient experience with objects moving away from us and coming toward us, the airplane simply seems to be receding into the distance and no inference or interpretation is required.

The first idea fits a philosophical reconstruction of our knowledge according to whether we receive data through our senses that are in themselves incorrigible (that is, we know infallibly how things seem to us) and we make inferences from these data to the reality that lies behind them (in this case, to the conclusion that the airplane is really going farther and farther away from us). According to this view, the mistakes we make about the world we perceive around us arise from the inferences we draw from incorrigible and indubitable data.

Opponents of this sense-datum view insist that it is impossible to isolate the pure datum of sense experience and distinguish it from all interpretations we put on it and from all inferences we draw from it. According to them, once we have had experience with receding objects, the objects do not appear to shrink when they recede; they simply appear to recede.

The disagreement between the two sides is important in epistemology, the theory of knowledge. The sense-datum view is obviously friendly to the idea that we could reconstruct all our knowledge of the world around us in such a way as to show that it rests on secure foundations, sense data. The other view considers foundationalism in epistemology naive and misconceived.

John Edgar's comment suggests that a much more nearly pure "given" is available to him than the critics of the sense-datum theory suppose is available. Moreover, his comment indicates that he may have put a wrong interpretation on his data and is in the process of working out another interpretation.

Do airplanes really shrink as they go up into the sky? If they did, how would they look, up in the sky, to the passengers they are carrying? Surely the passengers too would shrink. Looking at themselves and at the inside of the plane, they might be in no better position to detect the shrinkage than Alice was in Wonderland.

> Soon her eye fell on a little glass box that was lying under the table: she opened it, and found in it a very small cake, on which the words "**EAT ME**" were beautifully marked in currants. "Well, I'll eat it," said Alice, "and if it makes me grow larger, I can reach the key; and if it makes me grow smaller, I can creep under the door; so either way I'll get into the garden, and I don't care which happens!
>
> She ate a little bit, and said anxiously to herself "Which way? Which way?" holding her hand on the top of her head to feel which way it was growing, and she was quite surprised to find that she remained the same size.[4]

If John Edgar's conclusion is based simply on how things look in the cabin around him, his inference is just as shaky as Alice's. No doubt, however, he will soon have a look out the window. Perhaps he will see the airport from which the plane took off. He will see that the people and the planes still on the

---

[4] Lewis Carroll, *Alice's Adventures in Wonderland & Through the Looking-Glass* (New York: New American Library, 1960), p. 23.

ground have "shrunk" in much the way that airplanes "shrink" into the distance when he himself is on the ground. Reflection on these data may lead him to distinguish appearance from reality and to infer that receding objects seem to get smaller even though they actually maintain their size.

When I taught "Philosophy and the Young Child" at Smith College several years ago, one of my students decided to try out some of the questions we were discussing on her five-year-old brother, David. During spring vacation she interviewed him and recorded the exchange. In the transcript is an instructive moment of puzzlement over the concept of life:

> David worries about whether an apple is alive. He decides that it is when it's on the ground but not when it has been brought into the house.

Is the apple on the table alive? David is puzzled. If it is alive, then when we eat it, we eat something that is alive. If it isn't, how does it differ from an apple still hanging from a tree?

A common approach to the question of life is to list several "life" functions (digestion, elimination, reproduction, locomotion) and then say that an organism is alive if it is capable of performing several of those functions. David seems not to have had that kind of approach in mind. What did he have in mind?

Consider flowers. When we cut roses, bring them inside, and put them in water in a vase, we say that we are keeping them alive (at least until the petals begin to fall and the leaves to turn brown).

We don't put apples in water. We might put them in a cool place, but we don't say that we are doing this to keep them alive—only, perhaps, to keep them fresh. Do they, then, cease to be alive when we bring them indoors?

Are apples alive when they lie on the ground? Perhaps David thinks of an apple's being alive in terms of its life cycle. He may know that the apple contains seeds and nourishment for the seeds and that, if an apple is left on the ground, a seed may eventually germinate and produce a little apple tree. This little tree may grow into a big one and, in turn, produce apples of its own. In this way the cycle goes on.

Perhaps one could say that death occurs when the cycle is interrupted, for example, when the sapling withers so that it will not grow into a tree or when the apple is brought indoors so that its seeds will not germinate. This suggestion is an interesting one, an ingenious response to a very old and very persistent puzzle.

I am tucking my eight-year-old son, John, in bed. He looks up at me and asks, quite without warning, "Daddy, why don't I see you double, because I have two eyes and I can see you with each one by itself?"

What do I say?

First, I try to make sure that I understand what is puzzling him.

"You have two ears," I point out. "Are you surprised you don't hear double?"

John grins. "What is hearing double?"

"Well, maybe my-my voi-voice wo-would s-sound li-like thi-this," I say.

He reflects. "But your ears both go to the same place."

"And couldn't it be that your eyes both go to the same place?" I suggest.

He gets serious, thinks, then grins again. "You're just giving me another problem," he protests. "I want to think about the one I already have."

Fair enough. "Maybe," I suggest, "it's because the picture you get with your left eye comes together with the picture you get with your right eye. When they come together they make *one* picture."

We experiment with two fingers, one closer to our eyes, the other farther away. We try focusing now on one, now on the other. The aim is to see how, by focusing on the nearer finger, we can see the farther one double and vice versa. The moral is supposed to be that the two pictures don't *always* come together to make one, though they usually do.

My son is not satisfied. It turns out that he has constructed for himself, elaborating in various ways on what he has learned at school about vision and the retinal image, a complex theory of vision according to which one image comes through each eye, is reversed, rereversed, and then projected in front of the subject. No wonder he is worried about why we don't see double!

I suggest several ways of simplifying his theory, but he won't accept simplifications.

"I'll have to think about it some more," he says. "I'll talk to you again after I get it worked out."

John's question—"Why don't I see you double, because I have two eyes?"—mixes optics, neurophysiology, psychology, and philosophy. John, I discovered, had seen on television at school an episode in which a little man climbed into someone's eye to gaze at the retinal image. Ever since the retinal image was actually observed in the early seventeenth century, people have wondered why they don't see things upside down; after all, the retinal images reverse the objects seen. The seldom-spoken assumption is that what is really seen is the retinal image.

John insisted that the television program he had seen in school had not given him his problem, that he had already had the problem before he saw the program. He certainly seemed willing and able to think of the retinal image as being reversed by a later process in vision. His problem, he said, was to figure out how the images from the two eyes could merge.

Medieval theorists of vision, such as Alhazen and Roger Bacon, supposed that images travel from each eye through the optic nerve to the optic chiasma, where the two nerves cross and where, as Alhazen and Bacon supposed, the two images become one. It was a worry about why we don't see double even though we receive two images, one through each eye, that led to their theory. It is an answer to John's problem.[5]

In his brilliant *Paralipomena ad vitellionem* Johannes Kepler scathingly rejected this medieval account of vision. He said that it was optically impossible. Light doesn't behave in the way the medieval theory requires, he explained.

---

[5] See Gareth Matthews, "A Medieval Theory of Vision," in *Studies In Perception,* ed. P. K. Machamer and R. G. Turnbull (Columbus: Ohio State University Press, 1978), pp. 186–199.

Kepler took enormous strides in accounting for the optics of vision, but he did so at a price. He renounced all ambition to give an account of whatever it is that happens after the image is formed on the retina that results in someone's actually seeing something.

John wanted to explain how we see by supposing that we somehow project visual images in front. If we think of images as being projected in this way, somewhat like the image on a movie screen, nothing is explained, for we will want to know how the projected images can be seen. Doesn't that require vision, which is just what we first set out to explain? If, however, we think of the frontward projecting as the seeing, then there may be hope for a nonregressive explanation. But the explanation will not be helpful unless we are quite clear about the notion of projection that it uses.

Is John's puzzle a pseudoproblem? Suppose that it is. Then John may one day be sufficiently clear about the optics, neurophysiology, and psychology of vision that he will no longer be puzzled about why we usually don't see double. If that day arrives, he may want to know why he once mistakenly thought that there was a real problem. I hope he will. Trying to say why something one has puzzled over is a mere pseudoproblem is itself often a difficult philosophical task. But it can be rewarding, too.

Review of Arnold Lobel's
Frog and Toad Together (1985)

Frog and Toad Together, I often tell my students, half-jokingly, is a philosophical classic. They smile indulgently, as is appropriate for a half-joke. Then I elaborate.

Each of the five stories in the collection, I explain, introduces a philosophical problem, or set of problems. Thus "A List," the first story, illustrates an interesting worry about completeness. Toad decides to write down a list of *all* the things he will do that day. When the wind blows his list away he complains that he cannot run after it because running after it was not on his list of things to do that day. Would reading the list, or even following the list, be inappropriate because "Read this list" and "Follow this list" were not on the list either?"

Another story in the collection, "Cookies," takes up weakness of will. (See the very first of these columns, *Thinking,* Vol. 1, No. 1.) It invites us to puzzle over the question, "How could one ever try hard not to do what one really wants to do? If one tries hard enough to succeed at, say, *not* having another cookie, won't it be because one actually wants to stop having cookies?"

The story, "Dragons and Giants," explores the idea of bravery. Can I see in a mirror whether I am brave? Is there anything to look for? Must I do something dangerous to tell whether I am brave, something like slaying a dragon or facing down a giant? And suppose I am scared the whole time? Or don't realize how dangerous it really is? Or think it is dangerous when it isn't, really?

Review of Arnold Lobel's *Frog and Toad Together* by Gareth Matthews in *Thinking,* Vol 6, No 2, p. 1. Used by permission of Matthew Lipman.

The last story in the book, "The Dream," suggests familiar problems about deception and the dream world. "Frog," Toad asks after a dream episode, "is that really you?" Frog assures him that it is. If the reassurance is real, it is entirely appropriate that Toad should be reassured. But it might also be appropriate that Toad should be reassured. But it might also be appropriate *in a dream* that Toad be reassured.

The story I have left out, the second one, called "The Garden," is about inductive reasoning. Toad plants some seeds and, becoming impatient about their growth, shouts at them to grow. Alarmed at the noise Toad is making, Frog tells him that he is frightening the seeds. Toad is not amused. He burns candles to keep his seeds from being frightened. He sings songs, reads poetry and plays music to them. When these efforts produce no visible result, Toad laments, "These must be the most frightened seeds in the whole world." Exhausted, he falls asleep. Frog wakes him with the joyful news that the seeds have sprouted. Toad mops his brow and sighs, "You were right, Frog, it *was* very hard work."

The textbook name for Toad's error in inductive reasoning is given in the Latin phrase, *"post hoc, ergo propter hoc."* (After this, therefore because of this.) Even very small children laugh at Toad's comment and thus show some awareness that *post hoc, ergo propter hoc* is a fallacy. But it is difficult even for a sophisticated adult to be clear about what makes the reasoning fallacious. David Hume sometimes says that causation is conjunction plus a certain human expectation. ("We may . . . form another definition of cause, and call it, *an object followed by another, and whose appearance always conveys the thought to that other."—Enquiry 7.2.*) So why won't singing to seeds in the fervent expectation of bean sprouts be their cause so long as bean sprouts result?

Hume also speaks of "constant conjunction" (singing always followed by bean sprouts sprouting) and even suggests a stronger condition, a counterfactual requirement: singing won't be the cause of the sprouting of bean sprouts unless, *if* one were now to do such "hard work," seed growth *would* result.

Understanding causality is a difficult job, at least as hard work as making seeds grow. Though it is hard work, it can also be, as Arnold Lobel's story should remind us, lots of fun.

Questions

1. Discuss some of the philosophical problems in *Frog and Toad*.
2. Why are they philosophical?
3. In *The Philosophy of Childhood*, Matthews suggests that Sam's view may be superior to Plato's. Why?
4. What are the adult pretenses philosophers must give up?
5. What is a perfect circle? Why is it perfect?
6. Evaluate Matthews' evaluation of the stage/maturational model.
7. What is the problem of induction?
8. What is philosophical puzzlement?

chapter 16

Nel Noddings

TIME LINE FOR NODDINGS

1929	Is born in Irvington, New Jersey, on January 19.
1949	Receives B.A. in Mathematics and Physical Science from Montclair State College.
1949–1972	Teacher of mathematics and other subjects in schools of New Jersey; Department Chair, Curriculum Supervisor, and Assistant Principal.
1964	Receives M.A. in Mathematics from Rutgers University.
1972	Assistant Professor of Education at Pennsylvania State University.
1973	Receives Ph.D. in Educational Philosophy and Theory from Stanford University.
1975–1976	Director of Pre-Collegiate Education, The University of Chicago.
1977–1983	Assistant Professor of Education, Stanford University.
1983–1986	Associate Professor and Director of Teacher Education, Stanford University.
1984	Publishes *Caring: A Feminine Approach to Ethics and Moral Education* and, with Paul Shore, *Awakening the Inner Eye: Intuition in Education.*
1986–1992	Professor and Associate Dean of Academic Affairs, Stanford University.
1989	Publishes *Women and Evil.*

1990	Publishes *Constructivist Views on the Teaching and Learning of Mathematics.*
1991	Publishes *Stories Lives Tell: Narrative and Dialogue in Education.*
1992	Lee L. Jacks Professor of Education at Stanford University. Publishes *The Challenge to Care in Schools.*
1993	Publishes *Educating for Intelligent Belief or Unbelief.*
1994	Visiting Professor, Teachers College, Columbia University.
1995	Publishes *Philosophy of Education.*
1996	Publishes *Caregiving.*
1997	Lee L. Jacks Professor of Education, Stanford University and Professor of Philosophy and Education, Teachers College, Columbia University.
1998	Publishes *Justice and Care in Education.*

Introduction

Nel Noddings is the Lee L. Jacks Professor of Education at Stanford University and Professor of Philosophy and Education at Teachers College, Columbia University She is perhaps best known for *Caring: A Feminine Approach to Ethics and Moral Education* and for *The Challenge to Care in Schools.* Beginning with the "first wonderful accident" that "happened in the second grade," Noddings suggests that her professional life, like many other women, developed largely as a result of "various accidents and an awareness of opportunity." As a young child, Noddings remembers moving to a new town and finding herself in a "strange and much more demanding academic environment." Thanks to being placed into the top reading group by Miss Christ, her second grade teacher, school became her second home and provided her with emotional and intellectual support. Another such accident occurred in the seventh grade when, after another move, Noddings experienced another teacher who cared enough about her to attend her valedictorian speech upon graduation from high school. Noddings provides us with numerous life shaping "accidents" that contributed to her becoming a secondary math teacher and later an academic and philosopher. As she explains, "all of these accidents . . . involve love, or led to love, and these loves, like bits of colored sea glass, are the elements from which my life has been composed."[1]

Such accidents and the awareness and willingness to take advantage of the opportunities provided by them has enabled Noddings to reach the pinnacle of the academic world. While her academic and professional accomplishments are many, including serving as President of the Philosophy of Education Society, Noddings' success remains rooted in the caring relationships alluded to above and discussed in more depth in her "Accident, Awareness, and Actualization." In emphasizing the importance of caring relationships for teaching and learning, Noddings integrates her lived experiences with her academic and professional pursuits. In suggesting that children will work hard for people they like and trust, Noddings is both describing her own educational experiences and positing a significant educational principle.

Professor Noddings suggests that caring and courage are required to initiate the changes that our schools so desperately need. Noting that the social context has changed dramatically since she taught math in the public school, Professor Noddings contends that the established curriculum is not providing today's students with what they really need. To further illustrate this point, Noddings suggests that the outstanding curriculum projects developed in the aftermath of the "Sputnik" crisis were praiseworthy, but, as Jerome Bruner concluded in 1971, curriculum reform is not the answer. Bruner's MACOS (Man, A Course of Study) and many other outstanding curriculum projects represent significant achievements, but they are not capable of solving the malaise that grips our society.

If such outstanding curriculum projects as these were not the solution to our problems, it is not surprising, suggests Noddings, that our current disciplined and standards-based approach is failing. As an alternative, Noddings suggests incorporating themes of caring into our traditional subjects. Based on her work in the ethics of caring and from *The Challenge to Care in Schools,* Noddings offers examples of caring for the spiritual self, for intimate others, for strangers, and for plants and animals.

Professor Noddings explains, that, even in math, we can acknowledge that children care about spiritual questions. To illustrate, she suggests that a high school geometry class could critique Descartes' proof for the existence of God while Pascal's wager on God's existence could serve as a problem for a probability class. The value of infusing these and other examples into our curriculum is to help students understand that even the "great minds" struggled with spiritual questions.

Noting that responses to such questions as: What does it mean to be educated? have, until recently, been largely male voices, Noddings suggests that had women developed the disciplines, the curriculum would have been organized around the stages of life. For example, philosophy—until recently, a male dominated field—focuses on questions of death and an afterlife. Noddings suggests that questions of birth would be more prominent in a feminist-oriented philosophy and education. In language similar to that of Jane Roland Martin, Noddings suggests that a rigorous and challenging curriculum could be developed around the question: What does it mean to make a home? Noddings reminds us that John Dewey admonishes us to think of geography as the study of earth as humankind's home.

In short, Noddings suggests that an education grounded in caring is incompatible with the idea that there is *the* one or *same* curriculum for all. Noting that a mechanically-oriented curriculum can be as intellectually rigorous as any other, Noddings admonishes us to treasure the child who will become a plumber just as much as the child who will become a philosopher.[2]

Noddings argues that "liberal education (defined as a set of traditional disciplines) is an outmoded and dangerous model of education for today's young." Restating and updating the position John Dewey presented more than half a century ago, Noddings has no quarrel with literature, history, the physical sciences, or her own teaching field (mathematics), until and unless these subjects are used as weapons of an "ideology of control that forces students to study a particular, narrowly prescribed curriculum devoid of content they might really care about."[3] Noddings is particularly incensed by Mortimer Adler's recent attempt in *The Paideia Proposal* to revive Robert Maynard Hutchins argument that "the best education is the best education for all." Reminiscent of Dewey's opposition to Hutchins' argument that to be free human beings means mastering the traditional content that, according to Hutchins and Adler, constitutes the best that humankind has to offer, Noddings suggests that Adler and Hutchins confuse equality with sameness.

Noddings objects to Adler's statement that "there are no unteachable children," only teachers, parents, and schools that fail to teach them. Based on her own experience teaching elementary and secondary students, Noddings asserts "that no matter how fine the teaching, there will be considerable differences between what is achieved in, say geometry, by students most and least interested in mathematics." Realizing that not everyone—including many bright and good citizens—shares her passion for mathematics, Noddings understands that some students "will never understand the logic of mathematical proof or the power and generality of its greatest products."[4] While it is important, perhaps essential, that tomorrow's citizens "understand what it means to live in a mathematicized world," Noddings doubts that mastery of algebra is required for such understanding. She suggests that students could better achieve this necessary understanding of mathematics "through the study of social problems that really interest them."[5]

Extending her argument one step further, Noddings suggests that a traditional liberal education is the best education for no one. By focusing almost exclusively on linguistic and logical-mathematical reasoning, liberal education limits rather than liberates the human mind and spirit. By neglecting, if not ignoring, "feeling, concrete thinking, practical activity, and even moral action," an educational scheme grounded in the traditional liberal arts values the education of a philosopher more than the education of a plumber. In addition, such a traditional curriculum perpetuates a sexist society by largely omitting the "activities, attitudes, and values historically associated with women . . . ."[6]

Noddings proposes an alternative educational scheme based on caring. Her concept of "caring" is more fully developed in the selection that follows, but for now it is enough to suggest that it "speaks to the existential heart of life—. . . that draws attention to our passions, attitudes, connections, concerns, and experienced responsibilities." Rather than the traditional disciplines, the organization of this alternative vision for education focuses on kinds or domains of caring. Noddings' educational scheme is multidimensional and includes the domains of caring that all humans share: for self; for intimate others; for associates and distant others; for non-human life; for the human-made environment of objects and instruments; and for ideas.[7] She envisions schools where children and youth are grouped together in centers of care actively exploring and discussing topics of interest to them. In such an environment, individuals are encouraged to pursue that which interests them but since there are centers of care that all humans share, students learn to work collaboratively in developing their unique capacities or intelligences. Noddings argues that an educational scheme that builds upon what students care about will more likely develop adults capable of caring for themselves and the world they inhabit than will a revival of a discredited liberal arts tradition.

Notes

1. Nel Noddings, "Accident, Awareness, and Actualization" in Ann Newmann and Penelope L Peters, eds., *Learning from Our Lives: Women, Research, and Autobiography in Education* (New York: Teachers College Press, 1997), p. 166.
2. Information provided by Professor Noddings during a presentation at the University of North Carolina at Greensboro on March 17, 1994.
3. Nel Noddings, *The Challenge to Care in Schools: An Alternative Approach to Education* (New York: Teachers College Press, 1992), p. xii.
4. Ibid., p. 29.
5. "Accident, Awareness, and Actualization," p. 177.
6. *The Challenge to Care in Schools*, p. 43.
7. Ibid., p. 47.

From *The Challenge to Care in Schools: An Alternative Approach to Education* (1992)

The German philosopher Martin Heidegger (1962) described care as the very Being of human life. His use of the term is very broad, covering an attitude of solicitousness toward other living beings, a concern to do things meticulously, the deepest existential longings, fleeting moments of concern, and all the burdens and woes that belong to human life. From his perspective, we are immersed in care; it is the ultimate reality of life.

Heidegger's full range of meanings will be of interest as this exploration continues, but the meaning that will be primary here is relational. A *caring relation* is, in its most basic form, a connection or encounter between two human beings—a carer and a recipient of care, or cared-for. In order for the relation to be properly called caring, both parties must contribute to it in characteristic ways. A failure on the part of either carer or cared-for blocks completion of caring and, although there may still be a relation—that is, an encounter or connection in which each party feels something toward the other—it is not a *caring* relation. Even before I describe the contributions of carer and cared-for, one can see how useful this relational definition is. No matter how hard teachers try to care, if the caring is not received by students,

---

the claim "they don't care" has some validity. It suggests strongly that something is very wrong.

In *Caring* (1984), I described the state of consciousness of the carer (or "one-caring") as characterized by engrossment and motivational displacement. By engrossment I mean an open, nonselective receptivity to the cared-for. Other writers have used the word "attention" to describe this characteristic. Iris Murdoch (1970), for example, discussed attention as essential in moral life, and she traced the concept to Simone Weil. Weil placed attention at the center of love for our neighbors. It is what characterizes our consciousness when we ask another (explicitly or implicitly), "What are you going through?" Weil wrote:

> This way of looking is first of all attentive. The soul empties itself of all its own contents in order to receive into itself the being it is looking at, just as he is, in all his truth. Only he who is capable of attention can do this. (1951, p. 115)

To say that the soul empties itself of all its own contents in order to receive the other describes well what I mean by engrossment. I do not mean infatuation, enchantment, or obsession but a full receptivity. When I care, I really hear, see, or feel what the other tries to convey. The engrossment or attention may last only a few moments and it may or may not be repeated in future encounters, but it is full and essential in any caring encounter. For example, if a stranger stops me to ask directions, the encounter may produce a caring relation, albeit a brief one. I listen attentively to his need, and I respond in a way that he receives and recognizes. The caring relation is completed when he receives my efforts at caring.

As carer in the brief encounter just described, I was attentive, but I also felt the desire to help the stranger in his need. My consciousness was characterized by motivational displacement. Where a moment earlier I had my own projects in mind, I was now concerned with his project—finding his way on campus. When we watch a small child trying to tie her shoes, we often feel our own fingers moving in sympathetic reaction. This is motivational displacement, the sense that our motive energy is flowing toward others and their projects. I receive what the other conveys, and I want to respond in a way that furthers the other's purpose or project.

Experiencing motivational displacement, one begins to think. Just as we consider, plan, and reflect on our own projects, we now think what we can do to help another. Engrossment and motivational displacement do not tell us what to do; they merely characterize our consciousness when we care. But the thinking that we do will now be as careful as it is in our own service. We are seized by the needs of another.

What characterizes the consciousness of one who is cared for? Reception, recognition, and response seem to be primary. The cared-for receives the caring and shows that it has been received. This recognition now becomes part of what the carer receives in his or her engrossment, and the caring is completed.

Some critics worry that my account puts a tremendous burden on the carer and very little on the recipient of care. But we must keep in mind that the basic caring relation is an encounter. My description of a caring relation does not entail that carer and cared-for are permanent labels for individuals. Mature relationships are characterized by mutuality. They are made up of strings of encounters in which the parties exchange places; both members are carers and cared-fors as opportunities arise.

Even in the basic situation, however, the contribution of the cared-for is not negligible. Consider the mother-infant relationship. In every caring encounter, the mother is necessarily carer and the infant cared-for. But the infant responds—he or she coos, wriggles, stares attentively, smiles, reaches out, and cuddles. These responses are heartwarming; they make caregiving a rewarding experience. To see just how vital the infant's response is to the caring relation, one should observe what happens when infants cannot respond normally to care. Mothers and other caregivers in such situations are worn down by the lack of completion—burned out by the constant outward flow of energy that is not replenished by the response of the cared-for. Teachers, too, suffer this dreadful loss of energy when their students do not respond. Thus, even when the second party in a relation cannot assume the status of carer, there is a genuine form of reciprocity that is essential to the relation.

The desire to be cared for is almost certainly a universal human characteristic. Not everyone wants to be cuddled or fussed over. But everyone wants to be received, to elicit a response that is congruent with an underlying need or desire. Cool and formal people want others to respond to them with respect and a touch of deference. Warm, informal people often appreciate smiles and hugs. Everyone appreciates a person who knows when to hug and when to stand apart. In schools, all kids want to be cared for in this sense. They do not want to be treated "like numbers," by recipe—no matter how sweet the recipe may be for some consumers. When we understand that everyone wants to be cared for and that there is no recipe for caring, we see how important engrossment (or attention) is. In order to respond as a genuine carer, one does have to empty the soul of its own contents. One cannot say, "Aha! This fellow needs care. Now, let's see—here are the seven steps I must follow." Caring is a way of being in relation, not a set of specific behaviors.

I have put great emphasis on caring as relation, because our temptation is to think of caring as a virtue, an individual attribute. We do talk this way at times. We say, "He is a caring person," or even, "She is really a caring person, but she has trouble showing it." Both of these comments capture something of our broad notion of care, but both are misleading because of their emphasis on caring as an individual virtue. As we explore caring in the context of caregiving—any long-term unequal relation in which one person is carer and the other cared-for—we will ask about the virtues that support caring. But for now, it is important not to detach carers from caring relations. No matter how much a person professes to care, the result that concerns us is the caring relation. Lots of self-righteous, "caring" people induce the response, "she doesn't really care about me at all."

Even though I will often use the word *caring* to apply to relations, I will also need to apply it to capacities. The uses should be clear in context. I want to avoid a concentration on judgment or evaluation that accompanies an interpretation of caring as an individual virtue, but I also want to acknowledge that people have various capacities for caring—that is, for entering into caring relations as well as for attending to objects and ideas.

When we discuss teaching and teacher-learner relationships in depth, we will see that teachers not only have to create caring relations in which they are the carers, but that they also have a responsibility to help their students develop the capacity to care. What can this mean? For Heidegger care is inevitable; all aware human beings care. It is the mark of being human. But not everyone develops the capacity to care for others in the way described above. Perhaps very few learn to care for ideas, for nonhuman life, for objects. And often we confuse the forms of caring and suppose caring to be a unitary capacity that transfers easily from one domain to another.

Simone Weil is a good example of an outstanding thinker who seems to have believed that intellectual caring and interpersonal caring are closely related. In the essay from which the earlier passage was extracted, Weil observed that the study of geometry requires attention and that attention so learned could increase students' concentration in prayer. Thence, we may suppose, Weil concluded that closer connection in prayer would produce more sensitive interpersonal relations; that is, she believed that intellectual attention could be transferred to interpersonal attention. This is doubtful. Evidence abounds that people can attain high levels of intellectuality and remain insensitive to human beings and other living things. Consider the Nazi high command or the fictional Professor Moriarty (Sherlock Holmes's nemesis) who attended lovingly to his orchids but was evil incarnate in the human domain. So the varieties of care need analysis.

Unequal caring relations are interesting not only in the human domain but also in the realm of nonhuman animals. It is doubtful whether any animal can be a carer with respect to humans (although there are those who have argued the case for dogs), but many animals are responsive cared-fors, and taking care of animals can be a wonderful way to learn caring. In our interaction with animals, we also have an opportunity to study the forms of response that we value. Some animals respond with intelligence, and we usually value that. Some respond with affection; they like to be stroked, cuddled, held, or scratched. Still others respond vocally. All of these responses affect us and call forth a caring attitude. Further, certain physical characteristics that suggest the possibility of a valued response also affect us. Most of us feel sympathy for baby seals threatened by hunters, because they look as though they might respond in the ways mentioned. Creatures that are slimy, scaly, or spiny rarely evoke a sympathetic response in us. The nature of our responses will be seen as important when we consider the roots of ethical life.

In another sense of care, human beings can care about ideas or objects. An approach to education that begins with care is not, as I pointed out earlier, anti-intellectual. Part of what we receive from others is a sense of their interests, including intellectual passions. To enhance a student's understanding and skill in a given subject is an important task for teachers, but current educational practices are riddled with slogans and myths that are not very helpful.

Often we begin with the innocent-sounding slogan mentioned earlier, "All children can learn." The slogan was created by people who mean well. They want teachers to have high expectations for all their students and not to decide on the basis of race, ethnicity, sex, or economic status that some groups of children simply cannot learn the subject at hand. With that much I agree.

But I will argue that not all individual children can learn everything we might like to teach them. Further, the good intentions captured in the slogan can lead to highly manipulative and dictatorial methods that disregard the interests and purposes of students. Teachers these days are expected to induce a desire to learn in all students. But all students already want to learn; it is a question of *what* they want to learn. John Dewey (1963) argued years ago that teachers had to start with the experience and interests of students and patiently forge connections between that experience and whatever subject matter was prescribed. I would go further. There are few things that all students need to know, and it ought to be acceptable for students to reject some material in order to pursue other topics with enthusiasm. Caring teachers listen and respond differentially to their students. Much more will be said on this highly controversial issue in later chapters. For now it is enough to note that our schools are not intellectually stimulating places, even for many students who are intellectually oriented.

Few students learn to care for ideas in school. Perhaps even fewer learn to care for objects. I am not talking about mere acquisitiveness; this seems to be learned all too well. I am talking about what Harry Broudy (1972) called "enlightened cherishing" and what the novelist and essayist John Galsworthy (1948) called "quality." This kind of caring produces fine objects and takes care of them. In a society apparently devoted to planned obsolescence, our children have few opportunities to care lovingly for old furniture, dishes, carpets, or even new bicycles, radios, cassette players, and the like. It can be argued that the care of many tools and instruments is a waste of time because they are so easily replaced. But one wonders how long a throwaway society can live harmoniously with the natural environment and also how closely this form of carelessness is related to the gross desire for more and more acquisitions. Is there a role for schools to play in teaching care of buildings, books, computers, furniture, and laboratory equipment?

Caring for ideas and objects is different from caring for people and other living things. Strictly speaking, one cannot form a relation with mathematics or music or a food processor. The cared-for cannot feel anything for us; there is no affect in the second party. But, oddly, people do report a form of responsiveness from ideas and objects. The mathematician Gauss was "seized" by mathematics. The poet Robert Frost insisted that "a poem finds its own way" (see the accounts in Noddings & Shore, 1984). And we know that well-tended engines purr, polished instruments gleam, and fine glassware glistens. The care we exert induces something like a response from fields of ideas and from inanimate objects. Do our students hear enough—or anything at all—about these wondrous events?

Finally, we must consider Heidegger's deepest sense of care. As human beings, we care what happens to us. We wonder whether there is life after death, whether there is a deity who cares about us, whether we are loved by those we love, whether we belong anywhere; we wonder what we will become, who we are, how much control we have over our own fate. For adolescents these are among the most pressing questions: Who am I? What kind of person will I be? Who will love me? How do others see me? Yet schools spend more time on the quadratic formula than on any of these existential questions.

In reviewing the forms of care, it becomes clear that there is a challenge to care in schools. The structures of current schooling work against care, and at the same time, the need for care is perhaps greater than ever.

The Debate in Ethics

No discussion of caring today could be adequate without some attention to the ethic of care. In 1982 Carol Gilligan published her now famous *In a Different Voice,* describing an alternative approach to moral problems. This approach was identified in the voices of women, but Gilligan did not claim that the approach is exclusively female, nor did she claim that all women use it. Still, the avalanche of response from women who recognized themselves in Gilligan's description is an impressive phenomenon. "This is me," many women said. "Finally someone has articulated the way I come at moral problems."

Gilligan described a morality based on the recognition of needs, relation, and response. Women who speak in the different voice refuse to leave themselves, their loved ones, and connections out of their moral reasoning. They speak from and to a situation, and their reasoning is contextual. Those of us who write about an ethic of care have emphasized affective factors, but this is not to say that caring is irrational or even nonrational. It has its own rationality or reasonableness, and in appropriate situations carers draw freely on standard linear rationality as well. But its emphasis is on living together, on creating, maintaining, and enhancing positive relations—not on decision making in moments of high moral conflict, nor on justification.

An ethic of care—a needs- and response-based ethic—challenges many premises of traditional ethics and moral education. First, there is the difference of focus already mentioned. There is also a rejection of universalizability, the notion that anything that is morally justifiable is necessarily something that anyone else in a similar situation is obligated to do. Universalizability suggests that who we are, to whom we are related, and how we are situated should have nothing to do with our moral decision making. An ethic of caring rejects this. Next, although an ethic of care puts great emphasis on consequences in the sense that it always asks what happens to the relation, it is not a form of utilitarianism; it does not posit one greatest good to be optimized, nor does it separate means and ends. Finally, it is not properly labeled an ethic of virtue. Although it calls on people to be carers and to develop the virtues and capacities to care, it does not regard caring solely as an individual attribute. It recognizes the part played by the cared-for. It is an ethic of relation.

In moral education an ethic of care's great emphasis on motivation challenges the primacy of moral reasoning. We concentrate on developing the attitudes and skills required to sustain caring relations and the desire to do so, not nearly so much on the reasoning used to arrive at a decision. Lawrence Kohlberg (1981) and his associates, following Plato and Socrates, have focused on moral reasoning. The supposition here is that moral knowledge is sufficient for moral behavior. From this perspective, wrongdoing is always equated with ignorance. Gilligan explicitly challenged Kohlberg's scale or hierarchy of moral reasoning (suggesting a powerful alternative developmental model), but others of us have challenged the whole idea of a developmental model, arguing that moral responses in a given individual may vary contextually at almost any age. (The language used to discuss what one is doing and why may, of course, depend on intellectual development, but moral behavior and its intellectual articulation are not synonymous.)

Moral education from the perspective of an ethic of caring has four major components: modeling, dialogue, practice, and confirmation (Noddings, 1984). Modeling is important in most schemes of moral education, but in caring it is vital. In this framework we are not trying to teach students principles and ways of applying them to problems through chains of mathematical reasoning. Rather, we have to show how to care in our own relations with cared-fors. For example, professors of education and school administrators cannot be sarcastic and dictatorial with teachers in the hope that coercion will make them care for students. I have heard administrators use this excuse for "being tough" with teachers—"because I care about the kids of this state"—but, of course, the likely outcome is that teachers will then turn attention protectively to themselves rather than lovingly to their students. So we do not tell our students to care; we show them how to care by creating caring relations with them.

There is a second reason why modeling is so vital. The capacity to care may be dependent on adequate experience in being cared for. Even while a child is too young to be a carer, he or she can learn how to be a responsive cared-for. Thus our role as carer is more important than our role as model, but we fill both simultaneously. We remind ourselves when we are tempted to take short cuts in moral education that we are, inevitably, models. But otherwise, in our daily activities we simply respond as carers when the need arises. The function of modeling gets special attention when we try to explain what we are doing and why in moral education. But the primary reason for responding as carers to our students' needs is that we are called to such response by our moral orientation.

Dialogue is the second essential component of moral education. My use of the term *dialogue* is similar to that of Paulo Freire (1970). It is not just talk or conversation—certainly not an oral presentation of argument in which the second party is merely allowed to ask an occasional question. Dialogue is open-ended; that is, in a genuine dialogue, neither party knows at the outset what the outcome or decision will be. As parents and teachers, we cannot enter into dialogue with children when we know that our decision is already made. It is maddening to young people (or any people) to engage in "dialogue" with a sweetly reasonable adult who cannot be persuaded and who, in the end, will say, "Here's how it's going to be. I tried to reason with you. . . ." We do have to talk this way at times, but we should not pretend that this is dialogue. Dialogue is a common search for understanding, empathy, or appreciation. It can be playful or serious, logical or imaginative, goal or process oriented, but it is always a genuine quest for something undetermined at the beginning.

Dialogue permits us to talk about what we try to show. It gives learners opportunities to question "why," and it helps both parties to arrive at well-informed decisions. Although I do not believe that all wrongdoing can be equated with ignorance, I do believe that many moral errors are ill-informed decisions, particularly in the very young. Thus dialogue serves not only to inform the decision under consideration; it also contributes to a habit of mind—that of seeking adequate information on which to make decisions.

Dialogue serves another purpose in moral education. It connects us to each other and helps to maintain caring relations. It also provides us with the knowledge of each other that forms a foundation for response in caring. Caring (acting as carer) requires knowledge and skill as well as characteristic attitudes. We respond most effectively as carers when we understand what the other needs and the history of this need. Dialogue is implied in the criterion of engrossment. To receive the other is to attend fully and openly. Continuing dialogue builds up a substantial knowledge of one another that serves to guide our responses.

A third component of moral education is practice. Attitudes and "mentalities" are shaped, at least in part, by experience. Most of us speak regularly of a "military mind," a "police mentality," "business thinking," and the like. Although some of this talk is a product of stereotyping, it seems clear that it also captures some truth about human behavior. All disciplines and institutional organizations have training programs designed not only to teach specific skills but also to "shape minds," that is, to induce certain attitudes and ways of looking at the world. If we want people to approach moral life prepared to care, we need to provide opportunities for them to gain skills in caregiving and, more important, to develop the characteristic attitudes described earlier.

Some of the most fascinating work in contemporary feminist theory is devoted to the study of women's experience and its articulation. It seems likely that women's traditional experience is closely related to the moral approach described in ethics of care. Women, more often than men, have been charged with the direct care of young children, the ill, and the aged. They have been expected to maintain a pleasing environment, to look after the needs of others, and to mediate disputes in ordinary social situations. If we regard this experience as inseparable from oppression, then we might agree with Nietzsche that what I am describing is merely "slave mentality." But if we analyze the experience, we find considerable autonomy, love, choice, and consummate skid in the traditional female role. We may evaluate the experience as essential in developing fully human beings.

Women have learned to regard every human encounter as a potential caring occasion. In nursing theory, for example, Jean Watson (1985) defined the moment in which nurse and patient meet as a "caring occasion." It is not just that the nurse will provide care in the form of physical skills to the patient. Rather, it is a moment in which each must decide how to meet the other and what to do with the moment. This is obviously very different from defining a medical encounter as a problem-solving event. Problem solving is involved, of course, but it is preceded by a moment of receptivity—one in which the full humanity of both parties is recognized—and it is followed by a return to the human other in all his or her fullness.

If we decide that the capacity to care is as much a mark of personhood as reason or rationality, then we will want to find ways to increase this capacity. Just as we now think it is important for girls as well as boys to have mathematical experience, so we should want both boys and girls to have experience in caring. It does not just happen; we have to plan for it. As we will see, such planning is complex and loaded with potential pitfalls.

Some schools, recognizing the needs just discussed, have instituted requirements for a form of community service. This is a move in the right direction, but reflection produces some issues to worry about. The practice provided must be with people who can demonstrate caring. We do not want our children to learn the menial (or even sophisticated) skills of caregiving without the characteristic attitude of caring. The experience of caregiving should initiate or contribute to the desired attitude, but the conditions have to be right, and people are central to the setting. This is a major point, to which I will return.

Next, practice in caring should transform schools and, eventually, the society in which we live. If the practice is assimilated to the present structures of schooling, it may lose its transformative powers. *It* may be transformed—that is, distorted. If we were to give grades for caregiving, for example, students might well begin to compete for honors in caring. Clearly, then, their attention could be diverted from cared-fors to themselves. If, on the other hand, we neither grade nor give credit for such work, it may inevitably have second-class status in our schools. So long as our schools are organized hierarchically with emphasis on rewards and penalties, it will be very difficult to provide the kind of experience envisioned.

The fourth component of moral education from the perspective of caring is confirmation. Martin Buber (1965) described confirmation as an act of affirming and encouraging the best in others. When we confirm someone, we spot a better self and encourage its development. We can do this only if we know the other well enough to see what he or she is trying to become. Formulas and slogans have no place here. We do not set up a single ideal or set of expectations for everyone to meet, but we identify something admirable, or at least acceptable, struggling to emerge in each person we encounter. The person working toward a better self must see the attribute or goal as worthy, and we too must see it as at least morally acceptable. We do not confirm people in ways we judge to be wrong.

Confirmation requires attribution of the best possible motive consonant with reality. When someone commits an act we find reprehensible, we ask ourselves what might have motivated such an act. Often it is not hard to identify an array of possible motives ranging from the gross and grubby to some that are acceptable or even admirable. This array is not constructed in abstraction. We build it from a knowledge of this particular other and by listening carefully to what she or he tells us. The motive we attribute has to be a real, a genuine possibility.

Then we can open our dialogue with something like, "I know you were trying to help your friend . . ." or "I know what you're trying to accomplish. . . ." It will be clear that we disapprove of this particular act, but it will also be clear to the other that we see a self that is better than this act. Often the other will respond with enormous relief. *Here is this significant and percipient other who sees through the smallness or meanness of my present behavior a self that is better and a real possibility.* Confirmation lifts us toward our vision of a better self.

It is worth repeating that confirmation cannot be done by formula. A relation of trust must ground it. Continuity is required, because the carer in acting to confirm must know the cared-for well enough to be able to identify motives consonant with reality. Confirmation cannot be described in terms of strategies; it is a loving act founded on a relation of some depth. When we turn to specific changes that should occur in schooling in order to meet the challenge to care, I will put great emphasis on continuity. Not all caring relations require continuity (some, as we have seen, are brief encounters), but teaching does require it.

Confirmation contrasts sharply with the standard mode of religious moral education. There we usually find a sequence of accusation, confession, penance, and forgiveness. The initial step, accusation, causes or sustains separation. We stand in moral judgment and separate the other from ourselves and the moral community. In contrast, confirmation calls us to remain in connection. Further, accusation tends to produce denial or rationalization, which we then feel compelled to overthrow. But the rationalization may in fact be an attempt on the part of the accused to find that possible motive and convey it to us, the accuser. Because we have to reject it in order to proceed with confession, penance, and forgiveness, offenders may never understand their own true motives.. This sequence also depends heavily on authority, obedience, fear, and subordination. We can be harsh or magnanimous in our judgment and forgiveness. Our authority is emphasized, and the potential power of the offender's own moral struggle is overlooked.

I do not mean to suggest that there is never a place for accusation and confession in moral education. It is not always possible for us to find a motive that is morally acceptable; sometimes we have to begin by asking straight out, "Why did you do that?" or "How could you do such a thing?" But it is gratifying how often we really can see a better self if we look for one, and its identification is a first step in its realization.

This whole way of looking at ethics and moral education challenges not only parts of the religious tradition but also the ideas of Freud and like-minded theorists. Freud believed that our sense of morality develops out of fear. The superego, Freud said, is an internalization of authority—of the father's voice—and its establishment results from resolution of the Oedipal conflict. Sons fear castration by the father if they disobey or compete with him. Resolution of this desire to rebel and compete involves acceptance of the father's power and authority, and the superego (Freud's guide to acceptable behavior) takes up residence within the son. This account of moral development led Freud to conclude that women must be morally inferior to men. Because girls need not fear castration (having been born in that dread condition), their moral voice never attains the strength and dependability of men's.

Recent criticisms of Freud suggest that more attention should be given to the preoedipal period. Nancy Chodorow (1978) has theorized that girls and boys develop different psychological deep structures because females are almost exclusively the primary caregivers for both. Girls can find their gender identity without separating from their mother and, hence, develop a relational personality structure and perhaps even a relational epistemology or way of knowing (Keller, 1985). Boys, however, must construct their gender identity in opposition to all that is female. Here we have the possible roots of the different moral voices described by Gilligan. We will consider other alternatives as well.

Eli Sagan (1988) has also suggested that moral development begins and is strongly affected by preoedipal life. Without rejecting the Freudian framework entirely, Sagan recommends a shift in emphasis. If we give due weight to early childhood, we see that conscience (a sense of right and wrong, not mere internalization of authority) develops as much out of love and attachment as out of fear. Further, the primary fear is not of harm and punishment but, rather, of disappointing a loved parent and, at worst, losing that parent's love. This is a major challenge to masculinist psychology and a suggestion compatible with an ethic of caring and the model of moral education outlined here. Love, caring, and relation play central roles in both ethics and moral education.

I want to suggest that caring is the very bedrock of all successful education and that contemporary schooling can be revitalized in its light. Before describing a broad plan to make caring central in education, I need to explain why the current ideal is inadequate. Liberal education has been the Western ideal for centuries. Even when it is poorly funded in comparison with technical and professional education, it is still the ideal that puts pressure on precollegiate education. It is the form of education—done well or poorly—that most of us experienced. What is wrong with it, and why should it be rejected as a model of universal education?

Questions

1. Is caring a relation or a virtue?
2. What are the characteristics of a caring relationship?
3. Are intellectual caring and interpersonal caring related?
4. How is caring for ideas and objects different from caring for people and other living things?
5. Why does an ethic of caring reject universalizability?
6. How does traditional moral reasoning (Socrates, Plato, Kohlberg, etc.) differ from the ethic of caring?
7. What is the role of a carer in a caring relationship? Of the cared-for in a caring relationship?

8. Why is dialogue so important in a moral education based on the ethic of caring?

9. Is it possible to teach someone to care? Is it possible to develop the capacity to care for others?

10. What are the connections between the ethic of caring and the experiences of women?

11. Why is confirmation an essential component of the ethic of caring? How does this differ from more traditional, religious approaches to moral education?

chapter 17

Kieran Egan

TIME LINE FOR EGAN

1942	Is born in Clonmel, Ireland.
1961–1963	Taught high school in Warwick, England.
1966	Receives A.B. in Honours History from University of London.
1967	Receives Post Graduate Teaching Certificate, Goldsmith College, University of London.
1972	Receives Ph.D. in Philosophy of Education from Cornel University.
1972 to present	Assistant, Associate, and Full Professor at Simon Fraser University.
1978	Publishes *Ethics and Educational Policy*.
1979	Publishes *Educational Development*.
1980–1983	Director of Undergraduate Programs, Simon Fraser University.
1981	Publishes *The Erosion of Education: Socialization and the Schools*.
1983	Publishes *Education and Psychology: Plato, Piaget, and Scientific Psychology*.
1986	Publishes *Teaching as Story Telling*.
1988	Publishes *Imagination and Education* and *Primary Understanding: Education in Early Childhood*.

1990	Publishes *Romantic Understanding: The Development of Rationality and Imagination.*
1991	Receives Grawemeyer Award.
1992	Publishes *Imagination in Teaching and Learning.*
1997	Publishes *The Educated Mind: How Cognitive Tools Shape Our Understanding.*
1998	Publishes *Children's Minds, Talking Rabbits, and Clockwork Oranges.*

Introduction

Kieran Egan is as an educational philosopher whose emphasis on imagination, story-telling, and other tools of understanding offers new and provocative insights into what it means to be educated. Egan's work connects with and extends the storytelling approach exemplified by Plato in his allegories and in Rousseau's *Emile*. In addition his work supports Bruner's claim that "any subject can be taught effectively in some intellectually honest form to any child at any stage of development" and is compatible with the work of Lipman and Matthews. Equally important, his work illustrates the crucial connection between the philosophical question of what it means to be educated with the educational question of how do we teach for understanding. Born in Ireland, Egan received his Ph.D. from Cornel University in 1972 and has spent most of his academic career as a professor at Simon Fraser University in Canada.

Egan suggests that not enough attention is given to the role imagination plays in education or in our vision of what it means to be educated. Instead of imagination, the modern world has embraced a set of ad hoc principles which continue to "have a pervasive and profound influence on teaching practice and curriculum design." According to these principles education proceeds "from the concrete to the abstract, from the simple to the complex, from the known to the unknown, from active manipulation to symbolic conceptualization."[1] As Egan explains, our dominant model of curriculum and lesson planning coheres with a view of knowledge as a static entity, thus denying or minimizing imagination's role in the education process.

Egan offers numerous counter-examples, not to debunk these ad hoc principles, but to suggest that they are not always the most effective way to educate and that they do not encompass the totality of education. To balance the widely accepted dictum that "children learn best from concrete, hand-on experiences," Egan explains that much of the literature for young children depends upon the child's prior understanding of various underlying, but abstract, concepts. Using the story *Cinderella* to illustrate his point, Egan notes that five-year-old children have no trouble understanding and enjoying this story, though such understanding is dependent on their ability to grasp such abstract and conflicting concepts as fear/hope, kindness/cruelty, and good/evil.

Egan offers other examples drawn from children's literature to refute the position that "abstract concepts in general are difficult for young children." Egan suggests that "seeing the process of education as a development from the concrete to the abstract is a result of focusing on certain limited logical intellectual activities." The problem here is that the education of young children has been reduced to almost total reliance upon these ad hoc principles. Egan's argument is important for it adds credence to Matthews' and Lipman's claim that children possess sophisticated conceptual tools at a much younger age than the ad hoc principles allow. Their ability to make sense of rather complex fantasy stories suggests that children have the conceptual tools necessary to deal with abstract subjects as history and philosophy. Egan suggests that a learning tool observable in children "is the dialectical process of forming opposites and mediating between them." For example, in learning the temperature continuum, children tend to learn binary opposite concepts of "hot" and "cold". Next they mediate between these and learn the concept "warm."[2] A more detailed explanation of how such "mythic" cognitive tools as binary opposites assist humankind in learning about the world they inhabit is provided in the selection included in this text. But before reading that selection from *Teaching as Story Telling,* a brief discussion of a more recent and more philosophic work, *The Educated Mind: How Cognitive Tools Shape Our Understanding,* is needed.

Paralleling the modern world's over-reliance on the ad hoc educational principles discussed above is, suggests Egan, the modern world's irrational acceptance of education grounded in three significant and mutually incompatible educational ideas: (a) "that we must shape the young to the current norms and conventions of adult society;" (b) "that we must teach them the knowledge that will ensure their thinking conforms with what is real and true about the world"; and (c) "that we must encourage the development of each student's individual potential." According to Egan, the incompatibility of these three dominate educational ideas "is the primary cause of the continuing educational crisis."[3]

As an antidote for this crisis, Egan offers us a new theory that "describes education in terms of a sequence of kinds of understanding." Suggesting that human beings developed multiple tools for understanding their world, Egan characterizes several distinctive ways of understanding as the Somatic, Mythic, Romantic, Philosophic, and Ironic ways of knowing. In what is his most significant and provocative work to date, Egan explains how these ways of knowing evolve from and coalesce into one another. Egan realizes that the Somatic, Mythic, Romantic, Philosophic, and Ironic ways or tools of understanding have many dimensions, but concentrates on their linguistic aspects to sketch for us a composite of the human mind.

According to Egan, to be educated means to acquire "these kinds of understanding as fully as possible in the sequence in which each developed historically."[4] In short, Egan proposes a new kind of recapitulation theory which, when combined with insights from Vygotsky, leads to a new educational idea. Noting that all learning in a sense "involves people recapitulating, repeating for themselves, the discoveries and inventions that have accumulated through the history of that culture,"[5] Egan seeks to explain and characterize "the nature of the connection between cultural development in the past and educational development in the present." Embracing Vygotsky's notion that "we make sense of the world by use of mediating intellectual tools that in turn profoundly influence the kind of sense we make,"[6] Egan suggests that humankind's intellectual development can be better understood by focusing on the "role played by the intellectual tools available in the society into which a person grows" than by relying on Piaget's or others' psychological theories of development. In short, the mind is too complex, too dynamic to be captured or contained by simplistic theories of psychological processes.

From this perspective, to be educated means to acquire the intellectual tools provided to us by our cultural heritage and to use these tools to generate similar kinds of understandings "as existed for peoples using those tools in the past." In defense of this modern version of nineteenth century recapitulation theories, Egan argues that cultural and educational development are "connected by the tools that generate common kinds of understanding in both processes."[7] By thinking of education as an acquisition of these kinds of understanding in the sequence they developed historically, Egan suggests that we can break the education logjam created by our unthinking endorsement of the three incompatible educational ideas of socialization, the search for Platonic truths, and the development of each individual's potential.

While recognizing that knowing both precedes and transcends the development and use of language, Egan focuses on the linguistically based tools of understanding or ways of knowing. While Egan suggests that there is a progression from Mythic understanding to the Ironic understanding, he argues that even the most sophisticated ironic thinker uses and integrates the Mythic, Romantic, Philosophic, as well as Somatic ways of knowing. Egan suggests that traditional oral societies and the spontaneous discourse of young children in modern literate cultures share similar ways of knowing or tools for understanding. Basically, such tools as binary structuring, fantasy, reliance on metaphor, and attention to the rhythm and narrative constitute the framework of a story. Egan argues that in teaching young children we should develop pedagogical strategies and curriculum consistent with these tools for understanding.

In teaching older children, Egan suggests that we should employ tools associated with Romantic understanding. In explaining Romantic understanding, Egan refers to *The Histories* by Herodotus. Egan suggests that today's children's fascination with the extremes of experience is similar to Herodutus' desire to capture the grand and marvelous achievements of the ancient Greeks and barbarians. To illustrate teaching from this romantic perspective, Egan advocates replacing the moving from the known to the unknown approach that dominates the teaching of social studies in contemporary middle schools with an approach that concentrates on the limits of the social context being studied, the major events or achievements of the people or period under scrutiny, and the exotic features of that context.

To complete the educational process, Egan suggests that we focus—during the midteen years—on the "craving for generality" that characterizes the Philosophic tools for understanding bequeathed to us by Plato and Aristotle. For

Egan, the culminating yet neverending educational quest is the coalescence of all of these tools into an ironic understanding that both enables its users to appreciate multiple perspectives and empowers them to act in a postmodern world where absolute certainty is not possible. Clearly there are similarities between the ironic tools of understanding and postmodern thought—Richard Rorty's liberal ironist comes to mind—but Egan's ideally educated individual is one who integrates and uses the tools of understanding or multiple ways of knowing that both describe our cultural heritage and provide us with strategies for educating future generations.

In this brief introduction to Kieran Egan's contributions to the questions of what does it mean to be educated and how do we teach for understanding, we offer what our colleagues in literacy education refer to as an "advanced organizer." It is our hope that this and other "advanced organizers" of this text will assist you in unlocking the door to the thought of these creative minds. Once that door is opened, we encourage you to go beyond the selections included here. Our goal is to help, but to be truly educated *you* must, as Bruner suggests "go beyond the information given."

Notes

1. Kieran Egan, *Teaching as Story Telling: An Alternative Approach to Teaching and Curriculum in the Elementary School* (Chicago: University of Chicago Press, 1986), p. 28.
2. Ibid., p. 31.
3. Kieran Egan, *The Educated Mind: How Cognitive Tools Shape Our Understanding* (Chicago: University of Chicago Press, 1997), p. 3.
4. Ibid., p. 4.
5. Ibid., p. 27.
6. Ibid.,p. 29.
7. Ibid., p. 30.

From *Teaching as Story Telling* (1986)

Introduction

The critical comments about educational research in the previous chapter are meant as a caution against over generalizing from limited principles and from particular, limited results. No doubt most researchers are aware of the limits of their methods, but it is natural to try to stretch inferences from results as far as possible. We need whatever help we can get, and research on learning, development, motivation, etc., seems to offer some, if often opaque, guidance. The

From *Teaching As Story Telling* by Kieran Egan (Chicago: University of Chicago Press, © 1986), pp. 21–38.

problem I am mainly concerned with here is the imbalance in our image of the child that results from focusing very largely on a limited range of thinking skills.

The problem, I have suggested, is exacerbated by our focus having been directed by the dominant forms of research on those skills children are least good at. If, instead of focusing on development of logico-mathematical capacities, we were to focus on the development of imaginative capacities, we would no doubt produce a quite different profile of intellectual development. Indeed, the main result I suspect would be to point up similarities between children's and adult thinking. Piaget's influential focus on children's logico-mathematical thinking has pointed up the area where the difference between children's and adult thinking are most pronounced. Piaget's work has as a result, perhaps surprisingly, been most influential in education in a restrictive way. That is, most of the inferences one sees in education from his learning/development theory concern what children cannot do.

Some people might no doubt want to point out that Piaget has derived his theory from a study of play, dreams, and many other aspects of children's activity that are centrally concerned with imagination. The subject matter of his research has indeed included such material, but the aim has not been to study fantasy and imagination so much as to uncover from children's responses the logico-mathematical forms that underlie them. The free, imaginative content is typically given short shrift: "One would like to be able to rule out romancing with the same severity as (those answers designed to please the questioner)" (Piaget, 1951, p. 10). Similarly, most research on children's story comprehension misses their imaginative qualities and focuses on the familiar range of "graspable" logical skills (see, e.g., Stein and Trabasso, 1981).

If we continue to keep imaginative intellectual activity as our focus we might be able to construct a more hopeful and less constrictive image of the child as learner. Such an image would, it seems to me, be more in keeping with our everyday experience of children's creative intellectual energy than is the Piagetian view of relative intellectual incompetents. This is not to say that we will now ignore what children typically seem unable to do, but rather that we will focus on what they most obviously *can* do, and seem able to do best.

In the previous chapter, for example, it was noted that some Piagetian research suggests that children do not typically in elementary school years "develop" a concept of historical causality (Hallam, 1966, 1975). We can observe, however, that children clearly have available a concept of the kind of causality that keeps stories together and moves them along. Such a simple observation has an obvious educational implication. It is clearly insufficient to do a research study that concludes that "causality" is a "formal operational" concept, in Piaget's sense, and that young children thus cannot understand or use it, and then infer further that curriculum content requiring or using this concept should be excluded from the elementary school curriculum. Yet this very commonly is the kind of "educational implication" derived from Piaget's theory. Thus we see recommendations that in elementary schools we should always deal with experiences which "emphasise *direct* contact with the physical aspects of objects and events" (Wadsworth, 1978, p. 186).

There are two educational problems with such common "Piagetian" recommendations. First, the theme of the previous chapter, they take logico-mathematical thinking as the whole of thinking (their night sky is nothing but Piagetian moon). Second, they neglect the early stimulation and development of those concepts out of which the more formal logico-mathematical concept will grow. For example, the "formal" concept of causality may indeed be rare in young children, but a story-concept of causality is clearly common. The latter is hardly unconnected with the former, and ignoring the latter is hardly a sensible way of encouraging development of the former. We see that a concept like causality does not suddenly appear as a formal concept used in history at about sixteen years. Rather, it grows gradually from the uses we see in earliest stories to the more logical forms we see in history and science. Nor can we call the earlier form simpler than the later; it is rather just less specialized. Without use of the earlier forms the later forms will surely be less adequate. This same obvious point might be made about a whole range of concepts that young children are supposed to have no ability to use.

My alternative approach, then, is to focus on the kinds of conceptual abilities children clearly have and use routinely. I will consider just a few features of the kind of stories that children find most engaging, and observe what conceptual abilities must be in place for such stories to be meaningful. From this analysis I will identify those features of stories that can become parts of a model for planning teaching that more fully uses children's conceptual abilities by drawing on the engaging and communicative powers of the story form. If the story is considered as a communicative medium, we will also be able to use our observations about its power and effectiveness to show some of the inadequacies of the objectives–content–methods–evaluation model.

Story Rhythm

Stories are narrative units. That they are units is important. They are distinguishable from other kinds of narratives in that they have particular, clear beginnings and ends. The most basic story begins "Once upon a time" and concludes "they lived happily ever after." "Once upon a time" *begins* something and "ever after" does not refer to anything in particular except that what began is now ended. "Once upon a time" creates an expectation of a particular kind. We are told that at some particular time and place something happened. This something will involve a conflict or problem of some kind, which the rest of the story will be taken up resolving.

The story does not deal with anything except the problem set up in the beginning once it is underway. *Everything* in the story is focused on that central task. The weather is not incidental or arbitrary—it will affect either the action or the mood. If it does not, in a good story it will simply be ignored. Stories, then, have clear means of determining what should be included and excluded. We recognize as bad stories those that include things that do not take the story forward. Each such item lets interest sag, and if there are too many of them we stop reading, or watching, or listening.

"What happened next?" has to be answered by an incident or action that takes us towards some complication or resolution of the conflict set up in the beginning. There is, then, at the simplest level a rhythm in stories. They set up an expectation at the beginning, this is elaborated or complicated in the middle, and is satisfied in the end. Stories are tied beginning to end by their satisfying the expectation set up in the beginning. Anything that does not contribute to or fit in with this rhythm is irrelevant to the story and should be excluded. If in *Cinderella* we were to follow one of the ugly sisters through her daily round the story would sag: such events are irrelevant to resolving the particular conflict set up in the beginning of the story.

So we can observe a powerful principle of coherence and a criterion for selecting what is relevant at work in any good story. Such stories hold their power over us as long as all the events stick to and carry forward the basic rhythm. If we consider teaching in light of this cohesive principle of stories we may conclude that the general observation is hardly novel, but it encourages us to look at it in a new way. The principle of organizing a lesson coherently is obvious, but the comparison with the story form suggests new ways in which we might better achieve such coherence. How do we decide what and how much to include in a lesson? More material towards answering this will come in the next section, but here we might draw a first implication from the form of a well-wrought story.

In those stories which children find most engaging there are only those events and details which further the underlying rhythm. Other facts and events that might be connected to those in the story, even if interesting in their own right, are left out. Each irrelevant item, each item that fails to carry forward the story, lets our engagement sag a little. Most stories can obviously bear some of this, but too much and the story is lost. Think of the classic folk-tales. One thing that has happened to them in their centuries of transmission is that they have been honed down to the point where only essential details are included.

Classic folk-tales are, in this regard, a little like jokes. They both set up an expectation in the beginning that is ruthlessly followed to the end. The rhythms of jokes and classic folk-tales are clearly memorable. We might forget stories and jokes, of course, but once started on one the rhythm will usually carry us forward and fit the pieces into place.

A model for teaching that draws on the power of the story, then, will ensure that we set up a conflict or sense of dramatic tension at the beginning of our lessons and units. Thus we create some expectation that we will satisfy at the end. It is this rhythm of expectation and satisfaction that will give us a principle for precisely selecting content. Consider how much content is forgotten after a lesson or unit is finished. What purpose did that forgotten content serve? Well, no doubt, some purpose is served occasionally. We do not want to neglect the fact that some forgotten content nevertheless may remain in the structure of children's understanding of a topic ("I don't remember who opposed the settlement, but I know there was some opposition"). Nevertheless, it is surely reasonable to conclude that much forgotten content—and no doubt much that is remembered too—plays no significant educational role. It remains in Whitehead's sense "inert" (Whitehead, 1929). The implication from this reflection on the power of the story form is that we should concentrate more on simplifying and clarifying our selection of content according to the rhythm set up at the beginning of our lesson or unit. We need, then, to be more conscious of the importance of beginning with a conflict or problem whose resolution at the end can set such a rhythm in motion. Our choice of that opening conflict, then, becomes crucial. Our first consideration must be on what is most important about our topic, and we will identify importance in terms of those profound abstract concepts which children clearly already understand—good/bad, survival/destruction, security/fear, brave/cowardly, and so on.

The rhythms that stories follow are a reflection of further conceptual abilities of children. That is, whatever conceptual abilities are involved in recognizing conflicts and problems and following their elaboration and knowing when they have been satisfactorily resolved, children clearly have. Nor are these trivial intellectual abilities. They are complex and profound. As the study of linguistics has enlarged our understanding of the great complexity of the intellectual task of mastering language, so the study of poetics gives us some hints of the even greater complexity involved in mastery of the story-form. Our educational task is not to analyse these skills in detail, but rather to observe them and recognize more clearly something of the range and profundity of the learning power that children have.

Binary Opposites

One of the most obvious structural devices we can see in children's stories is the use of binary opposites. Embedded in the story or embodied by the story, are conflicts between good and bad, courage and cowardice, fear and security, and so on. The characters and events embody these underlying abstract conflicts.

These abstract binary opposites serve as criteria for the selection and organization of the content of the story and they serve as the main structuring lines along which the story moves forward. Let us consider these connected functions one at a time.

If we set up a story with a wicked step-mother and a good girl, like *Cinderella,* we begin with a conflict between these embodiments of good and bad. The selection of incidents and further characters, then, will be determined by the need to show the goodness of the one and the badness of the other. The incidents in which the step-mother is cruel to Cinders and favors her own unkind and vain daughters all elaborate the one binary pole. The unfailing kindness and self-sacrificing modesty of Cinderella place her as embodiment of the opposite pole. The story is the embodied conflict of the good and bad. In this way, then, the binary opposites that underlie our story serve as criteria for the selection of the "content"—the characters and incidents—which form the story.

These binary opposites, connectedly, provide the main structural lines along which the story moves forward. Having gathered the conflict at the beginning, we monitor the development of the story through the incidents showing the badness of the step-mother. She tries to frustrate all of Cinderella's wishes and to destroy her one modest hope of attending the Prince's ball. Our expectation is to see contrasting developments of Cinderella's goodness. Once these are vividly clear the conflict can then go forward through the actions of the good helpers, the attempts to frustrate these actions by the bad opposition, and so on to the final satisfying resolution in favor of the good. We even get some mediation in some versions of the story as the step-mother and ugly sisters recognize the error of their ways and, through Cinder's goodness, they too live happily ever after.

Wherever we look in children's stories, and in their own, no doubt derivative, narratives, we find such binary conflicts. We are not here concerned with psychological explanations, so much as simply observing their functions and power in making clear and engaging structures of meaning. Also we should not use such observations to suggest that these features of children's thinking are somehow unique to children. If we pause and consider how we make sense of events we hear about on the news, say, we can see these kinds of binary opposite organizers busily at work. They seem to be the first stage in our organizing and making meaningful new information. If we hear, for example, that there has just has just been a revolution in an African or South American state, we first search with our binary organizers to orient ourselves to the event. We want to know whether the rebels were supplied with arms by the C.I.A. or whether they had Cuban advisors, for example. That is, we first search for events or facts that allow us to fit the information into our already formed binary ideological structures. If we cannot fit the news account clearly into such structures it remains in danger of being meaningless.

Unfortunately perhaps, the news media that are eager to engage us tend to present information already embedded in such contexts. This tends to restrict our understanding of the world's complexity to the basic unmediated binary opposites of childhood. So our media present political information very much in terms of good and bad competing superpowers, and news-stories that can be fitted to that most easily engaging structure get prominent display, and those that cannot tend to get short shrift. In children's stories, however, the mediation that is appropriate for adults has not yet taken place, and so clarity of meaning requires that we structure information on binary opposites. (This does not mean that we have to present things crudely as good or bad, as I will show in the following chapter.)

So these binary opposites are not only of use in organizing stories, but we see them prominently in all kinds of areas in which we organize and make sense of things. If our concern in planning teaching is to communicate clearly an array of material we might wisely consider how binary opposites might be used to help. For my model then I will build in a way of using binary opposites as a means of organizing and selecting content. Because our aim is educational, unlike that of most news media, we will also want to build in a reminder that we should be seeking mediation of the binary opposites we start with.

Affective Meaning

Clearly stories are concerned with affective responses. A good story-teller plays our emotions, as a good violinist plays a violin. We resonate with the rhythm of the binary conflict, the events that carry it forward, and its resolution. Education, seen through the dominant planning and research models, is a largely logical and narrowly rational business. In this view, education is an area where there is little room for our emotional lives. For this reason, the "affective" is usually considered a matter only for the arts—the educational margin or "frills."

As I tried to show in the previous chapter, this view is a product of a misplaced empiricism and of a restricted conception of learning and, not least, of the child. We make sense of the world and experience "affectively" no less than "cognitively." Indeed the separation of the two is a product of the same research programs. Do we make sense of a story affectively or cognitively? Well, of course, both work together. We are not divided into two distinct parts. As we hear melody and harmony as one—though we can separate them in analysis—so we make sense of the world and experience in a unitary way—regardless of what distinctions we might make for research purposes.

The dominant model and its associated research programs have tended to suppress the affective aspects of learning. Consequently they have drawn on only a divided part of children's capacities. A further contribution to teaching that can come from drawing on the story form is a more balanced appeal to children's learning capacities. By using the story form in planning teaching we can reinstate this important and neglected aspect of children's thinking. How stories engage our affective responses, then, is important for us to notice. We will want to build such powers into our model as far as possible, allowing for the differences between typical fictional material and typical classroom instructional material. We can observe at least two ways in which stories engage us affectively.

First, we can observe that stories are largely *about* affective matters-they are about how people feel. These feelings can either provide the motives for actions or they can provide the point and result of actions. If Cinderella's motives were not kind, springing from generous feelings, much of the point of the story would be lost. Also we can readily understand such emotions as causal elements that provide the dynamic of stories. "Jack was angry and decided to get his own back. He stood up, crossed the room, and opened the door." Clearly Jack is going out to get his own back. Such causes of actions present no comprehension problems to young children.

From this observation we can see the importance of human emotions and intentions in making things meaningful. To present knowledge cut off from human emotions and intentions is to reduce its affective meaning. This affective meaning, also, seems especially important In providing *access* to knowledge and engaging us in knowledge. This lesson from our observation of stories will become particularly significant in the discussion of teaching mathematics and sciences in Chapter Four. These are the areas that suffer most from being stripped of their affective associations. We tend to teach mathematics and science as inhuman structures of knowledge, almost taking pride in their logical and inhuman precision. There are two problems with this approach. The first is that it is not true in any sense, the second is that it is educationally disastrous. Later I will discuss ways in which we can rehumanize mathematics and science, seeing the knowledge in its proper, living context of human emotions and intentions.

The second way in which stories engage us affectively follows from the fact that they end. I dwelt earlier on some implications of the obvious point that stories end; they do not just stop but rather they satisfy some conflict set up by their beginning. It is this wrapping up of the story that gives it also a part of its affective power, In life or in history there are no endings; just one damn thing after another. The patterns we impose in order to determine meaning are unlike those of the story. The patterns of our lives or of history are always provisional—something may happen to make us reinterpret, repattern, them. The uniqueness of the story form is that it creates its own world, in which the meaning of events, and thus what we should feel about them, is fixed. Even real-life ugly sisters are on Cinderella's side. We know we have reached the end of the story when we know how to *feel* about all the events and characters that make it up. What is completed by the ending of a good story is the pattern that fixes the meaning and our feelings about the contents.

From this observation we can see that our model needs to provide some way of ending a lesson or unit that has something more in common with the way stories end than with ending because we have "covered" all the content identified as relevant. Our beginning, then, needs to set up some binary conflict or problem and our end needs to resolve it in some way, if we are to take advantage of stories' power to be affectively engaging.

Metaphors, Analogs, and Objectives

In the ancient world and through the medieval period people felt their hearts pumping away in their chests just as we do. But they did not know what was going on in there. There are endless accounts in ancient medical speculation and in the myths and stories of the world of what that bumpety-bump in the chest might be. It seems so obvious to us. The heart is a pump. Blood comes out in spurts when we cut an artery because the pump is working at the rate the blood spurts.

The function of the heart became clear only after the invention of the pump. Indeed, as Jonathan Miller (1978, Ch. 5) argues, the function of the heart became *knowable* only after the invention of the pump. Once people understood how a pump worked, they could use that knowledge to make sense of the heart's function. With the advance of technology an analogy was provided which enabled understanding of things which were otherwise mysterious.

We have within us, of course, another functioning organ whose workings are not at all clear to us. We have no adequate mechanical analogs of the brain. We have seen constant attempts to make sense of it in terms of increasingly sophisticated technology. The earliest analogs were natural. Late medieval textbooks represent the brain as a kind of tree with knowledge categorized in various ways as leaves or branches from a trunk representing, often, theology. Later it is represented in terms of clockwork. Then, with a better understanding of the mechanics of the body, we find the brain represented as made up of parts that functioned like muscles—leading to faculty psychology. In this view, the parts, or faculties, of the brain grew and remained limber through exercise, much as a muscle does.

Once the telephone and then telephone exchanges were built we find those providing an analogy for thinking about the brain. This was considered especially appropriate as it was discovered that there was also some kind of electrical activity going on in the brain itself. It seems fair to say that behaviorism, as an overall theory about human behavior, owes more to the telephone exchange than it does to observations of behavior.

To say this about behaviorism is not intended as a contemptuously dismissive criticism. Our thinking is suffused with metaphors and analogies. There is an important sense in which we use the world to think with. We can use the telephone exchange as a tool with which to think about the brain. The analogy is hidden in the theory, but it has provided the means whereby we can get some conceptual grasp on it. We need, however, to be constantly concerned that our analogies are adequate. The pump is an adequate analogy for making sense of the heart. The telephone exchange is, it seems to be becoming increasingly recognized, an inadequate analogy for the brain.

In any scientific field, however, a bad theory is better than no theory at all. It is the inadequate analogy that yields a bad theory, but it is in perceiving the inadequacy of the theory that we can construct a better one. The demise of behaviorism, one might reasonably argue, owes less to the assaults of competing theories, and more to the development of the computer. The computer allows us, analogically, to think about brain functioning in a more sophisticated way than does the telephone exchange. The computer tends thereby to destroy the basis of behaviorism. But it is itself, of course, merely a relatively simple machine, and so provides us still with mechanistic analogies for thinking about the brain.

While it might be fun to continue with such notions, I should return to the point! These comments on metaphorical thinking and the use of analogies are intended as an introduction to reflecting on the adequacy of the dominant model used in planning teaching. In what way? Well, another great technical innovation in this century was the assembly line. Instead of building, for example, an automobile in one place, bringing the components to it and having the same gang of workers do all the different constructive jobs, the assembly line maximized efficiency by the methods now familiar to us all. The various bits and pieces of the automobile were gathered together at different places along the line ready to be slotted into place at the appropriate time. The workers each had specialized functions which they performed in time to the movement of the line. The initial design determined every detail of the process. It is perhaps trite to ask: What does that remind you of?

One thing it might remind us of is the curriculum. We have our overall aim and the problem becomes how best to organize its components into a sequence in order to attain that aim at the end of the process. Education is not so much like an assembly line as that the assembly line provides an analogy which people can use to think about education. Such analogical thinking need not be conscious. No doubt people could understand the heart without conscious reference to the pump, and behaviorists might even resist consciously connecting their conception of behavior with the telephone exchange. But once we understand the pump or the telephone exchange we can make sense of processes which we see in analogous terms. Even though the analogous connection may not be conscious, there is a strong tendency for the language associated with the comprehended process to invade discussion of that which it is used to comprehend. Thus Cubberly early in the century could write that schools are "factories in which the raw products (children) are to be shaped and fashioned into products to meet the various demands of life" (in Callahan, 1962, p. 152).

And so the process of planning teaching can be represented in a model that is an analog of the assembly line. We first design our final product or state our objectives, then we assemble the parts or decide what materials and content we will need in order to achieve those objectives, then we organize workers with appropriate skills along the line or choose the methods appropriate to organize most effectively the teaching of that content, and finally we arrange some means of determining whether each product is satisfactory or we evaluate whether our objectives have been attained.

Now this does not mean that there must be something wrong with planning teaching by means of a model that is an analogous extension of the assembly line. The pump made sense of the heart. The question here, however, is whether the assembly line leads to a model that is adequate for its educational task. The adequacy of such a model is not usually *raised*, however, because we forget that it is an analogous extension from a stage of technological development.

Let us, then, raise the question of whether the dominant model *is* adequate for its educational task. A number of points might be made that can leave us feeling at least uncomfortable about the adequacy of the model. Most generally, derived from the assembly line analogy, is the requirement that the first step in planning teaching requires that one prespecify precisely one's objectives. As the plan of the automobile determines every aspect of the assembly line so our "educational objectives become the criteria by which materials are selected, content is outlined, instructional procedures are developed and tests and examinations are prepared" (Tyler, 1949, p. 3).

Now if we use the dominant model, and its hidden, persuasive analogy, as the means to think about planning teaching, this first requirement will seem obvious. Of course you have to start with precise objectives or you will not know what to do—as you cannot organize an assembly line without a precisely designed automobile to provide the criterion for the construction and organization of the parts and the arrangements of the requisite tools and construction skills. What we have to do here, however, is try to use our understanding of the reality of education to reflect back on the adequacy of this model. This is difficult. Normally we use the model to think *with;* here we are to try to think *about* what we usually think with.

The first simple observation to make is that in education we do not expect, nor should we aim, to have each student become identical "products" in general and in particular we do not expect each student even to learn a particular lesson the same way as any other student. There are endless ways of being and becoming educated. We may try to specify certain necessary conditions, which may form a "core curriculum," but the sheer diversity of individual students and of social and cultural contexts makes even this a most problematic task. Our observation in the classroom shows us the endless and unpredictable ways in which students *use* knowledge. What we properly value in education are these unpredictable and spontaneously creative uses of knowledge. Clearly we can say that the imaginative creativity of children does not prevent us specifying certain objectives precisely. Children can then use in individually unpredictable ways what was the objective of the lesson. But the point here is that it is the unpredictable use, the spontaneity, the creative imagination that is at the educational heart of the matter. What the model does is leave this out in the cold, and suggest that the heart of the matter is the controllable, predictable, prespecifiable part. It is by such means that a model can deform an enterprise it is supposed to serve. This is not an argument against the model, in the sense of a logically convincing refutation. Rather it is one reason why we should feel uncomfortable with the model: what is most valuable is left out, and teachers are not encouraged to focus their attention on it.

Relatedly, if we reflect not just on the diversity of things a teacher might hope to have happen in an average class, but the ways in which all kinds of associations of ideas, particular hobbies or interests, wonder and humour, that might purely incidentally be stimulated, we may consider whether the reality of educational engagements is inappropriately represented as planned means working carefully along a prespecified path to precisely delineated objectives. Of course we can organize our curricula and lessons this way. But such a process seems not to *fit* some obvious features of education.

In the assembly line, and the analogous model, the product is made up of the pieces put together in the right way in the right sequence. The educated person is not merely the accumulated product of all that has been learned. The more basic problem at the heart of this objection is subtle and, again, not a compelling argument so much as a point of view from which the inadequacy of the model is pointed to. The assembly line model sees the educational product as a carefully planned accumulation of parts. Human understanding, however, does not seem to accumulate this way.

Perhaps I can better point to the inadequacy of the old-technology derived model by contrasting it by analogy with a newer technology. In the old model human understanding is represented as analogous to a two-dimensional picture. In order to compose the picture we need only get all the pieces together and fit them in their places. But if we think of human understanding as more like a hologram than a two dimensional picture, we see the poverty of the older view. If a hologram is broken in pieces, each piece contains an image of the whole. The laser will not show simply a part of the picture, but will show a fuzzy image of the whole. As pieces are added the whole picture becomes clearer. The curriculum is not adequately conceptualized if it is viewed as like a two dimensional picture that can be completed by putting the pieces together one by one. Rather it is a matter of coalescence and increasing clarity, in whose composition linear processes are inadequate.

My point, again, is not that the dominant model is in any sense *wrong*. Rather, it embodies a way of thinking about education, and encourages ways of thinking about teaching, that are in profound and subtle ways *inadequate*. The alternative I will describe in the following chapter is also, of course, inadequate, but its virtue I think is that it is less inadequate than what I am proposing it should replace. (Without the dominant model, of course, there could not have been this recommended alternative.)

The assembly line has become a fairly general metaphor for dehumanizing working conditions. Some automakers have tried a number of alternatives to the assembly line in order to reduce the deadening and deskilled routines it encourages. The assembly line is saved, however, by its perfectly attuned robot servants. The dehumanizing carries over, it seems to me, into the planning model for teaching derived by analogy from the assembly line. It has tended to reduce and deform education into a process of accumulating sequences of measurable knowledge and skills. It has tended to suppress, in the name of greater efficiency, the organic complexity of education, and to disguise the fact that we can adequately measure or evaluate only relatively trivial aspects of education.

In conclusion to this rather imprecise discussion—imprecise, because we are dealing with things we have no adequate analogies to enable us to make precise sense of—we might briefly reflect on how well the assembly line works as an analogy for telling a story. Part of my point is the sense of strain we feel thinking of a story in terms of an assembly line. And yet we can do so: we need to have our product or objective clear at the beginning, we need to organize the content, decide on our narrative procedures, and prepare some way of discovering whether we have successfully got the story across. The point is that this just is not a very useful way to think about how to plan telling a story. The analogy at the basis of the comparison simply does not fit very well. It misses the point of the story form in the way that a clockwork orange misses the point of fruit. What I will turn to now is trying to show that telling a story is a better analogy than the assembly line for teaching and that the story form provides a more adequate model for planning teaching.

Conclusion

Telling a story is a way of establishing meaning. Fictional stories tend to be concerned largely with affective meaning, whereas in education our concern is more comprehensive. We want "cognitive" and "affective" meaning together.

Because the dominant model has tended to emphasize the cognitive at the expense of the affective, drawing on some aspects of the story form for planning teaching can enable us to achieve a better balance. The result in practice of such abstract matters is clearer access to material for children and greater engagement with it.

The sense of story I am dealing with here is not so much the typical fictional kind, but something nearer to what a newspaper editor means when he asks his reporter "What's the story on this?" The editor is asking for an account of the particular events embedded in some more abstract context which readers already understand. The editor basically wants to know how the particulars fit into some binary conflict: How do these particulars give body to the ongoing story of good vs. bad, or security vs. danger, or political right vs. left, etc. The editor's question is one about how this particular knowledge is to be made meaningful and engaging to readers. So when I advocate use of some features of the story format it is in order to make new knowledge meaningful and engaging to children.

I will want to build into my model then some means of establishing at least some degree of story-like rhythm. This requires a particular kind of beginning that sets up an expectation, and a conclusion that satisfies this expectation. Such an overall form wraps the beginning and the end of a lesson or unit more tightly together than is usual. The new model also will be alert to the importance of underlying binary opposites for engaging interest and carrying it along. They also will provide a key criterion for the selection and organization of content.

I have spent some time discussing the inappropriateness of thinking about teaching by means of a model analogous to the assembly line because the major "heresy" of my model is that it does not begin with a statement of objectives. Indeed, objectives are not mentioned anywhere. In telling a story one does not begin by stating objectives, and yet stories are wonderful tools for efficiently organizing and communicating meaning. A major point of this book is that teaching is centrally concerned with efficiently organizing and communicating meaning, and so we will sensibly use a planning model derived from one of the world's most powerful and pervasive ways of doing this. Objectives based models are products of a particular phase of industrialization. They are the result of attempts to technologize teaching in inappropriate ways. They result in clockwork oranges. It is time to move to something more fruitful.

Questions

1. What are Egan's criticisms of Piaget and the educational implications derived form his research?
2. In terms of historical causality, how does Egan's approach differ from that of Piaget?
3. What is meant by the rhythm of a story?
4. How are classic folk-tales similar to jokes?
5. What is the relationship between the rhythms of stories and the conceptual abilities of children?

6. What are binary opposites and what role do they play in stories?

7. How do binary opposites assist us in organizing and making sense of our world?

8. What role does the affective play in enabling us to make sense of the world?

9. What is a metaphor or an analogy?

10. How do metaphors and/or analogies assist us in understanding otherwise mysterious things?

11. What distinguishes an adequate analogy from an inadequate one? What role do each play in furthering our understanding?

12. Is the comparison of education to an assembly line an adequate or inadequate analogy?

13. Is Egan's suggestion that human understanding is more like a hologram than a two-dimensional figure helpful?

14. Why, according to Egan, is telling a story a more effective tool for understanding than is an assembly line?

15. What role does or should story telling play in the Somatic, Mythic, Romantic, Philosophic, and Ironic tools for understanding?

chapter 18

Richard Rorty

TIME LINE FOR RORTY

1931	Is born on October 4 in New York City.
1949	Receives B.A. from University of Chicago.
1952	Receives M.A. from Yale University.
1956	Receives Ph.D. from Yale University.
1958–1961	Is assistant professor of philosophy at Wellesley College.
1961–1970	Is associate professor of philosophy at Princeton University.
1967	Publishes *Linguistic Turn: Essays in Philosophic Method.*
1970–1982	Is professor of philosophy at Princeton University.
1973–1974	Is Guggenheim Fellow.
1979	Publishes *Philosophy and the Mirror of Nature.*
1981–1986	Is MacArthur Fellow.
1982	Is named Vienan Professor of Humanities at University of Virginia.
1982	Publishes *Consequences of Pragmatism.*
1989	Publishes *Contingency, Irony, and Solidarity.*
1991	Publishes *Objectivity, Relativism, and Truth.*
1997	Publishes *Achieving Our Country.*
1998	Publishes *Truth and Progress.*

Introduction

Richard Rorty is one of the most influential and controversial American philosophers of the late twentieth century. Although Rorty has not devoted much specific
attention to educational matters, his consideration of and, in some ways, reinvention
of the work of John Dewey suggest that students of education may find things of
interest and value in his writing. In addition, if the life of the school somehow mir-
rors (or should mirror) the intellectual life of the community, it may prove helpful to
consult Rorty regarding one of the great shifts in Western intellectual life since
World War II, that is, the move from modernism to postmodernism.

A primary tenet of modernism, which begins with the philosopher Rene
Descartes (1596–1650) and continues into the twentieth century, is that reality has
a fixed character (it has certain qualities regardless of who is observing it). The task
of the thinker is to come up with a procedure for correctly describing the nature of
the real. That correct description, let us call it a narrative, is said to be privileged;
descriptions that conflict with the privileged narrative are, by definition, incorrect. If
for example, science is the privileged narrative, then Vincent Van Gogh's portrait of
the stars in *Starry Night* is somehow incorrect.

Postmodernism, as the name suggests, is a reaction against modernism. Where
modernism is essentially an exercise in description, postmodernism suggests that
rather than having a fixed character, reality is the outcome of inquiry. As the inquiry
shifts so too will shift the nature of the real. In effect, the physicist and the painter
are not in competition, are not trying to come up with a more accurate picture of
reality, but to the extent that they are involved in different disciplines, or avenues of
inquiry, are creating different realities.

Recent critics of American public education, such as Martin Benjamin and
Eugenio Echeverria, have suggested that the contemporary classroom is, in many
ways, a product of modernism.

> The conventional classroom presupposes a certain epistemology, or
> theory of knowledge, that has dominated Western philosophy since the
> seventeenth century. Knowledge, in this view, is acquired passively rather
> than actively, is more the product of careful observation than of prag-
> matic exploration. It is also largely individualistic; any singular knower
> with a properly receptive mind is, in principle, capable of acquiring knowl-
> edge of the world by him or herself. Education, therefore, has two princi-
> pal aims: first, to transmit all of the important knowledge that has been
> acquired firsthand by those who have preceded us . . . and, second, to
> make sure that the student's mind remains accurately aimed and highly
> receptive. . . .[1]

The student in that contemporary classroom is to serve as a mirror or a
piece of wax, standing at the ready, waiting to reflect the image or receive the

imprint from that which stands outside, fixed and immutable. The task of the student is to receive and accept the curriculum.

The good part, the comforting part, the part that is most appealing about the modern worldview, is that it satisfies what may be deep-seated human desires for order and progress, for certainty, for a clear distinction between mere subjectivity and objectivity, and for a differentiation between simple opinion and knowledge. The student in that contemporary classroom, if she or he was willing to work hard, if she or he was willing to be a good mirror or a malleable piece of wax, could be sustained by the belief that she or he was getting closer to the truth of things and was coming to see things in a more accurate fashion.

The problem that Rorty presents the student of American education is a rich, deeply philosophic one: If modernism is over, if we are, for better or worse, in a postmodern era, how will and should that be played out in the classroom? Rephrased in the form of another question: If the student cannot be sustained by a belief that her or his vision of things is becoming more accurate, what sort of belief will sustain her or him? Or finally, what does it mean to be an educated person in a postmodern era?

As mentioned previously, Rorty does not deal directly with educational issues, but his characterization of the roles of the disciplines, the nature of the thinker, and the redefinition of truth all have implications for how we might think about constructing a definition of the educated person.

For the postmodern thinker the disciplines are social and historical constructs. The rules of the disciplines, whether the disciplines of mathematics, physics, history, or art criticism, are not things that just emanate from the nature of reality. They are constructed by groups of people over periods of time as those groups try to make sense of their experiences. This is not to say that the disciplines are merely arbitrary contrivances, or that one discipline is as good as another. Disciplines do evolve and what may be considered reputable one day, for example, astrology, may at a later date fall into disrepute. Essential to the postmodern experience is a realization that disciplines are created by persons and, as such, are subject to all the foibles, limitations, and prejudices of any other human creation and of the need to come up with criteria for evaluating the worth of disciplines, for saying This is reputable and worth our time, and That is not. Translated into classroom practices, the curriculum has to be presented as a historical event agreed upon by scholars at this point in human history, and consisting of the things and the mechanisms that have been found to be useful in dealing with contemporary experience. Postmodernism does not necessarily change the curriculum, but what it does change is how the curriculum is viewed. The educated person uses it as an instrument for creating reality rather than as a mirror for reflecting reality.

As regards the nature of the thinker, if the modern thinker is, at heart, a discoverer, the postmodern thinker is basically a maker. Indeed, one of Rorty's preferred images is that of the thinker as cobbler, a person who, in consort with his fellows and using historical avenues of inquiries, cobbles out, hammers out, meaning and sense. People come together, agree on certain things (accept this standard of beauty or that way of measuring sound waves), and then try and talk or reason their way to a sensible conclusion. Again, translated into educational equivalents, the classroom becomes a place of active inquiry where, instead of simply learning some preexisting truth, scholars hammer out or cobble together a meaningful worldview. The educated person is the maker of meaning.

Finally, as suggested previously, the postmodern thinker does not jettison a notion of "truth," but she or he seriously redefines it. For the modern thinker, truth involves a correspondence between our beliefs (or, more precisely, the sentences are constructed to express our beliefs) and the way things really are. This, of course, assumes a fixed reality to which our beliefs correspond—precisely what postmodernism denies. For the postmodern thinker, reality is in a constant process of construction, and that which is warranted at one time may be unwarranted at another time. As the disciplines evolve, what is taken as true will evolve. In terms of education, the postmodern thinker sees truth as more of a resting place than a destination. One arrives at this conclusion at this time, one packs it into the curriculum as something to be learned and to be used, but the educated postmodern thinker is deeply aware of her or his own fallibility and the claim that truth, even when it is packed into the curriculum, is subject to scrutiny and to change. Using John Dewey's telling phrase, the postmodern thinker finds herself or himself in an "unfinished universe." The task of the educated person is precisely that of any worker confronted with an unfinished product, that is, to get on with the business of construction.

Contemporary philosophers are not agreed upon Rorty's relationship to Dewey and to the entire pragmatic tradition. The question phrased most simply is: "Does Rorty extend Dewey into the late twentieth century (and the early part of the twenty-first) or does he pervert Dewey?" We do not have a ready answer to that except to suggest that Rorty certainly reinvigorates the tradition. Rorty forces the reader to see the pragmatic tradition with fresh eyes and when one goes back and reads James on the nature of truth or Dewey on reconstruction of experience or Cornel West on the nature of social progress those works, somehow, seem sharper and better defined. Our text began with the most famous gadfly in the history of philosophy of education. It is fitting that it should conclude with an equally bothersome philosopher.

The selection from Rorty is a difficult one, but it does give the careful reader a fairly clear idea of what the context for education in the twenty-first century may be like.

Note

1. Martin Benjamin and Eugenio Echeverria, "Knowledge and the Classroom" in *Studies in Philosophy for Children*, ed. Ann Margaret Sharp and Ronald F. Reed (Philadelphia, PA: Temple University Press, 1992), p. 65.

From *Objectivity, Relativism, and Truth* (1991)

Postmodernist Bourgeois Liberalism

Complaints about the social irresponsibility of the intellectuals typically concern the intellectual's tendency to marginalize herself, to move out from one community by interior identification of herself with some other community—for example, another country or historical period, an invisible college, or some alienated subgroup within the larger community. Such marginalization is, however, common to intellectuals and to miners. In the early days of the United Mine Workers its members rightly put no faith in the surrounding legal and political institutions and were loyal only to each other. In this respect they resembled the literary and artistic avant-garde between the wars.

It is not clear that those who thus marginalize themselves can be criticized for social irresponsibility. One cannot be irresponsible toward a community of which one does not think of oneself as a member. Otherwise runaway slaves and tunnelers under the Berlin Wall would be irresponsible. If such criticism were to make sense there would have to be a supercommunity one *had* to identify with—humanity as such. Then one could appeal to the needs of that community when breaking with one's family or tribe or nation, and such groups could appeal to the same thing when criticizing the irresponsibility of those who break away. Some people believe that there is such a community. These are the people who think there are such things as intrinsic human dignity, intrinsic human rights, and an ahistorical distinction between the demands of morality and those of prudence. Call these people "Kantians." They are opposed by people who say that "humanity" is a biological rather than a moral notion, that there is no human dignity that is not derivative from the dignity of some specific community, and no appeal beyond the relative merits of various actual or proposed communities to impartial criteria which will help us weigh those merits. Call these people "Hegelians." Much of contemporary social philosophy in the English-speaking world is a three-cornered debate between Kantians (like Ronald Dworkin) who want to keep an ahistorical morality-prudence distinction as a buttress for the institutions and practices of the surviving democracies, those (like the post-Marxist philosophical left in Europe, Roberto Unger, and Alasdair MacIntyre) who want to abandon these institutions both because they presuppose a discredited philosophy and for other, more concrete, reasons, and those (like Michael Oakeshott and John Dewey) who want to preserve the institutions while abandoning their traditional Kantian backup. These last two positions take over Hegel's criticism of Kant's conception of moral agency, while either naturalizing or junking the rest of Hegel.

If the Hegelians are right, then there are no ahistorical criteria for deciding when it is or is not a responsible act to desert a community, any more than for deciding when to change lovers or professions. The Hegelians see nothing to be responsible to except persons and actual or possible historical communities; so they view the Kantians' use of 'social responsibility' as misleading. For that use suggests not the genuine contrast between, for example, Antigone's loyalties to Thebes and to her brother, or Alcibiades' loyalties to Athens and to Persia, but an illusory contrast between loyalty to a person or a historical community and to something "higher" than either. It suggests that there is a point of view that abstracts from any historical community and adjudicates the rights of communities vis-à-vis those of individuals.

Kantians tend to accuse of social irresponsibility those who doubt that there is such a point of view. So when Michael Walzer says that "A given society is just if its substantive life is lived in . . . a way faithful to the shared understandings of the members," Dworkin calls this view "relativism." "Justice," Dworkin retorts, "cannot be left to convention and anecdote." Such Kantian complaints can be defended using the Hegelians' own tactics, by noting that the very American society which Walzer wishes to commend and to reform is one whose self-image is bound up with the Kantian vocabulary of "inalienable rights" and "the dignity of man." Hegelian defenders of liberal institutions are in the position of defending, on the basis of solidarity alone, a society which has traditionally asked to be based on something more than mere solidarity. Kantian criticism of the tradition that runs from Hegel through Marx and Nietzsche, a tradition which insists on thinking of morality as the interest of a historically conditioned community rather than "the common interest of humanity," often insists that such a philosophical outlook is—if one values liberal practices and institutions—irresponsible. Such criticism rests on a prediction that such practices and institutions will not survive the removal of the traditional Kantian buttresses, buttresses which include an account of "rationality" and "morality" as transcultural and ahistorical.

I shall call the Hegelian attempt to defend the institutions and practices of the rich North Atlantic democracies without using such buttresses "postmodernist bourgeois liberalism." I call it "bourgeois" to emphasize that most of the people I am talking about would have no quarrel with the Marxist claim that a lot of those institutions and practices are possible and justifiable only in certain historical, and especially economic, conditions. I want to contrast bourgeois liberalism, the attempt to fulfill the hopes of the North Atlantic bourgeoisie, with philosophical liberalism, a collection of Kantian principles thought to justify us in having those hopes. Hegelians think that these principles are useful for *summarizing* these hopes, but not for justifying them. I use 'postmodernist' in a sense given to this term by Jean-François Lyotard, who says that the postmodern attitude is that of "distrust of metanarratives," narratives which describe or predict the activities of such entities as the noumenal self or the Absolute Spirit or the Proletariat. These metanarratives are stories which purport to justify loyalty to, or breaks with, certain contemporary communities, but which are neither historical narratives about what these or other communities have done in the past nor scenarios about what they might do in the future.

"Postmodernist bourgeois liberalism" sounds oxymoronic. This is partly because, for local and perhaps transitory reasons, the majority of those who think of themselves as beyond metaphysics and metanarratives also think of themselves as having opted out of the bourgeoisie. But partly it is because it is hard to disentangle bourgeois liberal institutions from the vocabulary that these institutions inherited from the Enlightenment—e.g., the eighteenth-century vocabulary of rights, which judges, and constitutional lawyers such as Dworkin, must use *ex officiis*. This vocabulary is built around a distinction between morality and prudence. In what follows I want to show how this vocabulary, and in particular this distinction, might be reinterpreted to suit the needs of us postmodernist bourgeois liberals. I hope thereby to suggest how such liberals might convince our society that loyalty to itself is morality enough, and that such loyalty no longer needs an ahistorical backup. I think they should try to clear themselves of charges of irresponsibility by convincing our society that it need be responsible only to its own traditions, and not to the moral law as well.

The crucial move in this reinterpretation is to think of the moral self, the embodiment of rationality, not as one of Rawls's original choosers, somebody who can distinguish her *self* from her talents and interests and views about the good, but as a network of beliefs, desires, and emotions with nothing behind it—no substrate behind the attributes. For purposes of moral and political deliberation and conversation, a person just *is* that network, as for purposes of ballistics she is a point-mass, or for purposes of chemistry a linkage of molecules. She is a network that is constantly reweaving itself in the usual Quinean manner—that is to say, not by reference to general criteria (e.g., "rules of meaning" or "moral principles") but in the hit-or-miss way in which cells readjust themselves to meet the pressures of the environment. On a Quinean view, rational behavior is just adaptive behavior of a sort which roughly parallels the behavior, in similar circumstances, of the other members of some relevant community. Irrationality, in both physics and ethics, is a matter of behavior that leads one to abandon, or be stripped of, membership in some such community. For some purposes this adaptive behavior is aptly described as "learning" or "computing" or "redistribution of electrical charges in neural tissue," and for others as "deliberation" or "choice." None of these vocabularies is privileged over against another.

What plays the role of "human dignity" on this view of the self? The answer is well expressed by Michael Sandel, who says that we cannot regard ourselves as Kantian subjects "capable of constituting meaning on our own," as Rawlsian choosers,

> without great cost to those loyalties and convictions whose moral force consists partly in the fact that living by them is inseparable from understanding ourselves as the particular people we are—as members of this family or community or nation or people, as bearers of this history, as sons and daughters of that revolution, as citizens of this republic.[1]

---

[1] *Liberalism and the Limits of Justice* (New York: Cambridge University Press, 1982), p. 179. Sandel's remarkable book argues masterfully that Rawls cannot naturalize Kant and still retain the metaethical authority of Kantian "practical reason."

I would argue that the moral force of such loyalties and convictions consists *wholly* in this fact, and that nothing else has *any* moral force. There is no "ground" for such loyalties and convictions save the fact that the beliefs and desires and emotions which buttress them overlap those of lots of other members of the group with which we identify for purposes of moral or political deliberations, and the further fact that these are *distinctive* features of that group, features which it uses to construct its self-image through contrasts with other groups. This means that the naturalized Hegelian analogue of "intrinsic human dignity" is the comparative dignity of a group with which a person identifies herself. Nations or churches or movements are, on this view, shining historical examples not because they reflect rays emanating from a higher source, but because of contrast-effects—comparisons with other, worse communities. Persons have dignity not as an interior luminescence, but because they share in such contrast-effects. It is a corollary of this view that the moral justification of the institutions and practices of one's group—e.g., of the contemporary bourgeoisie—is mostly a matter of historical narratives (including scenarios about what is likely to happen in certain future contingencies), rather than of philosophical metanarratives. The principal backup for historiography is not philosophy but the arts, which serve to develop and modify a group's self-image by, for example, apotheosizing its heroes, diabolizing its enemies, mounting dialogues among its members, and refocusing its attention.

A further corollary is that the morality/prudence distinction now appears as a distinction between appeals to two parts of the network that is the self—parts separated by blurry and constantly shifting boundaries. One part consists of those beliefs and desires and emotions which overlap with those of most other members of some community with which, for purposes of deliberation, she identifies herself, and which contrast with those of most members of other communities with which hers contrasts itself. A person appeals to morality rather than prudence when she appeals to this overlapping, shared part of herself, those beliefs and desires and emotions which permit her to say "WE do not do this sort of thing." Morality is, as Wilfrid Sellars has said, a matter of "we-intentions." Most moral dilemmas are thus reflections of the fact that most of us identify with a number of different communities and are equally reluctant to marginalize ourselves in relation to any of them. This diversity of identifications increases with education, just as the number of communities with which a person may identify increases with civilization.

Intra-social tensions, of the sort which Dworkin rightly says mark our pluralistic society, are rarely resolved by appeals to general principles of the sort Dworkin thinks necessary. More frequently they are resolved by appeals to what he calls "convention and anecdote." The political discourse of the democracies, at its best, is the exchange of what Wittgenstein called "reminders for a particular purpose"—anecdotes about the past effects of various practices and predictions of what will happen if, or unless, some of these are altered. The moral deliberations of the postmodernist bourgeois liberal consists largely in this same sort of discourse, avoiding the formulation of general principles except where the situation may require this particular tactic—as when one writes a constitution, or rules for young children to memorize. It is useful to remember that this view of moral and political deliberation was a commonplace among American intellectuals in the days when Dewey—a postmodernist before his time—was the reigning American philosopher, days when "legal realism" was thought of as desirable pragmatism rather than unprincipled subjectivism.

It is also useful to reflect on why this tolerance for anecdote was replaced by a reattachment to principles. Part of the explanation, I think, is that most American intellectuals in Dewey's day still thought their country was a shining historical example. They identified with it easily. The largest single reason for their loss of identification was the Vietnam War. The War caused some intellectuals to marginalize themselves entirely. Others attempted to rehabilitate Kantian notions in order to say, with Chomsky, that the War not merely betrayed America's hopes and interests and self-image, but was *immoral*, one which we had had no *right* to engage in in the first place.

Dewey would have thought such attempts at further self-castigation pointless. They may have served a useful cathartic purpose, but their long-run effect has been to separate the intellectuals from the moral consensus of the nation rather than to alter that consensus. Further, Dewey's naturalized Hegelianism has more overlap with the belief-systems of the communities we rich North American bourgeois need to talk with than does a naturalized Kantianism. So a reversion to the Deweyan outlook might leave us in a better position to carry on whatever conversation between nations may still be possible, as well as leaving American intellectuals in a better position to converse with their fellow citizens.

I shall end by taking up two objections to what I have been saying. The first objection is that on my view a child found wandering in the woods, the remnant of a slaughtered nation whose temples have been razed and whose books have been burned, has no share in human dignity. This is indeed a consequence, but it does not follow that she may be treated like an animal. For it is part of the tradition of *our* community that the human stranger from whom all dignity has been stripped is to be taken in, to be reclothed with dignity. This Jewish and Christian element in our tradition is gratefully invoked by freeloading atheists like myself, who would like to let differences like that between the Kantian and the Hegelian remain "merely philosophical." The existence of human rights, in the sense in which it is at issue in this meta-ethical debate, has as much or as little relevance to our treatment of such a child as the question of the existence of God. I think both have equally little relevance.

The second objection is that what I have been calling "postmodernism" is better named "relativism," and that relativism is self-refuting. Relativism certainly is self-refuting, but there is a difference between saying that every community is as good as every other and saying that we have to work out from the networks we are, from the communities with which we presently identify. Postmodernism is no more relativistic than Hilary Putnam's suggestion that we stop trying for a "God's-eye view" and realize that "We can only hope to produce a more rational conception of rationality or a better conception of

morality if we operate from within our tradition."[2]The view that every tradition
is as rational or as moral as every other could be held only by a god, someone
who had no need to use (but only to mention) the terms 'rational' or 'moral,'
because she had no need to inquire or deliberate. Such a being would have
escaped from history and conversation into contemplation and metanarrative.
To accuse postmodernism of relativism is to try to put a metanarrative in the
postmodernist's mouth. One will do this if one identifies "holding a philosophical position" with having a metanarrative available. If we insist on such a definition of "philosophy," then postmodernism is postphilosophical. But it would
be better to change the definition.[3]

Questions

1. What is modernism?
2. What is postmodernism?
3. How might a postmodern classroom differ from a modern one?
4. What is a metanarrative?
5. Why do postmodernists reject metanarrative?
6. Would you say that the natural sciences, as they are taught in school, constitute a metanarrative? Explain.
7. Do you think that postmodernism is committed to ethical relativism? Explain.
8. Assume postmodernists are right. Would it be necessary to change classroom practice? Explain.
9. Richard Rorty is a follower of John Dewey and, to a lesser extent, William James. Do you see any similarities between Rorty's stance on postmodernism and the writing of Dewey and James contained in this volume? Explain.
10. Consider the premodern philosophies we have studied—Socrates, Plato, Aristotle, Erasmus, Augustine. Would each be closer to modernism or postmodernism? Give reasons for your answers.

---

[2] *Reason, Truth and History* (New York: Cambridge University Press, 1981), p. 216.
[3] I discuss such redefinition in the Introduction to *Consequences of Pragmatism* (Minneapolis: University of Minnesota Press, 1982).

Name Index

Subject Index